Praise F

INFLUENCED: From Socia

"What sets Melissa's strategies apart is how she emphasizes importance of building strong relationships with your audience, and how you can use them to nurture a community that's excited to hear what you have to offer. If you're looking for a comprehensive guide to ultimately launch your product or service successfully online, this book is a must-read!"

-Amy Porterfield

Entrepreneur

NY Times Bestselling Author of

Two Weeks Notice

Content will not build a business for you. The heartbeat of any business is sales. And sales do not happen by randomly spraying out content into the world. You need a plan and a process to take people from your content, get them to raise their hand to tell you they're interested, and then lead them to conversion. This book shows you how to do just that.

-Jeff Walker

#1 NY Times bestselling author of

Launch

Oh, buckle up folks! You're in for a treat. I've had the distinct pleasure of watching Melissa and her husband Paul killing it with the material in this book. And let me tell you, it's been a real hoot. She's built an amazing business, and it's not only changed her life but is transforming the lives of thousands of others too. And now, she's spilling the beans in this book so that YOU can follow in her footsteps. Listen up here, cuz' when Melissa talks, I'm all ears. Get your mitts on this book, learn from her and put her teachings into practice. And when you're done, go ahead and read it again, and again. It's a hoot and a half!

-Ray Edwards

Communications Strategist & Copywriter

"INFLUENCED: From Social, to List, to Launch" is a game-changing guide for entrepreneurs seeking to make their mark in today's competitive world. This book reminds us of the essential, scalable strategies that empower businesses to thrive without sacrificing personal well-being. With its practical approach and actionable insights, INFLUENCED provides the foundation for targeting the right niches and delivering the perfect products. A highly recommended must-read for any aspiring entrepreneur.

-Wendy Mata

Founder of Bruja Power Botanica

"The frameworks and examples given make the material not just digestible but actionable. Putting the 104 Formula™ to work for you will reshape the way you communicate for a stronger and more relevant impact."

-Tracie Patterson

Indie Coaching

"What struck me was while so many gurus are out there trying to sell marketing alchemy, Influenced simply and succinctly delivers a system that works.

As a case study writer, I've seen so many first-hand examples of the success of your systems that I don't know if that colors my reading of the book... Regardless, it reinforces to me that those success stories aren't luck. They are doing the work and implementing a proven system that gets results."

-Amanda Perris

Case Study Queen

This is THE ONLY marketing book/course that you will EVER need! The information that exists between the front cover & the back cover will inspire you to rethink your marketing strategy. Influenced will give you the confidence & knowledge to speak into your expertise by helping you to organize your thoughts to connect to the people with whom you can solve problems for. Influenced is not fluff. It's real-world, actionable guidance to help you connect with your target market. Melissa Pruitt is the real deal. She's been in the trenches starting & running businesses. As a current coaching client of Melissa's, this is the piece of information that is connecting all of the marketing dots for me. This book comes from a place of personal experience, the good, the bad, & the ugly. I can't recommend this book enough. If you are struggling with connecting with your target market, get this book NOW and put the information to work for you that exists between the covers. You won't be sorry!

-Kelly Johnson

Kelly Johnson Photography

"Influenced: From Social, To List, To Launch," by Melissa Pruitt, is a must-read for all entrepreneurs. Melissa takes what seems to be the overwhelmingly complicated topic of marketing and breaks it down into easy-to-follow steps.

Her 104 Formula™ is a game changer and helps you create content that not only attracts your ideal customers but helps you engage with them at all stages of their journey.

I have worked with Melissa for over a year and have used what she teaches in this book to take my business to the next level by not only attracting new followers, but converting them to loyal customers. I know that anyone who reads this book can do that too.

-Katrina Oakley

Core Fitness For Moms

Melissa's book, Influenced, is an essential read for anyone selling a course or product online. She distills her years of experience and marketing know-how into an easy-to-follow, step-by-step process that will take you from identifying and speaking to your ideal clients' hopes and dreams through to planning, strategizing, and writing your content and even what to say and when to say it when launching a product.

Through her innovative 104 Formula™and Q Calendar, the fear of "I don't know what to talk about" will be a thing of the past—and the other 28 chapters are just as valuable!

If you sell courses online, this is the book for you.

-Stuart Tarn

Stuart Tarn Copy Ltd.

www.stuartwritescopy.com

Get Ready to Launch Your Business with the book Influenced: From Social, To List, To Launch.

Are you ready to launch or upgrade your business online? With the newly released book Influenced: From Social, To List, To Launch, you will have all the tools and resources you need to get started. Written by entrepreneur and digital marketing expert Melissa Pruitt, this book is an essential guide for anyone who wants to start their own online business. In this book, Melissa walks readers through every step of launching a successful online business. From setting up your systems and building a social media presence to creating an email list and monetizing it, she covers it all. "It's not a roadmap or a guide - it's an SOP for every online business!"

The chapters in this book are easy to read and consume and are like getting multiple in-depth quick-start course guides with actionable advice that can be implemented immediately. Whether you're just starting out or looking for ways to take your existing business to the next level, this book has something for everyone. With its straightforward language and easy-to-follow instructions, you'll be able to quickly understand the concepts and apply them right away.

This book is full of great advice on everything from driving traffic to monetizing an email list. I'm confident that anyone who reads it will come away with valuable insights that they can use in their own businesses. For aspiring entrepreneurs looking for guidance on launching their online businesses, look no further than book Influenced: From Social, To List, To Launch. This comprehensive book offers everything you need to know to get started. Get ready to upgrade or launch your own successful online business today!

-Phillis Benson

www.virtual-partner.com

www.virtualpartnerwebdesign.com

www.searchiehelp.com

If you create content just for the sake of creating content, with no real plan behind it, or if your conversions are lacking, then this book is for you. Not only will I send Influenced to all of my clients, but I'm also going to follow this clear roadmap, word for word, to build my own audience of raving fans.

-Ann Sheybani

Summit Press Publishers

I highly recommend Melissa Pruitt's Influenced book and class. I was reminded to be intentional with my marketing content and how to do so, rather than how I often do it by the seat of my pants on the fly. I got great concrete ideas. I love her examples and the way she reviews things, which helped me to remember them more. I resonate with the idea of reading book reviews on topics that my people would be interested in to get ideas for what they are thinking, feeling, saying, and doing. I never would have thought of that. I learned how to plan my year, plan ahead on marketing, and how to really segment my list so I am speaking to the right people in the right ways. People have different learning styles. Reading this book after taking the class really helped me get this. If you read the book first, taking the class next would really solidify what you read.

-Deborah Spiegel MT-BC

DBT Informed Board Certified Music Therapist

The Spiegel Academy: Music Therapy Continuing Education

www.TheSpiegelAcademy.com

"With her infectious smile and down-to-earth nature, Melissa is one of those people that you can't help but be inspired by. Passionate about helping others to achieve their dream life and to skyrocket their business, "Influenced" is a must-read for those looking to not only grow their audience but to create loyal, return customers. Including real-life examples, Melissa beautifully articulates and breaks down what can often be an overwhelming task into clear, actionable advice that is not only a joy to read but evokes a sense of excitement to implement."

-Kylie de Boer

Copywriter & Content Strategist

In her book, Influenced, Melissa Pruitt expertly guides readers through each step of getting traffic, connecting through audience conversations, and finally selling successfully to that audience. Each chapter is broken down into bite-size action items that make it simple and easy to apply her tactics and formulas to your specific niche. She lands the place on each idea so that you finish reading and know exactly how to implement her frameworks in your business and why they are so important. I finished the book with copious notes and action items that I'm excited to begin immediately. If you are looking to begin or grow an online business, Melissa's book is a MUSTREAD!

-Amy Small

Knit Collage

Melissa Pruitt's book Influenced is EXACTLY what entrepreneurs who are at the starting line need. I wish I had had this kind of straightforward, down-to-earth help when I was first starting out over 20 years ago. There are plenty of books out there to help you with VISION and lofty ideas when you start out. This book helps with straightforward sequenced tactical lists that are embedded in simple "why-to" language so that you don't have to spend hours getting up to speed on theory. It's a fast read and a must-read for newbies starting their online businesses. Melissa said in the book, "People don't want a checklist or a framework or a system. They want you to solve their problem." Guess what? Melissa just solved your problem with this book. Highly recommend it.

-Dr. Julie Helmrich

Psychologist in Milwaukee, WI

Co-founder IronPsych

"So many people think that building a platform for your online business is a matter of either a gazillion advertising dollars or pure viral luck. In this essential guide, Melissa debunks all that as she demystifies the process of building influence and shows how your roadmap to success is not just achievable; in fact, it's a very doable system. And she does it all in a friendly, approachable language that even the most overwhelmed entrepreneur can follow to success."

-Cathy Hay

www.FoundationsRevealed.com

"Finally! A fantastic book that teaches how to leverage social media to grow an email list and launch a thriving online business. Melissa's 104 Formula™is just brilliant!"

-Marco Scabia

Formula di Lancio Italia

If you're looking for an easy-to-understand while quite a thorough overview of online marketing, you need "Influenced: From Social, To List, To Launch" by Melissa Pruitt. Perfect for someone new to online marketing or starting an online business, this book provides the essential knowledge and tools to succeed in simple language and delightful diagrams. Better than a Marketing 101 class, this will get you oriented and implementing fast.

-Katie Hornor
Author of "The Flamingo Advantage: How to Leverage Unique, Stay Relevant and Change the World"

"I recently had the pleasure of reading Melissa's book, Influenced: From Social, To List, To Launch, and I have to say, I'm impressed.

As a fellow entrepreneur and member of the same mastermind group, I've always admired Melissa's dedication to helping others succeed, and this book is a perfect example of that. The book provides a comprehensive guide on how to build influence on social media, convert that influence into a list of engaged subscribers, and ultimately launch your product or service successfully.

Melissa writes with clarity and provides practical, actionable advice that will be easy to implement immediately.

What sets this book apart is Melissa's unique approach to building influence on social media, which is both refreshing and effective. If you're looking to build and leverage on social, I highly recommend you read Influenced: From Social, To List, To Launch."

-Alison Vidotto, MBA
Push! Business Training & Mentoring

If you want to simplify your content marketing and get results with a proven step-by-step system, this book is for you. Unlike many marketing books that are all promises and leave you hanging, Melissa has done an amazing job diving deep into content marketing strategies and practical steps to go from idea to launch; she holds nothing back. After using the strategies in this book, we went from marketing overwhelm to a clear content plan for our business. A definite must-read!

-Thembi Bheka

Digital Marketing On Demand

"To say that Melissa Pruitt has both a deep understanding of digital marketing, as well as the experience to move audiences in the real world, would be an understatement. She has the magical (and very rare) combination of a brilliant "tech" mind, a generous heart, and a down-to-earth communication style that makes even the most complex subject dead-easy to grasp. A great example is "The 104 Formula™," which she shares, which breaks down how to turn one piece of content into an endless asset library (and increasing the "influence") for any organization. That chapter alone, in terms of the marketing costs saved as well as the income it can generate, makes this book a "must-have" for any business owner or marketing director. "Influenced" will further be a valuable resource in the digital marketing space to review & implement for years to come... in the same spirit that "The E-Myth Revisited", "Profit First", and "Traction" have done in the entrepreneurial space as a whole."

-Mari Connor

CEO, Marigold Marketing Group

"Influenced: From Social, To List, To Launch," by Melissa Pruitt, is a practical guide to help entrepreneurs start and grow businesses across a wide range of industries. One of my favorite parts of the book is the section teaching entrepreneurs how to research their audience's pain points by looking at book reviews and by conducting client interviews. Melissa goes one step further by providing questions to ask clients during the interviews and ways to analyze themes and take action to solve client problems! There are amazing nuggets throughout the book that will be invaluable to both new and seasoned entrepreneurs."

-Mary Barbera, PH.D., RN, BCBA-D

Autism Mom, Behavior Analyst, and Best-Selling Author

MaryBarbera.com

If you want to master your digital marketing and feel good about yourself in the process, Melissa Pruitt is the person to learn from.

In Influenced, Melissa simplifies what others make complex and provides a repeatable system you can rely on for marketing results.

Whether you're looking to build your email list or turn them into buyers, Influenced is filled with gems to help you connect with your true audience and serve them in a way that creates raving fans. I can't wait to implement them in my own business!

-May Busch

CEO of Career Mastery™

"After helping hundreds of people launch and grow a business, I know that being able to attract customers and influence them to buy from you is a critical piece of your business success story. Melissa provides you with an in-depth look at how you can develop deep relationships with your audience so they are compelled to buy from you, and she packages it in a way that's easy to follow and even easier to implement. With a multitude of tools and examples to easily pull this through to your own business, you will be shocked at the speed and the impact it has on your business! Implement what Melissa tells you, and watch your business flourish with an ease you've never experienced before!"

-Jessica Miller

Founder of Jessica Miller Coaching and Sales

Growth Strategist

Melissa takes the best practices you could learn from years of sitting in marketing courses and on-the-job experience and neatly packages it into a simple and effective guide. If you're an entrepreneur wanting to go from novice to noticed by your ideal clients, this book has all the strategies you need.

-Kelli Thompson

Aaward-winning leadership coach

Author of Closing The Confidence Gap

Melissa makesoften complex and overwhelming marketing strategies seem absolutely easy and doable. I particularly found it valuable when she discusses how to build funnels differently based on where your customer is within their problem. This book can help new entrepreneurs and marketers to established online business owners.

Her writing is very easy to consume, and her expertise in these areas shines through and makes it all feel doable. Highly recommend!

-Angela Mascenik

Creator of the Stop Over-drinking and Start Living podcast

Womens Coach

I love what Melissa shares in this book! Building a business in service of your life, versus compromising your life to support your business - is something that so many entrepreneurs need to hear...and she gives you a step-by-step playbook to get there. I've watched Melissa and Paul walking the walk of what she teaches. Let her be your mentor!

-Jason Friedman

CEO CXFormula, LLC.

I've personally watched Melissa and her husband, Paul, do exactly what she teaches in this book. And it has been nothing short of remarkable. She's built an amazing business that supports her lifestyle and is having a positive impact on thousands of others. Now, she's created the playbook so that YOU can do the same. When Melissa has something to say, I'm listening. Read this book and do what she teaches. Then read it again... and again.

-Matt McWilliams

Bestselling author of Turn Your Passions Into Profits

Marketing is essential for all businesses, but it can be the biggest obstacle to success for many. There is so much information (and misinformation) on marketing today. Fortunately, Influenced can help you take the right steps in the right order to achieve the right results. As a serial entrepreneur, I've tried many marketing strategies and know the value of reliable, proven methods that work in today's market to attract the right audience and aligned clients.

In her book, Melissa Pruitt has simplified the complex world of marketing. She guides you through her decades of experience and proven strategies for repeatedly finding, connecting, and building relationships with your ideal clients, turning them into raving fans. Whether you are running a six-figure business or have yet to make your first sale, you will find value in this book. I highly recommend this book to anyone who wants to improve their marketing and attract more ideal clients (every business owner).

-Tina Brandau

Best-selling Author, Speaker, Coach

Success Coaching Solutions

Chasing followers to feel popular... chasing likes to be liked... posting without a plan... these are the traps you DON'T want to fall into if you're using social media to help you build a real business.

If you're tired of creating endless social media content without a coherent strategy or struggling to convert followers into actual paying customers, then Influenced by Melissa Pruitt is the book for you! Melissa's clear and actionable advice will show you how to build a massive following of raving fans who are ready and primed to buy your products and offers, so you can build a thriving and sustainable business in record speed.

-Julie Ann Cairns

Author of Amazon #1 Bestseller The Abundance Code

"In the game of marketing, there are people who follow the crowd and people who lead the way. Melissa Pruitt is one who has led the way for many years and not only created a business that fits her unique design and lifestyle, but also has enabled entrepreneurs around the world to do the same without sacrificing personal connection. Her out-of-the-box thinking, combined with radical generosity of spirit and commitment to the individual, really shines through in her new book, Influenced. I am honored to call her a friend and highly recommend this book for anyone who wants to learn how to impact the world with integrity and authenticity while making a great living at the same time."

-Matt Tommey

Artist, Author, Mentor & Entrepreneur

www.MattTommeyMentoring.com

Finally, marketing made easy. A reliable and repeatable system created by a professional of impeccable integrity who actually walks the talk. Influenced is your clear, concise, immediately implementable roadmap for building theat business of your dreams. The internet is replete with shiny marketing toys that glitter but don't deliver. Influenced works. Buy it, read it, do it now.

-Walt Hampton, J.D.

Executive Coach

Bestselling author of "Journey on the Edge: Living A Life That Matters, and The Power Principles of Time Mastery: Do Less, Make More, Have Fun"

Melissa Pruitt offers more than a marketing blueprint for entrepreneurs, coaches, and thought leaders in Influenced: From Social, To List, To Launch. She provides a formula for nurturing all relationships in your life, including the one you have with yourself. With authentic listening, thoughtful questioning, and intentional practices, she takes you on a "like, know, and trust" journey that builds rapport, confidence, and success. This book provides insight into the 'why' and 'how' of developing a successful marketing plan for your business.

-Lisa McGrath

International bestselling author, entrepreneur, and Book Coach at Pages with Purpose

Frankly, I'm blown away by the amount of actionable content in Melissa Pruitt's book, "Influenced." Now, I know my messaging is right, and it WORKS... from the very first social media post to the landing page to the lead magnet to the nurture sequence to my offer.

The messaging around my top offer was NOT easy. I work with people up to a year in advance before we head to the summit of Kilimanjaro to see (not climb!) Everest, or on a unique route to experience Machu Picchu. "Influenced" gave me the tools and focus to research where people ARE and then create the right messaging that brings them into my world... so they can see the TOP of the world.

Grab a notebook and pen and set aside some time to complete the proven step-by-step frameworks found in "Influenced." It WILL grow your business!

-JT Nelms

Creator of "True Purpose Adventures"

JTNelms.com

I am thrilled to endorse Melissa Pruitt's book, Influenced: From Social, to List, to Launch. As a small business owner myself, I understand the importance of marketing and finding new clients. Melissa takes us on a journey through her process of getting noticed by new people and converting them into paying clients and beyond.

Melissa and her husband, Paul, were instrumental in helping us start our photography business. They taught us the techniques outlined in this book, which enabled us to prove the naysayers wrong. Melissa emphasizes that marketing is not a scary thing, but rather it's simply about having conversations. This theme resonates throughout the book.

Whether you're just starting your business or want to give your existing business a boost, Influenced is a great read. It provides the foundations and process of finding new traffic, keeping it, and converting it to buyers. I have taken many classes and had several business coaches, but none have enabled me to move our business forward the way Melissa and Paul have using this method.

I highly recommend this book to any business owner wanting to improve their marketing. It's a must-read that will provide you with valuable insights and actionable strategies to take your business to the next level. Thank you, Melissa, for sharing your expertise and empowering entrepreneurs everywhere!

-Lori Keefer

Online Marketing Strategist & Co-Owner of Keefer Fine Art

When it comes to marketing and influencing, Melissa Pruitt is the person to learn from. Her book not only has real-life examples, but it has a step-by-step approach that helps you from starting your social engagement through launching and then keeping your lists in priorities that make sense.

I learned a lot for my own business, and I know you will as well. Thank you, Melissa, for sharing your knowledge in a quick and easy way.

-Kathy Lindert

Your favorite hypnotist

The Mental Edge, LLC

When it comes to marketing, Melissa and her husband, Paul, are experts at teaching exactly how to move people from being part of a general audience to paid clients. "Influenced: From Social, To List, To Launch" provides a practical, actionable roadmap that can be used to develop an effective marketing plan. I recommend this book to any business owner that's looking to start, grow, and scale their business.

-Peju Adedeji

Your IT Career

"Melissa does an amazing job of synthesizing and simplifying the specific marketing areas you need to focus on to quickly and effectively grow your brand online. You should not launch your product or service without reading this first!"

-Dave Gambrill

Founder of Digital Marketing Mentorship

Host of the "Unleash the Awesome" podcast.

Melissa has masterfully made the complex topic of marketing into an easy-to-understand framework that can be used by anyone who is building their own business or coaching practice - online or in-person. By providing practical business examples throughout, this book becomes immediately applicable to every reader. I'd recommend this for any marketer looking to streamline their list-building tactics and engagement and move toward action and conversion!

-Brenda Ster

Social Marketing Coach

TheEliteSuite.com

"As a small business owner with a limited budget, I have struggled for years to figure out how to organically drive potential clients from social media onto my email list. Not to mention how to effectively sell to them! This book was a game changer for my life and business. Melissa's methodology and 104 formula helped me grow my list with an intentionally aligned message to attract the right people and then convert that audience into paying customers! Regardless of whether you are a brick-and-mortar business, a service-based business, or an online business, this is a must-read!"

-Shelly Niehaus

Business Coach & Personal Brand Strategist

I've been lucky enough to work with Melissa for the past few years...so happy she is sharing her secrets in Influenced! Melissa's signature 104 Formula is the key to unlocking so many marketing decisions. Following Melissa's directions for creating the 104 Formula will make an incredible impact on creating content and programs for your business. Don't let this book sit on your bookshelf looking pretty! Take action immediately!

-Deb Mitchell

Senior Community Manager, Agorapulse, and Founder of Membership WOW

"I run a mission-based company and don't have a sales background, so a lot of mainstream marketing strategies tend to feel complicated, overwhelming, or a bit too salesy for me. The system Melissa teaches in this book is a breath of fresh air. It's simple, easy, and yet incredibly powerful. If you're struggling to attract the right people, or you can never work out what to post on social media, or how to convert those followers to buyers, you need to read this. Melissa shows you not just the high-level concepts but the nitty-gritty of how to get it done without burning yourself out. I came away from this book with a deeper understanding of my audience and knowing how to have value-led, natural conversations with the right people. I don't think I'll ever struggle for content ideas again!"

-Kate Bee

The Sober School

Just when you thought you had cracked the marketing code, along comes Melissa Pruitt with a host of excellent and, above all, original ideas for getting the word out there to your audience. A brilliant and all-encompassing guide to marketing in the new millennium, written by a super smart marketer. So many trade secrets, practical tips, and fantastic systems to learn. 100% worth your time. Good for beginners and seasoned marketers alike. I actioned multiple tips as I read it through the first time, and I will re-read it and work my way through the bigger ideas with my team systematically.

-Yasmin Boland

Award-winning astrologer,

best-selling author,

& Creator of Moonology

"Influenced is a must for anyone aspiring to build a successful online business. With her strategic insights, actionable advice, and genuine passion for helping others, Melissa provides a roadmap to connect authentically with your audience, create compelling content, and launch with impact. This book is a game-changer for entrepreneurs who want to build a thriving online presence and make a meaningful difference in the todays world."

-Dylan Ayaloo

The Inner Work Guy

"The only way Melissa Pruitt could make social media any easier is if she did it for you. Influenced is the ultimate playbook for founders and entrepreneurs who want a practical and proven profit path that harnesses the power of social media to maximize their business growth. Melissa expertly walks you through every step of every step to demystify social media and launching so you can find your right-fit clients, launch your offer, and fast-track your business growth. If you do the work (and she makes it easy), you will see results."

-Heather Campbell

Branding Strategist and Founder of Six Figure Founders

"As you dive into 'Influenced: From Social to List to Launch' by Melissa Pruitt, get ready to take copious notes and to embark on a journey that intertwines professional strategy with heartfelt authenticity. This empowering guide fills a void often present in the digital domain - a deep, sincere connection rooted in integrity. Melissa Pruitt goes beyond the conventional, guiding you on how to truly engage with your audience - resonating in their minds, touching their hearts, and sparking an enduring loyalty. Her approach teaches you how to converse with your audience on an emotional and psychological level, elevating 'Influenced' from a mere guide to a heartfelt and insightful manual for creating authentic digital connections."

-Linda Ezuka

Founder and CEO of CRA Today and the CRA Hub

"My favorite part of Influenced was the actionable takeaways that I could immediately implement into my business and see results. From the start of the book, Melissa jumps in with both feet, speaking to the Buyer's journey and how this is KEY to putting together a plan that keeps the perfect prospect moving forward and making sure you're meeting them where they're at in the journey. She also outlines how to have the right conversations in your content planning and shows you a simple roadmap to how you can easily create content by doing some quick research that makes putting these strategies into practice a snap! I would recommend this book to anyone who wants to create a successful marketing plan that is easy to implement and helps you have the right conversation with the right customer."

-Alena Wilson

CEO of Estimate Mastery

I am delighted to recommend this magnificent book on building an online business, which covers all the essential aspects of starting and growing a successful online venture. The author's comprehensive approach takes readers through the process of building a robust social media presence, creating a targeted email list, launching their product or service, and scaling their business to reach a broader audience.

With the rise of e-commerce and online businesses, this book is a valuable resource for anyone who wants to start an online business or improve their existing one. The author's writing style is engaging and easy to understand, making it accessible to both beginners and experienced entrepreneurs.

One of the book's strengths is its emphasis on building a strong social media presence. Social media is a critical aspect of any online business, and the author provides practical tips and strategies for creating a compelling online brand that resonates with the target audience.

Another strength of the book is its focus on building an email list. The author explains the importance of having a targeted email list and provides step-by-step instructions for creating and growing one.

The book also provides a detailed roadmap for launching a product or service, from creating a pre-launch buzz to executing a successful launch. The author's guidance on how to create and implement a launch plan is invaluable, and readers will learn how to maximize their launch's impact and reach.

Overall, this book is an excellent resource for anyone looking to build a successful online business. The author's comprehensive approach and practical advice make it an essential read for entrepreneurs at any stage of their business journey. I highly recommend it!

-Dr. Aleksander Šinigoj

Coach and author of "Breakthrough now"

"This book is a game-changer for the successful entrepreneur who is ready to take their business to the next level. Influenced is a powerful strategy and will become a key driver to deeply understanding your audience, speaking in a way that connects them to you quickly and helps you to create raving fans.

Melissa Pruitt's genuine passion for helping others build successful businesses shines on every page. Her expertise is evident throughout the book, as she provides practical guidance and real-world examples of successful strategies. What I appreciate most about this book is that it emphasizes the importance of building genuine connections with others.

Influenced gives you a one-of-a-kind, proven, and valuable roadmap for anyone looking to boost their sales through relationship marketing. Using Melissa's 104 Formula™, I have gone from having a chaotic and overly complex approach to marketing to one that seamlessly moves people from connection to list to sales. The organization this formula provides, the ease with which it becomes a long-term strategy, and, mostly, the clarity of connection to my audience it provides is genius.

Influenced is the secret weapon that separates successful entrepreneurs who simply survive from those who truly thrive. It's a powerful framework and strategy that not only sustains your business but also cultivates long-lasting connections that grow so your business will thrive."

-Laura P. Clark

wiselivinginstitute.com

As an investment professional who worked in corporate America for over 3 decades, I always had a marketing team that specialized in branding, messaging, and content creation. When I branched out to create my own wealth coaching business, marketing became another project I had to add to my "to-do" list. I found this book to be so well thought-out, covering all the things you've got to know to be a successful and authentic marketer. There are so many 'golden nuggets' and examples that could only come from someone who has walked the walk and built not one but several successful businesses.

The 104 Formula™ that Melissa outlines in the book is a game-changer for business owners who are looking for a blueprint to create engaging and educational content for their audience. No more staring at a blank page, wondering what to post today!

I highly recommend this book to anyone looking for a guide to help them use their unique influence to be better with messaging. I'm also enrolled in Melissa's Influenced course, and the Adaptive Inner Circle program, and the support provided is simply amazing! I'm more confident than ever in my ability to speak to the people who need to learn from me.

-Laurie Bodisch

Founder & CEO of Her Wealth Coach™

INFLUENCED

FROM SOCIAL TO LIST TO LAUNCH

Melissa Pruitt

INFLUENCED: From Social, to List, to Launch ™

Printed in the United States of America

ISBN: 979-8-218-19442-0

Dedication

To my loving husband, Paul, for his unwavering support and encouragement, and to the trailblazing online entrepreneurs who strive to make a positive impact in the world, this book is dedicated to you.

Influenced

From Social, to List, to Launch

The Influenced Course is a premium list building program to help you attract more of the right clients into your business. From your social media to your list builders to your launch!

I've seen how devastating it is for my clients to put the time, energy, and effort into a launch and not get the results they deserve.

Maybe you've bought other content creation courses that helped you create content for your social media but didn't lead your audience to buy your offers.
Or you purchased a list building course that got you started with your first lead magnet, but you haven't had luck converting those opt-ins into sales.

Perhaps you're having trouble connecting your lead magnets with your launches, making your content feel all over the place.

It's time to change all that!

With this course, I've created something dramatically different from anything else out there. I've bundled the best of my knowledge and experience, using the same advanced list building techniques that have led to the successes we've had in our multi-six-figure business.

I'm confident you won't find any other list building program like this one.

You'll learn real strategies to influence the right people to buy your offers, allowing you to build your business and positively impact their lives.

I must warn you though, this isn't a beginner-level course.

If you're ready to roll up your sleeves and get to work influencing your audience from social to list to launch...then enroll in the Influenced course!

Table of Contents

Preface

I remember the first time I sat in front of the computer staring at the screen, viewing the inbox of my future husband's photography business. "How in the world did he attract all these potential clients every single day of the week?" I wondered.

I'd already owned several businesses of my own. Throughout the years, I had my therapy practice, a martial arts studio, and other ventures too.

The one thing I could never figure out was how to influence people to walk in the door. So now here I was, sitting in front of this computer, seeing all these inquiries come in, and I couldn't help but wonder if this was possible for me.

Like, "Can you actually do this on purpose?" I asked internally. "Can you really create a business where people are banging down the door to come in?" The simple answer is a resounding yes!

Over the years, I began to realize that it takes a process. It's a system.

We used this system in our wedding photography business, where our calendar was booked solid every year. We received over 500 wedding inquiries per year and averaged over $7,000 per wedding, while others in our same market averaged only $1,500.

We eventually got so busy that we created another photography brand that included nine other photographers to shoot other weddings for us.

Then, in 2017, Paul and I got married and made the decision to take our weekends back, so we shifted our focus from weddings to headshots and, in less than two years, using the same methods to build our list and market to our clients, we created a multi-six-figure headshot business.

During this time, we were also keynote speakers on stage for the professional photography niche and stages in the internet marketing world.

In October 2019, we replicated our photography business income with our online business, achieving our milestone for closing the photography business. We then moved our business entirely online and never looked back.

You see, it is a duplicatable, replicable system. Before I met Paul, I never thought that was possible.

But now, I'm here to tell you business can be this easy.

We've had years of multi-six-figure launches for our courses and memberships and millions of dollars in online sales in just a few years' time. We are incredibly honored and privileged to serve thousands of clients.

What's interesting and important for you to know is we started at zero. Our current business began with zero following, zero lists, and zero offers. Yet, at four different times, each time using the methods I share in this book, we were able to influence people in a variety of niches to make an informed buying decision. Today, we're blessed to do this for ourselves and help other business owners—just like you.

So whether you are somewhat established and struggling to turn your list into buyers or starting at zero trying to build an email list, this book is for you! I've seen this system work too many times for far more people than just my husband and me. I know it can work for you too. Let's dig in!

Chapter 1

The Essence of Marketing

A lot of people think marketing has to be complicated. When they hear that word, thoughts of funnels, social media, and the tech it takes to bring in revenue all rush into their mind and overwhelm them. The truth is marketing is so much more than the machine that brings sales into a business.

To me, marketing is the best way to guide people into making an informed buying decision. There's no need for tricks and gimmicks and all the crazy tactics you see being used out there these days. While there are a lot of theories, strategies, and tactics that fall within the realm of marketing, perspectives can vary depending on who you follow. So, I want to make sure you and I are on the same page from the outset.

You see, my husband Paul and I have our own take on a lot of these traditional methods, and it's worked out pretty well for us. Currently, we run two very successful, high-touch, high-ticket memberships. We also offer several core courses, and we are top ten affiliates for other influencer's offers, bringing in nearly one million dollars of revenue each year. Not bad, huh?

I don't share any of that to brag or impress you but because I want to help you build a list that can lead to your business dreams, too. So it's important that you have a firm understanding and buy-in of marketing from my perspective in order for me to help you build that dream business.

When you follow the methods outlined in this book, you'll find that you are genuinely serving people, and from that place of service, potential buyers are able to decide what is right for them (and you end up with an awesome community of buyers who are right for you, too!).

Where to Focus

All the marketing procedures and processes you hear about are enough to make your head spin, right? Well, I'm here to share with you that marketing does not have to be complex and tricky. A lot of times, we make it more complicated than it needs to be. It's really quite simple. The essence of marketing comes down to three things:

1. Getting traffic
2. Keeping traffic
3. Converting traffic

If you focus on those three things with your marketing, it really makes it a lot simpler, and everything that you do with your social media, list building, and launches all fall into alignment.

Focusing on these elements of traffic brings the right people into our world—the people who would be perfect for our paid offers. As we continue through the pages of this book, you'll learn more about how to identify those perfect people and how to gain a really good understanding of who they are because, if we can speak to things that they want, it'll help us bring them in closer so we can deliver offers that are perfect for them.

Getting Traffic

The first piece is getting traffic. When it comes to getting traffic, there are two different ways you can attract people into your world.

- Organic influence
- Paid influence

Organic influence is everything that you do by your own effort. It's building a social media platform, podcast, or blog following that you can then send to people to your list builders. This method involves more of an investment of your time and energy resources. In just a bit, I'm going to show you exactly how to use organic influence to really attract and speak to the people that are perfectly aligned with your paid offers.

Another way to get traffic is through paid influence. For this, use things like radio or print advertising, Facebook ads, Google Ads, sponsored content, etc. There's a lot of paid methods out there. In this book, we're not going to focus on paid influence. Just know that when it comes to getting traffic, there are a variety of ways to do so. If you're looking for more information on how to utilize many of these paid methods, we focus on that in our Adaptive Marketing Program. The focus of this book is how to gain influence through organic traffic, as we find that is the best way for businesses in earlier stages to gain a list without a huge outlay of cash.

Keeping Traffic

Keeping traffic is really important because being drawn to someone is one thing, but staying is another. We must keep our people interested, excited about what we do, and curious for more. When it comes to keeping traffic, this is all about nurturing those relationships that you started.

The best way I know to nurture relationships is to have conversations. When we are building those relationships, we must always be thinking about how we can keep our audience's attention. How can we sustain their interest? How can we get them curious? What can we do to continue that conversation?

Conversations with your audience ensure that they understand exactly what we do and how we can help them. As you nurture that relationship, you're going to create even more interest and excitement. By having a natural conversation, it leads them closer to working with you.

Converting Traffic

Converting traffic comes down to making sure that your offers solve a real problem for your audience and that they speak to what they want. When you know your audience, the things that make them tick, the things that they want, their pain points, their desire points, and then we have an offer that's perfectly aligned with those, it's going to make sense for that individual to purchase and convert into a paying customer.

I'll show you all the ins and outs of the various types of conversations that will help you get, keep, and then convert traffic a little later on.

For now, focus on the simplicity of these three elements of marketing traffic. When you can keep these in mind, all of your list-building efforts are going to pay off in the end.

In the next few chapters, we'll begin to dive into how you can develop conversations to help you connect with your potential buyers on a deeper level leading to higher sales. But before you can do that, you'll need to align your audience, message, and offer. My main goal for you in this book is to help you get to know your people so well that they connect with your message, lean into your content, and ultimately buy your offers. Most importantly, I want you to know with your whole heart why these things are vital to you, your business, and, ultimately, the success of your clients.

Chapter 2

Phases of Conversations

As we discussed in the last chapter, marketing does not need to be complicated. It's all about the different things that we can do to get, keep, and convert traffic so we bring the right people into our world. And it all comes down to conversations. Conversations are the key to guiding people to make that informed buying decision. Having a two-way dialogue with each person gives you a keener insight into who they are and brings you into a deep understanding of their problems and desires so you can speak to those and convey how you can help them.

There are three phases of conversation that you're going to go through again and again as they travel through the various stages of the buyer's journey. Each of these conversation phases should be incorporated into your marketing plan. The conversation you'll have with each person will vary depending upon when you're meeting them, as well as where they are in the marketing and buying journey.

We go a lot deeper into this journey in some of our other courses and coaching programs. I hesitate to go fully into that here, as I don't want to overwhelm you. For our purposes in this book, it's important for you to have a basic understanding of the typical buyer's journey.

There are three main stages to the buyer's journey.

1. Awareness stage - The buyer becomes aware that they have a problem.
2. Consideration stage - The buyer begins to look for solutions to the problem.
3. Decision stage - The buyer evaluates and chooses someone to help them and then buys their solution.

To some degree, this is oversimplified, but these are the three basic stages you should be aware of as you begin engaging an audience. You want to create a variety of content so you can reach people at every stage.

As someone goes through this journey, there are six points where their mind is fixed in a specific direction when it comes to your product or service.

THE BUYERS JOURNEY

- Unconscious Point
- Observing Point
- Active Point
- Commitment Point
- Transformation Point
- Advocate Point

Here's a real-world example of the buyer's journey:

I love Instagram shopping. Whenever I see an awesome find on Instagram, I get really curious and interested. I've purchased beauty products, cookware, and specialty beverages. You name it, and I have probably bought it. And so, through my own experience with the buyer's journey, I want to share a story about how I came to find a really awesome purchase.

You see, I heard about an earring subscription that intrigued me. I had no idea that there was such a thing. I also had no idea that I needed these earrings or that they would become something that I would really love to wear and have as a regular part of my wardrobe. In terms of the buyer's journey, this is the Unconscious Point—the place where your potential buyer doesn't know they even have a problem.

These earrings are big and bold, and I love wearing them! When I am in Zoom meetings with clients, I always get compliments. When I first became aware of these earrings, I saw the business owner sharing her collection on social media. That moved me to the Observing Point.

I started to see this influencer show off all the different ways that she would incorporate them into her outfits. She also shared how her clients started wearing the earrings to stand out. I observed what other people were saying and how they incorporated them into their wardrobes, too, creating a signature look so they could stand out in a crowded marketplace. The more I observed, the more I became aware of this problem that I didn't even think I had.

The next thing I know, I'm thinking, "Ooh, wouldn't that be interesting if I started to incorporate a signature piece into my wardrobe that would allow me to stand out on coaching calls?" This is where I moved into the Active Point, where I really started to explore what this subscription service was and how it worked.

I went onto the website and looked at all the different options. I also looked at all of her social media pages as well, just to see how other people liked the earrings. I was actively looking to see if this product would make sense for me.

Eventually, I was ready to start incorporating these earrings into my wardrobe collection. First, I had some additional questions. Each was a potential objection to purchasing. She did a great job answering my questions and made sure I was comfortable making that decision to buy. I had reached the Commitment Point.

After purchasing, I was at the Transformation Point of the buyer's journey, where I got to experience what it was like to be part of the earrings subscription club. My first box included a handwritten note and ways I could share the collection on social media to show off how I was utilizing the earrings. It was an excellent experience with a wonderful first impression.

On top of that, the owner made a point to reach out regularly and always compliment me on my outfit and earrings. That made me feel really good. So I started wearing them more and more. Then, my audience noticed, and they gave me compliments too! Before long, I became a raving fan.

All of this, of course, got me to the Advocate Point, where I began recommending this service to my friends and clients (with tons of enthusiasm).

As prospects go through each of these points, there will be conversations you will have with them along the way. For now, it's valuable to note that there are three phases of conversation.

Audience-Building Conversation

First is the audience-building phase. Here, we're bringing people into our world. You may not have even met these individuals yet, so this is where we really focus on getting their attention by talking specifically to them, their likes, their desires, and most importantly, their problems. You should do this on all platforms where you are building an audience. Whether this is on your social media platforms, in your list builders, or when you're having a one-on-one conversation over coffee, you want to make sure that people are getting to know you and your area of expertise. They need to have an understanding of what you can do to help them, and you need to be speaking about the things they are interested in.

Remember to grab the attention of your audience and keep it. This is all part of the audience-building phase, where you are focused on bringing your perfect people into your world.

Launch-Building Conversations

The second phase is launch-building conversations. When you shift into this phase, the conversations you're having will also shift as you're ramping up toward a launch or timed promotion. This is where you're really speaking about a specific problem that your audience is having and the offer you are creating to help them solve that problem. During these conversations, you are warming people up and getting them interested in that thing you are offering through your launch vehicle. Think about how that shift happens and how those conversations start to shift. You want those people excited to take the next step into your paid offer. We delve a little deeper into the six phases of launch conversations later in this book.

Ongoing Conversations

Finally, we have the ongoing conversation phase. These are the conversations that we should be having all year long. The important part of this phase is that it helps build trust with our audience like nothing else can. They get a chance to know us as individuals and to really feel connected to us. We're not only speaking into the challenges and desires they have, but they're getting a real insight into who we are behind the screen. We're building that like, know, and trust with our audience, forming a real relationship with them. When there's trust, they are more likely to listen to what we have to say. This eventually makes them more likely to work with us and to refer their friends in the future.

Conversations are the foundational piece that guides people to make an informed buying decision. It's a really important component of influencing others and should always be a large part of your marketing strategy.

This is a simple overview of each of the three phases. We'll go deeper into each of these and how you can utilize them as you progress through the various aspects of list-building in later chapters.

Chapter 3

Audience Conversations

Conversations are a key piece to creating influence over an audience, but we should also keep in mind that not everyone communicates the same or likes to be communicated to in the same way. This is especially important to keep in mind as you move forward with your audience-building so that you can meet potential clients where they're at. Sure, you probably have a go-to method you prefer to use to communicate with people, something that you're comfortable with, and that's great. But you also need to expand your thinking and broaden your mindset so that you don't leave an entire group of people from your conversations.

There are quite a few different ways to communicate, but I'm going to share the various methods I use. You should find a use for each of them in your business to some degree. Remember, this is all about building and nurturing relationships. The various formats are here to help you have conversations with your audience in different ways to get attention so you can connect more readily.

A lot of people think the online marketing space is very complicated with all the technology and different platforms that are out there, not to mention the new ones that pop up. But having conversations with your audience and creating relationships with them is the focus. Beyond that, it's just a matter of where you'll be having these conversations. They are still the same conversations and still the same relationships you're nurturing and creating, just on different platforms and formats that may be different than what you might be used to using.

Social Media

Social media communication includes all of the posts that you make, ranging from simple paragraphs of text, video, and anything else that can help start a conversation with someone. Think about the things you're talking about on social media. Are they relevant to your audience? Are they things your audience would not only be interested in but would grab their attention? Is it visually appealing? Here's an amazing way to start a two-way conversation. When somebody leaves a comment, be sure to respond. This will provide a natural back-and-forth with little effort to get there.

Email

Another way to connect is through email. This helps people get one step closer to you. I want you to think of this almost like a letter to your audience. Write things in an interesting way to get their attention and start them thinking about the thing you want them to think about. In my emails, I always like to have some kind of call to action. This could be as simple as encouraging them to reply to me or directing them to check out a resource. Remember, while these are different forms of communication, they're still a conversation. You want to encourage a back-and-forth chat.

Offers

Your offers are yet another way to talk to people, and they can even help you build a relationship between you and your audience. With your offers, it's all about listening to your audience and creating a win for them. This can be something you do to help them in exchange for a fee, but it can also be a list builder in exchange for their email address. This way, you can continue to communicate and build rapport with them. What problems and challenges is your audience facing? How does your offer alleviate that pain? What kind of conversations are you going to have to help your audience believe you understand them?

When you solve a problem for your audience, and you speak about it specifically, people begin to feel heard, like somebody finally understands them. This helps them stick around for future offers, potentially even telling their friends about you.

Calls

Calls could be either by phone or by video over the internet. What I like about this format is that it allows me to have another level of contact with my audience. On a phone call, you can hear somebody's voice and inflection, and then react to them in real-time, removing the filter of ambiguous tone from social media comment sections.

With a video call, you even get to see their face and their mannerisms. By seeing their face, you're connecting with each other on a deeper level than is possible through most other formats. One major benefit of this type of conversation is that it allows you to talk to each other in a naturally flowing, verbal conversation. You can ask each other questions and respond instantly. You also feel more connected when talking to somebody who is sitting in front of you. Hearing their voice and seeing their body language gives you a frame of reference for who they are.

Messaging Apps

DM's or texts/SMS messages are a bit more intimate as they come straight from a phone or social media account. The way you "speak" written in a text may be different than what you would want to send in an email. Texts feel more personal, so they can make a lot of sense to write in a slightly less formal way than you would in some other formats. Because the message lands directly on somebody's phone, it makes it easier for them to respond, quickly sparking a back-and-forth conversation.

In-Person

Finally, we have in-person conversations. We all love when we have the ability to meet in person, as it's one of the best ways to talk to somebody.

You get to really know them, their personality, their body language, their inflection, etc. All of the things that make a person unique are present during in-person conversations. Any time you have the chance, I recommend you talk to people face-to-face.

Now that we've discussed all of the methods of communication that I use, do you find yourself leaning towards one communication method over the others? Is there one you're not as comfortable with? Which one is your go-to? Take some time to really think about this, and begin to stretch yourself. Not everybody communicates the same way, so it's up to us to come up with new ways to reach out to people and spark those conversations with them. This often means getting out of our comfort zone and using formats that can make us uncomfortable. We want to build relationships wherever we can find people, so think about the different conversations you're having now and how you can expand upon them by using these six methods of communication.

Chapter 4

Proper Research

While some of us may not enjoy it, conducting proper research is important in the modern business world. Now, I already hear you saying, "Ugh, research. That sounds really boring. I don't think this is really going to help me. I'm just going to skip to the next chapter." Don't do that.

This is the part where I want you to really pay attention to what I'm saying. Honestly, this is where I see people make some of their biggest mistakes. Research is going to help you with every aspect of your business. It'll help you with your offer, your copy, your social media posts, your free list builders, and so much more. Everything you do moving forward with your audience-building and then your list-building is going to stem from this research, as it will give you a better understanding of your client.

Unfortunately, experts like you and me can sometimes get in a mode where we forget what is most important to our audience members. One day not so long ago, we may have put our expert hats on and decreed ourselves as masters in our field. In doing so, we forgot what it's like to be in earlier phases of our expertise, like where our clients are today. When we get into this mindset, we forget about the challenges they face, the desires they have, and the pain points they experience.

Research keeps us aware of where our clients are in their journey. It also keeps us up to date on the trends that constantly shift in our ever-changing world. When you do this properly, you help people feel understood and heard, which builds trust and really helps to get your audience's attention.

Remember, the first goal is to get traffic, and we want to stay intentional about who we are bringing into our world. We want only the people who are perfect for our offers, as these are the people we can impact the most, which is why we must get to know them so well!

You never want to guess or assume when it comes to knowing your potential clients. Investigation and fact-finding are the only way you can guarantee you're informed as you continue getting and keeping the attention of your audience. It allows you to have the information you can use to speak directly to them and helps you understand one another.

Meet Kari, On Point Quilter

"I'm much better at targeting the right group of people and becoming more defined on what I need to focus on and what I need to do. But what's really interesting is that I've increased my profit percentage, not just my revenue. I've become much more efficient."

Scan Here To Learn More

Read more of this story at http://influencedbook.com/casestudies

As you conduct your research, there are three key factors you should focus on. These will help you get attention, connect better so you can keep their attention, and later convert those connections into sales. With our Adaptive Inner Circle members, we see that when an offer isn't converting as expected (offers aren't being purchased or people don't understand exactly what you do to help them), the problem is always caused by one or two of these three factors being out of alignment with each other.

Your Audience

While you're building your list, it's important to understand the people who make up your audience. You need to understand what a day in their life looks like. This includes knowing their struggles, challenges, goals, and their pain points.

- What are they thinking?
- What are they feeling?
- What are they saying?
- What are they doing?
- Where are they doing and saying it?

When we can collect enough information to truly know and understand them, we're going to reach them easier and more efficiently, building our list with only those exact right people. Then, the things we say will better resonate with them, as if we were cutting through all the noise in a crowded room.

Your Message

Now that you have a clear picture of who your audience is, it's time to really fine-tune your message to speak specifically to that person. The goal, as you continue, is to get deep into the head of your audience, almost to the point that they'll question how you know exactly what they are thinking and what they're going through. Ultimately, you want your message to feel like it's coming from a good friend.

Your Offer

When most people hear the word "offer," they think exclusively about purchased content or services. However, in list-building, this also applies to our free offers. Make sure that, whatever you're putting out in front of your audience, it's totally aligned with what they desire. When you develop your message, you should have a deep understanding of your audience and use that information to "speak their language."

Typically, when there is a disconnection between any of these three, you'll see a noticeable difference between conversions. For instance, maybe you've got a great message and an amazing offer, but you're broadcasting it to the wrong people. But when these three factors are in perfect alignment, that is when sales are made. That's when we can bring people into our world and get them to opt into our lists.

There is gold in the research, so you definitely don't want to skip this step. In the next chapter, we'll begin to talk about different ways you can conduct this research. Right now, it's important to build the right mindset. This doesn't have to be hard, and it definitely doesn't need to be boring. If we have the right attitude toward doing the research, we can later enjoy ourselves as we begin to connect with our audience on a deeper level.

Chapter 5

How to Do Client Research

Now that you understand the motivation behind why we want to research who our ideal client is, let's talk about the how. As you go into this, think of yourself as a detective, digging up info on the people that make up your market. It's all about finding clues. These clues point us toward what our client is thinking, what they're going through, the pain points they're talking about, the challenges they have, and maybe even the things they aspire to be, do, and have. As you begin your detective work, be mindful that the ultimate goal is to align your audience, message, and offer so that they will continue to do business with you.

Meet Patti, Rare Disease Coach

Patti found some amazing Facebook posts that provide insights into working with doctors, which were created by patients and others who shared their challenges, problems, feelings, thoughts, and actions with recommendations about getting care. This research allows her to create relevant content that connects with her audience.

Scan Here To Learn More

Read more of this story at http://influencedbook.com/casestudies

Social Media

Conversations

We touched a little bit on social media conversations earlier. This is where we dig into that area a bit more. There are many places where you can begin to search for clues as to what your audience is doing in their lives so you can also uncover the things they need help with most.

The first place you want to look for this data is social media. Look inside social media groups and on pages revolving around your area of business. The odds are good that you are already a member of a few of these and won't need to look very hard to find them. However, if you aren't already part of these social media discussions, your first task will be to find them.

Once you've selected a few groups and pages to look at, focus on the kinds of conversations that are being held within them, this is where you'll find a ton of clues pertaining to your audience's wants and desires. One thing to pay close attention to is which questions are being asked and how often they repeat. What are the biggest concerns they have? What are some of the wins that they share? Once you've found groups where your ideal client is hanging out, it's always a good idea to keep track of them and occasionally pop in to observe and take notes on these questions and concerns.

Eye Roll Posts

You also want to look out for what we call the Eye Roll Posts. Our good friend and mentor, Jeff Walker, recently asked us to give a presentation to his mastermind on this concept. He was so impressed by the training that, during his own pre-launch training series, he shared this tip with his audience of nearly 50,000 people on how to do this. His launch is typically one of the largest in the industry at around 5 million dollars each year. I share this with you because I want to impress upon you the value of this particular research technique.

Eye roll posts are the ones that you see again and again and again as you scroll through your favorite group's feed. It may not be worded the same way each time, but the sentiment is always the same. While the average reader who is actively engaged in this group may find these annoying (thus, the eye roll), to us marketers, these are little nuggets of gold. If this type of comment is common enough for people to begin recognizing them instantly, then it's a prevalent problem people within your community are facing. They desperately need an answer. This is one of those big clues that you should focus on.

Here's a great example. I've recently taken on a new hobby of doodling. It gives me a creative outlet. But it's not as simple as it sounds. I have a lot of questions about how to doodle correctly.

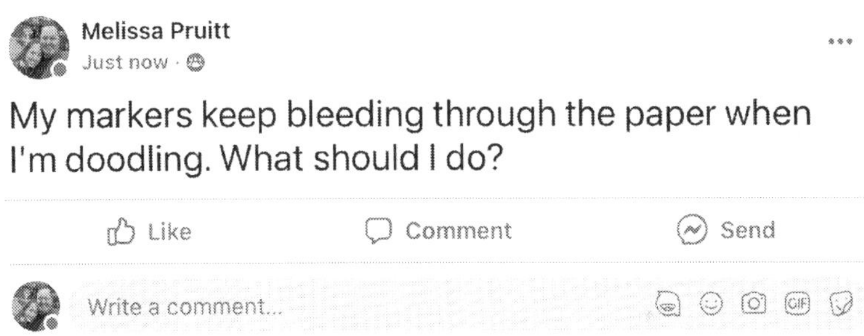

- What kind of paper should I use?
- Which markers don't bleed through the paper?
- Where is the best place to buy paper and markers?

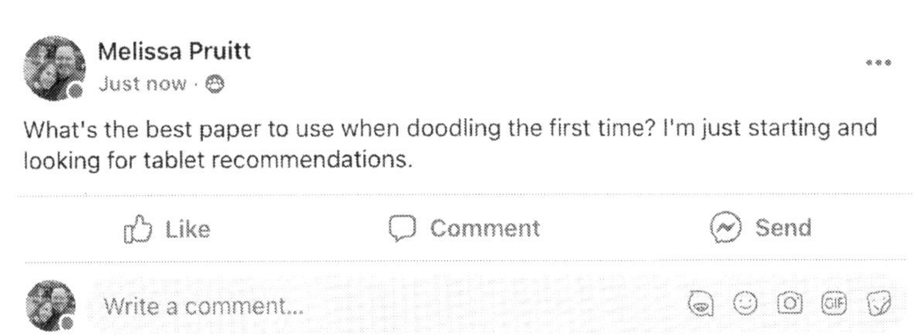

Basically, I have a lot of beginner-level questions that those more experienced doodlers in the group are probably tired of seeing. They most likely get frustrated with that because they've seen these questions asked over and over and over again, and there's probably already a resource somewhere that I didn't see.

The person I'm following has created a lead magnet for recommended markers, paper, and other resources as a result of these kinds of questions coming up over and over again. She also has a store that offers those resources l because she knows that those are the most commonly asked questions, and she knows this because of those eye roll posts.

Begin to keep a list of eye roll posts for your audience. These are the topics you'll want to speak about for your audience because they are relevant and specific to them, which enables you to create ongoing conversations about topics that they're actually interested in.

Relationships

Once you're in these groups, interacting and having conversations, begin to find ways to provide value in whatever way you feel comfortable. The key here is to not expect anything but to forge strong relationships within your community. If you see somebody asking a question that you can answer, feel free to jump in and talk to them. This might lead to more conversations with this same person or others that will help you do even deeper research, giving you even more insight into the places your audience members struggle.

All of this information will quickly begin to pile up, giving you a deep view of who your ideal client is because they're the ones who have told you. Through social media, you can really connect with people and peel back the curtain to see who is behind it. How cool would it be if you could take one of those eye-rolling posts and turn that common question into a list builder or resource that spoke to that concern that comes up all the time? It could end up becoming the key your audience uses to finally overcome that hurdle they've been facing, instantly building a deep sense of trust between you and your client. But you'll never be able to build that if you don't find these posts hidden within these public interactions.

Book Reviews

Book reviews are another good place to research your ideal client. Personally, I love book reviews, as they're a way to get direct comments from your audience about what it is that they want. Amazon is, of course, a great place to start, as they're one of the largest book and e-book distributors in the world. They're always going to have books, both old and new, and the reviews to follow. Look at books that speak to the topic you're helping people with. For basically any industry, there are already tons of books that exist to address your market. Go to that section, and begin to go through the books and their reviews. You may decide to look through new, hot-selling ones or tried and true classics.

The greatest part is people will tell you directly in their own words exactly what they thought of this book. They'll tell you what they loved, "This book taught me X, Y, and Z. I learned so much, and it solved this problem for me." Take note of the problems solved in these reviews, as it tells you the solutions your market is looking for.

tupelotina

★★★★★ **Great book full of incredibly helpful information geared towards the ...**

Reviewed in the United States on August 29, 2016

Verified Purchase

Great book full of incredibly helpful information geared towards the business side of photography. Coupled along with an amazing online forum of mutual photographers... The information given by Paul and Melissa is endless.

april

★★★★★ **A Must Buy**

Reviewed in the United States

Verified Purchase

This is literally my first review I have ever done on Amazon. So, let's get to the point. I own 2 paper copies and an ebook copy of this book. I absolutely love it. I orginally ordered one paper book but after a few hours it was covered in sticky notes and highlight. Than I forgot it at home so I got the ebook to continue on. Than bought the second paper book just to have one in my reference books that wasn't all highlighted. This book is great for beginners to pro. We all have something to learn. It's easy to read and understand no BS just a fellow photographer wanting to help out others follow there dreams too. Thank You Paul and Melissa you guys are amazing.

On the flip side, there will inevitably be books that don't have such great reviews. "I wish this book talked more about this subject." Or, "This book didn't mention this problem I have. I was disappointed because of X, Y, and Z." These reviews are equally as important as the reviews that solved all of your ideal client's problems and answered all of their questions, as you'll still see the pain points they're experiencing.

stephanie

★★★☆☆ **Really did not learn a lot from this book.**

Reviewed in the United States

Verified Purchase

Really did not learn a lot from this book. You can learn more or iust as much off Facebook groups for free

Sid

★★★☆☆ **Great book**

Reviewed in the United States

Good for inspiration ideas on starting a photography business. The author uses a background in sales as a tool for making his business successful. He has a lot of great points which are invaluable

Client Interviews

Another option that many don't think of is to interview past clients you've served. This is one of my favorites (and it's one of the most powerful). Your past clients are full of information about you, your offer, and how it helps people like them. As such, they are one of the sources you can research to really get an idea of what people in your niche are going through. These are people who you've already got a trusting connection with, who trust your work and can communicate with you. They're a source to turn to for insight into your market's thoughts and emotions while also getting a firsthand perspective from somebody you can trust.

Step 1: Reach out individually and ask for an interview.

Here's a little script you can use:

"Hey, I want to do some research. I know we worked together in the past, and I would love to pick your brain a little about how we worked together and how it helped you. Would you mind if I do a little interview with you and ask you some questions so I can get a better understanding of how I can continue to help others that are going through a similar situation as you?"

For the most part, people are more than happy to help you out with this.

Step 2: Schedule the interview call.

While it's possible, and not necessarily a bad idea, to do this over the phone, I'd recommend doing it on either Zoom or Skype. Doing it this way will make it easier to record your interview, allowing you to rewatch it later and retain all the information without having to take extensive notes during the call. It allows you to stay in the moment and give your interviewee your full attention. Plus, it will feel like a more natural conversation for both of you, which will give you better results in the long run.

Step 3: Have a set of questions ready.

During this interview, you're specifically targeting the pain points that you helped them solve or that they're still experiencing.

Here are some questions to get you started:

- What were you thinking, saying, feeling, and doing before you met me?
- What were your previous pain points? / Which pain points did we help you solve?
- What did an ordinary day look like for you before working with me?

You want to keep your questions conversational without being too intrusive while still getting a sense of where they are.

Then, you need to ask them those same questions but apply them to the current day.

- What results did you get from working with me?
- What about me made you decide to choose me to help you solve

this problem?
- Now that we've worked together, what are your current, new pain points?

The contrast between the two periods described in their own words will help paint a beautiful picture of what kinds of questions and problems your audience is having and possibly going to have. This is why it's important to record these conversations. Otherwise, when you translate their words into notes, you may lose out on important details that help the picture remain clear.

As you ask questions during these interviews, remain attentive and curious. Try to get as much detail as possible, and be sure to ask follow-up questions. The more information that you can capture, the more data you'll have to work with, and the better list builders you'll be able to make. This information will allow you to speak about the topics your people are interested in, address their problems and challenges directly, and make sure that your messaging reflects that. Here's a great example of an interview with one of our Adaptive Inner Circle clients, Noelle. Before joining Adaptive, Noelle struggled with building her audience. After over five years of hard work and struggle, she was only able to build her list to 900 people (less than 200 per year). After joining Adaptive, she built her list to 2,547 in less than a year. And in less than two years, she grew it even more to 4,687 and is still growing!

Melissa: Before you came into Adaptive, tell me a little about some of the types of marketing that you did to get your business out there.

Noelle: I had lead magnets. I offered free workshops. I just tried to build my membership, and so when I came to you, I had 900 people on my list and less than 30 members in my membership. And I came to you because that was the problem.

Melissa: So you were doing all the things, but in looking back now and reflecting, what do you think wasn't connecting for you?

Noelle: The thing that stands out the most for me is I'm giving away too much. My message isn't clear and concise, and I'm, I'm feeling like, "Oh, I need to provide all the things." You really don't. You need to provide that one thing that you can teach someone that they can have success with. And so, I laugh all the time when I see this freebie called, My 7 Favorite Interview Questions to Hire Your Next Great Teacher. It started with 110 when I showed up in Adaptive and talked to you or Paul and everybody, and you were like, "Whoa, you don't need to overwhelm them."

Do you see all the juicy data inside those two simple questions? Now, imagine what is possible if you have an entire twenty to thirty minutes with someone to ask questions like these. And when you can ask that same set of questions over and over until you've collected a group of five to ten people's responses, the insight you'll gain will blow your mind.

Other Resources & Solutions

At this point, you can spread out into other areas for even more research. In every industry, there are tons of resources and solutions already in the marketplace. You can Google a specific problem you have right now and find several answers and possibly even tools to help you overcome it.

Please allow me to give you a word of encouragement here. One big problem we see people face when they attempt to start a business is they enter a scarcity mode. They see the pre-existing solutions that others in their industry have already created, and they think to themselves:

- "Oh my gosh, I can't do this."
- "I can't build a course."
- "I can't create a program."
- "It's all been made already. There's nothing original I can come up with. It's all been done."

- "Nothing I can create will be able to help my people."

Don't get discouraged by all of that. The fact that there are already resources in your subject area is proof, beyond a shadow of a doubt, that there is a need for what you do.

The good thing is we all have different perspectives on life, and this often leads to different answers to the same questions. There is not only one solution to each and every problem in the world. In fact, most solutions work best for a specific group with a specific perspective and may not work for another similar group with a slightly different perspective. Often, both tactics work, even though they use different methods to reach the same conclusion.

Look to see what tools and resources others have already created to answer these questions and lean on them to give you clues to the questions being spoken to and the aspirations they address for your audience. All of this will only help you further get in tune with what your audience is thinking, saying, feeling, and doing. Next, we'll take all the information you've found and put your unique spin on it, so you can create content that provides your answers to these questions.

Chapter 6

The 104 Formula™

We've talked a lot about research and how that can help you identify and attract your perfect people. If you haven't yet researched your ideal audience, then the time to do so is now, as the data you find is going to be essential to you using the 104 Formula™. This research is just the starting point. Now, we are going to put it into action. In the next few chapters, we'll dive deep into my signature 104 Formula™ for creating engaging content and all the ways you can use this research to convert your information seekers into buyers.

The 104 Formula™ takes all of the things that our audience is thinking, feeling, saying, and doing and links them with all of the things that are relevant to them. This will help you easily create engaging content that is super intentional about reaching your market. You need this content to be specific, getting inside their head so that it speaks directly to them. If you can do this in a way that only speaks to the topics that your people are interested in, it makes them feel heard. It's like somebody finally understands them, and they'll want to hear what you have to say in return. From there, we can share our strategies and tactics. Of course, this includes your solutions, which take the form of your offers. Every single piece of content that you create should be linked directly to one of these, leading your people to the next step of your plan.

This ultimately allows you to better serve your audience and bring them along the journey through your world and your offers, showing them how you can help. It's an intentional way of list-building and makes sense to your audience.

The goal is to create 104 pieces of content, two topics for each week of the year. While you might be thinking, "Oh my gosh! I don't even know if my person has that many problems or challenges. There's no way I can come up with that many." I don't want you to stress yourself out. We're going to go through this step-by-step and keep this as simple as possible.

The greatest part of the 104 Formula™ is that once you begin to put it into practice, you'll never have to create new content again. After you've researched your ideal client, and you've picked their brain, learning their struggles and needs, you'll find they all have similar problems. So, you can recycle this content, using it over and over again, just tweaking it to say the same thing in different ways so that your audience will hear it based on their different circumstances.

A lot of times, people create content just for the sake of creating content, with no real plan behind it. They have no idea where they want to take their audience next. All they know is that they need to capture as many people as possible. While this is a great way to engage with and nurture an audience, you may find your conversions lacking if this is the only way you're promoting yourself. While you always want to put yourself out there as much as possible, getting people used to seeing you, you also need to have a clear goal on what you want them to do after they begin following you. Speak directly on that thing that they're stressing out about, focusing on their exact pain point. Then, focus on your next step, and lead them naturally to that, whether it's your offer or something as simple as hopping on a call with you. Whatever the next step is, you want to lead them there with your content. This is exactly what the 104 Formula™ was designed to do. It's going to help you stay intentional with your list-building while making your audience feel understood and more willing to listen to what you have to say.

Chapter 7

Audience Pain Points

Now that you know what your people are thinking, feeling, saying, and doing, you can speak to them in a way that they feel truly understood, as if you know everything they're going to say without them having to say it. As I've said many times, when people feel understood at this level, they're more likely to pay attention to what you have to say in return. You see, your audience comes to you from a specific perspective we call their pain point. They have a problem, a challenge, a stress, or something that they need help dealing with at that moment. It's important to speak about these challenges and experiences in our list-building content, saying, "Hey, we understand what you're going through. We get what you're thinking. We know what you're feeling. We hear what you're saying, and we get what you're doing." When we relay this message back to our people, they can sense that we truly care, and they'll know they aren't alone in this challenge.

I like to really "feel" what they are feeling, and I have an exercise that helps me connect with the way my ideal client is feeling. During this activity, I set aside time to think about what a day in that perfect person's life looks like, and I imagine what all of that feels like, allowing myself to feel those feelings, too.

A Day in the Life

Close your eyes and visualize your ideal client living out a typical day in their life. Envision it as though you are viewing everything on a big screen. Allow yourself permission to be creative as you do this.

- What are they going through?
- What's going on in their head?
- What are they feeling?
- What are they saying?
- Who are they talking to?
- What's going on in this scene?
- What actions are they taking?

Try to be as specific and clear as possible in this exercise, as this will help you stay as relevant as possible in your content creation.

The main reason I love this exercise is that it allows you to start from those beginning pain points and imagine and feel the feelings they'll experience and where they'll end up as the day closes.

For example, in our coaching program, Adaptive Inner Circle, a lot of times, we work with people that have a specialty in their field. They're considered the experts at what they do but still need a little assistance with marketing. Specifically, they need help with selling their products or services to get their offers out into the world. When someone like this initially comes to us, a lot of times, they're thinking, "I just don't know where to start. I can't figure out where to begin. This whole marketing thing is overwhelming to me. There are so many choices. Where do I go with this?"

Because these people are typically experts with all the habits and skills that it takes to be an expert, they're often used to figuring things out on their own. They know how to tackle problems and find solutions to them.

Like most of us, when they hit roadblocks, feelings can enter the mix. Not only are they confused by the vast world of marketing and all of the options they have at their disposal, but self-doubt and fear are screaming in their ear. While yes, they're experts who do what they do well, they may have never sold anything under their own brand before. This brings with it conflicting feelings, and dealing with those feelings can be scary. To work for somebody is one thing, but to put yourself out there to try and sell your service, product, or offer, is a vastly different challenge. Often, this manifests itself as being afraid of rejection, causing them to not even try to market themselves. "What if I put myself out there and nobody buys? What if people just won't like what I have to offer?"

Meet Sally, Coach for Moms of Defiant Adult Children

"I've tried other mastermind programs, which I got lost in because they're so large. I've worked with business coaches too, and while I gleaned good things from each, there was no support system. I'm also technically challenged, so I froze every time I had to do anything with technology and would have to pay people to help me."

Scan Here To Learn More

Read more of this story at http://influencedbook.com/casestudies

These are examples of challenges my audience members face. Since you're reading this book, it is something you've probably experienced too. When I sit down to visualize a day in the life of my perfect people, I play these conversations and experiences over that big movie screen in my mind. And I really think through how each of these thoughts and experiences may affect their entire day and what that might look like as it plays out. It forms an internal bond in me as I empathize with their plight. Later, that empathy and relatability will come through in my content.

As you continue this exercise, pay attention to the internal and external language being used by your perfect person. External language consists of the words we express to others verbally. It is what we hear as we work with our clients. These are things they say out loud. As an example, when our clients are in this state and need help getting started, they'll say to us, "I don't know how to do this. I'm clueless. This is totally new to me, and I just can't figure out where to get started. I just don't understand."

This is the external language they're using, and it often looks like trash talk directed at themselves. In their minds, the internal language they're using probably sounds like, "I'm not good enough to do this. I should never have started. What was I thinking? I'm just not cut out for this!" It's just as important to focus on what they're saying to themselves as you focus on what they say to you.

Lastly, you want to think about what your audience is doing. In our experience, when our potential clients and audience members put themselves into uncomfortable situations with marketing and selling their offers, they often end up procrastinating. They have ideas of what they're supposed to do, but instead of getting up and trying, their minds shut off, and they scroll through their social media feeds, doing anything else besides what they need to do to be successful.

They're doing it because they're in that uncomfortable starting position. They're overwhelmed, and they're afraid of what might happen. They're having conversations in their head, "I'm just not smart enough to figure this out. My voice is annoying, and nobody is going to like what I have to say anyways." This is often where people will sabotage themselves and start procrastinating.

Can you see how specific we've gotten with this? We've really gotten into our audiences' heads, and we can understand what they're saying, thinking, feeling, and doing before we've even talked to them. The more specific, the more relevant you can make this, the better-understood people will feel when they hear your message.

This can also be conveyed not just in your list-building content but also in all copy for your marketing. In everything that you do, you're going to be connecting with people and really letting them know you get it, that you understand them.

As you continue thinking about this movie in your mind, picture the screen and what the person is going through, "I need to lose weight. What should I do? Should I go keto? Should I go paleo? Should I go vegetarian?" As I picture these questions, I also think about where they're at. I can imagine them pushing a cart through the aisles of a grocery store and asking themselves these questions. They really want to create healthy meals for their family, but they can't figure out where to start or which diet to try. The worst part is that this isn't the only problem they're facing. Sure, in a world where food was free, you could just try everything until you found what works, but this family also has to stress about their budget. They can't afford to spend money on certain items, and many of these trendy diets can be expensive. This adds yet another factor to how they feel and another factor we can hone in on and speak to.

Externally, they may be saying things like, "I'm not a good cook. I'm not a good meal planner. I haven't done this before. It's all new to me." And while they have these conversations externally, what are they saying to themselves? "I feel like I'm letting my family down if I don't get this right, but I just don't understand how to make these delicious-looking recipes for healthy meals."

All of these things are reflections of how they see themselves and how they fear the other members of their family see them. And from these thoughts, they may begin to sabotage themselves. Maybe they stop going to the grocery store, choosing to get greasy, fried, fast-food because it's easier. This is how specific you should be taking your own mental movie as you experience a day in the life of your ideal client.

Maybe they want to write a book. They're excited because they feel like they have a really good idea for a story, and they want the world to experience it. The problem is, they haven't written in years, and that was only for college papers. They begin to doubt themselves, "Well, maybe that's a good idea, but I just don't have the skills to pull this off. Maybe it should just stay an idea." Externally, they're saying, "How do I even write this in a way that makes sense? I don't know where to start."

Internally, they may be saying to themselves, "No one's going to read this. No one's going to be interested in this story. They won't care what I write. It's copied anyways, and nobody wants something that isn't original."

Finally, they begin to procrastinate. The self-doubt and fear have taken hold, and they're now afraid to start, deciding it's easier to do nothing at all. They may begin to occupy themselves with anything that's not writing. Maybe they've begun to write a little bit, but they haven't taken action to turn it into something major. They may have a beautiful manuscript, but it just sits there on their computer, never going anywhere. Even though they really want to put this book out into the world, they simply can't bring themselves to do anything with it.

For a final example, let's think about what the day in the life of a brick-and-mortar business owner looks like. They have a real-life business, and they want more clients. They want more people knocking on their doors and coming into their world every day. They may be thinking, "I want more clients to come into my business, but I don't know how to get them in." They may be feeling overwhelmed about this because they don't know marketing. They're dealing with staff and all the other things that come with running a brick-and-mortar business. They may already be at their mental limit, all without trying to worry about marketing to grow their consumer base. They might be saying out loud, "I tried putting an ad in the paper. I also tried running ads on Facebook, but nothing works for me!" Internally, they're probably doubting themselves by now, "Am I cut out for this? I've been running this business for a while, but I can't get it to grow. Can I really do this? Can I keep this business afloat?"

Then, what are they doing? One of the things they may be doing is sabotaging themselves by working in the business but not on it. They might be focusing on their clients and staff so hard that putting themselves out into the market becomes a side thought, something that isn't important to chase.

Hopefully, these examples have helped you understand how to portray the movie in your mind as you do this exercise for your own audience. You need to have a deep understanding of your audience if you want to succeed, and this method will help get you the clarity you need to obtain that vision.

Chapter 8

Audience Desire Points

Let's shift gears and focus more on helping the people on our list achieve their desired results. This includes what they aspire to, what motivates them, and what they dream of on the other side of this transformation. The more specific you can get when addressing your audience, the better understood they'll feel, and when we put that into the content of our list builders and social media content, those people are more likely to pay attention.

The goal is to paint the picture of what their life is going to look like once they move past this struggle. You don't want to keep them focused on the negative in their lives. Nobody wants to stay in that pain. Focus on what they desire, what's going to motivate them to keep moving forward towards that end result that they really want.

This is equally important as addressing pain points. Sometimes when people are in pain, they can't even begin to imagine what life would look like without these burdens. They have blinders on that prevent them from imagining a better life, and they can only see things going one way. What we're doing here is opening up our audiences' minds to help them see how much better things can be. The more often we can do this, and the more specific we can be, the more likely our audience is to raise their hand up and say, "Yes, I want my life to look like that. I want to feel like that instead of going through what I am now."

This is a really important piece because you've already addressed the pain. Now you need to address where you want to take them, the place they start to believe they can be—final transformation. Everything in between these two points will be covered by your list builders, and these will be the steps your audience takes on the journey to that transformation. Conveying this to your audience is critical so that they really feel like you understand them. Then, your offer is going to help them get to where they want to be and will help them reach their aspirational point.

While this may seem like a bit of a silly example, it works. I want you to imagine one of those over-the-top infomercials. There's always a black-and-white shot of somebody hunched over in pain or doing something incorrectly. This is your audience in their pain point. The other side then is when the infomercial moves back to color, with the actor smiling, happy, and in a great place because they've solved their problem. Clearly paint the picture of pain for your audience, and then show them how much better life can be once they overcome this challenge that you can help them solve. Give them clear, specific examples so that they can truly understand this and begin to open their minds up to new possibilities.

Now, I'm going to go back to the examples from the previous chapter and show you how my husband, Paul, and I help our audience see what's possible in their futures. In our Adaptive Inner Circle and also in our Adaptive Marketing Program, we often have people come to us who are overwhelmed. There's so much to know and understand in the world of marketing. This usually makes them feel stuck and unable to get started. They're not feeling great about it, and there are a lot of self-doubts involved. While they may be an expert in their subject area, it can be difficult to declare that to the world, so there's a lot of fear. They may be afraid of rejection, and this often leads to procrastination. They're doing everything else besides marketing because they're afraid and so overwhelmed that they just can't bring themselves to start. This is often the point where they approach us, looking for a solution to their problems. But what does somebody's life look like after they've traveled our Transformation Track™ and made it to the other side?

Meet Sally, Coach for Moms of Defiant Adult Children

"After working with Paul & Melissa in their Inner Circle program, it's given me hope for once that I'm on the right track. I feel momentum for the first time in my business. I feel I'm actually gaining traction."

Scan Here To Learn More

Read more of this story at http://influencedbook.com/casestudies

They're thinking, "Wow, I really understand marketing now. I'm able to sell my offers, and I've gotten more time and more money." They may be feeling super proud of themselves and their business. They are also in a financial position to give to organizations and causes they really care about. They feel less stressed because they're not worried about all of the marketing pieces. They may be saying, "You know, I'm able to make an impact." They now have the confidence that they need to be a high-performing business owner, and everything within their business is serving them, their family, and their community. They're looking at the bigger picture, able to see the good that they can do because of their business' increased success from improved marketing.

They're traveling, spending time with their family, and paying off debts. They're doing the things they love to do because they now have the ability to do so. Their business is doing so well that they're not working all the time, and their business is now just a piece of life, and it's allowing them to do all the other things they want while still making an impact on the world.

They've made it to the other side of their problem. They now understand marketing at a much higher level than before, and they have more freedom in their life to pursue the things they enjoy. They no longer have that deep sense of overwhelm where they are worried about marketing or how the world may perceive their messaging. Their business is serving them now because they've had that transformation, they understand marketing, and they're getting the rewards for their hard work.

You can see how different the two stages are, from the overwhelming fear in their pain point to all of the wonderful things they're now able to do both inside and outside of their business. That's how we need to paint the picture of what life could look like on the other side of transformation.

Remember the example of preparing healthy meals? The individual wants to begin creating healthy meals for their family. They're overwhelmed because there are so many choices out there for food. They have a lot of self-doubts that they may not be able to cook impressive meals, so they feel like they're letting their families down. And like many families, they may have to adhere to a strict budget to make ends meet, adding another layer of complexity and stress to their already hectic schedule. They may be self-sabotaging, telling themselves, "This is too hard. I'm just going to order out and not even worry about any of this." But let's take a look at the other side of this pain point and paint a picture of what their life could look like on the other side of these problems.

At the end of this, they're likely not even thinking about meal planning anymore because it's just so natural to them. It's become second nature, so there's no stress or worry about it. It's become fun, and they look forward to it. They're excited about what they make for their family, and they're proud of it. Everyone loves the meals they're cooking. What's also exciting is the amount of money they've been able to save with meal planning, meaning they now have savings to do fun things like family vacations or future needs like putting money away in a college fund for their kids. With all the money they're saving on food, they're able to do what's important to them.

They may be saying, "I love this so much. I love to cook for other people, and now I have the confidence to do it." They're bringing food to share at family events or parties with their friends. They can now make a big impact with the things they're doing. Meals aren't a tension point in the house anymore because it's all about the meal plans they've created.

As you can see, when they came to you in that pain point, looking for ways to make healthy meals while staying on a budget, it was a big stressor. It was keeping them up at night, wondering just how they were going to be able to do this. Not only is it something that takes a decent amount of skill, but transitioning to healthy food is often expensive, adding extra stress to their plates. Yet now, it's a natural part of their lives. They're cooking meals and loving every second of it. They also have the added benefit of extra money to be able to save for things important to them and have a little bit of extra fun with their family.

What if they don't take action? On the surface, choosing to stay in pain will mean they'll continue to miss out on healthy meals, and they'll scramble around day-to-day trying to figure out what to eat. But on a deeper level, the true consequences, the ones that will keep them up at night, are the lack of energy, the time they are wasting trying to figure things out, and the level of stress that comes with declining health. Let's not forget about the agonizing guilt when family members experience declines in health as well.

Too many marketers focus on the pain they are in now and stop there, but if you keep going and also show them the future ahead for them if they don't take action and they don't buy your offer, this is often what helps them make the decision to move forward with you.

Going back to the example of the book, most people who want to become authors are under a lot of stress. Creating a book is a long process that requires hours of work. It's an overwhelming event if you don't know what you're doing, especially when you step back and realize just how much you'll have to write. This person isn't a natural writer, and they're worried they won't be able to write this book because they can't even figure out where to get started. They may have written a little bit of something, but it likely isn't much. They're not putting it out into the world. They're not talking about this dream with others. If this is the pain point, what does the other side look like?

They're thinking about just how excited they are. They've written their book, it's published and sold online or on store shelves, and they're already thinking about their next book. They're planning ahead, and they're super excited for the next one. They're thinking about all the different opportunities that they now have access to because of their book. They're being asked to be on stages, to go on podcasts, to share their ideas, and be a thought leader for the masses. They may even be walking down the street, and somebody might stop them for an autograph because they're so excited to meet and talk to them about the book.

They're proud of themselves. They're excited and looking forward to sharing new ideas in their future books. They're saying, "Hey, maybe I should go on a book tour and share this idea with an even bigger audience." They're sharing their ideas through their books, and they're owning the fact that they are now an author. They're writing more, making more time in their schedule to do something that they now love. From the royalties of the book, they now have more time to do things like travel and have fun while still sharing their message around the world. It's a big transformation from being overwhelmed, unable to start putting pen to paper, to when the book is out there, and they now have all of these opportunities at their fingertips.

For the final example, let's talk about the brick-and-mortar store owner. This person is struggling to find new clients, unable to get people in the door. They've tried some marketing in the past, but it didn't really go their way, so they're discouraged. "Oh, that won't work for me. I'm not even going to try again." They're so busy working in the business, managing team members, and taking care of existing clients that they can't focus on marketing. There are a lot of self-doubts, wondering if they can keep the business going or if they'll have to close the doors.

After the transformation, they're thinking about how excited they are. Maybe they've found new ways to run the business because they're so busy. The marketing has worked, and they now have so many clients coming in the door that they don't have enough hands on deck to handle them all. They're confident about their business and proud of what they were able to build it into. They've made an amazing work culture that everyone loves working in, and they always have inquiries from people because they've made such a huge impact on their community. They're excited to share their work stories with their friends, as they always have new people coming in. As successful business owners, they're helping to mentor others as well. Sharing what made them successful, generating an even bigger impact on people around them.

Now, the business is running on its own, allowing the owner to take more time off and relax. They're spending time with their family, traveling, and trying new things. The business has begun serving them to the point they may be considering a second location. It's a massive transformation from closed-minded marketing, where you don't make a ton of progress. Once the self-doubt is stripped away, it allows the business owner to begin putting themselves out there to the world, drawing in more clients.

This is the transformational piece that really allows us to speak to those pain points and show people just what's possible in their own lives. Our people know their challenges well, and they're struggling with them. When you're in that fight or flight mode, it becomes easy to let the darkness surround you, closing your mind to all of the opportunities around you. It's our job to help people begin to think creatively and desire these changes even more. When we can do this, our audience will pay attention to what we have to say. Again, this is all about the 104 Formula™. We need to create content that speaks to the challenges and aspirations of our audience, and our social media content and list builders are going to be the link between these two points. We're going to help people reach their transformation through our content. It needs to be relevant to them, or they won't pay attention to us, even if we truly can help them meet their goals.

Chapter 9

The Transformation Track™

People don't usually climb from a pain point directly to an inspirational point. There are steps that have to be completed between the two to reach the final destination. This is where the Transformation Track™ comes into play. People are going to buy our services, our products, and our offers to help them get from where they are to where they want to be. But there's a big gap between these two places, and our offers are the metaphorical vehicles that will carry them from location to location as they continue on their journey. Because of this, it's really important that we're always aware of the beginning and end points on the Transformation Track™.

When someone comes into your world, there are a lot of different things they can do to help themselves reach that desired result. Again, it's not going to happen overnight, and there are probably a ton of different steps they'll need to take in order to get there. Being aware of these desire points, as well as the different stages on the path to reach them, is going to help you celebrate the small milestones that your audience reaches on their journey and help them see what is possible.

For example, someone who wants to run a marathon for the first time has probably made up their mind that they're going to compete in one this year, but they haven't even started running yet. They don't have that skill in their wheelhouse. They don't run casually around the block, let alone competitively in a race. One of their first steps might be to start walking more and build up those muscles without burning themselves out. On the first day, they need to get up and just walk to the mailbox, something almost everybody can do. Then the next day, they might walk around their neighborhood, getting that daily movement in, but still not too challenging.

As they begin to build up their stamina, they'll start to jog and then for increasingly longer distances, going further and further each day. Eventually, that jog becomes a run. Before you know it, they are running that marathon. These are all points on the Transformation Track™ of a marathon runner. Each of these points needs to be crossed off in order to reach that end goal.

Nobody wakes up and says, "I'm going to run a marathon today with no preparation. Let's go do it!" They had to take many tiny steps to reach their destination. The same goes for what we want to do with our offers and the content that we put out with our list builders. We want our content to attract different people at different stages and to be relevant to people no matter where they are in that stage. This may be somebody who we are helping early on in their journey or somebody who has been committed to this for a while and still needs help getting clarity to reach the end. Whether it's somebody who's early on in their journey, looking for ways to start, or somebody who needs to be guided to their final step, the content we put into our social media and list builders should be able to speak to anybody, no matter where they are on your Transformation Track™.

The Adaptive Marketing & Sales Success System

	Audience	Message	Offer
Build	Create your foundational marketing assets that will position you as the expert in your field, so you attract the right audience.	Develop and test messaging so that you attract your optimal audience that will be aligned with your offers.	Develop and test different offers to help better define your initial core offer.
Launch	Creating a proper runway for your offer to properly identify the buyers within your audience.	Testing different messaging methods to properly segment your audience into buyers and non-buyers.	Develop and test different offers to help better define your Ultimate Offer.
Grow	Accelerate your audience growth through strategic partnerships, advanced exposure opportunities, and proactive marketing strategies.	Split testing messages and platforms, tracking for optimization, and creating systems to more properly align your audience and your offers.	Develop and test elements of a complete product suite, advanced funnel flow optimizations, and evergreen offers.

As you build up your list builders, you need to keep in mind what your audience is thinking, feeling, saying, and doing as they reach every individual stage in their journey. As you think about that Transformation Track™, remember that there's no predetermined amount of stages your track must have, and there isn't a limit to it either. It's always different, from person-to-person and from topic to topic. Think about everything that your clients will need to complete in order to reach their destination, as each of these will be a different step on your Transformation Track™.

For example, within our Adaptive Marketing Program, we help people with marketing and selling their offers. Nobody goes from having no clue about marketing straight to being an expert in the field. One of the first steps that they take on their Transformation Track™ is learning the kinds of questions to ask about marketing and where they can ask for help. While this is just one piece of their journey, it helps them move towards the desired result of having a marketing plan, one that will build their business to get the sales and results they want.

Speak to where they're at on your Transformation Track™, helping them to move from where they are to where they want to be and all the points in between. Your list builders should be attracting people who are at different stages and need your help to reach the end of their journey.

As you're going through the framework, keep in mind what your audience is thinking, saying, feeling, and doing. Be as specific and relatable as possible to the ideal person you're trying to reach. If they're within the early stages of your track, they'll feel more comfortable as they'll know that you understand their struggles. For those who are further along in their journey, their challenges may be different than they were in the early steps of your Transformation Track™, but this may not always be the case. If there are differences, address them as you see fit within your list builders.

At the end of the day, everybody is looking for their desired transformation as their end goal. Having a clearly defined Transformation Track™ will help you get specific and speak to the challenges your audience is facing and ultimately help you to push them towards their desired outcome. Once you connect with people through your list-building content, it's going to be a natural lead to your offers. Your offer is what's going to help them fill in the gap between where they are and the ultimate transformation they want. If you can really hone in on what they want and the challenges they face, then your audience is more likely to listen to you. So, get started on your Transformation Track™ and begin to map that out from start to finish.

Chapter 10

Ideas, Beliefs, Feelings, & Actions

Up to this point, we've talked a lot about what our people are thinking, saying, feeling, and doing from the perspective of when they first come to us with their struggles and the stress they feel as they make progress toward their desired result. Now, we're going to shift gears and talk about the ideas, feelings, beliefs, and actions they will experience as they begin to think about whether a transformation is possible for them.

Right now, your audience has a certain reality. They have beliefs, ideas, feelings, and experiences they've had in life. Empower your people by presenting a new set of ideas, beliefs, feelings, and actions. Currently, they are limited by their worldview and what they know about themselves. If they had all the answers, they'd have never come to you, right? Because of the ideas they've internalized, they may be holding themselves back without even realizing it. In a sense, we have to sell them, guide them, and help them to have a new way of looking at things. Where they're at right now, trapped in this pain point, is so far away from where they want to be that, without serious change, they won't reach the end. It might not even feel like a potential reality for them. Inside, they may feel like they will never have a chance of reaching their perfect outcome.

They're likely saying and thinking, "You know what? I can't even imagine what that life would be like, because I'm in so much pain over here, dealing with all these things. How will I ever make it to where I want to be if I can't even deal with this?"

By presenting new ideas and actions that they can take, we can show them that everything they want to achieve is possible once they buy in and let us guide them. If you can get people to accept this new way of thinking, then they're going to be far more open to what you present within your list builders, as well as your offers. If you don't do this piece, then your audience is going to be stuck in disempowering beliefs and ideas. They're not going to look at things with hope. This is what we're really doing for them, helping them to see things differently and to see the opportunities and possibilities before them.

In order to get there, we have to help them create a new reality. We must take them a layer deeper into our world and say things to help them adopt this new way of thinking.

Another really easy way to think of this is to imagine a funny phrase or meme. What would your people share? What would get them excited? What would allow them to have that new idea, belief, new feeling, or action? What would that phrase be that excites them to change?

Melissa Pruitt

@realmelissapruitt

"People don't want a checklist or a framework or a system. They just want their problem solved."

#quotes #inspirational

Within our list builders and content, we can use this phrase to empower our audience and help them begin to shift their thoughts with more hope for the future. Once this mindset begins to take hold, and they can believe there's a light at the end of the tunnel, they're going to be more open to the strategies and tactics you have to share. The first step to this is to make them aware there is a new, deeper way of thinking about things and to create that new reality in their mind.

So, brainstorm those one-liners that will get your audience excited. As you do this, focus only on what they need to hear from you to be inspired. What will keep them motivated after they hear it for the second, third, or fourth time? Take out a piece of paper, and dump all of your ideas on it for phrases that will inspire your audience.

There isn't a specific length or format that the ideas should fit. The only thing it needs to do is motivate your audience to get up and take action. Just get everything out of your head, and remember to keep in mind what your people are thinking, saying, feeling, and doing at this pain point in their lives.

Once all of your ideas are in one spot, then you can slowly start to separate them into different categories. Split them up into new ideas, new beliefs, new feelings, and new actions that someone in your market will need to take to become empowered.

If somebody wants to write a book, they may be wondering to themselves if they can even do this. "I don't have any formal education in writing a book. I don't know if I can make something good enough that people will want to read." They may not be putting themselves out there and haven't even begun writing. This is the pain they experience in this step of the transformation process. The desired result, you'll remember, is that they've written the book, maybe going so far as to have another book planned. They're speaking on stages and finding opportunities to speak on podcasts. People are stopping them to sign their books, begging for their autographs. They're creating an impact with this book and planning ahead for other opportunities to share their message. They're on a high because they were able to get that book out there into the world and can really help people with it.

That's the end game. It's the best-case outcome that somebody wanting to write a book can hope for. As you can see, there's a very big gap between these two stages in their life, and if you were still stuck being afraid of what other people might think of your book, you can easily see how the end result would look impossible from down there. They are so far away from the top of the mountain that they can't even see the peak.

This is where we take our exercise and the 104 Formula™ to help our people adopt the new ideas, beliefs, feelings, and actions that are going to get them a step closer to their goals. Guide them to see that new possibility because the better you help them see, the more likely they are to buy an offer from you. They have to believe in it. They have to buy in on it, and it's up to us to help motivate them to dream higher.

Let's walk through each of these areas, using our previous example of someone who wants to write a book.

Ideas

What's a new idea that will guide people and help them get where they need to be? Here are a few examples to help you better understand what these limiting beliefs may be and the answers that can be provided to challenge them.

This audience may be stuck in the disempowering belief that nobody will want to hear what they have to say, that they won't be able to find even a single person who will listen. But by convincing that audience that every idea is worth sharing, soon they may find themselves willing to sit down at their keyboard, writing deep into the night.

Maybe this person feels overwhelmed, daunted by the incredible length of time it would take to write a book. Another idea you could sell them on is that every book is written one page at a time. Sure, this may take a while, but if you never start, you'll never be finished. Focus on going one page at a time, and eventually, you'll get to see the end result of your work and hold your book in your hands.

Perhaps they're afraid to put themselves out there for others to judge. They may feel it's selfish to put the spotlight on themselves when others have struggled much more in similar ways. We all have stories worth sharing, no matter how much more others have suffered than us. It's not selfish to want to share your story. In fact, it might be selfish to keep it to yourself. By not telling people how you overcame the challenges in your life, you may be leaving others to struggle in the exact same ways you did.

Beliefs

Typically, when we talk about beliefs and when people work through beliefs, we find they have a lot of limiting beliefs. These are the thoughts that hold them back time and time again. While they can take many forms, at their core, they're entirely made of fear or doubt that overwhelms, paralyzing them with inaction.

Going back to our book example, a belief that an aspiring author may have is that writing a book could be a total waste of time. "Why should I even bother if no one is going to read what I've written? I'm not that important. There's no way I could even get even ten people to listen to what I have to say." Yet, if you could change one person's life with your book, wouldn't that make it all worth it? If they can really adopt that belief that one person's world would completely change from their book, it may inspire them to find the motivation to keep moving forward, even when it all feels like too much.

With our list builders and within the content that we put out, we need to be challenging these limiting beliefs. Only by convincing our audience that there is hope for them can we motivate them to make drastic changes in their life that they need in order to get to their goal. Once they make that shift in their mindset, they're more likely to be open to what we have to say in our list builders and then eventually the offers we have to help them.

IDEAS WE'RE SELLING

Problem	Solution 1	Solution 2	Solution 3
Example-Running a business doesn't need to be stressful	Being intentional with your time	Being intentional with setting boundaries	Ask yourself, "How much is enough?"
Success leaves clues. Others are doing what you're doing. They have consistency so you can too.	Success leaves clues because there are others doing what you're doing and they have consistency so you can too	Consistent effort allows you to measure results, which allows you to fine tune your processes.	Staying focused on something long enough allows you to outcompete vour competitors.

BELIEFS WE'RE SELLING

Problem	Solution 1	Solution 2	Solution 3
Example-You don't have to work hard, hard work doesn't equal more money	Your belief of how your parents grew up and that you have to work more hours and harder for more money	Creating a solution to a problem people want solved at a price point people are willing to pay	One to many model: You can save time while serving more people and making more money
Example-There is an easier way	Your belief that you have to trade time for money	There are other people solving the problem you are and they're making money and doing less work.	Recurring income model gives you consistent revenue while allowing you to save time and energy.

Feelings

When an individual settles on their desire to write a book, it can be an overwhelming task. There's so much to do. Even with a clear topic or concept, it can feel like an impossible task to get it all done. They don't have a background in writing. They're just in the weeds with no clear way out, no direction to head in, and they feel stuck. But by giving them the ability to reframe this task in their mind, you can easily change that into the excitement that they haven't figured everything out yet. "I'm excited because I'm going to be trying something new, and I'm going to be putting myself out there." If you can get people excited about the challenge before them, changing their perspective from fighting a terrifying beast to solving a tricky puzzle, their mood can shift drastically, giving them the energy to continue forward to find the solution. With that excitement, they'll be drastically more likely to take an interest in what you have to say, and come to you for answers to more of their problems.

Meet Katrina, Certified postpartum corrective exercise specialist

"I've had Melissa work through all my email sequences and tell me what I missed. I was missing the emotional side. I'm a go-getter and a very practical person. Melissa said, "That's great; you've told them exactly what they will get. But you've not told them why that will be helpful for them. And you haven't shared the story and the joy of their transformation." She helped me learn how to write about joy and transformation so that story comes to life."

Scan Here To Learn More

Read more of this story at http://influencedbook.com/casestudies

Actions

Maybe after the initial excitement fades, the extreme feeling of overwhelm returns. They might have stepped back and realized the monstrous amount of work ahead of them, paralyzed by how much is left to do. They've realized how many chapters they still have left to write, and it's beginning to feel like an impossible task to tackle. There's simply not enough time in the day to do all that they need to and write this book.

Instead of treating this like it needs to be all done in one sitting, the easiest way to empower somebody would be to help them break the book into manageable chunks. If you could get through even two or three pages a day, in two months, your book could be finished depending on how long you want it to be. And to achieve this, you could get up an hour earlier and do your writing before you leave for work. This changes the impossible task of writing an entire full-length book into something that's not only possible, but it's also easy.

When the tasks ahead of us feel manageable, we're more likely to try to accomplish them. If we can begin to change how our audience perceives their challenging tasks, they'll have the motivation they need to see it to the end.

We're empowering our people to really shift their mindset, to adopt this new set of beliefs, ideas, feelings, and actions. You already know what they're thinking, saying, feeling, and doing at the beginning of their journey, as well as where they want to go. As you move along the Transformation Track™, make sure to include the new set of ideas, beliefs, feelings, and actions that they need in order to reach that step toward their ultimate goal. What do they need to shift their mindset to in order to get where they want to go?

If you can make your audience look at even one aspect of their challenges differently, it can completely change the way they look at their situation, shifting the possibilities that are available to them.

While this is a little bit of deeper-level work, this is also going to help you understand your audience better. When you can really understand this concept, your people, and the root of their problems as you write out your list-building content, you'll create a much deeper relationship between you and your people. Challenge old beliefs and provide new ideas. The main thing to focus on is inspiring your audience by telling them what they need to hear in order to achieve their desired state.

FEELINGS WE'RE SELLING

Problem	Solution 1	Solution 2	Solution 3
Example- Entrepreneurship isn't easy and that's ok.	If it was easy everyone would do it.	Because everyone isn't doing it, more people in the market are willing to buy.	We're the crazy ones and innovators.
Example-You don't have to feel overwhelmed.	Ask yourself "Who are you racing?"	Ask yourself "How much is enough?"	Small consistent actions every day lead to the the next right step

ACTIONS WE'RE SELLING

Problem	Solution 1	Solution 2	Solution 3
Example- Take your first step	Go from thinking to doing changes everything	Every successful business created by someone who decided to take first step	The book with story to success starts page 1
Example-Progress over perfection	Just get going	Imperfect action is better than no action	Feedback is through imperfect action

Chapter 11

The Problem / Solution Framework

The Problem/Solution Framework is the tool that will help you to pull together all the work you've done so far. The thing to remember when creating a list builder is that the ones that are most attractive to our audience are the ones that solve their problems. Our audience is coming to us specifically because they have a problem. We already know what they're thinking, saying, feeling, and doing within that pain point, and our list builders, when designed right, solve those problems.

Remember, being intentional about our content and our list builders translates directly into deeper connections with our audience. As we completed our research, we're now able to see more clearly what they're thinking, feeling, saying, and doing at both the pain point and aspirational points of their lives. Then, we started to expand what our people believe they're capable of accomplishing. We're able to break through their old way of thinking and get to the deep roots of what they're interested in, allowing us to truly help them out.

When we present new and interesting solutions or alternative ways of looking at things, our people will pay attention. They're going to join our list so that they can follow along with us, and because they're following us, they're going to be more likely to purchase our offers.

As you work through the Problem/Solution Framework, think about the ideas, beliefs, feelings, actions, and problems your audience faces. Redirect them to actions and ideas that will empower them, and show them how you want to help them come up with new solutions.

Paul and I believe you don't have to work long hours and have a business that's a big hassle. You can actually have a very successful business without stress consuming your life. We are very intentional with how we run our business. This intentionality shows up in the way we create our daily routine. We have work days where we serve our clients on a high level. We also have days that we block off for free time. This allows us to go deeper with fewer people, which leads to a business that serves well. As a result, our current members are raving fans and have become great referral sources.

The solution to working long hours is having deeper relationships with your clients. That's it. It truly is that simple. With the 104 Formula™, you'll begin having rich, in-depth conversations. We've seen that with our audience, and these connections allowed us the opportunity to work with more people in high-touch programs. This enabled us to work less while still making more money in our business (and having a greater impact).

And that's just one way you can expand on an idea to change the way somebody looks at a situation.

For another example, let's go back to the idea of that person wanting to write a book. That person who wants to begin writing is caught in the idea that writing a book takes a very long time, and they're not sure if they're able to dedicate that much to it right now. That's an old, disempowering belief that they have. When we introduce a new, empowering belief to them that they only need to devote enough time to get a page or two done a day, it opens their mind to new possibilities.

To expand on that thought and give them a solution, we can show them how to write a book one page at a time. We can give them tactics and strategies, things they can do to break up the large task of writing a book into smaller, bite-sized processes that are easy to get through. This keeps things from being overwhelming, allowing the brain to only focus on what's in front of it, just getting through one page before worrying about the next.

By giving them this solution, we're easily expanding their mindset, breaking their old patterns and habits, and helping them to adopt new ones that can empower their lives.

Throughout this section, we've talked a lot about our book writing example and how we can take that overwhelming feeling and reframe it into something exciting. If somebody is facing something daunting, then a solution could be convincing them to leave their comfort zone. This could be trying a new writing method or just simply getting really creative with what they're writing. The goal is to open their mind to new possibilities, to expand that original problem, and give them a solution to work towards.

As this person writes their book, they may begin to feel afraid to make mistakes. Once this book is published, there will be no going back. While they can always create a revision and update it, once those original books are sold, even something as simple as a spelling error will permanently reflect on their own ability within those copies. They feel that they can't even begin to write, as there will inevitably be mistakes the first time they do anything.

One way to challenge this would be to help them see that only through making mistakes can we become better at anything. Mistakes are the quickest way to learn something. They're a way to test things out and get feedback to do things better the next time we try.

As you can see, by challenging old ideas, beliefs, feelings, and actions, we can help transform those disempowering thoughts into something new, something that gives new opportunities. Now we're expanding upon them, giving our audience potential solutions for those challenges, and letting them reframe things in their mind so that their goals seem possible.

As you give them strategies to work through, it's going to expand upon the solutions, giving you more content to create as you connect and later make your list builders.

Chapter 12

The Secret Weapon for Content

A consistent theme throughout this book has been the need to keep your content intentional. Often, when I see people first start to create content, they struggle to understand what their audience really wants to hear. They're guessing at what their audience might like, trying to keep things moving hard and fast, which leads to creating content on the fly with little to no planning ahead. While this will produce a piece of content, it usually leads to posts that get little to no engagement. Not only is this frustrating, but it can be demoralizing. Writer's block may set in as you second guess yourself, wondering what to say. It's circumstances like this that push some people to quit trying altogether.

Another trendy theory is that nothing matters as much as consistently posting content, even if you don't fully know what to say. They're just putting things out there because saying something is always better than saying nothing, right? Not so.

It's important that you're intentional about every single post that you make. The things you put out into the world will begin to attract an audience, and it's crucial that the free content you upload is perfectly aligned with the list builder you will eventually offer. Otherwise, the people you attract may not be interested in your list builder, meaning all of the time working on not only that lead magnet but your marketing and website will all go to waste, which is why we'll eventually get into creating that list builder in alignment with everything else you've done so far.

I know you've probably experienced this at some point, where you're trying to make content, and the only thought in your head is, "What am I supposed to create today?" You're stuck, scratching your head, unable to come up with anything relevant for your audience. My secret content weapon will stop you from creating content from scratch and on the fly. It leads to direct, intentional content that will appeal to your audience and speak to their problems.

Be a Producer

Before we go into that, we need to talk about consuming versus producing and how that relates to your output of content. As a consumer, you're spending most of your time on social media mindlessly scrolling and endlessly absorbing other people's content. Many who do this have convinced themselves that this helps them stay up to date on what's going on within their community. It can be exhausting working like this, leading to you being overwhelmed and burned out. This mindset is restrictive. It causes you to waste precious time that could be used to create amazing content for your audience.

So, we've got to shift your perspective to that of a producer. Instead of endlessly trying to keep track of what's being said by who, you want to be the one starting conversations. As a producer, you are the leader. You are the one who puts out engaging content that gets people talking to you and with each other. They love hearing from you, and your content is something that they can really connect with on a deep level. You're paying attention to their needs by sharing your knowledge and experience, and you're speaking about their pain points.

If you look at the social media pages of top leaders and influencers, they all have one thing in common; they follow very few people in contrast to how many followers they have. This is because they are only focused on producing engaging, high-quality content that their audience loves. They're not interested in keeping up with everything going on in the world. Making this mental shift will reduce stress and give you back the processing power to focus on creating effective content.

While this is only one piece of the puzzle for building your list, it's an important one that puts the power back into your hands.

Batching

Now that you understand this very important mindset that you need moving forward, it's time that I introduce my secret weapon to you. In order to create all of this amazing content in a timely manner, we're going to create it in batches. This means, in one sitting, we're going to produce all of the content that we can, at least a few days' worth or more if you're able. Personally, this method of content creation has saved us a lot of time and energy and allows us to focus on what we're producing for our audience so that we create everything with intention and purpose.

Paul and I make an "event" out of batching. It's fun, and we look forward to it. Every Tuesday is dedicated strictly to content creation. First, we take a full day to write out all our ideas, set the outcome we want, and write the goals we have for this content. The following Tuesday, we write the details for each of those topics with the exact bullet points we want to cover.

We include ideas on what to teach, stories to share, and the call-to-action. On these creation days, Paul and I go somewhere fun where it's not distracting, like a quiet table at one of our favorite restaurants. We've even gone to a winery in the summer months to create content outside on a sunny day. Then, we go to our recording area and pump out videos (including wardrobe changes). It's a seamless process and allows us to quickly create the content our audience wants.

When you set time aside specifically for creating content, you're giving it the attention and energy it deserves. Whether it's writing Facebook or blog posts, sitting down to record audio, or even filming videos, whatever kind of content you're making, you need to set aside time to be intentional with it.

Because you've already gone through the 104 Formula™, you know your audience's problems, and you have some solutions. You also have an idea of what they want to hear more about because you know what they are thinking, saying, feeling, and doing. You're never going to run out of things to say that are relevant to your audience.

Now, take your 104 Formula™, and select the topics you're going to focus on today. Then, set aside that time to batch-create your content. In later chapters, we'll talk further about how you can incorporate this into your schedule, but for the first time, simply try a day of batching content this way.

One thing that I love about batching is that it allows you to focus specifically on creating value. Because you're not creating content on the fly, panicking about what you're going to say, you have time to take a breath and focus. If you're out and about and you see something that you want to share with your audience, you can record that video on your phone in real-time and then save it for when you create your next batch of content. It allows you to quickly go back to enjoying that moment for yourself while still being able to show and tell people about what you saw. You're not stuck creating content for the rest of the day. You've given yourself the freedom to enjoy living in the moment.

Another thing I love is that you can rinse and repeat these ideas you've come up with for years to come. The struggles and aspirations of your audience will continue to arise as new people enter your circle of influence. As they come into your world, they will keep going through all the different stages, so you can reuse the content over and over, tweaking it a little each time. In this way, batching content frees up even more of your time because you don't need to keep coming up with new topics year after year. For somebody who is dealing with this challenge for the first time, it's all new to them, so it allows you to nurture them no matter which step of the journey they're on.

When you take the time to be intentional with this step, your content is going to better reflect your audience. They're going to hear you because you're focused on them and their problems, not keeping up with the rush of creating content. You're free to speak about their challenges, problems, and aspirations. The harder you push yourself to create content in real-time, the harder it is to be intentional and keep all of your content connected together under one plan. But now you will be able to enjoy life instead of feeling like you always have to be producing content to keep algorithms happy. As you move forward, remember to focus on producing instead of trying to keep up with every tiny thing that's going on within your community. Once you make this mindset shift, I promise it's going to change a lot of things for you. It's going to reduce your stress, and it's going to help you produce even better content that attracts only the perfect people.

Chapter 13

Theme Days

To further streamline your content creation, I'd like to introduce you to the theme day. For most people, especially entrepreneurs, we're doing a number of different things throughout the week. We jump from ten different ideas and roles, constantly changing what we're working on. You might start your day by checking your emails. Then, you have appointments in the afternoon where you're scheduled to meet with clients. After, you're going to record some content, then you're going to do administrative work at the end of the day. This can leave you exhausted and feeling a little all over the place. When you're going from task to task throughout your day, it actually takes a lot more energy for your brain to do that. It leaves you overwhelmed, and it's something many people struggle with once they begin running their own businesses.

Instead, we should get ourselves into a state of flow where we're focused on only one task, allowing us to fall into a well-moving rhythm. You've probably found yourself in a state where you get set into doing something, enjoying yourself for what feels like twenty minutes, only to realize that hours have passed since you first sat down and entered that flow state. This is what the theme day is meant to produce and how it's going to help you the most.

A theme day is a day where you allow yourself to focus on only one subject. While this is amazing for many areas of your business, it truly accelerates content creation. Start by choosing a day when you really dig your heels in and focus only on making amazing content for your social media platforms. This will give you the time to step back, breathe, and make sure you're speaking into those problems and challenges that your audience is facing.

When Paul and I do this, we are able to accomplish a lot of things in our business. Every day is a theme day for us, and it's helped us become more efficient. Monday, for example, is our day for coaching. This is when Paul and I are on calls coaching our members, really helping them overcome their challenges. Tuesday is our content day. This is when we focus exclusively on creating all of our content, whether it's for external use, like posts for our social media accounts, or internal, like exclusive training for our members. For Wednesday, we have one-on-one appointments with members or potential new people coming into our world. Thursday is our dedicated flex day. This gives us a breather to focus on catching up with the areas that got out of hand on the other days of the week. It allows us to be free from panic when something goes wrong and maybe even take a little time off if things go better than expected. Finally, Friday is a day dedicated to learning because we're always working on improving our skill sets, and we also do administrative work. As you can see, we've mapped our week out very well, and we know what we're getting into each day, with very little room for surprises.

Of course, sometimes life happens, and things don't go as planned. I remember one time we had an "opportunity crisis" where Paul and I had a chance to speak on the virtual stage for a major leader in the online marketing space. With little notice and no desire to pass on the opportunity, we put aside the theme for that day so we could focus on our presentation. We had a fantastic experience and received a lot of compliments from the audience and this leader's team.

Afterward, we were able to easily pick right back up where we left off with our theme days. Having your time already allotted this way keeps you organized and allows you to always know what you're coming back to when you return to your normal routine.

This is especially helpful for content creation because it's one of those things where we can have the best intentions and still wind up creating it on the fly without a plan. It ends up not being intentional, and then we're just throwing ideas at the wall, praying for something to stick. If we don't follow our 104 Formula™ when speaking to our audience, then we're going to struggle to capture their attention, and then they won't get interested in what we have to say, no matter how much it may help. Instead, we want a day where we can sit down and focus on nothing other than creating intentional content, whether it be free content on our social media or our list builders and paid offers.

Think of it as business-building time, especially when it comes to social media content. Make sure you're getting this time each week, and remain dedicated to it. These posts are all about nurturing relationships with your audience, building trust, and allowing them to get to know you better, so they become curious about what you do. This takes them deeper into your world and allows your list builders to do their job and carry people to your paid offers.

You can think of your content as though it were split into two different buckets. The first contains your internal content. This bucket comprises everything that you are doing that is not outwardly posted on your social media accounts. This may include prep work like recording videos or writing posts, or creating content for those already in your world, such as your email lists or those in your courses or memberships.

The second bucket contains everything that is going to be posted externally. This contains the content that is ready to be delivered and is, for all intents and purposes, your social media presence. If you're only focusing on delivering content to those already within your community, then you're going to be invisible to the outside world, unable to find new clients and fans. You need to strike a balance between external and internal content so that you can both find new community members and keep established ones satisfied. Because of this, you may decide it's best if you have two different days where you focus on content, one where you create and another where you post and talk to your audience.

With this theme day, I want you to know that you don't have to do all of your content creation in that single twenty-four-hour period. For example, for one theme day, you might just spend the entire day working on your 104 Formula™, getting very clear on those problems your audience has. You might not even sit down to write content on that day. You're just going to do your research and fill out the formula. Then, the next week you come back to your content day and map out all of your content on your calendar, still not writing out or recording any actual content. Then, on a separate day, you actually begin recording videos and writing content, allowing yourself to get into a flow. Because of your prior prep work, there's little thought each video needs. You know exactly what outfits you're going to wear for each one. You have your scripts or notes. All you need to do is sit down and speak into a camera. You're not switching from task to task, you're getting into a rhythm, and it's going to let you do a lot more with your content. This process allows you to be specific and intentional about every decision you make as you speak to your audience.

Everything we do needs to be aligned with all other aspects of our business and with the challenges our audience is facing. When we work with this strategy, it gives us the time we desperately need in order to think through each decision without feeling the immense stress of rapidly switching tasks. It gives us permission to focus only on what we want to do that day, and our content is going to see a big improvement because of it. With these theme days, begin to think about how you're going to incorporate them into your schedule. Dedicate however many hours you want to set aside on each of these days, put these into your calendar, and treat them like a real appointment with a client. Just like any other appointment, you won't allow yourself to miss it and leave somebody hanging, and you can't leave yourself hanging, either. Getting into this cycle is one of the most important things you can do for yourself, and you need to take it seriously. It's not only going to improve the quality of your content, but it's also going to free your mind and give you the energy that you need to focus on your business.

Chapter 14

The Content Creation Framework

Now that you've created space to crank out engaging content that's aligned with everything your audience is interested in, it's time to begin using the Content Creation Framework. We've utilized the 104 Formula™, so we know we're speaking about topics that are really relevant to our people. Again, you want to remember those problems that they are struggling with so that you can speak on the challenges they face, as well as their aspirations and wants.

With all of our content, we're lining everything together, from our social media posts to our list builders and, finally, our paid offers. When our audience comes into our world, everything will perfectly align, seamlessly transitioning them through our pipeline until they reach their end goal. This pipeline is based only on what's interesting and relevant to our ideal audience, and it makes perfect sense to them as to why they would want to take a deeper look into our world and begin working with us.

Now you might be wondering, "How do I actually create the content?" This is where the Content Creation Framework comes into play. Moving forward, this is what you will use to create every single piece of content you need, and it will streamline the process.

First, select a topic from the completed 104 Formula™ that you filled out earlier. You don't want this to be something random. It needs to be something that addresses a clearly defined problem that your audience is saying they need help with.

No matter what kind of content you're creating, the framework will keep you organized, and every decision you make will be with intention. It's also going to keep your solution aligned with your audience's problems so that you can stay relevant. The end result will be content that keeps your audience excited and, at the same time, provides them with real value.

Hook

First up is the hook. This is that big opening line or statement that grabs people's attention and gets them curious to learn more. This is debatably the most important part of your content, so it's important that you spend a little bit of time thinking about and getting this right.

Because you've already done the research and have everything mapped out within your 104 Formula™, you have an idea of what your audience is thinking, saying, feeling, and doing and can therefore take that into account while you're creating your hook. You want to try and use some of the same language that your audience is using, as this will help capture their attention quickly. This is a piece that you're going to have to experiment with a little bit to see exactly what works best for your specific audience, so feel free to play around with these a little bit as you settle into creating your content.

Discussion or Story

Next, you need to have your discussion or story. This is the foundational piece of your content and the main reason people will stick around to hear what you have to say. These are your opinions, tips, and strategies. You may also choose to share a simple story that relates to your main topic. For example, this may be the story of somebody you worked with and how you helped them reach a goal through your process. The main goal is to speak about your chosen topic and expand upon it while providing lots of value and ideas.

Be sure to keep it clear and concise. You want to give enough information so that people really understand where you're going with this, but not every piece of knowledge that you have on the subject. Stay relevant and streamlined so that your audience can understand the information you're passing on to them. This will draw them a little closer into your world because they're going to feel like you understand what they're going through. The more you can relay this to your audience, the easier it will be to convince them that you can see them through their problems. Basically, provide something that can be implemented easily without giving away the entire solution.

Destroy a Limiting Belief/Empower with a New Belief

The next piece of the framework is really important and something you definitely don't want to skip over. You want to destroy a limiting belief and rebuild it with a new empowering one. What exactly does that mean?

You've already completed a deep exploration into their beliefs and know which ones are holding them back from greatness. You know what's getting in their way, which means you also know what they can change to excel. It's up to us, in our content, to address those limiting beliefs head-on. We want our audience to buy in and feel not only compelled but empowered to be able to take on whatever you're leading them to do. They can do this, they have the ability, but they have such a limiting belief in their mind that they believe it's not possible. They're putting up many obstacles in their way of working with us, so we need to destroy those limiting beliefs. We need to call them out in a way that's compassionate while still shining a light on them.

This allows us to shift their mindset towards something new, something that will serve them as they move forward to better things. We've filled out the Transformation Track™, so we know the things they'll face along the way, as well as the different ways their thoughts and feelings will start to shift as they continue. Address this in your content, and talk to your ideal client about those limiting beliefs. Let them know that they have the power to overcome them, and help them rebuild their mindset with something that will propel them forward.

Next Steps/Call-to-Action

The fourth step within the framework is telling them what you want them to do next, as well as how they can do it if it wasn't already addressed within the body of your post or video. Keep this step simple.

An example of a simple next step could be to download your list builder. Because all of your content is aligned with your audience's struggles, as well as your other pieces of content, the transition should be natural. It should make sense that your audience is interested in your list builder and that they want to go deeper with you and see more of what you can offer them.

The next step could also be to purchase your paid offer. It could be as simple as leaving a comment sharing their thoughts on a social media post. The purpose is to get people in your audience to engage with you. Whatever your next step or action is, you need to keep it simple and easy to do so that your audience is always moving forward and connecting with you.

Summarize

After all of this, you recap everything that you said in the main body of your content. Review and tie everything together with a neat little bow. "Hey, we talked about this today. I gave you these tips, and we spoke about this belief. Here's a new way to think about it. Here's what I want you to do next."

This helps cement people's understanding of your content and leaves it fresh in their minds so that they can digest the information you gave them.

Close-out

The final piece is the close-out. This is an inspirational or informational way to finish your piece of content. You can think of this as your closing statement. For our podcast, we close-out, "You're just one step away from becoming an Adaptive Marketer." It's a very simple tagline that allows us to convey our overall message about marketing, and we use that to sign off on each and every episode of our podcast. The goal is to keep things simple while still speaking into the piece of content that you just created.

Following the Content Creation Framework, your audience is going to really appreciate the consistency they can expect from you, and it'll be clear to them why they should continue following you. And, because you're building content off of the 104 Formula™, your content will align with all of the other steps you're using to build your list and promote your offers.

If you want to see our content creation framework in action, I encourage you to check out the Online Marketing Podcast. This is where Paul and I share strategies on marketing and selling your courses, memberships, and coaching programs. Each episode goes through the framework, and we share ninja tips and strategies with our listeners. It's an easy framework to follow, so you can listen and implement what you learn on the show, and we frequently share free resources, as well.

ONLINEMARKETING
PODCAST

Welcome to the Online Marketing Podcast, where we help Course Creators, Membership Site Owners, & Coaches market & sell their offers.

Chapter 15

Content Squeeze™

Now that you've worked through the Content Creation Framework, you've got many pieces of content planned out, but how do you go about creating each individual piece? This is where I'd like to introduce you to the Content Squeeze™, an amazing way to help you repurpose old content into new, fresh takes.

People all digest content differently. Some learn visually, such as through watching videos, while others discover new information through reading written text. When you can take your content and transform it into different mediums, you'll appeal to even more people because they'll be attracted to the types of content they prefer to consume. This is where the focus of your social media ecosystem shifts.

Echo the messages within your content onto all of your social media platforms to catch people wherever they're at. We want our videos, the sound of our voice, or reading our posts available so they can see us in the medium they prefer most.

Unless your content goes viral, less than six percent of people will see your posts. This is why echoing the same messaging in different places is so important. We're going to reach different types of people and, therefore, more people overall. When you use the Content Squeeze™ Framework, you'll be able to easily turn your content into different formats, helping you to reach new audiences who otherwise may have never found you.

This may sound exhausting, but that's the last thing I want you to feel. The Content Squeeze™ will help you not only move your content in a way that's intentional it'll help save you time and effort.

Think of this framework like making orange juice. Your first piece of content is a ripe, fresh orange, and the juice within is the message behind your content. By squeezing the orange harder and harder, we can get every piece of value from it, making the most of our time and allowing us to easily share it on various platforms. The Content Squeeze™ is a press that will help save you effort and get the "juice" out more quickly.

To begin, create your first initial piece of content. Because you've used the Content Creation Framework, everything is already mapped out. You know the challenges you want to speak about and how everything combines together into one aligned vision. Remember to give them a piece of information to help solve a challenge and include a call-to-action at the end, inviting them to continue working with you. From this initial piece of content will come the other versions that we'll put onto different platforms, so it's alright to spend some time here making sure your messaging is really ironed out and clear.

As you create this first piece, think about how you best connect to your audience. Which format is your favorite way to create? Follow this path of least resistance, as it will be the easiest for you. If you're a natural writer, your first iteration should be something written, like a blog post. If you love to make videos, then start there. The point is to remove as much thought as possible. Make this not only quick but easy.

From there, it's time to start squeezing that content dry. You want to take that initial piece of content and put it onto any platforms that make sense. A blog post can easily be used as a social media post, and the pictures you use can be repurposed on different social platforms. Think of every possible place where you upload content and spread it to all of those places.

With our first piece of content uploaded to as many places as possible, it's time to start changing the formatting so that we can spread it further. This is the part where you can get really creative to squeeze it into new forms and capture new eyes.

If you had a written piece of content, then you could take that and put it into audio form. From there, you can upload it to any platform that makes sense to you. You may choose to upload it to Instagram as a story or on your website as an episode of a podcast. If it was a video, putting it on Facebook can be a great way for people to connect to you as they hear your voice and see your face. There are so many possibilities for what you can do. The only true limit is how much time and creativity you want to pour into each iteration of content.

Now that you've pushed yourself, moving from the easiest format for you to work into multiple different kinds that stretch your abilities, is there anything else you can do with it? Are there even more iterations of content that can be pulled from that first piece?

A great example of this would be quotes. Perhaps in your written blog post, you had an amazing one-liner that was sharp and interesting. Something that would grab people's attention or provide a small but powerful punch of information. You could easily take that quote and turn it into a visual image, allowing you to continue reusing that first piece of content into helpful, informational posts.

Working in this style helps you to keep producing content for all of your platforms quicker and easier. As you continue to squeeze your initial piece of content, get creative and repurpose it in as many different ways as possible. When you can get into a rhythm with this and get your content into that same rhythm, you're not going to be working as hard. You will free up time by designing content that is easier to squeeze into additional formats, and keeping everything aligned will be easier.

One of the things that Paul and I do for our content is set aside a day to batch-create videos. From one of these days, we can get about a month's worth of videos in a very short period of time. We'll start by recording an initial video. Then we'll upload it to both Facebook and Instagram pages. This is where we are already starting the squeeze and getting our content onto as many platforms as possible. From there, we'll send the video over to our podcast director, who extracts the audio and uses it to create our podcast. Now that we have an audio file, we can squeeze that further to create a transcript of our video. With that transcription, we'll turn the video into a blog article that gets posted to our website and use it to accompany our podcast. Typically, this blog post is also broken down further into email content that we use for our email list. We also take the transcript and use the text to create all our social media captions and quote posts.

From one single piece of content, we're able to break everything down into smaller and smaller pieces that still provide huge value to our audience. I want you to really think about the possibilities that you have at your fingertips and how you can squeeze the most value out of your content as you move forward.

All of the content that I mentioned continues to stay aligned with our core messaging and stays relevant to our audience. None of it is accidental or done on the fly. All of it stays consistent with our audience's challenges and aspirations and allows us to speak to them wherever they're at on our Transformation Track™. As you use this framework, you will create the same kind of results.

Taking Your Content Squeeze To The Next Level With AI

In today's fast-changing business world, one thing we cannot ignore is the amazing help we get from AI, which stands for Artificial Intelligence. It's like having a super smart tool that makes our work better and faster, especially with creating content for our social media and list builders.

One of these AI tools is ChatGPT, which is like a helpful computer friend that's great with words.

ChatGPT can understand your questions and help you with all sorts of writing and information. It's super handy for creating content and finding answers to your questions. Just type in what you want to know or ask for help, and ChatGPT will do its best to assist you. It's like having a clever buddy in your computer.

It is crucial to remember that while ChatGPT is a fantastic tool, it should not be your one and only source for content creation. It is like having a trusty compass, but you still need to explore the terrain yourself.

Before you start chatting with ChatGPT, take the time to do your research including the 104 Formula™ and other resources I have shared with you in this book. Understand your audience's preferences, pain points, and interests. Get a solid grasp of your niche and market. Then, use ChatGPT as your creative assistant to refine and enhance your content.

By combining your knowledge with the power of ChatGPT, you will be well on your way to creating content that truly resonates with your audience and drives your online success. Remember, it is the teamwork between your expertise and ChatGPT's capabilities that can lead to outstanding results.

Here are four quickstart ways you can use ChatGPT with the principles you have learned in Influenced:

1. Understanding Your Audience

To create content that really connects, you need to know your audience inside and out. ChatGPT can help you dig deep into research. Just ask it questions like, "Tell me about my audience's problems," or "What do they like to do for fun?" It will provide you with valuable insights that you can use to create content that speaks directly to your audience's heart.

2. Creating List Builders

Building a list of potential customers is super important. ChatGPT can help you brainstorm ideas for freebies or lead magnets that will make people want to join your list. It can suggest topics, titles, and even help you write the content for your opt-in pages. You'll have a list building machine in no time.

3. Crafting Social Media Magic:

Social media is where you connect with your audience daily. ChatGPT can help you come up with creative and engaging social media posts.

Just tell it what you want to talk about, and it can provide you with catchy captions, fun facts, or even jokes to keep your audience interested.

4. Writing Heartfelt Emails

Connecting through email is crucial for building trust. With ChatGPT, you can draft friendly and relatable emails that your audience will look forward to reading. Whether you're sending updates, promotions, or just saying hello, ChatGPT can help you sound authentic and caring.

In a nutshell, ChatGPT is your helpful sidekick in creating content that matters. It is like having a friendly expert by your side, ready to assist you with research, list-building, social media, and email writing.

So, don't be shy; chat away and let ChatGPT make your content creation journey a breeze. Using ChatGPT as a tool and the information you have learned in Influenced, you will have an advantage of creating intentional and relevant content for your audience.

Chapter 16

From Social to List

Within these last few chapters, we've been talking about how you can create influence over your audience and then use that to lead them to an informed buying decision. One of the first steps in this process is to use our social media content as a way to help our audience connect, get excited, interested, and maybe even be a little curious about what exactly it is that we do. When your social media content is aligned with your list builders, then you're going to attract only those who will be perfect for your paid offers. But how do you take that step? How do you get your audience from your social media onto your email list? In this chapter, I'm going to share with you some of the ways that you can do just that.

Call-to-Action

Now, the first thing you will do once you have a list builder to offer is to make sure there's a clear call-to-action. At the same time, don't overwhelm your audience with too many steps all at once. Create social media posts designed to get your audience one step closer to working with you. Let them know the problem you're solving, the solution you're presenting, and give them a clear call-to-action to accept your offer (such as signing up for your list builder). When you can do all of this, your audience will be reassured that you're going to be able to help them. They won't walk away confused because they have a million little things to focus on. You're giving them one perfectly clear action to put all of their focus into, and that is downloading your list builder. That list builder will help them solve that problem. Remember, your list builder should speak to only one of the problems you discovered with your research. Keep it simple, giving your audience one quick win. The purpose of your list builder is to create curiosity for your paid offers.

Billboard Effect

One of the big ways you can get followers to go from social to your list is to utilize something I call the billboard effect. This is all about leveraging your social media platforms as much as you can to show your audience your list builders, similar to posting yourself on a billboard on the side of the interstate.

Imagine yourself driving down the highway and seeing the different billboards along the way. You may see a series of billboards about a particular store. There may be multiple billboards about that specific store and all it has to offer. It makes you aware and builds excitement, sharing all the different things that this store offers. These bring awareness that there is one at the next exit.

You want to do the same thing with your social media posts. Get creative and think through all of the different ways that you can passively put your list builder onto all of your social media platforms in a variety of formats.

Personal Profile

This includes your personal profile banner or cover image. While it may not seem like an obvious choice to utilize, as you may have many friends that aren't interested in your business, you never know if friends or even friends of friends will be interested. Take advantage of the option to put your list builders in front of new audiences. You may even want to include a little piece in your bio. If you're not doing a lot of business on your personal profile, you could still share with your friend list precisely what you do with a call-to-action, presenting your list builder to them that way. Just remember to balance what you share on your personal profile as you want your content to not overwhelm your friends with too many call-to-actions, and you want to still keep your personal profile conversational and approachable.

Facebook Pages

Other pages can be used to obtain the billboard effect as well. This is most obvious on your business pages. You can include a cover image in the bio section of your profile, making sure that the list builder is easily found within the descriptive text.

Facebook Groups

If you manage any groups as part of your business, it's another amazing place to share your lead magnets. You could put a pinned post at the top of your page so that everybody who comes to chat or ask questions can see it. This way, when people stumble upon your group, they're inevitably going to end up finding your list builder. Anywhere that you can put your list builder in front of people (when applicable), that is exactly where you want to put it.

You want to expose as many people as possible to what it is that you do, how you can help them, and to the solution found in your lead magnet.

Social Media Posts

Another way to get people to transition from social to your email list is through posts. I want to tell you here that, number one, no matter what you do within that post, you want to lead with value. You always want to be giving your audience something that they can think about and ponder on, increasing their curiosity. You may even want to include a little bit of a quick win or a takeaway from the post before you give them the opportunity to get your list builder.

You don't want to just post and say, "Hey, come grab this awesome list builder! It's amazing! You want to go get it right now, and give me your email address while you're at it." While you may get a couple of people to sign up this way, you're never going to gain a continuing relationship this way. When you lead with value, the natural next step is for your audience to continue forward, looking for more solutions to the problems you've answered, leading them to your list builder, and, subsequently, giving you their email address to be on your list.

Other People's Groups

On your own social media platforms, you can do what you would like to do when it comes to sharing your list builder directly. But when it comes to groups owned by other people, you want to be aware of the rules set in place by the admins. A lot of times, it's frowned upon to immediately join a group and start advertising yourself. While this is technically promotional, it's frequently considered spam.

We don't ever want to do that. We never want to cause alarm in the group and anger the admins. We want to enter these other groups and spaces with the respect that they deserve. Lead with value and nurture relationships, which you should be doing anyway. Give without expecting anything in return. You don't need to share your list builder directly within their group. If you're going in, talking to people, answering questions, and really getting to know them, eventually, somebody will ask, "Can I work with you more?" Or "Do you have any more tips about that?" They're going to click on your profile, and guess what? Because you've done the work to utilize the billboard effect, they're going to immediately find your list builder in all of these different places. This is why it's so important that you take the time now to set up your billboards in strategic places. If you're set up and have your billboards in many different places, people will eventually find it naturally, and they'll sign up. Then, all you have to do is go and create relationships. Through all you do on social media, your list builder should always be the next natural step toward working with you.

Chapter 17

Q Calendar Framework

The Q Calendar allows you to be even more intentional with your list builders and launches. It helps you place your launches on your calendar at just the right time for you and your business. You'll know what to say and do all year long, keeping you from being overwhelmed with all of your launches, list-building, and everything in between.

When you set up your Q Calendar correctly, it leaves ample time for you to build, nurture, and serve your audience. The key is to set everything up correctly so that you make space for all of the time needed for each of those stages.

Quarters

The first thing I like to do when setting up my calendar is break everything down into quarters. It allows me to visually see my calendar in manageable segments. To create your Q Calendar, sit down with a piece of paper. Break it into four pieces. Label each piece Q1, Q2, Q3, and Q4.

Q1 begins in January and ends in March. Q2 begins in April and ends in June. So on, and so forth, until all four segments are filled in with each month. This is the basis of the Q calendar and is what we're going to use to get hyper-specific, filling everything in that we need for the year. Of course, you don't have to start with January. You can begin this at any point in the year.

I remember the first time I used this framework. I was planning our launches, along with travel plans and events. Everything was stacked with tons of overlap. Even on quick turnaround travel where we were off the plane, washing clothes, repacking, and out for our next trip, there was simply not enough time to do it all.

The Q Calendar gave me perspective to quickly realize the need to change our schedule to provide a good experience for our members. It also gave us room for personal downtime, which is needed just as much as the time spent in our business.

Once the calendar is in place, you may occasionally find that some things take longer to complete than expected, things out of your control may happen, or maybe you just realized something would be more efficient in a different order. This can leave your calendar off course. I encourage you to make adjustments when needed to keep everything flowing smoothly. Be sure to go back to your calendar each quarter so that you can evaluate whether anything needs to be moved around.

Big Rocks

Once you have everything broken down neatly into quarters, the first thing you want to focus on is your "big rocks." These are the things that you don't have any control over when they happen. This is where I like to pull out my normal calendar to see what is already scheduled for the future. This might include trips to conferences, events that happen annually at the same time each year, and holidays. The main point is to sit down and look at all the things that are a priority to you and simply cannot be rescheduled. The last thing that you want is to schedule one of your launches the same week you agreed to be part of somebody's promotion, leading to massive overlap and splitting your attention into too many directions.

Personal

After you place the big rocks, it's time to schedule your personal time. This consists of vacations or long periods of time when you know you want to rest. I always say that you want to do personal time before business because it's important for your health that you have downtime. If you aren't intentional about setting the time aside now, you simply never will. You'll eventually get overwhelmed and burned out as the stress piles up. I don't want that to happen to you. Your business needs to be built to serve you, so pay attention to your personal time when scheduling your Q Calendar. If your family already has events planned, then get that down right away.

Business

Now that your personal time is in, it's time to get started on scheduling your business items. This consists of things like launches as well as events and promotions. Anything that is going on in your business, you want to set aside time for those things.

By this point, your calendar is mostly filled in. You can take a step back and absorb everything visually. Before long, gaps between all of these scheduled events will be obvious. This is the greatest part of the Q Calendar; being able to break everything down into manageable chunks that you can see and interact with. These gaps are the perfect place for you to schedule launches and everything leading up to them.

Themes

One important thing to pay attention to as you look at your Q Calendar is the themes. There will be parts of the year when you're extremely busy and others where you have time to breathe and focus. During the hectic times on your calendar, you don't want to schedule a lot, as you've already got so much on your plate.

Other Considerations

While you may not celebrate them, there are many holidays around the world that happen year-round. If you have an international audience, it's important to remember the dates for these, as your audience will be less active during this time. You also want to consider your launches themselves. It's important to remember that not every launch is the same, so after you map everything out on your calendar, you should consider the difference between them. Your launches can be broken down into two groups: primary and secondary launches. With your primary launches, you want to go all out. This is when all hands should be on deck, and your entire focus should be on doing any and everything you can to get people into your launch. These take a lot of time and energy, but they also should bring in the most customers of the year. With a secondary launch, things are much more relaxed. This is a smaller launch, one that you may only advertise in one way, such as through emails. This one isn't designed to attract as many people as possible. Instead, it serves as a way to bridge the gap between larger launches. While this is still a promotion that keeps your audience active and engaged, it isn't as hectic, requiring all hands on deck to handle the massive amount of time and resources that a primary launch takes. Within your Q Calendar, you should be able to see exactly where the different types of launches will fit best for you.

You also want to be aware of the time it takes for the different phases of your launch, such as the open and closed cart phases. These typically require the most energy of the entire launch sequence, so you don't want to have them packed too tightly near any other events.

Your main goal with the Q Calendar is to find the gaps in time where everything fits together perfectly. This means that you need to include breathing room not just for yourself but for your audience as well. You don't want your audience to go through launch fatigue, where they get burned out hopping from promotion to promotion. Create time in between for them to absorb the information you've already given them. If you constantly exist in launch mode, not only will you not have ample time to serve your audience, but they'll get overwhelmed and may decide to leave in search of somebody else who can help them.

Now it's time to put the Q Calendar into action. Go ahead and take out a piece of paper and get started. You'll need this information for the next chapter, where you will begin to discuss a tool that will help you nurture relationships with your audience on a deeper level and ensure you have time for everything that you will have going on in your life.

Chapter 18

Conversations Calendar

The most successful business relationships start with a conversation! The Conversations Calendar gives you one engaging question to invite your audience into a two-way dialogue with you every day of the year! This calendar will not only create real conversations with your audience but will also facilitate planning your calendar.

By now, you know that conversations are necessary for influencing your audience to make an informed buying decision. It's the single best way to create a relationship with your audience.

Meet Lori & Jerry, Keefer Fine Art - Automotive Photography

"I can figure out how to market to just about anybody. It's all about relationships and being purposeful and intentional. Melissa and Paul have helped us learn that growing the business is about playing that long game, building relationships, and being intentional."

Scan Here To Learn More

Read more of this story at http://influencedbook.com/casestudies

With your Q Calendar, you also have an idea of what your entire year is going to look like, mapping it out with social media posts, your list builders, and your launches, along with everything else in your personal and professional life. The question is, with these conversations between you and your audience, what should you be talking about?

This is where the Conversations Calendar comes in. This tool is going to help you have ongoing conversations with your audience between launches, no matter where you're at in your business. You need to be in constant contact with people in order to connect and build those relationships. By talking with them regularly, you build trust.

A lot of times, people mess up when they don't know what to say, but you're not going to do that. You'll know exactly what to say to your audience that will nurture a connection between the two of you so that when it comes time to offer your list builders and launches, they're primed and ready. Everything will lead naturally into the next step, and it will all be perfectly aligned to finish with your paid offers.

The key to conversations and the key to creating that relationship is having a two-way dialogue with your audience. This means not just you talking "at" them but having them respond in a genuine manner so that you really connect.

Connect

There are three aspects that you should maintain with your audience to keep things flowing smoothly all year. The first of these is connection. By simply reaching out to form a connection, you can build that like, know, and trust effect, letting you get some real insight into who they are and also allowing them to get to know you too. When your audience trusts you, they're going to feel more connected, like they know you as a friend, not just the silhouette behind a faceless brand, and they'll be more likely to listen to what you have to say.

This means opening the door sometimes and showing them a little bit more about yourself. You want to create a dialogue and provide real value. Share things about yourself and your business. The more you pull the curtain back to a level that's comfortable for you, the more your audience will know and trust you. This is something that you can do all year long and will pay off when it comes time for you to present your offers.

Invite

Next, you want to invite them to work with you. Just like connecting, this involves sharing a little bit about yourself and what goes on behind -the-scenes. You may want to show people what your day is really like, such as how your office looks, even during the messy points. This helps you to be relatable, as nobody else in the world has a perfect grasp on keeping everything neat and orderly 100% of the time. One thing that is definitely important is to set healthy boundaries with what you're comfortable sharing with your audience. This is all personal preference, as some are completely okay laying everything bare with nothing to hide, and others feel uneasy with strangers knowing so much about them. You never want to put yourself in a situation where you don't feel authentic or not quite right about sharing something. Pay attention to the boundary, but if it's something you feel like your audience would appreciate seeing and you're comfortable sharing, then put it out there. Your audience will love it.

In this phase, the goal is to invite your audience to work with you. Throughout the year, there will be points in your conversations where it feels natural to do this. You may not be in the middle of a launch, but you still feel like it's the right decision to share your list builder with somebody. You could even invite them to have deeper conversations with you, potentially involving something like a one-on-one call. Or, if it's local, you may decide to meet in person. Inviting people into your world is an amazing way to have these ongoing and engaging conversations throughout the entire year.

Position

The final aspect is to position yourself correctly. This helps you show your authority on a subject, growing your credibility. When you position yourself as an expert at what you do, it shows your audience that you have their backs. You know exactly what it is that can help them, and you're going to share the tactics that help them overcome their challenge.

Some people feel uncomfortable doing this, like they're bragging to the world about how great they are. The main difference between positioning yourself and bragging is that you're showing your expertise and experience in a way that shows exactly what you're capable of and nothing more. You're not claiming to be the absolute best in the world, but you're confident in your abilities and need people to know that you are an expert. If you can share your experiences, letting them know everything you've done up to this point, they will believe you have their best interests in mind. This gives your audience a massive amount of reassurance that working with you is going to be a great experience.

In this piece, you also want to educate people about your brand and business. They may not know all of the things that you do, so tell them. Show them exactly what you do, how you can help, and what kinds of solutions you can bring to the table. This is also a great opportunity to teach your audience something and give them a quick win. You could also share a strategy that also positions you as an expert.

Oftentimes, I hear from people, "Well, I'm not bad at what I do, but I'm definitely no expert." This is where I want you to challenge how you perceive yourself. You're exactly where you need to be, and you have the knowledge, skills, and experience that nobody else has. It's alright to toot your own horn and let the world know that you can do what you claim. You have something important to share. Never take that for granted.

These three aspects combine together to help you create great conversations with your audience year-round. Get to know your audience, and start that two-way dialogue. When you have that, and you're asking questions, it's going to build trust between you and your audience in a way that can't be captured through other methods. They're going to get to know you a little better, and they're going to be primed to listen to you later when your launches start rolling out. If you're doing this all year long, you're going to be on people's minds, pushing them to take the next step and work with you through your offers. It all starts with those conversations.

Chapter 19

List-Building Foundations

Before you dive into the ins and outs of list-building, it's important to set yourself up for success. You might be thinking, "Well, I don't have a list," or, "I've got a really small list, and I just don't know what to do with it." It's easy to get deep into your thoughts and sabotage your success without realizing it. This is where I see most people get frustrated and discouraged from even trying because they feel like they are spinning their wheels without seeing any progress. At the end of the day, it's important to always keep in mind how and why you are building your list. This is all about being intentional. You're not trying to build a big list, but one of quality. No matter how much you want to help people, you'll never be able to do that unless you've got the right people on your list. So, be intentional about how you do it and what you are aiming to achieve. The entire goal is to have a list that is made up of your perfect people.

Key Factors To Remember

Everybody starts with the first subscriber.

Every email list that has ever been made in this world started off having exactly zero people on it. If you've been building your list, and you're at a point where you've hit a standstill, that's okay. This has happened to just about everyone. Keep pressing forward to find your perfect people.

If you're applying the right methods, you will eventually have a long list of folks who are best served by your product or service.

I remember back when I built my very first list builder. It was right after I published my first book back in 2015. I crowdsourced people who I knew on my social media accounts and people that I met at networking events. Anywhere and everywhere I went, I was pulling people onto my email list. First, it was just my immediate family and friends. Then, slowly I built it up to several hundred people over the course of a year.

As I look back, it's interesting to me that I didn't have an offer. I didn't know where I was taking people, but they did subscribe, and I did 365 Days of Intentions, which was based on the book I created at the time. So I sent just a little bit of inspiration to them in their email box each and every day throughout the entire year.

I put all this time, energy, and effort into building a list, but I didn't do anything at all that I've shared with you in the pages of this book. At that time, I wasn't aware that I needed an offer. I had no idea that I needed the right people nor how to guide them into a proper offer later on. So it was very humbling that, after collecting these several hundred people, I realized I did not have the right people. I did not attract the right people for what I wanted to offer the marketplace. It was a tough lesson to learn.

So guess what I did? I started all over again at zero.

Later, going into 2016, I started helping my love (who is now my husband Paul) with his photography business. I also helped him with his workshops, and we both had speaking opportunities for photographers, teaching them about marketing and selling their photography services.

And we started at zero with our email list for that too. Between speaking engagements online as well as offline, podcasts, and other opportunities, building Facebook groups and social media accounts, we actually grew that email list to over 30,000 people. From that list, we did very well. We made several hundred thousand dollars a year with our courses and memberships and the offers that we had in the marketplace during those years.

And the interesting thing is, in 2018, we decided to pivot and go in the direction of a new market. Because we had a lot of success with our courses and memberships, a lot of people from that niche approached us.

Now that sounds great, but the thing is, the 30,000 photographers that were on our email list did not have an interest in learning about courses, memberships, and online marketing. So we had to start over at zero all over again.

Since then, we have created an incredible mentorship program called Adaptive Inner Circle, where we've helped many of our members go from zero upwards to over 40,000 plus people on their email lists.

We accomplished that by coaching our members through their own launches, summits, lead magnets, Facebook ads, SEO, blog posts, YouTube videos, and other social media opportunities.

One of our members, Kay, was really struggling with building her email list when she originally came to us. Using our methods and guidance, which adds onto what I share within this book, she started getting leads at six cents per lead on Facebook ads. Incredible! She was able to do this because her message and her offer were very aligned with the audience that she was attracting.

We've had other members come to us, like Breanne and Kristina, who had a moderately sized email list when they came into our world, but nobody on their list was converting into paying clients, plus they were struggling to get the price point that they really wanted.

They were spending nearly a full-time effort maintaining a free Facebook group. With our guidance, they were able to switch their format and their Facebook group and also started building their list of potential buyers, and at the same time, raising their prices to a high-ticket offer that they presented to their members.

When we first met them, they had a $15 per month text messaging membership, and we helped them transform into a several hundred dollars per month coaching and support program for the parents of high school and college athletes.

List-building takes time.

Stay focused on getting the perfect people on your list. I would much rather you have fewer of the right people than have a larger number of the wrong people. Being in business, you're offering a product to people in an attempt to help them with some problem they are facing. Stay mindful that the key to being successful in business is remaining focused on the people you serve. Behind every email address on your list is a real, live person who created it, and they deserve to be treated as more than just a number you collect to increase your social proof.

**Meet Kristina & Breanne,
Elite Performance Coaches**

"So it's not just us giving and giving, but also creating something that we love to deliver and that our people love. We've tripled our return. The numbers prove that it was worth our investment."

Scan Here To Learn More

Read more of this story at http://influencedbook.com/casestudies

Of course, it's easy to get caught up in vanity metrics. We all want a big list of people because it makes us feel successful. The problem with that is we may not actually be as successful as those numbers seem to indicate. It's simply a way of obtaining validation that we're proceeding in the right direction. But those numbers can be deceptive, even if we're the only people who ever see them. Remember, a long list of wrong people won't serve you, and it certainly won't serve the majority of those who are on it. List-building takes time, and it's alright if it takes you a while to capture that perfect audience.

Marketing is testing.

Just as with any other skill you're learning, in marketing, you'll sometimes feel stuck, like you're not making any progress no matter what you try. When this happens, it's easy to throw your hands up and say, "That's it! I quit. I can't do this anymore. This just isn't for me, I guess."

It's in these moments that I encourage you to dig your heels in and give it another shot. Growth is always uncomfortable, and you may find yourself trying something that doesn't come naturally. Often, the greatest success comes from moments where you put yourself out there and stick with it. When you hit these moments of friction, remind yourself, verbally if needed, that this is just a moment of growth. Take a deep breath and try again. Try something new, and keep moving forward. If you get stuck, push through it!

Marketing is all about testing the waters and seeing what works with your specific niche and clients. It's up to you to try out new techniques, show yourself to the world, and see what works. This may take more time than you like and certainly a lot more time than you may think it should.

Just remember the tortoise and the hare. This isn't about going fast. It's about finding the right people. That is what will make you a winner in the end.

One of the common mistakes that we see is people rushing to build their list and their social media following as quickly as possible. The interesting thing with that is you typically don't have a strong relationship established with the people that you are collecting. By taking your time and going at a steady pace, you'll actually nurture the relationships better. You'll get better feedback from the people that you do have following you, and you'll be more strategic in how you grow your list with the right people. By growing too fast or doing creative things in the marketplace just to game the system, you find out that you have a lot of people that are really not interested in what you offer. You just did random things to attract large groups of people that are not aligned with your offers.

So one of the things that we like to look at, and you might see this in some of my videos, are the pictures positioned behind me of the tortoise on one side and the hare on the other. Now, as we all know, the story goes that the hare runs the race fast, gets tired, and takes a nap, and the tortoise just takes its time, methodically taking one step over and over again all the way to the win.

Just like everything in life that's worthwhile, true success takes time. It's the building of small successes stacked one upon another that gets us to a worthy goal. Now, the great thing about doing this is we're not skipping steps. We're not going to compare ourselves to the marketplace. We're going to go at our own pace, not worrying about what everybody else is doing, and take the next step that we need to take for ourselves and our business.

So don't get caught up in everybody else's race and what they're doing. Focus on your own lane. Focus on the next step that you need to take. And understand that this is about long-term relationships, not short-term ones.

Chapter 20

Segmenting Your List

Having different lists (sorting your main email list into smaller categories) sets the stage for intentional list-building and helps you create unique conversations with those who are on your list. Over time, people will join your list for many different reasons, and because of that, the dialogue you have with them should be tailored to each group.

At the beginning of your business, having all of your subscribers on one list can be a great strategy. You have a million things on your mind, and it can be overwhelming to keep track of them all. The last thing you need is one more detail to keep an eye on.

While your list is small, having it in one area means you can still keep up with the conversations you are having with each person. This will also enable you, in real-time, to quickly identify which list builders are working and which aren't. However, keeping things organized like this as your business grows is a mistake.

As your list gets bigger and bigger, and you begin to speak to more and more topics, it will get exponentially more difficult to be intentional with the people who are subscribed to your email list. Before long, you'll find yourself in a place where it's nearly impossible to track who is interested in each service you offer or why they're even seeking your expertise.

This is why it's so important to segment your list.

Segmenting your list simply means that you separate all of your subscribers into different buckets. Eventually, you'll want to do this so that the conversations you're having with each person will revolve around the topic that they joined your list to learn more about. You want this topic to be a major, if not the only reason somebody approached your business for help. This allows you to nurture those relationships deeper, helping each person feel like you really understand them and that they can truly turn to you for help.

We experienced the importance of segmenting our list when we moved from serving photographers with their businesses to helping online entrepreneurs market and sell their courses, memberships, and coaching programs. When we first started the transition, we had everyone on one list together. But, we found that our new messaging didn't resonate as much with the photographers, so we began segmenting our list. This way, we could have separate conversations with our photographers from those with the online entrepreneurs as we shifted and eventually leaned into serving online entrepreneurs exclusively. When you don't segment a growing list, it leads to more confusion and frustration for your audience, and they'll be more likely to unsubscribe. For instance, if you have somebody talk to you who is looking for help with list-building,

but the only conversations you're having with them are about their personal brand, then they can quickly become confused as to why they came to you in the first place. This can lead to someone being turned off from you completely, ultimately unsubscribing from your list.

Remember, you don't want each name on your list to be nothing more than a mere number to you. By having conversations with each subscriber revolve around the specific reason that person entered your list, you'll help them feel valued, and they will walk away from your email feeling like they've been heard, that somebody understands their problem, and they aren't alone, because you are somebody who has been exactly where they are and overcame it.

4 Key Lists

For our purposes here, I'm going to keep everything simple and give you four key lists that I believe every online business owner should have in their list-building toolkit. Of course, if you desire, you can segment your list even further, but it's best to keep it simple in the beginning and add more when you see fit for your individual needs.

House List

This is typically the list most people start with, and they may never realize it has a name. This is your catch-all list, the one that has every single subscriber on it. The House List often has people who have many different reasons for wanting to know more about what you have to offer. These might be people who were interested in your podcast and wanted to hear more. Perhaps you offer an email-based subscription, and this includes those members. You might have offered a free product to capture emails in an attempt to market to more people. Once again, this type of list is perfectly fine to have in the beginning. But as you progress, continue to segment your list further into the other categories, as the conversations you'll be having will need to become more specific for each one.

Launch List

From your House List, you'll want to begin building your Launch List. This type of list is exclusively composed of individuals who have opted into one of your launches, whether it be a list of members from your previous launch or those eagerly awaiting your newest one. All conversations for this list should be centered around your upcoming launch, as everybody on your launch list wants as much information as they can to make an informed decision on whether to buy into your service. When addressing this list, you want to build excitement and speak about the different aspects of your launch that will entice members of this list to become customers.

Waitlist

If you have a program that opens to new customers for one part of the year and closes for the rest, then the Waitlist is an important piece of the puzzle. During the time your offer is closed to the public, there may still be people who are interested in hearing more about your product or who are eagerly awaiting your cart to go live again and want a reminder. The Waitlist captures these individuals and helps you get them excited and then keep them excited while they wait. Your main goal here is to build anticipation, hopefully taking as many people as you can through your launch sequence.

Buyers List

The Buyers List is only for those who have bought from you, whether they are current clients or past. This is one of the most valuable lists you can have. Using this type of list helps you keep track of the varying pieces of work you've done with and for each person on the list. The reason this is so important to keep track of is that those who have already purchased from you are already proven to be interested in your products, and therefore they are more likely to buy from you again.

What's most exciting about this list is that these people already know you on a deeper level than even those who are eagerly waiting to purchase from you. Because you've worked with them, you've already had more intimate conversations than you've been able to have with those who are a part of any other list of yours. People who are brand new on your waitlist may not know a whole lot about you, but those on your Buyers List have worked side-by-side with you in some capacity and can give you an increased social proof showing that you can do what you claim you are capable of doing.

The main takeaway that I want you to hold onto is that having separate lists will help you more easily track where people are in their journey with you, and that will help you serve them on a deeper level than you would be able to with only one list. While you could simply dump everybody into one list, that would homogenize the conversations you'd have with your potential clients and will keep those individual relationships weak, which means they may not move forward.

The conversations you have with somebody from your Buyers List are going to be drastically different than with those who are on your Waitlist and have barely heard of you. You'll need to share more tips and strategies with your Waitlist to help build trust compared to somebody who has already worked with you and walked away a satisfied customer.

Segmenting your list is only powerful when you manage to pinpoint the reason somebody has entered your world, and people will come to you for many different reasons. You want to continue to speak to those reasons and make it your primary mission to keep from ignoring them. When you do this, people are more likely to feel heard, understood, and more connected to you. This creates a much richer experience for your clients as you take them on the journey of working with you at increasingly higher levels.

You can always add more segments to your lists later. For now, focus on these four:

- House List
- Launch List
- Waitlist

- Buyers List

This is a great head start and allows you to see more clearly which segments you still need to add, if any.

Chapter 21

Research Into Action

We've talked a lot about list builders and how creating one with intent helps us speak into the problems our audience members are facing. We've also talked a little bit about pain points, moving from the challenges your people are facing and moving to the end goal, their transformation. People don't just move directly from point-to-point. There are often many small steps involved, which are covered within your Transformation Track™. Now, it's time to put all of that research into action as we create your list builder.

List builders should always speak to people at different stages of your track. If someone's further along in their journey, the list builder that speaks to them and their challenges is going to be greatly different than one that will be best for somebody who is fresh at the start. The purpose of every list builder is to solve a specific problem and ultimately lead people to our offers.

The right list builder will attract only the right people to you, which is why doing research on your audience early on in the process was so important. If your list builder is not aligned with what your people think, say, feel, and do, then they're not going to be able to understand what you have to say, even if you truly can help because you're not speaking their language. This imperfect list builder may not even attract anybody, or worse, it could attract the wrong audience to you.

A lot of times, the challenge that I see my clients experience as they begin creating their initial list builders is that they focus on making them eye-catching and beautiful without caring at all if it's relevant for their ideal client. But, when it doesn't tie into the problem they solve with their offer, interest from their leads remains low, with few purchasing.

From a high-level overview perspective, the end goal is to create several list builders, each one meeting people at the various levels of your Transformation Track™—eventually. Your initial lead magnet is the first spoke on your wheel, so to speak. This "spoke" leads directly to your paid offer. Once that is created, you'll test it out in the real world, then create another list builder for a separate problem, still related to your offer. This will be another spoke on your wheel, once again leading directly to a paid offer. The goal is to make several of these, with each passing one giving us more information on what our audience is looking for and what helps us make more conversions. All of them need to speak into separate problems while staying seamlessly relevant to your offers.

None of the problems you're solving with these list builders are going to be pulled from thin air. All of them will come from the research you've done on your ideal client from earlier chapters and should be pulled specifically from those top problems that keep showing themselves time and time again. The end goal of each of these list builders is to successfully get people to give you their email address, allowing you to nurture that relationship and lead them directly into your offers.

As you test your lead magnets, you may find that one is an especially great hit and that the problem it solves seems to be common enough that almost everybody wants help with it. This process is awesome for you to get that information because you're going to know even more about which messages resonate with your audience. This allows you to fine-tune your messaging, not only within your list builders to come but within your offer as well as everything you do in your marketing.

Offer Wheel

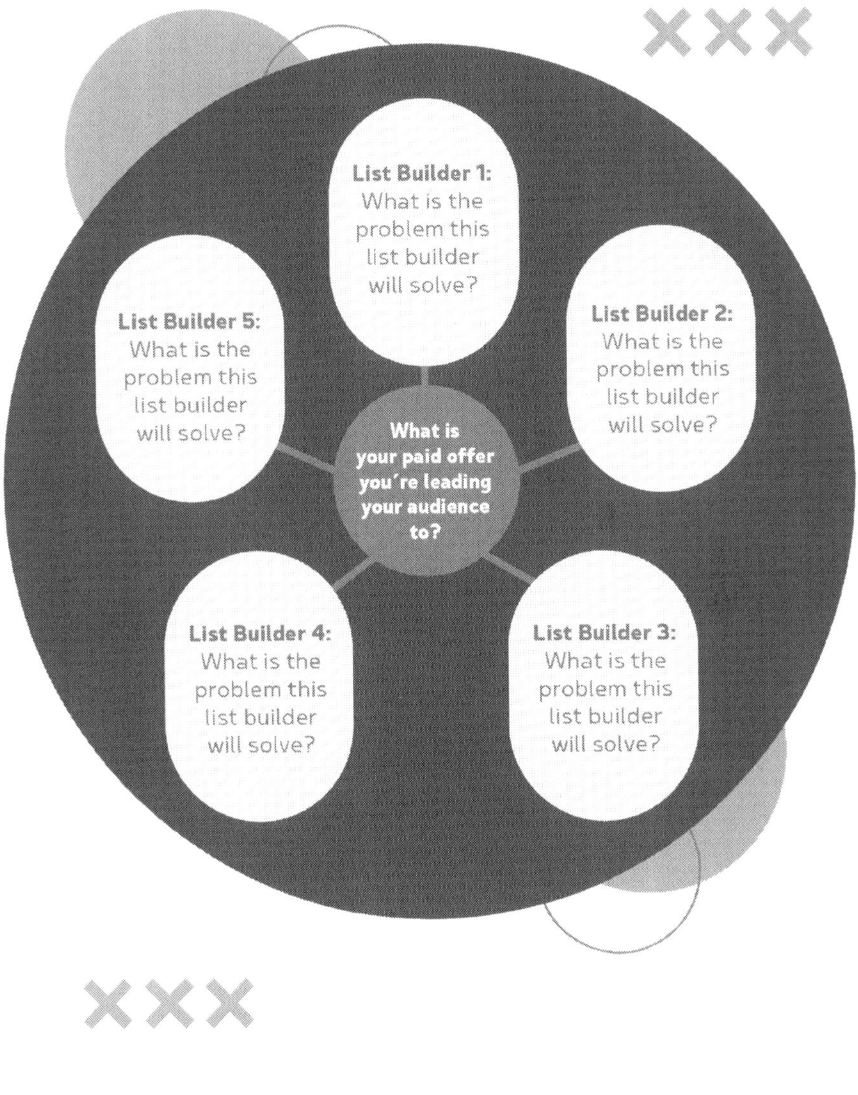
List Builder 1:
What is the problem this list builder will solve?
List Builder 2:
What is the problem this list builder will solve?
List Builder 3:
What is the problem this list builder will solve?
List Builder 4:
What is the problem this list builder will solve?
List Builder 5:
What is the problem this list builder will solve?
What is your paid offer you're leading your audience to?

Don't be overwhelmed, thinking that you have to create all different kinds of list builders that appeal to all different kinds of people at one time. That would be very confusing for anybody to deal with. Choose one problem to help your audience overcome, and start with that. This is going to serve as a test to really see what resonates with your people. Choose the pain point you understand best, and create that list builder, putting it out into the world for others to see.

Not all problems are equal, and some problems may weigh heavier than others. Sometimes, we think that our audience is coming to us for one specific reason that we push, but they're interested in something else that we help solve. This first lead magnet will be your first test to truly see what your audience is interested in and will allow you to see what resonates with them.

Chapter 22

Types of List Builders

When we first start designing our lead magnets, it can be tricky to wrap our minds around what they will look like from our audience's point of view and what would make sense to them. If we remember the purpose of a list builder, its primary reason for existence is to solve a problem for our people. They've raised their hands, asking for help with this challenge, and we're creating something that speaks to that pain point. That's going to get them curious, and we follow up with our lead magnet giving them a strategy to overcome that challenge.

We're surrounded by list builders all the time, even if we don't realize it. Imagine you're at the boardwalk on a nice summer day, and you walk by a small candy store you've never been to before. Outside, there's somebody holding a tray of free fudge samples. Personally, that's going to get me to walk in the door. That plate of free fudge acts as a lead magnet, pushing me towards the candy store by giving me something small that holds real value to me as the consumer. That's going to get me to raise my hand, or in this case, I'll walk over and grab that piece of fudge before I walk inside the store to see what else they sell.

When we talk about our list builders being perfectly aligned, the person standing outside of the store understands their audience and what they want. Just thinking about that fudge makes me want to browse for more candy. It puts me in the mood for something sweet. But how weird would it be if I opened the door and, instead of more candy, I found a pizza shop? While they're both foods, contextually, the fudge primes me to want more sugar, and I'm going to be disappointed to find something savory on the other side of that door. In the same way, your list builder should be a free sample to get people excited, interested, and curious to enter your store (whether virtual or brick-and-mortar).

Of course, real-world examples don't stop at just food. In the area I live, when you go into a convenience store, there are a lot of publications for anyone that's looking for a home. The magazine will have a large collection of homes for sale, along with prices, square footage, etc. I've also seen similar guides for wedding shows, where they'll provide a list of vendors to help couples find the ones that are relevant to them. This ranges from dresses and tuxes to flowers, cakes, and more. It's a beautiful magazine that helps couples save time during an already hectic and fast-paced period of their life. Both of these are perfect examples of lead magnets. They help generate interest in their areas of business, drawing people one step closer to their world and priming them to make a sale.

Now, let's shift gears once again, looking at how you may have already experienced somebody leading you into an offer. I think many people reading this book have bought a course of some kind. Initially, you knew nothing about the course. You didn't even know it existed. But everything changed when somebody offered you a free guide, and all they asked for in exchange was your email address. The next thing you know, you're reading through their emails and starting to trust that person. Eventually, an email comes in, promising to help you learn a new skill, and before you know it, you are in their course. And it all started with something as simple as signing up for a free guide. The same thing can happen to you with all of your offers.

Your lead magnets don't need to be complex. In fact, it can help if they're simple, easy to understand, and cut straight to solving the problem. Simple lead magnets make information easier to digest, helping people to truly understand the concepts that you're teaching. Remember, the goal is not to teach everything all at once. It's to give your audience one win, one eye-opening piece of information to get them onto your email list, so you can nurture a relationship with them. Don't make this too complicated. Keep it super simple.

When you're teaching information, you should know that there are three main learning styles, which we will dive into in a moment. Each person learns in a different way, and the format you decide to use should be dependent on your audience and the problems they face. If you're helping people learn to write books, then it makes sense that they enjoy reading, so using text for that audience makes sense. You may also decide that you want to mix any of these mediums together. The only thing you need to focus on is whether or not your chosen formats are perfectly aligned with your audience based on the research you've already done.

Text-Based List Builders

Using a text-based list builder is especially powerful for audiences that highly enjoy reading. Some examples include a checklist to help your audience organize their thoughts, a step-by-step process on how to accomplish something, or even a template. Templates have been especially popular lately because your audience will only have to focus on creating rather than intricately planning something out, quickly solving their problem, and giving them a big win.

Audio-Based List Builders

Audio is great because some people process information easier through listening than in any other way. Spoken content can also be easier, if not quicker, to produce than other formats, as there are little to no visual components that need to be designed. An audio-based lead magnet could look like a private podcast that's specific to those who have opted into your list builder or an audiobook that gives your audience a portion of what you teach. An additional benefit of using audio as your vessel of communication is that it can help people feel closer to you, as hearing one's voice creates a direct connection between them and their listeners.

Visual-Based List Builders

The majority of people learn visually. Visual list builders are often created from video, but pictures can also be used. With this format, you could teach something in the form of a short video training, where you help your audience learn a new skill or solve a quick problem, and they watch the video along the way.

Other Considerations

The best part is you don't need to feel restricted to choosing one format per list builder, as you can create combinations that mix the best parts of each format to make something stronger than choosing either exclusively. You may decide to choose to create a training video, but alongside that is a series of emails that expand on the information presented within the video.

Give yourself permission to get as creative as you want when you begin planning and designing your list builders. The first and most important rule is to keep things simple. Think about that one type of transformation you're going to give the individual through your list builder and start mapping that out. What would be the best way you can give your audience that experience while still solving that problem?

As you're planning your lead magnet, make sure that everything is aligned with your offer. We've done this through our Facebook ads course. For someone perfect for that course, we want to make sure that our list builders are aligned with teaching our audience about Facebook ads. One great list builder we use for that is our 50 High Converting Headlines. This is an easy download where they receive fifty different templates that help the recipient create an eye-catching headline. It's absolutely free, and if somebody wants to grab it, all it takes is to give us their email address.

If you'd like to see this opt-in in action, you can check it out on the next page:

Snap Up More Sales & Incredible Clients With This FREE Fill In the Blank Headline Templates PDF!
50 Headline Templates For Your Business
50 HIGH CONVERTING
HEADLINE
TEMPLATES

From there, we put the people who sign up for it into our email sequences, nurturing that relationship with conversations, as well as letting them know about the opportunity to join our Facebook ads course. Everything is perfectly in alignment, guiding our audience down the path of transformation, seamlessly blending into one another.

Now, it's your turn. Begin thinking about the different kinds of list builders that you're excited to try, and continue on to the exercise ahead.

Chapter 23

Quality & Design

Your list builder is your chance to make a good first impression on your audience, as this is how many people are going to find you and your work. It's a way for your people to get to know you, to get a true understanding of your expertise, and how you can help them. I remember when I created my first list builder. It took me hours to make this simple PDF. Even though I had expertise in the subject matter, there were other areas where I lacked experience and expertise. First, I had to write it. I consider myself to be a good writer, but this was my first piece of content I ever created for the purpose of building my list. Copywriting and leading clients to take action was a different style of writing than I had been doing up until then.

Next, I had to go through the design process. I'm not a professional graphic designer, and I didn't even own design software, let alone know how to use it. I spent a lot of time making a logo, selecting colors, and it was so hard getting all the text to fit on the page. When it was complete, I was so incredibly proud of my new creation. I marveled at how nice it turned out.

Looking back now, I recognize it was a very amateur version, and I know if I had sent it to a pro, it would have looked a lot more professional and taken much less time than I took to create it. And then, of course, I had to struggle with all the technical pieces. Beyond all the struggle with skills or lack thereof, what I didn't understand at the time was this is often the initial impression and beginning of building a connection with someone who I wanted to trust me enough to eventually open their wallet and buy from me.

Your lead magnet opens the door for a relationship and is the first step towards the path of greater opportunities, guiding your audience to work with you on deeper levels through your offers. The best way to make that good impression is to have great quality and design. Before you begin designing your first list builder, there are some considerations that you should think about that will help you to create a stronger first impression.

Outsourcing

The first thing to consider is whether or not you want to outsource any areas of your list builder. While you may be an expert in everything that you know, it's always important to remember your limitations. I know this can be hard for some of us because we want to have hands-on experience as we create our list builder. We have a great idea that we want to see come to life in the specific way we're imagining. But, if things like graphic design or copywriting—elements every list builder needs—aren't our strong suit, it may be a good idea to outsource that to somebody who is an expert in that area.

Of course, you can do this yourself, and you can absolutely create something that generates interest with your content alone. But if your layout and design aren't in good form, then it can detract from your message, potentially leading some to write you off entirely as a novice. This is why I highly recommend that you hire professionals to help you with any elements that are outside your area of expertise.

You need this list builder to have a strong impact to cause that amazing first impression. In order for us to create that impression, it may take us hours of learning and even more hours of work when a professional could get it back to us in a fraction of that time, potentially at a higher quality than we could make ourselves.

Copywriting

One prominent area that people outsource is copywriting. Conveying your message in a way that other people can understand is a difficult task and one that many people aren't skilled in. Copywriting is a skill that you learn over time through many hours of practice. And while it's a skill that many can learn eventually, when it comes to creating our list builder, it can be important to keep things moving.

A copywriter's job is to take your message, your ideas, and your thoughts and convert them into a professional block of text that conveys what your list builder is going to do to help that individual. Your copywriter will translate your idea into simple language that everybody in your audience can understand. All of the research you've done up to this point will also help your copywriter identify your audience, enabling them to convey your message in the language that they understand best.

If you're not a copywriter, then this is an area I'd most strongly recommend you outsource. The success of your list builder relies heavily on how well your message is received by your audience, and that's exactly what a professional copywriter can help you achieve.

Graphic Design

Another type of professional you may consider hiring would be a graphic designer. While this is something that we can do ourselves, it can take a lot of time to learn if this isn't already a skill we have. A good graphic designer can save you so much time and frustration. They are especially useful if you're producing a written text lead magnet, as the design and layout can be challenging to get right. A graphic designer will make sure that the important areas of text pop out and make themselves known to the reader.

When the design within your list builder is done well, it really accentuates that you are a leader within your niche, helping your audience pay even more attention to what you have to say.

Additional Design Tips

Technical Pieces

Depending on the format you choose for your list builder, certain things will need to be decided before you can begin with the design work.

The most common file format for a text-based lead magnet is PDF which is the one I recommend. However, this comes with some technical considerations. One thing that makes PDFs so attractive is that you can make them fillable. For example, if your PDF contains a checklist, some people will choose to print it out and physically write on each line with a pen. Others enjoy having everything in one place on their computer. If the PDF is designed correctly, you can give your audience the ability to digitally sign each of those lines or boxes with text, leaving their answers on the PDF with no extra work on their end. While this is a small thing, it can leave such a huge impact on the enjoyment somebody gets from your product.

Brand Colors

You should always keep your brand colors consistent, and within your list builder, it's no different. Every good lead magnet needs to be professional, clean, and easy to read. You want everything, from the moment they land on your website to the time they read your lead magnet, to have a congruent, high-quality feel.

There's nothing worse than opening a PDF and having trouble reading it because the font is just a bit too small or the text and background colors clash, making everything difficult for the eyes. These types of decisions can create a ripple effect on the quality of your list builder.

Image Tips

Within a text-based lead magnet, images are incredibly important for conveying thoughts quickly or helping to set the mood. Consider the kinds of images you want to use, including images of yourself. These set the tone and can make you feel approachable and down to earth when done right. Depending on how long your viewer has been following you, this may be their first exposure to you, so including professional pictures of yourself allows your audience to connect with you. It may be a good idea to contact a photographer to help you update your brand's photos, letting you incorporate them not just into your list builder but in places like your website and marketing materials as well. This, along with matching colors between your different products and projects, helps to keep your brand congruent.

As you design your lead magnet, the way it's formatted can drastically change the size of the file. If the file size becomes too large, it can be difficult for your audience to easily download and use, potentially causing frustration and leaving a negative opinion. A pro will know how to compress images in a way that they look good and also don't take up large file space.

Text-Based Tips

With a text-based lead magnet, I heavily recommend splitting everything up into multiple pages. When too much information is crammed into one, it can begin to feel overwhelming, making everything hard to keep track of, even if there's a healthy amount of content within. By breaking your text up into multiple pages, it's instantly easier to digest, even though the amount of content hasn't changed. This should be done by putting everything within three sections.

Welcome Section

Within your first section, you first want to welcome your audience to your lead magnet, telling them how you aim to help. The main focus is introducing the topic that you're sharing. This is also your opportunity to position yourself by talking about your expertise.

Information Section(s)

The next area is where you share about the topic itself. This section is full of the information your audience came looking for when they signed up for your list builder. It's where you provide the value you promised and help your people overcome a challenge they've been facing.

Next Steps Section

Finally, your third section is going to be about the next steps your audience can take. After going through this list builder, your audience has had one challenge solved, but they've likely got more questions now. Tie everything up with a nice little bow that tells the user how they can continue to work with you. You can add a little more positioning here to present you as an expert, increasing their desire for that next step.

It's important that you include links to places such as your website to help people easily find you. Not everyone is tech literate, and it may be difficult for some to find their way back to the original URL of your list builder without links. Meanwhile, this file will forever be (unless deleted) within their computer. Take advantage of this, and make it as easy as possible for them to find you. Never lose out on the opportunity for somebody to find and contact you. Having all of this information within your lead magnet is vital.

Audio and Video Tips

If you're creating a list builder that's focused on audio or video, the biggest piece to get right is the quality. There's nothing worse than trying to watch a video, only for the audio to be low quality making it hard to understand what's being said, or the picture is so fuzzy you can't make out what you're looking at. You want your audio and picture quality to be crisp and sharp. This may necessitate buying a new microphone or using lights to make your set bright so you can be clearly seen.

When recording, keep your environment as quiet as humanly possible. When you're filming, you don't want a barking dog in the background causing a distraction to your audience. Instead, make sure it's a pleasant environment to be in, especially if it's going to be seen by hundreds of people.

If you haven't recorded very much live-action content, you'll want to practice pacing yourself to make sure your content is easy to understand. Don't talk too fast or too slow to the point it's distracting.

You should also be aware of what you're wearing as you film your video. Wearing an eccentric pattern can look great in person but will often look terrible in a video. Focus on wearing mostly solid colors for a reliably good look.

If there are areas outside of your expertise, it's best to hire someone to help figure out what you need to do to increase the quality of your audio or video.

At the end of the day, make sure that the quality and design of your list builder is top-notch. You've done a lot of work to help find the perfect people. It would be a great shame to throw all of that away because your attention to detail was lacking at this point, and you tried to scrimp on resources for the design of your list builder. Create something amazing that your audience is going to love, and it will form an amazing, lasting first impression. We're working towards a strong relationship with our audience, and this is the first step of building one.

Chapter 24

Landing Page

By now, you've created an amazing list builder that speaks to a problem your audience is having. Now, it's time to create a page where your audience can opt into your email list and grab it.

The landing page should emphasize the visitor's desire for help and convince them to opt in. They'll give you their email address, and that allows you to communicate on an ongoing basis and build a relationship.

Normally, when meeting someone new, we make an effort to impress. The same goes for your landing page. This is your audience's first impression and could be your only chance to get them excited about what you do. It should grab their attention and get them excited to fill out your opt-in form so you can help them with the transformation they're seeking. Remember, first impressions count, which is why this page is key!

Every good landing page has several components that make them successful and are absolutely required. One thing to keep in mind is that your landing page can be simple and still be effective. This doesn't need to be a long page, especially if it's your first.

Headline

The first component you need is a solid headline. This functions as your opening statement and needs to be a real attention-grabber. This is your big, bold promise that you're going to make and follow through on with your list builder. It's always great when you have a headline that speaks to your audience because that will grab their attention most effectively. In a sense, you want people to read your headline and raise their hands up, saying, "Yes! That's it. That's me!" Whatever your headline is, it should speak to the transformation that your audience desires.

Last chapter, I mentioned that you should consider hiring a copywriter while designing your list builder if it's not your area of expertise. The same applies here. If the wording of your headline is weak, your entire landing page, and therefore lead magnet, could suffer.

Subheadline

Below your headline is your subheadline. This is a little bit of text that speaks into the transformation and helps to support your main headline. Where your headline is the promise you're making, the sub-headline tells how you plan to help your audience achieve that goal. This is another way to grab the attention of your audience, once again creating desire.

When in doubt, check back to the 104 Formula™. Look into the problems your audience is having, and speak in their own words as you describe the challenge they're facing and the result they are after.

Photo or Video

Often, landing pages contain some form of a visual element. Most commonly, this is a photo, but you could also choose to include some type of promotional video as well. For example, if you offer a PDF template, then an image of the completed template can show how it's used and give life to your landing page. If you don't have an image of the list builder itself, then something that relates to the desire or transformation can be used to drum up additional interest for your page.

Supporting Copy

You're likely going to have some additional copy that helps to support the desire for your list builder. This copy explains why your audience needs your lead magnet, how it's going to help them solve the problem they face, and why it's important that they opt in now. You can talk about some of the benefits they'll get from your list builder, such as what they'll learn. This is where you want to hone in on the transformation they'll receive and explain why they need this list builder right away.

Call-to-Action Button

The final item is the call-to-action button. The text of this button should help drum up visual interest in your audience, driving all of their focus into clicking it. Ideally, people will get excited that they're clicking it, preparing them to receive something from you, bringing them one step closer to solving one of their problems.

Your call-to-action button should appear above the "fold" of your page. This means, on a computer, it's visible to everyone who visits your landing page without needing to scroll down the page. This keeps things in a quick-to-digest format, making it as simple as possible for someone to sign up for your list builder, ultimately leading to more opt-ins.

This is the Above the Fold section of your landing page that should include your headline, sub headline, photo or video, supporting copy, and call to action button. This section is visible to everyone who visits your landing page without needing to scroll down the page and makes it simple for someone to sign up for your list builder.

This is the below the fold section of your landing page that includes supporting copy that creates interest and desire for someone to opt in for your list builder. Include text, photos or video and additional call to action buttons to encourage your audience to opt-in

Additional Components

While all of these components are necessary for any good landing page, there are additional elements you can add to increase visual interest and potentially help convince more stubborn readers. With all of your landing pages, it's important that you test out different lengths to see what works best for your audience. The pieces that I've already given you, when combined, create a very short landing page, only large enough to fit onto a screen without scrolling. While this works for many instances, in some cases, you might want to add additional information.

Social Proof

Perhaps you want to add social proof about transformations that have happened for people who have worked with you. This also applies to people that this list builder has helped. Even something as simple as a quote from somebody, "I downloaded this PDF, and it helped me do X, Y, and Z." This shows visitors to your page that if you've helped others, then you can also help them. You may also include social proof of people that have worked with you in other programs or services, ideally in the same subject that your list builder is in. Additional social proof could look like logos, such as if you've had opportunities to speak on certain stages or if you've contributed to magazines, blogs, or other forms of publications. One I always include on my pages is the TEDx logo because I am a previous TEDx speaker.

Having social proof on a landing page is incredibly powerful, as it's a real-world piece of evidence that you have the expertise you claim to have. It gives authority to your words and helps to cement you as an expert in your field.

About Me/ Meet the Expert

Related to the section on social proof, you may decide to add an "about me" section to your landing page. Here, you would talk about who you are, who you've helped in the past, and what you've accomplished. Be sure to include a high-quality headshot to help your audience make a connection with you quickly. You may also want to include a little note here about how you can help the reader and how your list builder is going to help with their problem.

Branding

Within your landing page, one thing you want to maintain is brand congruence. Make sure all of the colors are consistent with other products and websites in your brand while staying clean and professional.

Tracking Codes and Pixels

If your hosting service doesn't already do this for you, including several trackers on the back end of your website can be enormously helpful. This allows you to see not only how many people are visiting your page but how many people are opting into your list builder. This helps you see if your page is actually converting and, if not, shows you that something is wrong and needs to be fixed. Maybe your messaging isn't captivating enough, or you need to change your headline. Either way, the tracker will help give you more information about your situation, allowing you to make changes as needed. It's important to note that these types of trackers aren't visible to your viewer, and the information is only available to you.

If setting up this tracker isn't in your wheelhouse, you can always outsource this task to somebody with the expertise to help you out.

URL Title

Often, when people are first starting out creating websites, they don't consider the length of the URL when they're creating their landing pages. This leads to long, complicated URLs that are hard to say, especially if you're out and sharing your list builder with the community on podcasts, interviews, or in person. The longer the name of your landing page is, the harder it will be for people to find it after you've told them about it. They won't be able to remember where they're supposed to go, and it can lead to awkward situations. You want a URL that's easy to say and remember. In this case, you could do something like buy a custom domain and point the list builder landing page to that domain. That way, all you have to do is tell people the domain name, which is far simpler to convey. It's something you can mention in interviews, in groups, or just simply write out easily.

The last thing I'd like to remind you of is that your landing page is part of your first impression, just as your list builder is. This page needs to be able to guide people to opt-in easily while still looking good and creating excitement. Get rid of any distractions that pull people away. I don't recommend putting any of your social media contact information on this page. Don't lead them to other websites, even those you own. Keep them on this page distraction-free, and focus on your lead magnet.

Chapter 25

Thank You Page

Your thank you page, while not quite as prominent as the landing page, is still a crucial part of your audience's first impression.

Once someone has gotten excited by your landing page, they go ahead and give you their contact information. They've officially made it past the "stranger danger" phase, where they're evaluating to see if you're trustworthy. Immediately after clicking the call-to-action button, they should be redirected to a page that thanks them for signing up and lets them know their list builder is on the way.

This page helps create a relationship with your audience right away. You don't want anybody to opt-in and then become confused, not knowing what to expect next. This has happened to me several times in the past where I opted into a free offer and then wasn't sure if my information went through because I never received an email.

One time, I opted into a free offer and didn't have a great experience. At first, I wasn't sure if my information went through because nothing happened after I clicked the submit button. I checked my email and didn't see anything. I went back and signed up again because I wasn't sure if it went through. It left me feeling confused and frustrated, having to go through the process over and over. I just wanted my free thing!

I'm sure at some point you've also had this experience and may have had similar feelings. You want to avoid this happening to your people by making it really clear what's going to happen next.

Lead Magnet Delivery

There are a couple of elements you should include to keep things simple. The first of these is to let your audience know exactly what to expect. Congratulate them, continue to build that excitement, but let them know that their lead magnet is on the way and where they can find it. Leave no room for confusion. Make sure to be as precise and direct as you can within these instructions. This is also where you want to include information about how they can have their email resent in the event it never arrives. Mistakes happen when you're working with automation, and there will inevitably be someone who doesn't receive their email for one reason or another. We don't want our audience to feel lost if they never get their list builder, so we need to include a recovery option that's easy to find.

Sometimes, people will receive the email, but in a location, they don't expect it. Occasionally when an email is sent, it will be wrongly flagged as spam or put into their promotional folder. It's always a good idea to remind people to check these if they don't receive their list builder.

Visual Element

You may also want to include a visual element on your thank you page. This may be a photo or video that you use to continue the conversation and excitement for what's to come. It's another way to increase the experience for your audience and really push things from good to great.

Next Steps

Finally, your thank you page needs to include some kind of next step. You don't want to overload them with options. Just choose one thing that they can do to further your relationship. We want to keep this simple so as not to confuse people. This could be an opportunity to work with you in another way, or this could be an invitation to a Facebook group with the link built into the page.

In some cases, while this is a little bit more advanced, you could choose to have a low ticket offer for them. Something that's going to help carry them through the transformation. They just opted into your freebie, that's going to solve their problem, but here you offer a solution to another challenge that you identified when you used the 104 Formula™. While I won't go into too much detail here, as you build out more list builders, keep in mind that it is a valid strategy to try and expand upon them right from the get-go in your thank you page. You want this offer to be low-priced to make it more enticing while still connecting everything from your list builder to your further offers.

The thank you page is a short, simple page, but one whose use cannot be underestimated. Be sure that you pay attention to it because the entirety of your list builder is about first impressions, and this page helps take that to the next level. Think about the kinds of elements you want to include on your thank you page to make people excited about what they opted into, and let them know the next steps of what they can do to work with you.

Chapter 26

Nurture Email Basics

At this point in the process, somebody has gone to your landing page and decided to opt-in. They've been redirected to your thank you page and have a solid grasp on what they can do next so they can continue working with you. Now, we're in the part of our sequence where we continue to nurture that relationship through emails, talking to our audience about future paid offers. This step happens after your audience has received their free list builder, but that doesn't mean that they've completed the "first impression" stage of interacting with you.

Communicating regularly with the people on our list is the only way that we can build trust. It also helps us pass along information about our upcoming offers, allowing them to naturally gain interest.

This part seems to be a common problem for many people that I see. We do a lot of work to get people onto our landing page, fighting to get them interested in our list builder so that we can get their contact information. But after the opt-in, it's a dead end. There's no more communication. Nothing happens. The audience is ghosted, and they don't hear from us again. This is the main thing we want to prevent. We need to continue to nurture that relationship right out of the gate, talking with our audience on a regular basis.

These nurture emails should be created ahead of time and placed into an email automation campaign to be delivered based on when someone has opted into your list builder. By having your nurture sequence automatically delivered, you'll create an excellent client experience, so your audience knows what to expect, and you won't have to write follow-up emails with your audience on the fly.

Meet Wendy, Founder at Bruja Power Botanica

Wendy experienced one of her biggest launches just by adding a nurture email sequence after her coaching week to continue the experience for her audience and give them another opportunity to work with her. She's excited that this sequence can be used again in future launches and she doesn't have to recreate them.

Scan Here To Learn More

Read more of this story at http://influencedbook.com/casestudies

Lead Magnet Delivery

There are several emails you want to have as a baseline once someone has opted into your email list. These will help you build conversations and lead people to your paid offers. The first of these is the delivery of the lead magnet. This is an incredibly important email, as it's the main reason someone has decided to join your email list. When you deliver this, it is going to create excitement and should reaffirm why they decided to opt-in. In this email, talk about how this list builder is going to help them and the things it's going to do to help them reach that transformation they want so badly. You could even talk about some of the features that are included or some of the benefits that your specific list builder provides over others. When you can link the two features and benefits, it helps everything tie directly back into the transformation.

Within this email, you should also make it clear how they can access their list builder. Depending on how you have things set up, you may decide to have the list builder attached directly to the email. Or, you may have a link within the email that goes directly to the lead magnet that's hosted on your website. Whatever the case is, make sure it's entirely clear how to access your lead magnet. If the process is more complicated than grabbing a link, you should include step-by-step instructions to avoid as much confusion as possible.

Did You Get It? Email (4 - 24 hours later)

After they've received their list builder, I recommend you send out another email between four and twenty-four hours later. This is going to be a very simple text email where the only purpose is to keep the conversation flowing. Check in with the recipient and make sure they have access to their list builder. Ask them to reply whether they have or not. This helps to create that initial communication loop, keeping the conversation flowing back and forth naturally. Sometimes, the email making sure your audience has received their list builder gets lost in the promotional or spam folders, so this will help double-check everything is flowing as it should be.

This is a great way to check in on your people in a natural, conversational way. You don't want to include any pictures or anything like that. Just leave it as a short, sweet, text-based email.

Once you receive their reply, you can even keep the conversation going further. If they didn't receive their list builder, of course, you want to reply and help them get things straightened out. But once you're told that they received it, you can talk about how excited you are to help them solve this problem they're facing and that you can't wait to hear what they thought once they've finished going through the list builder. This strategy allows you to talk to people in a natural, genuine way, furthering your relationship early on.

What Do You Think? (1 - 2 Days after Did You Get It?)

In your third email, ask what they thought of your lead magnet. This should be delivered about one day after the second email has been sent.

Some possible things you can ask to get the conversation going:

- What did you think about it?
- How have you started to apply it?
- Has it opened any possibilities for you?
- Is it clear where you can find new opportunities?

In this email, you can also include another tip or strategy that's related directly to the list builder. This is a great opportunity to show your expertise and poses yourself as an authority who provides value to their community.

Whenever I send this email, I try to be as direct as I can in my questions. "Hey, let me know what you think. What was the biggest takeaway from the resource?" This is another way to deepen relationships with your community and will continue that two-way conversation where they reply and write out a response to you, giving you another opportunity to communicate back with those who have sent you emails.

Bridge Email (1-2 days after What Do You Think?)

Within email marketing, there are a ton of strategies that you can utilize to push relationships further and communicate on deeper levels. I suggest you send out one more email at minimum to really bridge the gap between the topic you discuss in your list builder, then transition into what's coming up next in your regular email list. Let people know how often they're going to receive emails from you and what you typically discuss. You want to warm up the individual to your upcoming launches, but you have to prepare them for what's coming next. We wouldn't want to put them on that list without any kind of transition, marketing to them right out of the gate. This could not only lead to a great deal of confusion but can also cause direct frustration.

Make it absolutely clear that from this point forward, you will begin your regular communication through your email list. You can also, as a bit of a more advanced strategy, lead them directly into another offer through a series of email sequences directly from this nurture sequence. For right now, focus on those four basic emails.

At the end of the day, this is all about warming up your audience, continuing the conversation, and building relationships. If we don't take the time to nurture these relationships early on, then when it comes time to launch our offer, they're going to have their guard up. We want them to know who we are, get them familiar with us, and begin to like, know, and trust us, maybe even feeling a little bit of excitement at the prospect of working with us again because they've seen the results we've already given them from this free opportunity.

Focus on the nurture emails in this sequence, and spend time thinking about what kind of emails you're going to write to really take your person through this process as they bridge into your regular email list. Your main goal here is to establish an ongoing two-way dialogue to help them get comfortable with you and know you better.

Chapter 27

Launch Conversations

When it comes to taking your list conversation to the next level and bridging to a launch conversation, I always advise beginning with the end in mind. As I've said throughout this book, the simplest way is to make sure that your offer is aligned from the start with the rest of your plan. You want to guide people to your paid offer one step at a time, from social to list to launch. Make sure you have great alignment with all the things you've created so far leading up to launch time. If you don't, return to the 104 Formula™ and get to work realigning everything. Make sure you're speaking to your audience where they're at on your Transformation Track™ and that your messaging aligns with that perfectly. Once that's in place, you can lead your audience directly into your paid offer. Getting this alignment right is really important, as, without it, we won't be bringing in the right people for our launch.

This is why the concept of launch conversations is so important. It allows us to guide people into our launch and beyond. When you're talking to somebody about your paid offer, it shouldn't come off as a sales pitch. It should feel just like you're casually talking about an opportunity to work with you. It should seem like the natural next step for that person to take because you've been having these conversations all along.

Here's a real-world example so that you can start to plan what you do with your product online. Pretend you're driving down the road, and you see a huge billboard to your right. This billboard is advertising a store, one that you know has exactly what you need. You detour off of the main highway just because this sign caught your attention. Now that you're off the highway, you see the sign that leads you to the parking lot of the store. While it's smaller than the billboard, it still has the same name and information about the store. It draws you in, and you park your car. As you're approaching the store, you see signs in the windows telling you more about what's in the store, preparing you for what to expect once you get inside. This creates a sense of excitement and a further sense of curiosity about what awaits you.

Once you get inside, you look around and see all the different aisles and all the products each has to offer. Each aisle has its own signs, letting you know what's on them, and even signs showing where every section of the store is located. All of this helps to create curiosity and gets you excited to see everything this store has to offer. After a while, you locate the original product that pulled you in, and you decide to buy it and anything else you find that catches your eye.

As you can see, there's a lot of different messaging there. It all started with a billboard on the highway that drew you in with a captivating offer. There were lots of signs that pointed toward all different kinds of products. You can think of each of these signs as a conversation, different points that you'll have as you interact with your audience. As you take them through a launch, you're going to have that initial messaging that really draws them in and grabs attention from their busy lives. You need something that gets them to make that detour off of the highway. Once they're off, you need additional signs that keep them interested, excited, and engaged. If you've done this the right way, by the time your audience reaches the store that represents your offer, they should be super excited and ready to buy because you've already nurtured them along the way with these different kinds of conversations.

Don't forget, all along the way, you've had previous conversations on social media. You've spoken into the things that they are thinking, saying, feeling, and doing. That content is going to draw them in and get them curious because they feel understood by you. They finally see somebody else who gets it, who really understands their problems. You brought them a step closer to your world with your list builders, and now they're ready to convert.

This launch conversation should continue well after you've gotten people onto your list. It shouldn't feel like a forced decision. It should feel like a natural conversation with someone you know. It's all about getting your messaging right and making sure you touch along all of those points as you continue talking with your audience. Make sure you're taking them from the billboard on the highway, all through the different signs they'll encounter as they make their way to the register and check out of your store.

As you engage in launch conversations, you'll find there are six phases. Each of these phases necessitates a different conversation approach that is a natural lead into the next subsequent step of your launch. Be intentional with these conversations as you go through each phase.

We don't want to come off like the old cliche, "Hi, I just met you. Will you marry me?" We don't want to come out right away and hit our audience with a big proposal. "Hi, please buy my stuff now!"

It feels gross to start a relationship like that, and it can come off as manipulative. But, when you do this the right way, it makes perfect, natural sense to your audience. It's the obvious next step to take, and it's going to help solve many of their problems.

Chapter 28

6 Phases of Launch Conversations

Think of this plan like a GPS, where you lead your audience to a specific destination that you have mapped out. In order to reach the end goal, we first need to know where that is. Then we can map out the directions to get there.

One of the road trips Paul and I love is our drive from Delaware to Key Largo, where we stay for the winter. It's a seventeen-hour drive, and we like to enjoy sights along the way, but we don't want long stretches of driving. So we plan our entire trip working backward from our final destination. We allow time each day for driving, pit stops for meals and gas, and then for finding a safe and comfortable place to sleep before we start the next leg of our trip. Before we step foot out of our home, we know where we are going and every step we are taking along the way. This is exactly how your launches should be.

When you plan your launch conversations this way, you'll know exactly where you are leading people. That way, all of your decisions can be intentional, allowing the pieces to blend together seamlessly. Remember to be purposeful with your conversations, keeping them perfectly aligned with your audience's journey.

Pre-Pre Launch Conversations

The first phase is the pre-pre-launch. These are the conversations and topics your audience is interested in that will bridge the gap in your offer. You probably have an idea of some of these topics already from the 104 Formula™. The main goal of your pre-pre-launch conversations is to transition people from your ongoing conversations and get them primed for your upcoming launch. We typically start these conversations roughly thirty to forty-five days before the start of our launch vehicle.

Pre-Launch Conversations

Next, we have the pre-launch phase. This gets your audience one step closer to your offer. The purpose of this phase is to create curiosity about what you do and get people excited to go through your launch process. This kickstarts all kinds of conversations that you'll be having throughout the entirety of your launch cycle, so it's the tone-setter.

In the pre-launch phase, the conversation is aimed at filling up your launch with the people who want to attend. Typically, for us, our pre-launch is about ten to fifteen days before the launch vehicle begins. Your launch vehicle is the event that leads to open cart, such as a challenge, workshop, or coaching week.

When you're first beginning this phase, go back to your 104 Formula™ and look at those hot topics. What is your audience interested in learning more about? This is what you want to focus on as you continue into your pre-launch conversations, especially if these relate to the topics covered in your actual launch vehicle. Doing so helps everything feel even more connected and keeps that transition seamless.

Launch Vehicle Conversations

After that, we take them into our actual launch mechanisms. This is what's going to lead people to your offer. These conversations consist of getting people excited about taking the next step, whatever that may be in your case.

The key for these conversations is to destroy limiting beliefs, overcome objections, and show your authority while speaking to the different stages of transformation they can expect from your program. The main point is to hype up your launch and tell people exactly what challenges they can expect to have solved with your help, leading them right into the open cart period.

Open & Closed Cart Conversations

This is the phase that often creates a lot of excitement. Here, you're opening the opportunity of buying your offer, allowing your audience the chance to work with you. The conversations in this phase consist of telling people not only how you can help them but asking what you can do to convince them to make a decision and buy your offer. Of all the phases, it can be argued that this one takes the most energy and focus, and it's also debatably the most important to get right.

During open cart, the goal is frequent conversations that keep the energy flowing high throughout this entire period of time. This is an exciting time, and we want to make sure that everybody is in on it. Think about how you can show up for your audience in this phase and how you can create that excitement in your community.

The final day of your open cart period, known as close cart, is usually another very exciting day because this is where a majority of sales will come in. Show up strong on this last day with multiple emails and social media posts to bring in those stragglers and last-minute decision-makers.

Post Launch Conversations

After the opportunity has opened and closed, what do you say to your audience? As the name suggests, this phase happens immediately after your launch. Unlike the other phases, the conversations in this phase are divided into two different audiences—those who bought your offer and those who did not.

Your conversations with each person will depend on whether they've moved forward with your offer or if they've elected to wait until later. While you want to keep those who have signed up happy and excited for what's next, you should also continue nurturing the relationship with the people who haven't signed up.

A big mistake people often make is focusing only on the buyers, and then they fall silent with everybody else. We don't want to do that. It's really important to focus on both types of individuals.

Ongoing Conversations

Finally, we circle back to ongoing conversations. These are the conversations that are happening all throughout the year, outside of your launch. This phase is where everything will come naturally to you because you've been working so hard on your 104 Formula™. The ongoing conversations phase is simply your 104 Formula™ in its purest state.

Keep these conversations related to the topics your audience is interested in. Use the 104 Formula™ to continue nurturing relationships with your people until it's time, once again, to start up your next set of pre-pre-launch conversations.

I go much deeper into all of these conversations and how to make it all happen in my course, Influenced. But for now, I wanted to at least provide you with this overview so you understand what to do and why we do it.

So far, we've kept everything smoothly flowing together. From our social media posts to our list builders, and now we're lining those up with our paid offers using these different types of conversations to pull people deeper into our world so we can convince them that we're the perfect person to solve their problems. But there's one more conversation that we have to delve into, and it is definitely the most complex. We'll discuss that in the next chapter.

Chapter 29

The Sales Page Conversation

In terms of launch conversations, I'm going to take a side step for a moment. One of the most important pieces of your launch is having a sales page that easily speaks to your audience and shares the transformation that your offer is providing so well that they are willing to pay for it. While it isn't a conversation in the sense of having words going back and forth, it is a one-way conversation between you and the voice in their head. Your goal is to be the prevailing voice.

There's a template that I follow whenever I'm creating one of my sales pages. I've used these blueprints for all kinds of digital offers, including paid memberships and courses. What's great about it is that it can be used for all kinds of offers, from physical products, opt-ins, lead magnets, and everything in between.

Unfortunately, a book doesn't give me adequate space to go into all the complexities of building a sales page. I do go into that inside my Influenced course, however. But before you get started building your sales page, I want to help you at least understand some of the fundamentals behind creating a sales page that converts.

Remember, all of the elements on your sales page need to convey the transformation that you're promising. That means all of the copy on this page needs to reflect that. You want to speak to your audience on both an emotional and logical level. Every person who approaches your sales page will be looking at it through a slightly different lens each time, making their buying decisions based on their individual criteria and what is important to each of them. We want to convince as many people as possible that working with us is truly a good step to take, so we need our arguments to spread out into multiple different facets.

As you begin to build your sales page, you may find that you don't yet have all of the assets required. You may be missing certain testimonials or don't yet have all of the pictures you want to include. That's perfectly fine. You can use what you have now and add them to your sales page later. Your sales page is something that will continue to evolve and shift over time, so you can continue to fine-tune it well into the future. The important thing is to start now and improve it later.

3 Steps to Creating a High-Converting Sales Page

1. Gather Your Resources

The first of these is to gather all of your resources into one easily accessible place. You want to get all of your photos, testimonials, case studies, etc., and put them all together. This will save you a lot of time and energy when you actually begin designing your sales page. As part of this step, you want to be super crystal clear on the transformation that you're promising, as it will make writing your copy out much easier and will help to keep everything consistent across the page.

2. Write Your Copy

The second step is to begin writing out your copy. Although this may feel like it should be a part of step one, I separate them in order to help keep my mind focused on one task at a time. This keeps things from being too overwhelming and confusing. Great copy is best written when you avoid feeling like your brain is split into too many areas at once. When we work on our copy, we want it to be as clear and concise as possible, so it needs to be the only task on our minds. Just like I said earlier about building web pages, writing copy is a skill that takes time to develop. If this is not yet in your wheelhouse, this page is the most important one of them all, and it's worth considering hiring a professional copywriter.

3. Assemble Sales Page Online

With the writing done, the final thing is to assemble our sales page. This is where we take all of the assets that we've gathered, including our freshly written copy, and place everything exactly where we want it. A great benefit of working this way is that we're able to see any gaps in our page quickly. You may find a spot that's missing a picture or somewhere another case study would fit perfectly.

This formula for creating your sales page makes the design process so much easier in the long run. It helps you to save a lot of time by keeping your mind focused on one task at a time, as opposed to tackling such a huge project all at once. The biggest piece to remember is that you need to adequately convey your message to your audience, clearly showing them your promised transformation.

Writing a winning sales page is complex. It always takes longer than we think it's going to take. And most of us are so close to our offer that we sometimes go into writing a sales page with assumptions that our audience sees the benefits we're providing and will automatically buy. Or we focus so much on all the features of our offer that we fail to convey the true transformation that we're promising. At the end of the day, people don't want the checklist, template, course, membership, or whatever our thing is. That's just the vehicle. They really want the transformation. They want their lives to be better. They desire more fulfillment, more happiness, and an easier way. So it's imperative that we convey this on our sales page.

Chapter 30

New Beginnings

You are one of the few who made it to the last pages of this book. Congratulations!

Here you are at the finish line as the tortoise, not the hare. As you continue on, don't get overwhelmed. Don't think of all the things you need to do. As the old saying goes, the way to eat an elephant is one bite at a time (I'm not encouraging you to eat an elephant, but this phrase is very powerful!).

You've read about all the successes that I've enjoyed with Paul. Keep in mind they didn't happen all at once. They were realized slowly, over time, as we went at our own pace. Sometimes we started over. Sometimes we had to pivot. Other times, we had to make new decisions and go in different directions while some things were outside of our control.

Remember, what we can control is how we think, the things we say and feel, and the way we do things. We need to take that power and make new decisions every single day because whatever has happened in the past doesn't matter.

It's a new day. We are making new decisions and taking a new step forward in the direction we want to go. As I'm sitting here now writing out the words on this page, I reflect back to where we started our journey together. I recall sitting in front of the computer, looking at Paul's business happening, and just thinking of all the decisions, all the steps that we took, the highs, the lows, the laughter, the tears, the issues, the challenges, the problems that happened, all the high five moments and celebrations along the way, coming full circle to being here right now, able to share this knowledge and expertise with you.

I am so happy to give you an advantage that we didn't have. You see, I had to spend all those years going through all these trials and tribulations so we could figure out the formulas and the steps and the processes that I'm sharing with you through this book.

Now, you have the power to make similar choices without having to go through everything that Paul and I went through.

So I challenge you. Don't just put this book down and go about life as usual. Instead, step forward. Take action, and make this happen for yourself. Then, even on those tough days when you think things aren't going to go the way you want, you'll push through and make a new decision and take another action, again and again, and again.

In the next iteration of this book, I want to share your success. I want you to be my next case study. So take that first step and lean into making new decisions one step at a time. No racing anyone else. You're going at your own pace.

Now here's the thing, this format has its limits, and I can only cover so many things within this book, but I want to bless you even more. Because while you've come a great distance from where you began, there is so much more to learn, be, do, and have.

So, I encourage you to take the next step and join me inside my course, Influenced, where we take everything you've learned inside this book and help you fully implement it. Completing will separate you from 99% of your competitors. I cannot express how much I want you to experience this gift to yourself.

Because conversations, proper planning, and great copy that converts doesn't happen by accident. It takes time and continuous effort to develop these habits, and you don't have to do it alone. This is an opportunity to get guidance as you research your audience, refine your message and your offer, and guide your people to make an ethical buying decision with you.

What you've learned here in this book is foundational. Now, I invite you to expand upon what you've learned to not only build your email list and social media following with potential buyers but to become a better communicator with your audience to show them the possibility for positive change in their lives so they can experience real transformation.

Let's keep the journey going. I can't wait to see you on the inside.

Influenced

From Social, to List, to Launch

The Influenced Course is a premium list building program to help you attract more of the right clients into your business. From your social media to your list builders to your launch!

I've seen how devastating it is for my clients to put the time, energy, and effort into a launch and not get the results they deserve.

Maybe you've bought other content creation courses that helped you create content for your social media but didn't lead your audience to buy your offers. **Or** you purchased a list building course that got you started with your first lead magnet, but you haven't had luck converting those opt-ins into sales.

Perhaps you're having trouble connecting your lead magnets with your launches, making your content feel all over the place.

With this course, I've created something dramatically different from anything else out there. I've bundled the best of my knowledge and experience, using the same advanced list building techniques that have led to the successes we've had in our multi-six-figure business.

I'm confident you won't find any other list building program like this one.

You'll learn real strategies to influence the right people to buy your offers, allowing you to build your business and positively impact their lives.

I must warn you though, this isn't a beginner-level course.

If you're ready to roll up your sleeves and get to work influencing your audience from social to list to launch... then enroll in the Influenced course!

HERE'S WHAT YOU GET IN INFLUENCED:

Module 1: List Building Foundations

Your Takeaways:

» Discover why you don't need a big list to be successful.
» How to find out what list-building methods work for you.
» The 4 key lists that you should have.
» The 3 factors that allow you to connect better with your people & increase conversions.
» How to find out where your ideal client is hanging out in the online space.
» How to get a first-hand perspective of what your clients are going through.

Module 2: The 104 Formula

Your Takeaways:

- How to create content that resonates with your audience and is linked to your offers.
- Understanding the internal and external language of our clients.
- Empower your audience to shift their feeling of overwhelm to excitement.
- Speak into the things that your audience desires with inspirational and motivational content.
- Map out the key points in your transformation track to really connect with your people no matter where they're at on their journey of transformation.
- Create list-building content that speaks to what your audience is thinking, saying, feeling and doing.

Module 3: Content Framework

Your Takeaways:

- Create content that's consistent, engaging, and aligned.
- Reach different audiences through different mediums.
- Spend less time on content creation and be more intentional.
- Shift your mindset from being a consumer into being a producer.
- Create content that grabs your audience's attention and gets them curious.
- Help your audience have buy-in and feel compelled and empowered that they can actually do whatever you're leading them to do.

Module 4: Perfectly Aligned List Builder

Your Takeaways:

- How to create a quick win that doesn't give away too much with your list builder.
- Align your list builder and offer with your audience's problems to attract the right audience.
- How to position yourself as an expert and level up your authority without bragging
- Ensure a high-quality standard and congruent branding with your list builder.
- Make your audience understand how your list builder helps them through a simplified copy and a precise layout.
- Build Like, Know and Trust to warm up your audience for your additional paid offers.

Module 5: Perfectly Aligned Launch

Your Takeaways:

- Use your audience's hot topics that are related to your launch topics as pre-launch conversations.
- Have different types of conversations to connect with your audience during different points of your launch.
- Don't just focus on the deliverables of your offer but also portray the benefits of the transformation your audience will achieve by going through your offer.
- Start a seamless conversation that carries through into your open cart and avoid suddenly switching into "selling mode."
- Handle objections and limiting beliefs throughout your launch conversation, so your audience will have that buy-in and be more open to the possibilities.
- Create an amazing onboarding experience for buyers and continue to build like, know & trust with your non-buyers.

InfluencedWorkshop.com

About the Author

Melissa Pruitt is an online marketing coach and educator who works together with her husband and business partner, Paul, helping entrepreneurs market and sell their courses, memberships, and coaching programs. Their mission is to help ambitious entrepreneurs build a business they love.

She is a TEDx speaker, three-time published author, and featured guest on multiple publications and platforms, including the Huffington Post, various podcasts, summits, and events, whose passion is sharing her knowledge and expertise to help entrepreneurs connect with their audience, fine-tune their message, and get their offers in front of the right people.

Her degree in Psychology and NLP certifications give her a unique perspective in the marketing world as she bridges human behavior with marketing strategy, showing her clients how to create deeper connections with their audiences.

When she's not coaching entrepreneurs, Melissa enjoys travel adventures with Paul, spending time with family and their dog Bentley, intent on being fully present with each other as they treasure every single moment of a happy life together.

Be sure to connect with Melissa on Facebook and Instagram:
@RealMelissaPruitt

HOW TO TELL IF YOUR K-9 IS A DEMON

TRISTA RICKETTS

For more information, email: trista@tristaricketts.com

Contributions:

Editor: Vallie O'Hara

Cover Art: White Rose Publishing Service IG: @siennas.coverart

Also By

Other titles available

MODERN LEGENDS OF DRAGONS AND SHADOWS SERIES

Lahaina Noon (Book 1)

Circles in the Sand (Book 2)

The Waters Edge (Book 3)

Silver Belles (Book 4)

Ashes of Eternity (Book 5)

Coming 2026

COMPULSIONS OF THE DAMNED SERIES

Arcane Fate (Book 1)

Arcane Conflict (Book 2)

Arcane Resolution (Book 3)

Dedication

In 2025, I was lurking in a social media forum for lovers of Fantasy and Romance books. Someone posted a picture of a female police officer kneeling next to her K-9, a solid black dog who was "smiling" for his photo. The caption read, "Imagine you're running from the police, and you hear 'Fetch me his soul', then you turn and see this." The person who posted it commented they would love to read that book. A lot of other people chimed in saying the same. I commented and said, "I'll write it!" Now I wish I had saved that post so I could thank that person for the prompt because otherwise, Malachi might have been adopted by someone else.

And it goes without saying, thank you Joel for putting up with my crazy ass and making me forty-six paw print devil hearts. You're a good boy!

Content Warning

Content Warning:

As with any book, there may be topics that some readers may find offensive or triggering. This one is full of offensive things. It also broaches on some subjects others may struggle with. I'll list them here, so you have an idea of what you're getting into:

Murder (mostly off page, there is the one minor character)

Kidnapping

Foul language (I mean, he's a demon)

Open door spicy time

Accidental demon adoption

Discussion of bondage

Questionable fashion choices

Singing of Nickelback at karaoke

Don't worry, no animals die

Contents

1

Black Souls and Bacon

Being forced into the body of an animal that licked its own genitals wasn't the most dignifying of ways to reclaim my position in Hell, but it wasn't that bad as punishments went.

Lifting his hind leg and scratching behind his large, pointy ear, the demon Malachi rolled his eyes as the crowd of little girls outside of his cage oohed and aahed. He was too damn cute for his own good. Baring his teeth, he snarled, not wanting to be adopted by the fucking Cleaver family. The mother eyed him warily and pulled her children away to another cage where a wrinkly ball of fur that could barely walk without rolling was doing its best to get their attention. It looked like a fluffy potato.

Grunting, he flopped down and heaved out a gusty sigh; he hoped it sounded like the icy winds of the frozen sections of Hell whipping across the barren land. In reality, it sounded like the sweetest huffed-out doggie breath ever. A dog. A flipping fuzzy-assed canine. Cute. Fluffy. Adorable. At least he was solid black. Hoping his eyes were glowing crimson-red like a Hellhound, he turned and stared into the metal water dish to check. He groaned; they were the most pleasant shade of melt-your-heart chocolatey

brown that ever existed. This sucked worse than the time cave lice ran rampant through his legions and their nether regions.

"Hey, Chuck, look at this one. It's black, like your soul," came a male voice just out of sight of the cage where Malachi was being held at the animal rescue center. He remembered the last scream of rage from his demon Ward Commander before he was whisked away to suffer his punishment. Welcoming the blackness as it closed in on him, because black was, of course, his favorite color, he was confused when he opened his eyes and gazed around. Low to the ground, in a cage with a concrete floor, metal bars between him and the outside world. The noise and stench overwhelmed him at first, and sensory overload swirled around until a whimper slipped from his throat. The sound shocked him so much that he paused and began taking stock of his body. Where his nose would normally be, he found a long snout instead. His fingers and toes were now furry paws, and a tail waved from his behind like a hairy flag. He finally figured out where and what he was, to his everlasting dismay.

But now he was intrigued. *A black soul? That sounds like my ticket out of here.* The owner of the voice came into view, and Malachi studied the man who had spoken. He looked like a strong, capable dude that would have fun getting into trouble with a demon, maybe even do a little soul corrupting along the way. That would for sure get Malachi pardoned. Then he took in the man's clothing, noting it was a police uniform. *Ooh, corrupting an officer? Even better!* He glanced at the person the man had spoken to—the supposed black-souled Chuck—expecting another man to run around creating chaos with.

His gaze settled on a slender woman, and he dropped flat, backing up in terror at the burning, glowing visage of the angel standing there, glaring at the man who now smirked mockingly at her. The black police uniform,

tightly encasing her body, did nothing to subdue the soft, bright light emanating from her skin.

Black soul, my unholy ass! Malachi thought frantically. Trying to summon his shadow power, he nearly howled as it wouldn't respond. His demonic magic was locked down. He scrunched himself into a small ball of shadow and tried to disappear into the corner, hoping she wouldn't notice him. Black dogs and cats were the least likely to be adopted. If he was still enough, he might get out of this one. He glared at the man who had suggested him, now thinking the ruggedly handsome man was a douchebag of epic proportions.

The woman turned her warm gaze to Malachi and frowned, a cute pout of her lips as her brows drew together. "I don't know, Jaxon; he seems kind of timid. How do you think he would handle it if someone threatened him or pointed a gun at him? Poor fluffer would probably piss himself then hide under the bed."

I would not! Take that back, you lying bitch! Malachi snarled the words at her, but of course, all they heard was aggressive barking. *Ugh, even my bark is cute.* He debated vomiting on her shoes in protest, but decided to piss on Officer Jaxon, the douchebag, instead. Lifting his hind leg, he aimed at the man's shiny boots.

Jaxon jumped back, startled. "Oh, what the hell?" He groaned and shook the liquid off his pant leg before he stomped away to get some paper towels.

The woman squatted down and stared at him. "Why did you do that... um,"—she paused and read the paper in his cage—"Noble. Huh. You were found behind a Barnes & Noble bookstore, untagged and unchipped. Poor baby. So why did you pee on him? I'm the one who called you puny, but you're a feisty fellow, aren't you?" She waved a clerk over. "Hey, can I take Noble to the play yard? I'd like to interact with him to see if he'd fit the need."

Need? What need? He wondered as he studied the woman, interest piqued. She didn't seem to recognize that he was a demon. He was confused; most angels would smite him on sight, but she didn't. Which was good, because smiting hurt like a son-of-a-bitch. She seemed intrigued by him, and he realized he had a burning curiosity about her as well. She had rich mahogany hair, cut short in a pixie style, tapering at her neck. Her eyes were a deep brown, much like his own. She was like no angel he'd ever seen. Where was the shining blonde hair? The blazing eyes of blue? The wings? He tilted his head and stared. She was pretty, being of average height and shape, nothing overly noticeable. Just a pretty girl next door who happened to be carrying a gun and handcuffs. His tongue lolled out then. Handcuffs were always fun, even if they couldn't hold him long.

"Sure. Noble is super smart and playful. A real sweet boy," gushed the perky volunteer who bounced cheerfully over to open the cage.

He smirked; she was thinking of the dog they'd taken in before it was replaced by a demon. Idly, he wondered what happened to the actual dog, then decided he didn't care. He was a demon; he wasn't supposed to care. Eagerly, he stepped forward towards the opening, getting ready to make a run for it when the officer asked the volunteer an interesting question.

"Does he bite? I mean, I want him to bite, but only on command."

Pausing, Malachi sat back and tilted his head, studying her again. Biting on command had potential. Just like the handcuffs. *Color my black heart intrigued. What are we doing here, Officer Angel?*

The volunteer glanced at her with concern for the strange question, then took in the uniform. "Oh, are you wanting a trainee for a K-9 unit?" Her expression turned bright and cheerful again, and Malachi felt slightly nauseated.

Officer Angel nodded slowly. "I'm looking for a K-9 partner. One we can train to fetch criminals on the run. Normally, we get our service dogs

from a specialized breeder overseas, but I got permission to use a shelter dog for active retrieval. We're looking to spotlight our partnerships with community organizations to show that even shelter mutts can be loyal and helpful."

Who you calling a mutt? He growled, wishing he could access his dark powers so he could smudge that soft glow surrounding her frame.

The female officer glanced back at him and smiled in amusement. "Sorry, buddy, I guess you didn't like being called a mutt? Apologies, Noble. Wanna go play?" Reaching through the crack in the door, she ruffled the fur between his ears and grinned. "Wow! He's way softer than I thought he would be. What breed is he? He kind of looks like a Belgian Malinois, but his fur is like silk."

The volunteer bobbed her head. "We suspect he is, but of course, being from the street, we can't confirm. I hear Malinois make good police dogs, and solid black ones are rare."

Nodding absently, the officer knelt down and clipped a leash on the collar around his neck as she stared intently at him. "Well, come on, Noble. Let's see what you've got."

She gave a small tug on the leash, but he just sat there, staring at her in disdain. He was not some poodle bitch to do her bidding just because she had a piece of rope. He was a demon. Lieutenant of the Sixth Ward. He had a legion under his command. *Had* being the operative word. Dropping his head in shame, a low whine escaped his throat. He was currently commanding no one.

Officer Angel held out a piece of what smelled like bacon. "Come on, Noble, want a snack?"

You bet your wingless ass I do! He licked his chops. He might not walk on a leash, but he would do some pretty shady stuff for bacon. Inching forward, his nose quivered at the delicacy in her slender fingers. His first

instinct was to chomp her hand just to see the blood fly. Hello, demon. But he gently took the treat, and his eyes rolled back. This was too good to be true. *Is this what H-Heaven's like?* It might not be, but it was as close as he would ever get. He licked his lips again and stared up at her, releasing a small whimper designed to play on her sympathies.

"Alright! Typical man, the way to your heart is through your stomach. Come play with me a little, and there's more snacks where that came from. Okay, buddy?" She tilted her head and smiled at him.

He nodded his head before remembering dogs didn't do that and flopped out his tongue instead, putting a stupid expression on his face as she frowned, looking closer.

"I swear he just..." She shook her head slowly, eyebrows raised. "Never mind. Come on, Noble, let's go find Jax and see what you can do."

Malachi grinned; he couldn't wait to pee on Jaxon again.

2

Of Chuglets and Deals

In the play yard, Malachi glanced around with a dubious eye at the other dogs running through the area, trying to convince the humans that they were a perfect fit for their families. He huffed out a disgusted breath, determined that he was not doing any of that. It was downright degrading. He stood there studying the exits, about to make a break for freedom, bacon or not, when something cold and wet was forcefully shoved against his ass.

What the fuck! He shouted with indignation in a loud bark. It would have been righteous indignation, but demons can never be righteous, so he had to settle for being suitably pissed. He whirled and found a small brown hot-mess-express of a dog sticking its nose in his behind. *Yo, not that I don't enjoy a little foreplay, but do you mind?*

The other dog stared vapidly at him, tongue out, panting and grinning. It was a short, stubby, brindle-colored breed that seemed to be a strange cross between a chihuahua and a pug. He studied it intently, realizing then that the dog couldn't speak to him because it was just an animal. Sighing, he laughed at the floppy ears and underbite, telling it, *You look like a right*

little psycho. He smirked at the other dog, actually liking the idea of an insane companion to run amok with. His mind drifted to a scene in a movie he'd seen once about witches. A blonde witch with the smokin' rack was jumping around singing, 'Amok, amok, amok'. He loved that visual and was daydreaming of it when he heard Jaxon's voice.

"Decided to check out the demon, huh?" The man grinned wryly at Malachi as he moved next to Officer Angel of the Not-So-Black-Soul.

Malachi was so startled, he plopped down on his butt as his hind legs involuntarily gave out. The human knew he was a demon? Whoops, this might not go over well with the angel cop. He glanced back at her, and she frowned at Jaxon. Here it came, let the mighty smiting begin. He hung his head as he braced for impact, a whine escaping his throat.

"Jaxon, you hurt his feelings!" she scolded her friend, flicking him between his now-wide eyes. "He's not a demon; he's a sweet boy who just needs the proper handling!" She glared at the man as he cursed under his breath, rubbing his forehead. She squatted down next to Malachi. "Don't you listen to him. He's just mad because you peed on him. You're a good boy, aren't you?" She reached out and placed her hand on his head, scratching it, rubbing between his ears.

Malachi realized with relief that the man was just calling him names; they didn't know that he was, in fact, an actual demon. The angel cop was petting him now, and it felt glorious. He closed his eyes and whimpered in ecstasy before looking around to see if anyone noticed. The goofy brown dog that had invaded his personal space still stood next to him, panting and staring into the distance, eyes empty and unfocused as if listening to voices on the wind. He eyed the strange specimen briefly before turning back to the woman as she began speaking again.

"Hey, Noble, my name is Kelly. Kelly Charles, but everyone calls me Chuck. I need a partner; someone I can count on to have my back and help

me do my job. What do you think, buddy, wanna help me catch some bad guys?"

Her warm, kind eyes moved something inside of him, and he wanted nothing more than to keep staring into them. He nodded quickly. *Sure!* What she heard, of course, was a short bark, but she'd seen him nod again, and the smooth space between her eyebrows pinched slightly. *Shit, I need to remember to act more like a dog.* He jumped forward, putting his paws on her shoulders, and licked her cheek.

Laughing, Chuck pushed him down. "Okay, Noble, can you fetch?" she inquired as she pulled a tennis ball from a nearby basket and held it out to him as if that would entice him. She tossed it and watched to see what he would do.

He flopped down and stared at her like she was stupid, shaking his head in disbelief. She really expected him to get excited about a piece of rubber covered in felt that some other dog had probably drooled on? That bitch was crazy—disappointing, really. He sighed and yawned, bored now. Glancing back at her, he realized he'd been acting distinctly non-doggie again.

"Would you do it for another snack?" she asked lightly, trying not to laugh as she held up one of the delicious bacon things she'd offered earlier.

His ears perked up all on their own. Thinking about it, he shrugged then woofed low. He'd always loved the gluttony level of Hell, where it was all-you-could-eat, but you were never full, so you ate until you burst. He didn't get full anyway, and bacon had always been a favorite.

Chuck's eyes narrowed, and she slipped him the snack. "Okay, Noble, you got it, now bring me the ball?" she requested quietly.

Malachi sighed heavily as he stood and trotted over to where the ball lay in the corner of the yard. He groaned at the thought of putting it in his mouth, but leaned down because he'd agreed and Chuck had come

through with the bacon. A deal was a deal. The little brown dog that had been standing near him, staring into space earlier, had followed him and now barked at the ball like it was a ferocious beast from the lower levels of Satan's realm. He stared at the dog, thinking it might just be an idiot after all. Shaking his head again, he picked up the ball gingerly between his teeth, trying to keep his tongue free of the dirty material. *Gross, I hope no one sees how far I've fallen. Ugh.*

He hurried back to Chuck and dropped it into her hand. He tried to spit out the taste but couldn't figure out how to make his muzzle work like that. Pawing at her knee, he woofed, demanding another snack for having performed well.

"Oh, you want another snack, do you? Think you've earned it?" She chuckled and watched him closely. The glow of angelic grace around her brightened slightly with her quiet laughter.

He nodded vigorously, the smell of the bacon seasoning making his lips quiver and a small string of drool drip from his jaws, angel glow be damned. His tongue flopped out, and he panted heavily.

She leaned in. "Okay, Noble," she said as she squinted consideringly. "You did earn this. But I'm going to make you another deal. I'll adopt you and take you in as my partner. You can have all the bacon snacks you want. But you're going to have to work hard and tell me how you can understand me so clearly. Because I don't know what you are, but you are certainly more than just a dog someone found behind a bookstore." She smirked at him. "Deal?"

He squinted back, realizing she'd caught on to him not being a full dog, but still didn't know he was a demon. This might be beneficial to him because he was beginning to suspect she didn't know she was part angel. He slowly put his paw in her offered hand.

"Are you talking to the dog now, Chuck?" Jaxon asked incredulously. He shook his head. "The guys are gonna love this. Chuck, the K-9 whisperer." He laughed, pulling out his phone to take a picture. He crouched in front of Malachi. "Say cheese, you dumb dog." He chuckled.

Malachi bared his teeth and growled. He would show that puny human who was dumb. He took a menacing step towards Jaxon, who backed up nervously, then shrieked, high-pitched and unmanly as something brushed his legs. It was the pug-chihuahua mix that had been hanging around. Malachi chuckled. The other dog—he really needed a name for it—was coming in handy after all. He studied it closely. *Pug-huahua? Chihug? Chug?* He snorted, *Chuglet*. It was now the Chuglet. He turned back to Chuck and gently took her hand in his mouth. She'd been watching the exchange with him and Jaxon, wry amusement in her expression. He carefully pulled her to the Chuglet, put a paw on its back, and barked.

"Is that a warning that you're a package deal with her?" she asked him quietly.

Her? Okay, so apparently the Chuglet was a girl. He responded with a soft woof. Putting his paw on her back again, then putting it on Chuck. He would go with her and work for her, unlimited bacon a requirement of course, but the Chuglet had to go too.

Smirking, she nodded back. "Okay, Noble. You, me, and"—she checked the tag on the collar—"Reena makes three. Hang out here like a good... boy, I guess? I'll go do the paperwork." She made her way to the volunteer to let her know she wanted to adopt them.

Boy? He growled furiously. *I'll have you know I'm not a boy. I'm a full-grown man—a whole damned demon. Ugh, you'll see, I'll figure out how to get my body back, and you won't be calling me 'boy' anymore.* He grunted and absently scratched his ear before turning towards a panting sound. The vapid expression of the Chuglet was fixed on him, and she seemed to be

smiling. *So... Reena? Well, you're going to have to help me spread chaos and fuckery. Are you down for that?*

Reena the Chuglet barked happily in response, which caught him off guard. It seemed she was able to understand him after all. She lifted a paw and touched his leg, panting in sheer joy. Her little curly tail wiggled so hard her whole ass shook like the belly dancer he'd seduced about a century ago. He liked this spunky little psycho. Grinning, he turned to see Jaxon studying him curiously.

"So, Noble, umm, good doggie?" Officer Dumbass offered cautiously, giving a half-hearted wave.

Malachi rolled his eyes. *Dude, don't be a little bitch, or I'll piss on you again.*

Reena let out a wheezing sound that seemed suspiciously like a laugh.

Oh yeah, Reena was going to be a lot of fun. He laughed too as she leaned on him and snorted her happiness. He could see Chuck across the yard, nodding and pointing at them both, to the volunteer's obvious surprise. Eventually, the woman shrugged, gave Chuck the forms, which she quickly filled out, then approached with the leashes in hand.

"Reena, Noble, welcome to the Charles family. Let's go home!"

3

That's Not my Name

Malachi sat in the passenger seat of Chuck's car, happily blinking his eyes and hanging his head out the window. *Man, now I get why dogs do this. It's freaking awesome.* Groaning in pleasure, he sighed and glanced down at Reena, wrapped around his hind legs. She was too short to enjoy this; the window only rolled down a small amount. He guessed Chuck was nervous about the dingy dog falling out. Watching her chase her curly little tail earlier, he figured the officer wasn't entirely wrong. He turned to study Chuck, thinking it was an odd name for a woman. He figured it must be a nickname, a play on her last name, Charles. As if feeling the weight of his gaze, she glanced over.

"Hey, Noble, you doing okay? Need something?"

Sighing with irritation, he rolled his eyes and turned his back to her. He was going to have to figure out a way to tell her his name wasn't Noble. There was no way he would answer to that name. Bookstores were cool, and he was a voracious reader. He especially liked dark romances and epic fantasy when no one was looking. But his name was Malachi, and it represented his family heritage.

"What's the matter, Noble?"

He growled, low and menacing in his chest.

"Noble? Is that it? Noble isn't your name?"

He turned towards her with alacrity, perking up his ears with an excited woof. *Yes! C'mon Chuck. You're smart, you can figure this out.* He placed a paw on her arm to let her know she was on the right track.

"Okay, okay, so it's not Noble. Got it. But what on earth could it be? It could take years to guess. Umm... let me think about it, okay?" She hummed to herself for a bit.

He huffed, impatient, wanting to communicate now.

"I'm working on it, keep your pants on." She snorted, then chuckled. "Pants, you don't wear pants." She laughed harder now, her glow bouncing with her shoulders.

Ha ha, Chuck, laugh it up. If I were in my man form and not wearing pants, you'd be on your knees begging me... He paused as he pictured that. His tongue lolled out at the thought of an angel on her knees in front of him.

"Hey!" Fingers snapped in front of him. "Earth to doggo!" She laughed again. "Where'd you go just then?" She shook her head. "Where'd he go? I'm talking to a frickin' dog," she murmured to herself.

WOOF! The stern bark echoed in the car before he growled, then shook his head.

She smiled softly. "Okay, sorry, um, do you know the alphabet?"

He barked once, softer this time, excited about this approach.

"Wait, is that a yes or a no? Okay, one bark for yes, two barks for no. Let's test. Are you Reena?"

He barked twice and followed it with a wheezing laugh.

"Okay, and are you a handsome boy? A big, silky, black, handsome boy who loves bacon?"

He gave one loud, excited bark at the mention of bacon.

She laughed and tossed him a treat, slipping one to Reena as well. "Okay, good, back to the alphabet; do you know your ABCs?" She glanced at him as they came to a stop at a red light.

Barking once, he stared at her harder, hoping that if he concentrated enough, she would hear his thoughts. *C'mon, Chuck, let's do this. I do not want to be called Noble or good doggie. I'm Malachi, Lieutenant of Darkness and Legions of the Sixth Ward. Demon extraordinaire and seducer of women. I am death and destruction, smoke and shadows, chaos and insanity.*

Reena snorted in amusement at his words, her strange wheezing laugh indicating he was overdoing it a bit.

Rolling his eyes, he turned back to Chuck. *Okay, well, Malachi is good to start with.* He paused, glancing at his canine companion again. *Hey, Reena, is that your real name? Or do you have another name too?*

She grunted and ducked her head.

Okay, Reena, got it. It's a good name, ya little psycho. Ready to spread that chaos and fuckery as we discussed?

Her tail thumped on the seat, and her eyes rolled around, accompanied by small pig-like snorting noises.

He chuckled and faced Chuck, who was watching them in amusement.

She began to rapid-fire questions at him, laughing incredulously as his barks confirmed and denied various things. "Okay, okay, slow down, you. Let me get this straight. She's Reena, she's okay with that name. She can understand you, but she can't speak the way you can. She's just a regular dog. We think. And then there's you. Your name is Malachi? Am I right so far?" At his confirmatory bark, she smiled. "Okay, so, Malachi. Odd name for a dog," she mused, then grinned at his growl. "Right, still your name. Gonna have to figure out what's going on here, but for now, here we are,

home sweet home." She parked the car and came around to open the door, so Malachi and Reena could jump out and see their new living quarters.

The small brick home was quaint but well-kept. The yard was tidy; the shutters were painted and in good shape. The bushes were trimmed in a way that made him suspect Chuck had hired a landscaper to maintain them.

Malachi began sniffing the air as Reena ran in wild circles chasing her own tail in her excitement. He chuckled; he could certainly use her in his legion. She had just enough craziness and detachment from the real world to make a fantastic demon.

"Halloo, Officer Charles!" came a sharp hail as an older woman scurried across the sidewalk to speak to Chuck. Her neon yellow muumuu, absolutely slathered with pink hibiscus flowers larger than dinner plates, flapped in the slight breeze.

Sensing his partner's displeasure at the intrusion on her property, especially noting how her glow dimmed, Malachi promptly aligned himself next to Chuck. He gave the visitor a stern, pointed glare, making clear his disgust with her choice of leisure wear. She slowed immediately, much further back than she had obviously intended. Eying him warily, she started forward again, determination in her expression. He lifted his upper lip in distaste, a bit of fang showing. She came to a sudden halt, windmilling her arms with the effort.

"Hello, Muriel," Chuck called politely, nodding at her neighbor. Her lips twitched while she attempted to keep a straight face as the older woman was clearly maintaining her distance from Malachi. "I'd like you to meet my new housemate, Reena." She gestured to the spinning dervish of insanity. "And my new K-9 partner, Malachi." Here she laid her hand on his head, rubbing gently between his silky ears.

He nearly moaned with pleasure at the touch, wondering if all human hands were this soft or if it was because she was part angel. He'd decided on the drive here that she truly wasn't aware of her angel heritage and wasn't a full celestial being, thus the muted glow and lack of wings. He focused back in on Muriel, who was eyeing him now in contempt, a sneer distorting her chin, which was sorely in need of plucking.

"Malachi?" Muriel drawled his name out like a dirty word. "What kind of name is that for a dog? He better not bark all night or mess in my flowers," she grumped, as if being a dog was a derogatory thing, unworthy of her attention.

Growling, Malachi pressed himself closer to Chuck. He did not like Muriel and was going to make sure she knew it. Reena hurried to Chuck's other side, releasing a yipping snarl that was too cute to be threatening but still sounded unhinged. He was proud of her efforts.

Chuck laughed as Muriel took a quick step back. "Well, Malachi is a special breed, and he's very sensitive. He can sense fear and dishonesty. He's highly trained to detect liars, nuisance spreaders, and con artists. He'll alert, then growl."

Almost overcome with laughter in his head at Chuck's machinations, Malachi took her cue and stepped forward. He unleashed an unearthly, desolate howl, a call for a legion of the damned to step forth. Then he slowly lowered his head and glared at Muriel before letting another low warning growl enter his throat. He struggled to keep a straight face as Reena began to howl in solidarity. Her offering sounded more like the summoning of evil clowns from an asylum, but it still worked. He almost bit his tongue as Muriel grabbed at her throat and stumbled back. If she'd had pearls, they would have been firmly clutched.

"Didn't you need something, Muriel?" Chuck inquired innocently.

"No, no," the unpleasant woman answered quickly, almost stumbling over her own feet to get back to her yard. "Just wanting to say hello. Have to run. Oven's on. Tea's boiling. I'm sure my iron is still plugged in!" She called this frantically over her shoulder as she ran back inside her home like Satan himself was on her tail, still eyeing the black dog who hadn't stopped glaring at her.

A rub between his ears again as Chuck laughed quietly. "Good job, Malachi. I can tell we're going to be a great team. Now let's get inside and get you set up. You too, Reena, although that howl of yours needs some work."

Reena snorted, then sneezed so hard her curly tail straightened for a moment. She made a wheezing sound and smiled vapidly as she blinked at them both.

Malachi stared at the furry little psycho with pride. Chuck stared at her in considered apprehension.

Chuck led them inside and showed them where their food and water dishes would be, a doggie door so they could go out to 'potty', and finally where their dog bed was. "Sorry, Malachi, you'll have to share with Reena until I can get another one. I wasn't expecting to have two of you." She shook her head, laughing, the subtle glow flickering like dappled sunlight around her.

Malachi simply rolled his eyes, trotted to the bedroom, and jumped on her bed. There, he flopped down and stared at her bemused expression as she watched him with hands on her hips. *I'm not sleeping in a fucking dog bed, princess. I'm a Lieutenant of the Legion of Demons, Sixth Ward. I will sleep in the bed. You're lucky I'm in dog form, or we'd do more than sleep in here.* He eyed her up and down, appreciating her figure more than on his initial inspection. Officer Angel was actually pretty hot now that he wasn't worried about being smote.

She, in turn, was staring in exasperation, her eyes narrowed as she pointed at him. "Malachi, I don't know who you think you are, but you are *not* sleeping in my bed. Not happening, mister." Dark flickers of irritation burst across her glow.

He arched an eyebrow at her and laughed, then settled down onto the soft comforter, sighing happily at the feeling of the squishy fabric under his paws. He might be in dog form, but that didn't mean he had to give up his creature comforts. Maybe if he explained to her that he didn't need to eat, so she'd save on dog food? He *could* eat, he just didn't need to, and there was no way he was going to debase himself on that dry, noxious pellet crap that most people gave their dogs. Bacon, though, that was another story.

Sighing, Chuck shook her head. "Okay, we'll have this debate later. For now, though, I need to take you to the station to register you as my K-9. What do you say, buddy? Ready to meet the rest of the squad?" At his affirmative woof, she smiled and turned to the Chuglet. "Reena, sorry darling, you'll have to stay here. I can't have two partners, and I don't think you meet the requirements for K-9 duty anyway. Will you be okay alone for a while?"

The fun-sized monster spun in circles and yipped. She wagged her tail at Malachi until he heaved a sigh and followed her. Curious, Chuck followed them as well. In the living room, Reena yapped at the television until Malachi sniffed out the remote and brought it to Chuck.

"Are... are you saying Reena wants me to turn the TV on for her?" she asked incredulously.

Reena burst into a chorus of excited yips and yowls, spinning around again but this time in the opposite direction. Malachi glanced at Chuck, who huffed out a short laugh and flipped it on. She started to set the remote down, but Malachi grunted softly. He looked to Reena and sighed; he had a

feeling she was a reality TV slut. He nudged the remote and gazed at Chuck with his best rendition of puppy dog eyes.

She began flipping channels until she came to an episode of *Real Housewives,* and he woofed. He glanced at Reena, who was now entranced by the absolute brain-deadening trash on the screen in front of her. He snorted and nodded at Chuck. His suspicions were correct.

For her part, Chuck was staring in open-mouthed disbelief. "Okay," she murmured. "So, one of you is literate, and the other binge-watches daytime TV. I don't know what I've gotten myself into here, but I'm pretty sure I can't share this with anyone because they won't believe me for a second."

4

Retrieving a Douche

The police station was a hive of activity and noise as Malachi had expected. But the actual setting was boring compared to what the television shows he watched depicted. The walls were greige, and the floor was worn yellow linoleum. The lingering odor of old burnt coffee created a heavy miasma in the air, which at least lived up to expectations. He didn't hear a single typewriter, which wasn't too surprising, but he did hear a lot of computer keyboard clicking and complaints about the wi-fi signal. His attention was captured by a woman sitting on a bench, her thigh-high fishnets ripped, mascara flaking, and the hem of her short skirt showing exactly what she was advertising. Tongue lolling out, he eagerly made his way towards her.

"Malachi," Chuck warned quietly and tugged his leash, pulling him back to her side.

He grumbled in disgust at her for raining on his prostitute parade.

She squatted next to him and whispered, "Hey, look, I get it. You're not the average dog, but we made a deal, and while we're at work, you have to act like one. When it's just you and me, or we're at home or the park,

fine, act like yourself. But not here. Got it?" She gave him a stern, expectant glare.

He huffed then nodded once before catching himself, so he panted and let out a soft woof instead.

"Good boy." She smiled and scratched behind his ears.

He moaned in pleasure. Leaning into her, the moan became a louder rumble in his chest.

"Oh, you like that, do you?" she gushed and scratched harder, joy in her tone, until she was hailed from across the room.

"Chuck!" A large beefy man called, his booming voice echoing over the din. "Get your ass in here!" He pointed at his office, not looking terribly pleased.

Sighing, Chuck straightened and pulled on the leash. "C'mon, Mal, we gotta go meet the boss. Be on your best doggie behavior. We have to impress him, okay? No peeing on him, no humping anyone, and for the love, please, don't roll your eyes, you little smart ass. Deal?"

Trying not to laugh, he gave a wheeze of understanding and heeled by her side. He was determined to impress the boss so he could stay with his Chuck. She may have adopted him on paper, but she belonged to him now.

"So, Officer Charles, let's get this boy registered. Office Raifson tells me his name is Noble and that he's a bit defiant. For this to work, we need a trainable animal, an agreeable one. Now is not the time for a struggle." The head of the K-9 unit, Lieutenant Jeffers, stared at her with disapproval. Apparently, Jaxon had already notified him of her selection of a partner.

"Well, sir," she spoke loudly to cover up Malachi's low growl. "There was a misunderstanding at the shelter. His name is actually Malachi. He doesn't respond to Noble, but he's very responsive and well-behaved when using his actual name. I know he'll learn quickly. He's already shown an impressive response to commands and retrieval."

Lieutenant Jeffers tilted his head, and his expression relaxed into a smile. "Jaxon told me the only thing the dog has accomplished is pissing on him. For that alone, I'm inclined to like the fella. Well, let's take a look at him." He turned to the black dog watching him with silent consideration. "Hmm, he definitely has the right build and look. Kinda surprising to find a Malinois at a shelter." He finally grunted and patted his knee. "Come, Malachi."

Malachi glanced at Chuck to check if this was something he should do. She gave a slight nod, so he trotted warily to the large man on the other side of the desk and promptly sat, waiting for the next command.

"Hmph," Jeffers grunted, then tilted his head. "He looked to you first. That indicates there's already a strong bond, which is incredible given you just got him today." He leaned over, holding out a squeaky toy, and tossed it. "Malachi, retrieve."

Looking once again to Chuck, who repeated, "Retrieve." He hurried to get the toy, restraining his groan at the taste of slobber and plastic, before dropping it in her lap. "Thank you, Malachi, but please take this to Lieutenant Jeffers."

Once again suppressing his internal groan, he picked it up gingerly and took the toy to the waiting officer. Passing it to him gently, he sat waiting for his next order.

Lieutenant Jeffers' eyebrows rose so high that if he weren't bald, they would have touched his hairline. "Now that's impressive." He pursed his

lips in consideration, then his lips curled mischievously. "Malachi." He pointed at Jaxon, who had just walked by. "Retrieve."

This time, Malachi couldn't help the smile that crept over his canine features and took off like a shot after Jaxon. He grabbed the man's pant leg and growled, causing the officer to freeze and stare at him in alarm.

"Chuck!" Jaxon hollered in a slightly panicked tone. "Call your dog off!"

Others in the office gathered around to watch, amused at the stand-off between the ferocious-looking black dog and the cocky officer about to spill his coffee. Cheers erupted as the Malachi slowly began to pull an indignant Jaxon towards the lieutenant's office.

"Chuck! Chuck!" Jaxon yelled, his agitation causing his voice to crack.

Smothering a laugh, she leaned in the doorway. "Sorry, Jax, I can't call him off. Boss ordered him to retrieve you. He's just following orders like a good officer. Might as well go along with it before he tears your uniform."

Sighing in embarrassment, Jaxon gave in and allowed Malachi to drag him into the office.

That's right, you punk-ass bitch, get in here. I'm retrieving you, Malachi chuckled. He stopped in front of the lieutenant and eyed him in question without letting go of his prey's leg, waiting for his next order.

"Good boy, now release!" the laughing man told him, shaking his head. "Well, Officer Charles, I'd say you've got yourself a mighty fine partner there. I have a feeling he'll breeze through training. This will be great for our social media and community feel-good presence. You two are going to be the poster children of rising to meet a challenge." He glanced down at the dog, who was now surreptitiously peeing on Jaxon's leg. His chest bounced hard as he roared in laughter.

Malachi huffed out his own doggie laugh. He'd been able to piss on the man again without him noticing. He glanced at Chuck, who was also

trying to cover up a laugh. She winked at him, and he flushed all over, warm and excited by her approval.

Jaxon, however, was less than enthusiastic. "Jesus Christ, Chuck! Your dog is a lunatic!" he yelled as he jumped back from the puddle forming around him.

Invoking that name almost made Malachi vomit, then he decided, *why not,* and promptly barfed on Jaxon's shoe. He woofed with pride, noticing the splash had neatly fallen in the shape of the Sixth Ward of Demonic Legion's seal.

"Fuck! Chuck! Seriously?" Jaxon was shaking his shoe, nearly purple with rage now.

Chuck's laughter was drowned out by that of the other officers who'd gathered to watch the spectacle.

The lieutenant let out his own booming laugh. "Officer Raifson, it would appear you've offended Officer Malachi. I think you should consider apologizing." He shook his head in mirth.

"Apologize?" Jaxon sputtered incredulously, eyes wide. "To a dog?"

Malachi snarled ominously and lifted his lips, showing his impressive fangs.

Jaxon reeled back, almost stumbling over his feet. "Okay, I'm sorry. Let's start over, buddy. Huh? What do you say, Malachi, right? Can we be friends? I'm sorry I made fun of you."

That's right, you lame, whiny bitch. I own you, Malachi woofed and bared his teeth. Sitting, he lifted his paw.

The officer leaned down warily and took the offered paw, giving a gentle, tentative shake. He meekly replied, "Good boy."

Malachi leaned towards him. *When I figure out how to get back into my other forms, I'm going to eat your soul.*

Jaxon blinked, as if confused. Straightening, he stared at Malachi with a slow horror dawning across his face, contorting his expression into a comical battle between his true feelings and the need to keep up a brave appearance for his peers. He cleared his throat. "I've got some reports to finish, I'll uh..." he stared at the dog in front of him. "I'll catch you later, Chuck." He hurried out of the office, laughter trailing after his obvious retreat.

Chuck watched Malachi with quiet consideration while Jeffers finished up the forms. She stared at him, sizing him up, then a soft smile crept over her lips. "Good job, Mal," she whispered.

He winked at her and lay his head on her lap while the lieutenant gave instructions on the training program.

5

Who's a Good Boy?

It had been four months since Malachi came to live with Chuck and Reena, the psycho Chuglet. He spent a lot of his days with Chuck, training with her and two other traditional K-9s. In the evenings, he romped with Reena, regaling her with stories of the legions of Hell. In the car, Chuck would often sing along with the radio. She wasn't bad, but she wasn't very accomplished either. So Malachi started singing along with her, laughing when his howls made her wince. She finally gave up telling him to hush and just sang louder. Their days off were spent running through the park and watching scary movies curled up on the couch. Often, Chuck would talk to him about various scenarios or ask for his opinions, and they would laugh at her clumsy interpretations of his answers. Every day, the conversations went deeper, her understanding grew sharper, and he knew she was aware that he was not truly a dog, but she didn't mention it. Neither of them seemed ready to push the issue.

At first, Chuck had been a bit miffed at him because he managed to get the other K-9s to form a union of sorts, striking while demanding higher wages for bacon snacks. Although the dispute was resolved amicably and

bacon demands met, she'd scolded him furiously for his involvement. He'd rather enjoyed that part as well, but he didn't want to make her so mad she'd cancel their deal. Training had shown him he was going to get to hunt down criminals and fetch them. Possibly even bite them. He really liked those classes and was enthusiastic on days he got to attack the volunteer in the padded suit.

Reena loved hearing his stories about training and what mischief he got up to. She especially enjoyed his recounting of the great Bacon Rebellion. Truly, she was the perfect companion. She liked to listen, she didn't talk back, and she was always up to spread chaos. A particular favorite was chasing their neighbor Muriel's cat. It drove the woman crazy, but she didn't dare speak against Chuck. Malachi ensured that, snarling and howling like he was summoning an army of the undead anytime she came near. Reena's favorite toilet was Muriel's begonias.

The lieutenant seemed impressed with his progress and fast-tracked his graduation. Tomorrow was going to be a big day. Chuck and Malachi were going on the news for a local feel-good story, then on their first official patrol as partners. He was actively looking forward to it.

"Off the bed, Malachi," came Chuck's irritated voice.

He snorted and rolled over, showing his belly, which she rubbed like she always did. *Sucker,* he sang and heard Reena's wheezy laugh.

"Seriously, Mal, you know the rule. Only I get to sleep in the bed." Chuck rolled her eyes.

He rolled his eyes right back. They had this same argument every night. She didn't want him on the bed. He wasn't sleeping on the floor. She would fuss at him. He would whimper. She would smile and say...

"Fine... but this is the last time. Tomorrow you're in your dog bed. Got it?" Her lips curved gently; she knew the game too. Especially since she had never actually bought another dog bed, she laughed as he gave

a small happy rumble, then flipped the blanket back and yawned. She crawled into the bed while he made room for her. As she snuggled down under the comforter, she smirked when he flopped next to her. As they did every night, she talked about various things, telling him bits about her life, her friends growing up. He dutifully listened and would woof quietly at intervals to show he was paying attention. She would mumble to him until her eyes started drifting. Tonight was no different. "Goodnight, Mal," she called sleepily and rubbed the silky spot between his ears.

Goodnight, Chuck, he thought as he started to drift off, too. He heard the piggy snort, meaning the Chuglet wanted on the bed. Another thing that wasn't allowed but was often overlooked. He groaned as he had almost been asleep. Dragging himself to the edge of the bed, he gently picked Reena up in his mouth, hating the taste of fur, but not having opposable thumbs limited his options. Dropping her unceremoniously on the mattress, he curled back up with Chuck. He laughed when Reena snuggled against his butt and sighed with a happy wheeze. Her tail thumped a few times before her breathing indicated she was asleep. The little thing seemed attached to him, as if he were her savior. In a way, he was. No telling who she would have ended up with if they'd left her there at the rescue center.

The following morning, Malachi and Chuck were up extra early to report to the news station. Leaning down to straighten his spiffy new vest, she gave him some last-minute reminders. "This is it, Malachi, best behavior. No starting riots, no organizing revolts, and absolutely no peeing on anyone."

He grumbled under his breath and rolled his eyes before licking her hand in agreement. *Fine, but only because you asked so nicely.* He trotted alongside her; the leash held limply at her side because she didn't actually need it. It was just the requirement. He stared in interest at the scene around him, always on the lookout for ways to corrupt people despite his promise to Chuck. After all, he agreed to today only; tomorrow was a different story. Or when he got back to his man form. The newsroom was a prime location for corruption. Politics and power plays ruled the day, and they decided what the people heard and thought.

They were directed to a set with a perky platinum blonde woman and a handsome man with thick, coffee-brown, wavy hair that somehow stood tall but looked weightless. Malachi studied him intensely; he didn't like the way the man was ogling Chuck.

"Officer Charles?" the woman squeaked. "Hi, I'm Candy Morgan. This is Buck Perkins. We are just so incredibly excited to meet you! And who is this handsome fellow? Oh my gosh, isn't he just the sweetest wittle baby ever? Look at him! Malachi, right?" She squealed in a high-pitched tone and began to baby-talk him.

Malachi stared at her in horror. *Oh hell no, that bimbo better not be calling ME a wittle baby. Wait, is she going to pet me? Ugh!* He tried to back up, but Chuck cleared her throat and pulled on his leash, giving him a subtle reminder to act like a dog. Groaning internally, he sat, then panted and held out a paw for the blonde twit to shake.

"Oh, isn't he just the sweetest gentleman!" the reporter gushed. She reached out and shook him, then dug her fingernails behind his ears, giving him a good scratch.

Oh, wait, keep doing that! He moaned and leaned into her, scooting closer. He licked her cheek and decided she wasn't too bad after all.

Buck leaned down. "Big fellow, huh? Bet his bite is worse than his bark, right?" he chuckled before he continued in a smarmy voice that set Malachi's teeth on edge. "Officer Kelly Charles, my my, if I'd known such beautiful women were serving on the force, I might have chosen a different career path. The city's finest indeed." He raised an eyebrow and cocked his head in a pose that someone had probably told him was sexy, smiling with all his overly whitened teeth on display. Even worse, he took her hand and kissed the back of it like the star of the daytime soap opera Reena liked to watch.

Chuck's mouth dropped open, and she leaned back, cringing at the sheer cheese factor of the situation. She may have been coached by the PR department for the interview, but no one warned her to school her face when Buck acted like—well—Buck.

Malachi coughed to cover his laugh at her reaction.

"Bless you, sweet baby!" Candy cooed at him. She turned a dirty look on her co-anchor, snapping, "Buck, mind your hands. I'm sure Officer Charles wants to keep our interactions as professional as possible."

"Sure, Candy," he gritted through clenched teeth. "No offense intended, Officer. Just always good to see strong women in positions that have typically been male-dominated. Very impressive, my dear. The audience is going to love this message of positivity and community outreach."

Smooth. Malachi admired the man's recovery, although he still didn't like the way Buck was oozing on Chuck. *Heh, Buck and Chuck. Wait, ew.* He grimaced and stuck his nose in Chuck's hand, trying to nudge her away from the slimeball anchor.

Chuck dropped to a knee and rubbed his head, effectively moving away from Buck. "I know, buddy." She turned to Candy. "Malachi is a little confused about all the lights in here. Where should we set up?"

Don't blame me, he huffed as the reporter led them to a set with cozy chairs and decorative tables that were too low to actually be useful. At least the rug looked soft. *If you would just let me bite him, the problem would be solved already.*

"Shh," Chuck cautioned firmly. "No biting." She stopped in her tracks and stared at him; her eyes slightly widened. Her grip tightened on the leash, and her hand trembled for a moment. Squaring her shoulders, she continued her march towards the set. The anchors indicated a chair, and she called softly to Malachi, "Heel, Sit," she said, before taking her own seat.

He was still too stunned that she seemed to have heard his thoughts to even consider being contrary. Plopping down with an ungraceful thump, he stared at her intently, chanting, *Chuck, Chuck, Chuck, Chuck.* He wanted to growl in frustration. If she heard him, she was doing a good job of pretending she didn't. Turning back to Candy, he idly wondered if that was her real name or a stage name. He was willing to bet she stripped to pay for college because that rack was certainly not real. Those tits were one hundred percent financed.

He glanced at Buck, who was once again openly appreciating Chuck, and narrowed his eyes disdainfully. His upper lip lifted slightly, showing one fang. Buck noticed the stare and leaned back warily. Malachi slowly winked at the man who jumped out of his chair and swallowed heavily before scurrying away, calling for makeup. Chuck squinted at Malachi in suspicion, but he let his tongue loll out and panted innocently. He was a very good boy, and one of these days, she would know how good.

Malachi turned back to Candy and listened intently as they gave Chuck instructions, while the rest of the crew wired her with a microphone. Another lackey came over and asked if she could brush him. He turned eagerly to her, knowing it would feel awesome, and he was certainly a

creature who enjoyed his comforts. A small, wicked smile curved his lips as he noticed the tiny crucifix dangling around her neck; he would love to corrupt her. Sitting perfectly still while she ran a comb through his fur, he waited until she was done, then put his paws on her lap and licked all over her face.

"Oh, aren't you just the sweetest baby!" she gushed and rubbed his head. She squealed as he stuck his snout down her blouse and licked over the top of her bra. "Oh!" she exclaimed again as he pulsed dark energy into it. He sat back and watched the flush creep over her face at the sensation it had given her.

One corrupted intern, check, he chuckled. Sitting back, he pondered further on what just happened, surprised it worked. He'd been trying to use his demon powers since he woke in the shelter without success. Now, today, they seemed to be almost within his reach again. He smirked at the young woman who still stared at him, confused by what had happened. Wagging his tail, he gave his best good boy happy bark. He put a paw out to shake, sitting up on his haunches.

"Look how cute!" cried Candy, the former stripper.

The young woman jumped to her feet and hurried away, looking back over her shoulder at the large black dog who had just put a smudge of darkness on her soul. She shook her head as she wandered off.

"Behave," came Chuck's low warning.

Malachi huffed out a frustrated breath. Chuck was raining on his corruption parade yet again. He turned and sat next to her, determined to be a good boy until they left. He didn't want Chuck to be too mad at him.

Soon, the cameras were rolling, and they were live.

The interview was boring for him since they didn't ask about his opinions. He enjoyed hearing Chuck brag about him and his skills, how smart he was, and what an asset he was going to be to the squad. The rest was

gross, a feel-good story. One of those heartwarming ones meant to make people soften up towards shelter dogs and cops, then donate to both. Barf. His concentration wandered a bit, and he caught a glimpse of something dark.

As a lover of all things dark, his attention snapped into focus, and he quickly zeroed in on the source. He saw a man hunched in an oversized coat that seemed a little out of place in the large studio. The man was glancing about furtively, but no one was paying attention to him. They were all focused on the broadcast. Malachi had a cold pit in his stomach; it wasn't a feeling he was used to having. Causing, yes. Experiencing it on his own? Not so much.

He watched the man a little longer, trying to figure out what was creating the feeling. Then it hit him. The furtive man intended harm, and Malachi was fairly certain the creep was going to cause it. A deep rage boiled inside the stranger, his soul oozing malice. Malachi narrowed his eyes, concerned the man wanted to hurt Chuck as well. He was not going to let that happen. Whipping his head to Chuck, he gave a soft woof.

She stared at him, startled. He wasn't supposed to be doing anything right now, and it had caught her off guard. "Not now, Malachi, heel." She smiled reassuringly at the anchors and cameras. She gently placed her hand on his head and rubbed, trying to calm him.

Malachi grunted in frustration and glanced back to the man who was now creeping up behind a cameraman. No one had noticed him yet. He whined lightly and turned frantically to Chuck. He slapped his paw on her leg.

Now she gave him her full attention. "What's the matter, Malachi?" Ignoring the anchors who were trying to redirect the interview, worried about what this would look like live, Chuck was focused solely on him.

Grateful for her attention, he stared into her eyes and thought hard. *DANGER, DANGER.* Assuming his 'alert' position, a low rumble built in his chest.

She blinked once. "Retrieve!" she commanded as she unclipped the leash.

Like a shot, Malachi took off, an unearthly snarl ripping through the studio as he rocketed across the stage and ran straight at the ill-intentioned man. With a leap and a howl, he tackled the would-be attacker and incapacitated him like he'd been taught, holding his arm away from his body. The man was screaming, fear and pain mixing as Malachi bit down harder on his limb.

Shouts and screams erupted from the crew as the cameras panned to the man, while Chuck ran over in full officer mode, assessing the situation before calling, "Release!"

Malachi let his captive go and lay next to him, growling in warning that the man shouldn't even think of making a move towards his Chuck. *Hurt her, and I'll eat your soul,* he thought at the now sobbing man. Sure no one else could see, he flashed some Hellfire through his eyes to drive his point home.

"I won't!" the captive yelled, his voice trembling with terror. "I won't touch her!" he cried, sobbing and hiccupping now. He obediently held out his hands towards Chuck and let her turn him on his stomach with his hands behind his back.

She searched him efficiently and found two pistols in his waistband, along with a wicked-looking knife in a sheath on his leg. She cuffed him and pulled him to his feet. "I think this interview is over, Candy, Buck. We appreciate it, but my partner and I have work to do."

The entire studio broke into applause, and Malachi was praised for his quick thinking, detecting trouble before it started. The whole incident had been captured live.

Candy ran over and dropped down, kissing Malachi's head. "Sweet baby! What a good boy!" she glanced at the would-be attacker and froze. "Randall?" she squeaked. "That's Randall Johnson, he used to work here! He was fired for filming women in the dressing rooms." Her tone was now so frosty, ice practically dripped from her words. She glanced at the cameras and continued in her professional voice. "That's right, ladies and gentlemen; Randall Johnson was terminated from this network and is a registered sex offender. He came in with multiple weapons, no doubt intending to do harm. But this brave, amazing K-9, Officer Malachi, and his handler, the intrepid and fearless Officer Kelly Charles, have stopped what would likely have been a mass casualty incident. So be sure to support our local police department and shelters. We'll break here and be back with more at nine!" She flashed a syrupy sweet smile and waited until she got the signal that they were off air.

Buck ran over and grabbed his co-anchor by the shoulders as he shook Candy. "Are you insane? Why would you say all that? He can get a case of defamation against us!"

Malachi leapt to his feet, snarling and shoved himself between Candy and Buck.

The anchorman stepped back fearfully. "Whoa there, buddy, I'm not trying to hurt her!" He glanced around and realized everyone was watching him with wide eyes full of concern. "Right." He cleared his throat and straightened his tie nervously. "I'll be in the prep room." He turned and stormed off with a stiff posture and an embarrassed flush creeping up his neck.

"Thanks, Malachi," Candy called softly as she bent down and placed another kiss on his head. She glanced at Chuck. "You've got a keeper there." She smiled and ruffled the fur between his ears, laughing when he licked her hand.

"Yeah, he's the best." Chuck smiled fondly at him. "And now, please truly accept our apologies, but we need to give our friend here a lift to the station. I've called it in; one of my partners will be taking statements." She pointed at the other officers entering the building. With that, she whistled, calling Malachi to her side as they made their way back to the squad car.

6

Biting Felons is Fun

At the station, cheers and whistles greeted Chuck and Malachi as they arrived, their captive walking sedately in front of them. He kept darting nervous glances at the dog trotting alongside him, licking his chops as if waiting for him to step out of line. Malachi was practically prancing as he strutted next to Chuck. She'd praised him as the best boy and promised him a steak for dinner tonight for his actions. Now she turned the prisoner in to booking and answered the summons to the Chief's office.

She knocked on the frame and waited for the gruff command to enter. As she opened the door and went in, Malachi followed close on her heels. He noticed she gulped when she saw the Chief's office was packed. He recognized her lieutenant and the K-9 trainer, listening closely as the others were introduced as the PR lead, another detective, and the mayor herself. He was impressed as Chuck squared her shoulders. "You asked for me, sir?" she declared, her eyes straight forward.

Malachi could tell this was important, so he pressed close to her side, lending her support. It was a new sensation for him. He'd never had anyone depend on him before. He'd never wanted to support anyone. Fervently,

he hoped this dog body wasn't making him soft. When the Chief began speaking, he listened closely.

"I'm not sure if you realize the impact your actions will have on this department." The Chief was staring at Chuck, his expression blank and indecipherable. "Officer Charles, what on earth tipped you off that there was enough danger to justify releasing your untested K-9? On live television no less."

"Sir, Malachi alerted me to the threat. He's very well trained, and he signaled with confidence. I confirmed with him and knew time was of the essence. I released and immediately followed, where we successfully and without further incident subdued the suspect and took him into custody." She continued to stare straight ahead and relayed the information with a steady, detached clinical tone.

Malachi pressed in harder and thought to her, *I've got you, Chuck. He looked suspicious, and I could sense he had bad intent.*

"So, your untested partner, fresh out of training, alerted you, and you released him on live television without any confirmation he was correct?" the Chief repeated incredulously.

"Yes, sir. He may be new, but I have a deep bond with him, and I trust him. With my life," she stated with full confidence.

"Have a seat, Officer Charles. You did good work today." The Chief was now grinning, and the others in the office broke into applause. The K-9 trainer kneeled next to Malachi and gave him a good rub down.

"Who's a good boy? Yeah, you are, yeah, you are! I've got a whole bowl of those bacon treats for you, buddy." He laughed as Malachi lay low and moaned in excitement.

Chuck's quiet laughter reached his ears, and she winked at him.

A few hours later, Chuck was driving her patrol, and Malachi was sitting quietly behind her, licking the rest of the bacon off his lips. The trainer had been true to his word and rewarded Malachi handsomely for his efforts. "You know, I don't understand. You don't eat dog food, which is fine, saves me money, but you love bacon. What is that? Don't get me wrong, I love bacon too." She shook her head. "Malachi, one of these days you're going to have to tell me what's going on. I trust you. I hope you trust me. I've really enjoyed our time together, and I don't want that to change."

A quick woof in the affirmative made her smile. He did trust her, but he didn't want to admit he was a demon. Malachi wasn't ashamed, but he didn't want her to push him away. He really enjoyed being around Chuck, spending time with her, and helping her. Hanging with Reena and watching trashy TV on Chuck's days off was another highlight of his life. He was living a good, comfortable existence. Was he constantly corrupting others? Not as much as he used to, but he still got in some corruption here and there. Just enough to not lose his D-card, and today he even seemed to be getting some of his dark mojo back.

The radio suddenly squawked, signaling Chuck that there was a call for her and Malachi. "Saved by the radio." She smirked and picked up her com. She signaled back to dispatch for information. After getting the location and details, she confirmed to show her attached to the call, then hit her lights and siren. "Okay, Mal, this is it, first real call together. You ready, buddy?"

I was born ready, he grinned, then made a happy noise she had no trouble interpreting.

"Okay, there was a robbery, and the suspect fled into a nearby neighborhood. He got out of the car and fled on foot, so we're going in to find him." She pulled up to the scene and saw the lead officer directing the others. She parked and tapped the release button to let Malachi out of his compartment, then took him to the command post. "Officer Charles, K-9 Malachi ready, sir."

They were given their lead, and Malachi sniffed the car where the suspect had been. He closed his eyes and let his senses roam. Soon, he picked up a whiff of fear, pain, and the stale sweat of terror that marked the man they were looking for. It was in the opposite direction to their assigned location. Malachi turned and started towards where he was sure the man was hiding.

"Malachi, heel, that's not our search grid. That area's already been cleared," she called.

He shook his head and narrowed his eyes. He woofed twice. His signal for no. He started again towards that area.

"Officer Charles, get your K-9 under control. That's not the area you're assigned," came the sharp, frustrated order.

She studied Malachi as he stared at her.

Chuck, p-please, he implored, not used to saying that word, but he *knew* the suspect they were looking for was this way.

She raised her chin. "Sir, Malachi is alerting this way. I believe the suspect could have circled back around. I promise, sir, he's caught something."

The lieutenant didn't look pleased, but he studied the dog, who was now using his alert signals towards the area they claimed was clear. He gave one short nod and clenched his jaw. "He better be right."

Chuck reassured him. "He will be." She turned back to Malachi and repeated quietly, "You better be."

Malachi snorted and trotted forward, traveling about a block and a half down before turning to the left, then going another block. Without warning, he dropped to his belly and let out a low growl.

Chuck called out her identity and ordered the suspect to present and surrender. There was no response. She repeated it, adding that she had a K-9 she would release. Still no response. She glanced down at Malachi and shrugged before quietly radioing her position.

He knew the guy was there; he could hear his heart beating rapidly. He nodded at Chuck and gave a quiet woof. Yes, he was still there.

She smiled grimly. "Malachi, retrieve."

He grinned, showing every fang in his mouth. Launching hard, he bolted towards a dilapidated storage shed that was leaning haphazardly to one side, looking like a wayward house for orphaned snakes and spiders. Wood splintered, flying everywhere as he barreled through the door. He snagged the pants legs of the terrified criminal who was screaming in abject fear. Huffing with laughter, he dragged the man to Chuck, who was standing right outside, waiting to cuff him.

As she called to release and knelt to secure the suspect, Malachi developed a sinking feeling, deep in the pit of his stomach. She had her eyes on the man on the ground in front of her, and the other officers were closing in. A low whimper escaped his throat before he could help it.

Her eyes darted to him as her hands stilled. "What? What do you know, Mal?" she whispered.

Head whipping side to side, Malachi shifted uneasily from paw to paw before his senses locked in. There was another man—possibly a partner—sneaking up on Chuck from her blind side. A matte black gun loomed in his hand, and he raised it above her bent back while she kneeled by the prone suspect.

Without waiting for the command, Malachi leapt. Snatching the man by the throat, he slammed him to the ground and shook him just hard enough to incapacitate but not kill. He knew from training that killing was a big no-no, but it took every ounce of strength in him to not close his fangs through the tender flesh of the man's neck. The smallest amount of blood oozed into his mouth, and he nearly moaned in pleasure, but the sight of Chuck's shocked expression had him slowly easing back.

"Mal," Chuck choked out, her voice quivering slightly. "Good boy!" Her shoulders shook as she radioed again, alerting them to the additional suspect her partner had subdued. She didn't mention that he'd saved her life, but he saw it in her gaze. Shaken but grateful, she reached out and gripped his shoulder. "Thanks, Malachi."

A swarm of officers reached them then, yanking the two men from the ground. Someone bagged and tagged the weapon of the sneak attack partner, while another officer roughly dragged him to his feet.

"Boy, you just couldn't resist racking up the felonies today, could you?" the officer growled in a fair impression of what Malachi would have done in his demon form. "Armed robbery, assault with a deadly weapon, and now attempted murder of a peace officer? You're never going to see fresh air again."

Malachi added a snarling bark to emphasize the other officer's point. *That's right, you boil on a lower demon's ass! You're lucky I didn't kill you for trying to hurt Chuck! She's mine!*

"Chuck!" came a relieved voice, which then firmed. "Get your partner under control."

At the scene lieutenant's words, Malachi snapped his jaws closed and dropped the defensive position he'd been holding in front of her. He realized he was blocking the other officers from checking on her. Moving next

to Chuck, he nuzzled her neck. *You're okay, right?* he whimpered, unable to stem the wave of concern for her well-being from flooding through him.

"I'm okay, buddy." She ruffled his fur. "Good job." She threw her arms around his neck. "Thanks for saving my ass there, Mal, you get extra bacon for that one."

Back at the station, Chuck was filing her reports, and Malachi was getting even more bacon treats.

"Damn, Chuck, that mutt of yours really came in handy today, huh? Now aren't you glad I pointed him out?" Jaxon chuckled as he perched his hip on the corner of her desk. "Good job, Malachi. Thanks for looking out for our girl."

Eyeing the smarmy officer with disdain, Malachi thought about barfing on his shoes again for the mutt comment. His stomach was a little queasy from the number of bacon treats he'd inhaled. But the idiot did truly seem thankful, so he decided to just roll his eyes instead.

"Did he just..." Jaxon stared hard at Malachi.

"Hmm?" Chuck murmured distractedly.

Shaking his head and pinching the bridge of his nose, Jaxon closed his eyes briefly, then muttered, "Nothing... just been a long day."

7

Revelations During Cuddle Time

"You know what, Malachi? I'm too tired for the game tonight. We both know that no matter what I say, you're going to jump up on the bed. Reena too. So go ahead, get comfortable, I'll be back. Just leave space for me." Chuck sighed listlessly and grabbed her pajamas before heading into the bathroom to get ready for bed.

Malachi stared after her in concern. Chuck seemed off tonight. She'd been quiet at dinner and hadn't flipped on the news like she usually did. He thought she'd be happy. At the end of their first two weeks on the job, they had several big collars already. He really enjoyed riding around with her and chasing down the bad guys. Slowly, he was getting some of his demon powers back, and he was putting the fear of Hell into the suspects he retrieved for her. They usually went quietly after that, being extra compliant.

Noticing it was suspiciously quiet in the bathroom, Malachi trotted over and gently nudged the door open with his nose. His fuzzy eyebrows bunched together when he saw Chuck sitting on the floor, arms wrapped

around her knees. Her delicate shoulders were shaking as she wept against her skin, trying to muffle the sound. Her aura was solid blue, streaked with swirls of black. With a soft whine, he eased up to her and wedged his head under her arms, laying it on her chest.

The gesture was foreign to him, one of comfort, which was something he didn't normally do. Near panic seized him, thinking he must have done it wrong, when she started crying harder. He tried to back up, but she flung her arms around him and buried her face in the soft scruff of his neck. Malachi froze, unsure what to do, but Chuck just held him tighter, so he dropped his body to the floor and lay in her lap, trusting she would let him know what she needed.

Finally, her tears subsided, and she leaned back, smiling at him. "Look at you, big softie." She ruffled his ears, then more quietly said, "Thanks, Mal, that was just what I needed." Sighing, she thumped her head against the wall. Her fingers stayed bunched in his fur, kneading his neck. "It's stupid, I shouldn't get so damn maudlin like this. But... no, you don't want to hear this."

Without understanding why, he sat up and licked her face. Then, tongue hanging out, he put one paw on her shoulder. *I do want to know, why are you sad?*

"Huh, maybe you do." She flashed him a watery smile. "Today is my dad's birthday. Or would have been if he hadn't been killed in a failed raid a year ago. He was an amazing officer. Why I went into the force. You'd have liked him; he loved bacon, too." She sniffled and stared at the wall. "I still don't understand how those bastards knew he was coming. My dad and his partner both died that night. The investigation never turned up a leak, but I just can't shake the feeling that something weird was going on." Another heavy sigh as her hands dropped. "I guess I'd better get ready for bed, I'm not sleeping on this floor."

Malachi backed up slightly. Normally, he didn't follow her into the bathroom; she always shut the door behind her, discouraging company. When she stood, she stripped her shirt off before he could leave. His jaw dropped at the sight of her there in her bra and the lounge pants she'd put on when she got home. His eyes followed her hands as she pushed them down, her slender fingers skimming her thighs as the material slithered to the floor. Stepping out of the cloth puddled at her feet, she bent to collect it and toss it in the hamper. The sight of her bottom, covered in surprisingly delicate lace panties, almost wrenched a whimper from his throat. He might be in a dog's body, but he was still a demon male. He knew how to appreciate female anatomy, and her anatomy was worth the appreciation he was giving it.

Her slim arms reached behind her back to unhook her bra, and Malachi fervently wished he still had opposable thumbs so he could help her. His tongue fell out of his mouth, hanging down as he panted heavily.

Chuck paused and turned a concerned gaze on him, noticing the intensity of his stare. Her fingers fell nervously away from the band. "Malachi, I keep ignoring it, but you're not just a dog, are you?" She swallowed heavily before crossing her arms defensively over her chest.

Debating quickly on truth versus keeping up his charade, Malachi sighed and hung his head, shaking it slowly. He wanted to lie. It was in his nature to lie. But he couldn't with her for some reason. His body shook and trembled in fear. He didn't want her to send him away; he really liked working with her. He liked *her*. Dropping flat, he crossed his paws over his eyes so he couldn't see the disappointment—or worse—rejection in her gaze.

A soft hand ruffled his ears. "It's okay, Malachi, I always suspected. But I'm still not sure what's going on. I guess we should talk." She

snort-laughed then, the sound surprising him so much he peeked at her. Her fingers were covering her lips, and she giggled.

The sound was like music to his ears, and he eagerly sat up, staring at her. *Do that again, make that sound again.*

To his delight, she did.

"Oh, Malachi, people would think I'm crazy, telling my K-9 partner we should talk, but I know you're so much more than that. I do think you need to step out and give me privacy while I change. Then we can figure this out. Okay?" At his head tilt, she narrowed her eyes and jerked her thumb towards the door. "Don't act like you don't understand me. Out."

Giving up all pretenses, Malachi sighed then turned, dragging himself slowly from the room. He glanced over his shoulder and woofed low at her. *You're beautiful.*

Ten minutes later, Malachi lay on the bed, head on his paws. He was staring at the door, listening to the comforting sounds of Chuck preparing for bed. Water running, the toothbrush settling back in its holder before she spat out the toothpaste. The clink from the lid of the jar that held her nighttime moisturizer. It had a pleasing lavender scent that he enjoyed.

In the plush dog bed on the floor behind him, Reena was already asleep. Her little snores rasping in the quiet of the bedroom were the only other sounds. She'd had a long day terrorizing the neighbor's cat.

Finally, the bathroom door opened, and Chuck stood on the threshold. Silhouetted in the soft light behind her, she looked even more angelic than ever. Her gaze caught his, and she offered a soft smile. "Thanks for saving me a spot." After flipping the overhead light off, she made her way to bed, climbing under the sheet and settling against the headboard. "Okay, Mal, c'mere." She patted her lap.

Slowly, he crawled to her and gingerly rested his head on her thigh. His ears trembled, and his eyes searched hers. *Don't ask questions you don't want answers to, Chuck.*

Absently running her fingers over his back, she stared out into the darkness of the room. The only illumination was a small lamp on the nightstand. "Alright, so we've put this off too long. I think I didn't want to know, because I don't want to lose you, Mal. I'm scared that if I figure out the truth, everything changes. You've become part of my life, and I can't see going forward without you in it."

A soft humming sound came from his throat as he thought, *I don't want to lose you either, Chuck.*

"But..." she blew out an unsteady breath. "I can't ignore this anymore. It's not fair to you, and it makes me selfish when you're so giving. So, not fully a dog, but what are you?" she mused. "I don't think you want to hurt me. You're obviously very smart, and you understand human language. Are you an alien?" She glanced at him, smiling at his disgusted huff.

An alien? Please. Not even original. I don't go around abducting and anally probing people! Well, not in the last few decades at least.

"Okay, so not a little green man. Got it. Hmm. Are you a familiar? Like for a witch?"

An eyeroll for this guess.

"Geez, calm down. Guessing here." Tapping her finger on her lips, she stared at him hard. "Are you cursed?"

Malachi sat up slightly. Technically, he was cursed. He grunted low, and his ears swiveled to her in 'alert' mode like he'd been taught.

"Wait, you are cursed? So... were you ever a dog?" she exclaimed, sitting up quickly.

He nodded, then shook his head side to side. Frustrated, he groaned; this was hard.

Squinting, she nodded too. "Okay, right. I asked you two conflicting questions. My fault. Let's do this one at a time. Are you cursed?"

A nod.

"Phew. Okay. Were you always a dog?"

Negative head shake.

"Not a dog..." she whispered and leaned back, her eyes growing round in surprise. "So... what were you?"

He whimpered now. For the first time in his existence, he didn't want to admit his demonic heritage. Not if it would make her send him away.

"I guess that wasn't a yes or no question. Hmm. Are you a... person?" she asked hesitantly.

He nodded vigorously; he did have a human form.

At this, Chuck jolted upright and clenched her fingers in his fur. "You're a person trapped in a dog's body? How... why... how...?" She trailed off again and stared. Her face went pale, and her hands began to tremble. "I... I don't understand." She gasped, "Are you a werewolf? Weredog? Oh my god, you watched me undress!"

Wanting to reassure her, Malachi placed a paw on her leg and whined low in his throat, ducking his head.

Slowly, her breathing steadied, and she tentatively ruffled the fur between his ears. "I'm sorry, that wasn't fair. You were trying to comfort me. You've never been anything but good, well, except when you're around Jaxon, but he makes me want to puke on his shoes, too." She smiled at him softly.

Wheezing out a laugh, Malachi inched closer and nuzzled her shoulder, searching her face for acceptance. When he saw it, he sighed in relief and flopped next to her.

"Right, so you're a person trapped in a dog's body somehow. Who the hell knows how or why, and now the question is... how do I get you back to normal? Do... do you want that?" came her worried words.

Malachi didn't know any of those answers and didn't want her digging too deeply. He burrowed against her side and sighed again, hiding his face.

"You're right," came her sleepy reply. "It's too late to think these philosophical things. Too much to unpack right now. Let's get some sleep, and we can talk more tomorrow." She slid down under the comforter and shuffled around until she was comfortable. "Mal?" came a quiet whisper.

His ears perked up, and he raised his head slightly.

"No matter what, I'm here for you. I care about you a lot."

He made the smallest happy woof he could, *Me too.*

"Reena?"

This time, he huffed out a small laugh and hummed low in his throat, a clear negative.

"Right. Just a crazy dog who likes reality TV, then. Okay. Night, Mal."

8

Yes, You're Still Pretty

Malachi woke in the middle of the night to a cold, wet nose shoved against his own. He bolted upright, almost knocking Reena ass over teakettle off the mattress. *Geez, short stuff, don't scare me like that.* A wheezing laugh came from the other dog as she righted herself. A quiet yip from her had Chuck fretting in her sleep. Reena and Malachi both paused to study her until she settled back down.

Jumping down to the ground with an undignified grunt, the smaller dog glanced back over her shoulder like she wanted Malachi to follow.

He was curious. Reena had never acted like this before. Intrigued, he gently stepped over Chuck and quietly lowered himself to the floor before trotting after the Chuglet. He watched her curly tail wagging as she hurried to the back door, pausing to glance at him again before squeezing through the flap to the backyard. His interest was on high alert, although an oppressive feeling was slowly working its way over his body. An unexpected ripple rolled over his back, and his hackles raised on their own. Tension squeezed him tightly, and a sick sense of dread streaked through his veins as he poked his head through the plastic door.

Sitting in the grass, pulling on a tug rope with Reena, was his former commander, Hyacinth the Destroyer. It was quite possibly one of the worst and most un-demonly names possible, but no one dared say that in his presence. Malachi wasn't sure whether he was named that because of his bulbous shape that resembled the actual flower bulb, or the fact that he reeked of dead flowers instead of brimstone. Regardless, it was his name, and no one cracked a smile towards it.

"Malachi..." Hyacinth crooned quietly. "Come. Face me."

With steps dragging only slightly, Malachi reluctantly continued his trek towards the higher demon who had placed him in the dog's body.

Hyacinth chuckled as he lifted the rope in the air, Reena dangling from the other end. Her teeth were clamped around the toy as she growled and snorted, refusing to let go. The demon shook the rope, laughing harder as Reena's piggy noises grew louder and her eyes rolled wildly. "So much fire and spite in this one. She'd make a fine demon!"

Agreed, sir. I said as much when I met her. That's why I petitioned to keep her around me, so I could bring her along when I get back to the sixth ward.

"When..." Hyacinth drawled. "So bold of you to presume. Maybe I'll just give her your post instead."

Reena suddenly let go of the rope and plopped on the grass. She stood and shook herself on wobbly legs before trotting over to Malachi. Turning, she faced the other demon, lifting her stubby snout in a snarl.

Booming laughter escaped the shriveled lips, wafting the smell of a decaying spring garden over the two canines. "Oh yes, all the feisty best in that tiny creature. Look how loyal she is to you. I have much to think on small one, but be at ease. I have a proposition for your Malachi."

Snuffling, Reena relaxed and scampered off to water the garden.

"Well, well, Malachi. You've done surprisingly well in this form. It's not nearly the punishment I expected it to be. But it has brought some rather

good news to us. You managed to attach yourself to an angel. I'm assuming she doesn't know what you are?" Arched hairless brows over the blazing yellow eyes of the higher demon advised Malachi what his answer should be.

No, your unholiness, he offered as he bowed deferentially. *She knows I'm not a regular dog, but she believes I'm a human cursed into this form. Like a werewolf. I have not shared with her my true nature. I do, however, spread corruption and chaos whenever I am able, with the limited power you have disgracefully allowed me.* He continued to stare at the grass under his paws. Not daring to meet the Hellish gaze concentrated on his neck, burning his skin like the midday sun.

"Werewolf." The demon commander chuckled. "I like that. Wait... your power?" he snapped as his voice rose, thundering now. "I have not given you any powers!"

Swallowing hard, Malachi thought furiously. If Hyacinth didn't give him access to his power, where had it come from? Unfortunately, right about the time he realized the answer—and that he shouldn't have revealed that bit of information—Hyacinth came to the same conclusion.

"The angel," he hissed, like a radiator leaking pure menace. "Her grace must be eroding the spell on you. Tell me, Malachi," the demon taunted. "Have you been a good boy for her? Does she think you're well behaved?" An evil chuckle accompanied his words.

Sorta, Malachi replied. *She doesn't know she's part angel. She's a police officer and made me her partner. So, I get to chase down criminals and bite them. When I do a good job, she tells me that. I think that's what's happening. I've been using it for nefarious purposes, though, sir! I slip chaos into their minds, making them crazier. Sending them visions of Hell and roasting in the fires. They'll be prime specimens for our dark lord in no time!*

Hyacinth tilted his head thoughtfully. "Hmm, doesn't know she's an angel. That has promise." He scratched at the giant wart on his nose and scrunched his face harder. Slowly, like an oil slick spreading over his face, a terrible smile curved his wrinkled mouth. "This is just what we need. You've gained her trust; now you can corrupt her, and we'll get an angel soul in Hell. Imagine the rewards!" The demon's slitted eyes closed in bliss, and he licked his lips in an obscenely gleeful way.

The sight sickened Malachi, which was just as shocking. He should be cheering, too! Why was he against the idea? Not wanting Hyacinth to catch on to his true feelings, Malachi quickly chuckled as well. *Wonderfully evil idea. I'll keep working on warping her virtue and turning her grace dark.*

"Not enough," muttered Hyacinth, cracking his knuckles, causing a flurry of soil to fall like dirty snow. "She might catch on." The upper demon studied Malachi consideringly. The gaze was so intense that Malachi wanted to squirm, but he knew better. Suddenly, Hyacinth's shriveled lips curved into a grin significantly nastier than usual. "You said she thought you were a werewolf?" A laugh that sounded like a cross between a piece of metal caught in a shredder and a wet phlegmy cough issued from the demon's throat. "I think that's just what we need. Canine by day, man by night. Corrupt her, twist her, claim her!" He sneered. "But do *NOT* let her know what you truly are. Play on her sympathies, let her try to save you, but she's the one who's going to need saving. Oh, this is diabolical. I bet I'll get the Dark Lord's personal commendation for this one." Slapping his withered knees, the chuckle wheezed through the night.

Malachi's legs were trembling, but he held himself still. *Diabolical idea, oh evil one, but I cannot change into my human form anymore.* He ducked his head in supplication.

A mucous-filled snort echoed over the small yard as Hyacinth glared at Malachi in derision. "Do not toy with me, you smear of slime. You know

what I intend. It's almost as if you don't want to collect her soul." He squinted in suspicion. "You aren't... going soft, are you?"

Fuck no! Malachi insisted vehemently. *I'm trying to corrupt a fucking angel for evil's sake. I just wanted to be sure you understood I can't pull the werewolf routine without my human form. I'm ready to prove myself to our dark lord. I mean, I'll do it in canine form; it will just take longer.* He sneered at his commander, his tone matching the other demon's disdain.

Nodding, Hyacinth smirked. "As you should, I'd hate to have to smite you before we collected the angel. Well, no, I wouldn't hate it. I would thoroughly enjoy it. But I'm going to give you one chance. Don't make me regret it, or I *will* send you back to the lowest level of demon-kind, and you will spend the next five centuries trying to get an opportunity for me to *think* whether I will grant you access to the next level.

Malachi shuddered at the visual threat it brought. He did *not* want to be demoted to an entry-level demon. They were the true bottom feeders, the scum on Satan's shoes, the dirt under the filth. It was a fate worse than death. It was quite possibly the worst punishment in Hell other than absolute destruction. Some demons opted for final death rather than demotion to level one. *I won't fail you, Hyacinth. I will corrupt the angel and gain her soul for the ingloriousness of Hell and all demon-kind.* He bowed low for good measure, scraping his muzzle on the ground.

"See that you do," Hyacinth growled. He reached out with one jagged, filthy claw, caked with soil and grime.

Malachi braced himself, and with a sharp rap, the gnarled finger tapped him between his furry eyebrows. A burning pain like a blazing inferno raced through his veins, boiling and searing, before dropping him to the ground. Writhing in agony, a low whimper burst from his throat, and he clenched through the scream that wanted to escape him. Spasms had his body thrashing in the grass before it mercifully stopped. He panted in

exhaustion as the feeling of his powers returning soothed the aches that had bent his limbs at awkward angles.

A heavy sigh eased from his lungs before he could stop it. Stretching, he moaned with pleasure as his demonic magic suffused every part of his body. He opened his eyes and blinked, noticing his perspective had changed. He no longer saw a fuzzy snout in front of him. He held up his paws and grinned. They weren't paws. They were hands. Human hands. Five fingers, neatly manicured nails, with a light dusting of black hair on the backs. "Oh, fuck yeah!" he cheered and quickly stood on two legs, swaying slightly.

Wheezing snarls had him whirling to find Reena curling her upper lip at him, a sudden stranger standing in her territory. Holding up his hands, Malachi took a slight step back. "Reena, it's me. Malachi. It's me, Re-re. Here... smell!" He held out one hand for her to sniff.

Cautiously, Reena leaned forward and took a whiff, then tilted her head in cute doggie confusion. A small yip and excited rumbling followed as she rubbed against his legs before glaring at Hyacinth. She growled once and ran back through the doggie door, no doubt heading for the comfort of her plush bed, far from the weirdness occurring in the backyard.

Turning back to the squat wrinkly demon, Malachi glanced down and thanked the evil fires below. He had a human form that was pleasing. He barely managed to keep the judgment from his face as he studied his demon boss. Bowing low at the waist, he murmured, "My eternal wishes that all of your line command the Hellfire with spite and fury." A standard demonic thanks, because demons just didn't do that kind of thing.

Malachi caught a glimpse of his reflection in the window and his smile stretched from ear to ear. His human form was made to capture the eye. His mother was a winged ash demon, his father an incubus. The result was that he had an incubus form with wings and smoke magic. Something that had served him well until he had accidentally seduced Hyacinth's daughter.

It hadn't been intentional; he thought her just another loose female. But his superior hadn't seen it that way, taking it as a personal insult.

Tossing back his shaggy black hair from his face, he was pleased to see he had maintained his figure during his time confined to dog form. His arm muscles were toned, and he still boasted six-pack abs. A sharp jaw, sculpted cheekbones, and full lips that would easily curve into a sinful, knowing smile, accented by a single dimple on the left, greeted his ecstatic grin upon regaining his body. His eyes—normally a gorgeous turquoise—had inexplicably stayed chocolate brown. Frowning, he leaned closer to the glass to study this, but Hyacinth cleared his throat in irritation.

"Yes, you're still pretty. That's what got you in this mess. Now, use that for some good. Go in there and charm her!"

Spinning to face the other demon, Malachi grimaced. "Yeah, pretty high on the list of that's not how that works. She's a *cop*. A strange man waltzes into her bedroom in the middle of the night; she's more likely to pop a bullet in my head than drop her panties. I need to let her think she's 'curing' me." He made finger air quotes with a smirk. "And then I'll be her reward for her hard work. She'd be more likely to succumb to my charms if she pities me. Poor, cursed Malachi, starving for attention. Boom. She thinks she's the hero savior."

Squinting suspiciously, Hyacinth finally growled his agreement. "Fine, but don't let this take too long. If I even suspect for a second you're drawing this out on purpose..." He stomped his stubby foot and dug his heel into the ground like he was crushing a cigarette.

Nodding with alacrity, Malachi promised, "I know! I won't let you down. I'll get her to drop her guard, then I'll have her soul. You'll see! I've always been your best, most reliable soldier. Until our... misunderstanding!" He blinked and grimaced, realizing belatedly he probably shouldn't have mentioned that last part.

"*Were*. You were. Now you need to earn it again. I want a report in one week. Don't disappoint me, Malachi." His name was said with a mocking emphasis that left no doubt he was high on his commander's shit list. With a stench of rotten egg and putrid squelching noises, Hyacinth melted into the grass and disappeared.

Sighing in relief, Malachi dropped to his knees and let the shivering and trembling he'd contained earlier ripple through his body. After a few minutes, when it all subsided, he turned to the house and wondered what to do next. Shrugging his shoulders, he willed himself back to dog form and shook out his coat. He hurried through the doggie door, then crawled back into bed with Chuck, watching over her for the rest of the night. He didn't dare sleep for fear Hyacinth would drag him kicking and screaming through the floor. Carrying out his promise to reduce Malachi to a level one demon.

The occasional shudder rippled over his body, keeping him awake long after the darkness ebbed and dawn crept over the horizon.

9

Finally, the Right Frequency

Chuck snuck glances at Malachi all morning as she ate breakfast, on the drive to the station, and now on their patrol. Usually, they would sing along to the radio, or she would tell him about a favorite movie or memory. Today, it was silent; uncomfortably so. Finally, he couldn't take it anymore and whimpered, ducking his head. The noise brought her eyes to his, and she pulled over, sighing.

"I'm sorry, Malachi. I just don't know what to make of all this. I mean... did I imagine the conversation last night? Are you really a person cursed into a dog's body?" She shook her head in disbelief, her eyes tired and worried.

Sitting up quickly, he gave one short bark, an affirmative.

Chuck leaned her head back and lay it on the seat, rubbing between her eyes as if she had a headache. "Okay, it wasn't just some messed-up dream then."

Two barks, negative.

"Then here's my problem, Mal. I can't keep using you as my K-9 partner. You're a person. Not a service animal." Her eyes met his again; this time, tears welled in them.

Panic shot through his body at this unforeseen complication. A flurry of rapid barking broke from him. *NO! Chuck no! I like being with you. I want to help you, don't send me away. P-please don't!*

Startled, she jerked to the side, her eyes wide and lips parted. "Okay, okay, settle down, buddy. I didn't mean I was getting rid of you. I would never. I feel like I'm taking advantage of you." She opened the gate and let him jump to the front with her, wrapping her arms around his neck. "I'm sorry, I didn't mean to scare you. I don't want to abuse you when you're already in a tough situation."

Two short barks, a negative. *Chuck, you aren't abusing me. I'm your partner. I want to do this.* He put a paw on her thigh and stared deep into her eyes. Thoughts of Hyacinth and his threats the night before crept in, and he dropped his head low, shaking with fear.

"Oh, Mal, don't do that! I'm sorry again. I promise, I'm not giving up on you. I want to figure out how to uncurse you and get you back to normal. I just... well... are you happy being my partner until then?" Her tone was uncertain and quivered just a bit.

Malachi sat up and barked one loud, happy *YES!* He began licking her face excitedly and bouncing on the seat. No small matter in the confined space. *Yes, Chuck! I'm your partner. No one else, just me. I'll keep doing this as long as you'll have me.*

"Okay, alright!" She laughed, trying to push him back a bit, her aura now sparkling pink. "I got it. You like the work. I appreciate that. And honestly, that makes me feel better, Mal. It tells me you're a good person and you don't deserve this!"

At her words, his ears dropped, and a small grumble escaped his throat. He hadn't earned her high opinion of him. She didn't know his ulterior motive. *I'm not good, I don't deserve your... f-f-faith,* he managed to choke out the dirty word.

Rubbing between his ears, she smiled softly. "Yes, you do." Her hand stilled. "Wait, how did I...?" Her eyes went large again. "Malachi..." she said slowly, "are you speaking to me in my head? I keep hearing snippets of words here and there, and I thought I was imagining it. But I'm pretty sure I just heard you say you don't deserve my faith." Searching the depths of his gaze, she asked, "Am I going crazy?"

No, Chuck, I've been talking to you all along, but I didn't think you could hear me. Can you? He tilted his head.

A small nod. "Yeah, I can."

Holy shit! This is incredible! Chuck, I have so much to tell you! Like how much I like being your partner, and what a douche Jaxon is, and that you don't need to worry about Reena and...

Laughing, she put her hands on his shoulders. "Slow your roll there, turbo. I didn't catch all of that. But I agree, Jaxon can be a douche sometimes. I can't hear all of it. It comes in and out, like radio static." She gestured towards the car's radio face plate. "A crackling interference for some reason, but it's getting clearer." She leaned back and studied him, a small smile gracing her lips. "You have a very deep voice, it's nice. Soothing almost."

Malachi flinched as her subtle angel glow brightened momentarily. It did that when she was making monumental decisions.

"We are going to fix this. But we need to figure out how it was placed. Can you tell me—"

Her next words were interrupted by the squawk of her radio, a call to attach herself to an ongoing situation. She immediately shifted back into

officer mode and confirmed she was en route. "Okay, Mal, more later, we've got to help out with a suspect who's on the run. Hang on!"

The vehicle lurched forward, and Malachi stumbled a bit trying to keep his balance on the cushion of the front seat. He woofed happily at the action then loosed a small victory howl.

"Mal!" Chuck shouted, "Not in the car!" She chuckled at his sheepish grin.

Within minutes, Chuck pulled to a stop and leapt from the car to find out what the plan was. Shortly, she released him, and he heeled at her side. *Who do I get to bite today? What scumbag am I taking down?*

Chuck shook her head slightly, waving at him to quiet down. He sat with an exasperated huff and took small pleasure in the way her lips tightened, trying to fight off a smile at his reaction. Deciding to mess with her, he stuck his wet nose in her palm that was hanging at her side. Disappointingly, she didn't flinch. He lightly bit one finger and licked her hand.

Squishing his nose in her fingers, she shook it slightly and cleared her throat at the arched eyebrow the scene lieutenant gave her.

"Problems with your K-9?" the man asked with a dry drawl.

"No, sir, he just knows there's bacon when he's successful, so he's anxious to proceed." Chuck turned to face him. "After… Malachi, not yet. Be a good boy." She widened her eyes and frowned, silently telling him to cool it.

Malachi sat up straight and waited at attention as a good dog should. *I'll show her who's a good boy once she sees my human form,* he thought carefully so she wouldn't hear it. Listening closely, he tuned in to the conversation. The suspect was a male who had taken a neighbor's child hostage in an attempt to keep officers from arresting him on drug charges. He was now hiding somewhere in the neighborhood where they'd lost track of him. A helicopter buzzed overhead, but they had no line of sight either.

Chuck led him to the suspect's car and let him take a good whiff. Scent firmly locked in his nose, Malachi woofed to confirm he was ready. Backing up, he closed his eyes and let his mind roam, sensing those around him, searching for a dark evil soul.

"Hey, Chuck," came a familiar douchey voice. "What's he doing? Meditating?" It was Jaxon.

Malachi lifted the edge of his upper lip, and a small snarl slipped out. His eyes stayed closed as he frowned. He could sense two dark souls, but one wasn't their suspect. The scent was wrong. His eyes flew open as he realized who it was, and he took a step back in shock.

"Got him, Mal?" Chuck asked softly.

Yeah, sorry, got distracted. Chuck... you should know, I think...

"Get that dog moving, Chuck!" came the lieutenant's booming call. Frustration in his tone was clear that Malachi wasn't scenting the way the other dogs did.

Rolling his eyes, Malachi resolved to talk about it with Chuck later, but for now, he focused on the suspect's scent and trotted in the direction it was strongest. Confident now that he was on the right track, since the odor led towards the other darker soul, he picked up his pace. Finally, he tracked it to a grove of trees gathered next to a small pond in a nearby park. Several ducks floated serenely on the surface in direct contrast to the nefarious deeds unfolding nearby. Pausing, he alerted Chuck and waited for her command.

Crouching next to him—hand on his collar—she called out to the man to surrender, advising she would release her K-9 if he didn't comply. A rustle of leaves followed by silence was her only answer. She inhaled and called again, her fingers gripping his shoulder with tension.

This time, a muffled cry belonging to a little girl was followed by a gruff voice advising that if she released the dog, he would kill the child.

Malachi heard the quick catch in Chuck's throat and felt the brief tremble of her hand before she took a deep breath. He nudged her thigh with his nose. *Let me circle behind, I can sneak up on him and take him before he realizes it. I won't let the child get hurt.* He could tell she was about to decline; this would be breaking protocol. He placed a paw on her knee and turned his eyes on her, giving her his best Puss in Boots impression. *Chuck, trust me. At least let me look, and I'll let you know what his position is before I move. If you like what you're hearing, say... brimstone, and I'll know you approve. Please, Chuck, let me try!*

She hesitated, then nodded once and whispered, "Brimstone? Dammit, Mal, this better not blow up in our faces. I won't be able to answer any hard questions." She ruffled his ears and nudged him forward as she called out loud. "Okay, sir, I'll hold my dog, but please, will you consider letting the girl go? She's innocent."

With half an ear tuned to Chuck's pleas, Malachi used his demonic power to silence his footfalls and trotted a wide circle around the bank of trees, appearing to leave the area. Once he was far enough away, he loped around behind the copse with unnatural speed and closed on the suspect. Moving nearer, he quickly located the man who was squatting behind some overgrowth, peering out furtively. The suspect had his hand over the child's mouth and was pointing a gun at Chuck.

Malachi's blood ran colder than the frozen tundra of Hell at the sight. The man was threatening HIS Chuck. *Chuck,* he sent furiously, *this fucker is pointing a gun at you. He doesn't see me. I can reach his gun arm, but he may fire. When I count to three, throw yourself flat on the ground. I'm not letting you get hurt. This asshole is about to eat dirt. Are we good?*

The silence stretched for so long, he began to fear she hadn't heard him. He strained his neck to see her through the brush, frustrated by the lack of visual. He was just about to return to her when he heard her speaking.

"Hey, George, can I call you George? Do you smell that? It smells like..." She took a deep breath. "Brimstone."

10

Hellfire and Dude Bros

With a wicked grin, Malachi snuck a little closer. His heart began beating wildly in his chest with excitement. Not only for the action to come, but also that Chuck trusted him enough to let him act. Taking a deep breath, he charged forward, moving so quietly and quickly that he was a noiseless blur. *One, two, three, DUCK!*

His jaws latched onto the man's wrist and clamped down. As expected, the man screamed and tried to fire the gun, but Malachi didn't want to chance Chuck getting hit, so he used his power to jam the trigger. Screaming even louder now, George let go of the little girl and tried to pry Malachi's jaws from his wrist. Snarls erupted from Malachi's throat as he warned the man to stop fighting. Briefly, he let his eyes flash red with Hellfire, which had the desired effect of freezing the suspect so Malachi could slam him to the ground. He lay across the man's chest and growled in his face. *Try it. Try to get up motherfucker, I'll eat your soul and drink the blood from your carcass.*

A small whimper caught Malachi's attention, and from the corner of his eye, he saw the little girl covering her eyes with fear. Quickly, he called to Chuck, *suspect secured, get the kid!*

A rustle in the branches announced Chuck as she burst through, squatting quickly to check on the child. She gave continuous reassurances to the little one, promising her it was now safe. Radioing her position in, they were quickly surrounded by other officers who took charge of the girl and cuffed the now sobbing but compliant George.

"Demon!" the man shrieked, pointing a bleeding, trembling finger. "El Diablo!" He backed up and begged the officers to take him away.

Malachi simply sat and tilted his head in average dog fashion, letting his tongue hang out like he was just the neighbor's pet. He did his best to look as innocuous as possible. Panting, he released a friendly bark and did a silly dance in front of the child. As expected, she giggled and threw her arms around his neck. He licked her face and let her hold him tightly.

"Yeah, that's a devil, alright!" chuckled one of the officers, dragging George to the waiting car. "Watch out, big spooky puppy coming in hot!" The other officer laughed and grabbed the man's other arm to assist in removing him from the scene.

The scene lieutenant eyed Malachi with a narrowed gaze, slowly shaking his head. "Damn fine officer you got there, Charles. Keep him healthy." He spun on his heel and hurried away.

Soon, another officer collected the child to reunite her with her family. Finally, it was just Chuck and Malachi at her vehicle. Chuck was absently rubbing his ears and staring up at the single small fluffy cloud gently floating past in the otherwise clear sky. She sighed and shook her head before dropping to a knee by him. Her aura was such a confusing mix of colors and was so tangled, he gave up trying to decipher it.

"Malachi, you did a good thing today. I don't know how you managed that, but I'm impressed and grateful. Also,"—she blew out a heavy breath laced with worry—"I'm in a lot of trouble. My body camera will pick up that I let you off-leash and go against protocol. I would do it again, without a doubt, to save that kiddo, but I have a feeling that might have just ended our partnership."

A loud whine slipped from his throat before he could stop it. *No! Chuck, I'm sorry! I didn't want you to get in trouble! I just wanted to help!*

"I know, Mal. I know. But what's done is done. Don't worry, I personally adopted you, so I'm pretty sure I can keep you. But your days as a K-9 may be limited. I just don't know." Her troubled gaze met his, and her lower lip trembled. "Dammit, I'm so sorry. I know you've enjoyed this. And we could've made such a difference!"

Malachi growled then. No one was taking him from his Chuck. *Fuck that!* He told her. Laughing as she blinked in surprise, he stuck his nose on her body camera then shot a bolt of Hellfire into it, melting the inner workings and destroying the recordings. *I got you, babe,* he thought to himself as he chuckled in his head.

Chuck gasped, "What did you do? Malachi?" She grabbed the camera and unhooked it from her vest. Holding it in front of her, she dropped it as the heat from the melted glass and plastic scorched her fingers. She blew on them and eyed him warily. "Shit, Malachi, I appreciate the gesture, but how in the hell did you do that?"

Lowering his head, he replied, *I'm sorry, Chuck, I didn't mean to hurt you. I just don't want you to get in trouble. I... I don't know how I did that. I was worried about you, and it happened. I'm scared, Chuck. What if someone takes me away from you? You're my only chance to find out what happened to me. The only one who would help me. And I like you; I care about you.* For good measure, he covered his eyes with his paws and moaned

miserably. To his utter surprise, mixed with a bit of horror, he realized it was true. He *did* care about her and wasn't sure how he was going to balance it with trying to corrupt her soul.

A shaking hand landed on his neck. "No, Malachi, it's okay. I don't want anyone to take you from me either; you're my best friend. I want to help you. I *will* help you." She plopped onto the ground and pulled him close, burying her face in his fur. "No one is taking you from me. We are going to figure this out." Her aura glowed bright gold with certainty as he relaxed in her embrace.

Friend, he thought quietly, happily. He'd never had one before.

After she filed her report, Chuck requested to leave for the day and let Malachi have a rest to which their lieutenant readily agreed. They'd already proven indispensable in his eyes, and he didn't want to wear them out.

A quick change of clothes later, Chuck grabbed Reena and whisked the three of them off to their favorite park to relax. Reena romped happily in the grass, snapping at butterflies and growling at crickets. Malachi lounged next to Chuck, where she was sprawled on a blanket. On her stomach, her arms crossed under her chin, she watched Reena with a soft smile. "At least Reena is carefree," she murmured to him.

Not hard to be conflict-free when there's not a lot of thoughts in your head, Malachi snorted.

Coughing into her arm to hold back her laughter, Chuck glanced at him. "So now that we can talk—I guess this is talking—tell me more about

what's going on. Who did this to you? How long have you been like this? Who were you before? Or I guess you're still *you* but like... as a person."

Malachi hesitated, unsure how much to reveal.

Misunderstanding his quiet, she murmured, "It's okay, Mal, if it's too painful to discuss, you don't have to."

Shaking his head, he sighed heavily. *It's not that, it's just that I don't know all the answers. I mean, I can tell you what I look like as a human, and that I woke up in this dog body right before you saw me. I was a dog for all of about five minutes when you walked up to my cage. I'm not sure how it happened or who did it. All I can say is it was someone with some dark, powerful magic for sure.* Sighing heavily again, he settled his chin on his paws. *I wasn't a good person, Chuck. I'm sure on some level I deserved this.*

"Don't say that!" Chuck demanded fiercely, sitting up slightly. "No one deserves this. Malachi, you are a good person. Look how much you help me! And that little girl today. You saved her life, and mine. You saved those people at the news station. And you look after Reena, too! No one who does all those things is a bad person." She rubbed the back of his neck. "Tell me what you look like. How old are you? Are you tall? Do you have black hair as a... man?"

Chuckling, Malachi leaned against her. *Yeah, I have black hair, but my eyes were blue before. I don't know if they'll stay brown or go back to blue eventually. I'm tall, about six feet four. I'm not trying to be conceited, but I've been told I'm a good-looking guy. I'm only two hund—um, twenty-eight.*

If Chuck heard his near slip-up on his age, she didn't mention it. He figured the static she mentioned before might have muffled it.

"Hmm, sounds like the kind of guy I'd want to date," she muttered, before her eyes went wide. "Umm, that didn't come out right. I'm not saying I want to date you. I meant that you sound like a handsome guy. You're a handsome dog, so that makes sense. And wow, that didn't come

out right either!" She buried her face in her arms, cheeks burning, aura swirling with orange and a hint of red.

Malachi studied that glow intensely, surprised to see affection mingling there. He decided she liked him as a dog—a good boy. Not wanting to embarrass her further—another foreign concept to him—he changed the subject. *What about you? Tell me more about your family. Where's your mom? What was your dad like?*

Seeming grateful for the change in subject, Chuck sat up and crossed her legs, toying with a leaf. Starting at it while lost in thought, she began to tell him about growing up in rural Wyoming, watching the seasons change, and romping through the wide-open spaces. She was a bit of a tomboy. Her mother, Carla, was quiet and kind, a gentle woman. She'd always wanted Chuck to follow in her footsteps and become a teacher like her, but Chuck was stubborn and feisty, the near opposite. Her dad, Gavin Charles, had always been the steadfast stoic one. Her mother died of cancer when Chuck was eight, so her dad moved them away from the area, claiming the sight of the flowers and the fields was too painful.

"So, we ended up here. My dad joined the force and would take me to the station to see the guys. His partner, Roger, was always bringing me treats and presents. They were both there to see me off on my first date, to Homecoming, Prom. Even to graduate. A lot of the guys in the squad came to see me graduate from college as well. I've always been part of that family, and my dad was this larger-than-life hero to me. I looked up to him so much because even being a single parent with a wild little girl, he always made sure I felt loved and cared for while balancing his strong sense of justice." She sighed wistfully and twirled the leaf in her fingers absently. "I know everyone processes death differently, and people tell me I should let it go. Maybe it's just me grieving, but I can't shake the feeling that my

dad and Roger were set up. I mean… the timing, the weird smudges, the feathers…" She shook her head. "It doesn't make sense."

Feathers? Malachi tilted his head as a cold wave washed through him.

"Oh yeah, it was weird. When the responding officers arrived, there was a large pile of gray feathers under my dad. They don't know how he fell on them without scattering them, or where they came from. I don't think they could even tell what kind of bird they came from. But there was a large ring of soot around him, and he was lying on those feathers. Honestly, it sounded like some kind of ritual."

Quietly, Malachi sat next to her and trained his gaze on Reena, who was now chasing a leaf that was blowing across the grass. He didn't want Chuck to see how much this news affected him. He'd assumed one of her parents was an angel, but he thought it was her mother. Now he was absolutely certain it was her father, and he never told her his heritage. The feathers and soot were from his wings when his grace left his corporeal form. Furthermore, whoever killed him was someone who knew how to destroy an angel because they couldn't be killed through normal means. A gunshot wouldn't be fatal, a knife to the heart would just tickle. Angels had to be stabbed with a forsaken blade, and there weren't too many of those lingering on Earth.

Stomach churning, Malachi stole a glance at Chuck from the corner of his eye. She was still lost in her memories, her nose scrunched, eyebrows furrowed. She suspected there was more to her dad's passing than what the investigation showed, and she was correct. He'd been targeted. Malachi was certain of it. There's no way some random street criminal had a forsaken blade just lying around in case an angel just happened to show up. Acid rose in his throat, and for one horrifying moment, he thought he might puke.

"Reena!" came Chuck's sharp snap.

Eyes flying to his companion, Malachi noted with amusement that she was snarling and growling at another dog easily ten times her size. The bored Doberman was staring down at her with his head tilted in irritation. He gave one mighty bark, no doubt intended to warn her off. That only served to send Reena into a circling frenzy of yowls and yips. Malachi realized the larger dog was standing on her leaf and didn't seem to care that she wanted it back.

I got her, Malachi sighed wearily to Chuck as she watched nervously. He stood and stretched lazily before making his way over to the pair, taking his time with a leisurely pace. A whimper escaped Reena then as the other dog bared his teeth and snapped like he was going to bite her. Launching himself like a rocket, Malachi barreled into the other dog at top speed.

Back the fuck off, my Chuglet, you cock sucking piece of horse shit! he growled. The Doberman fell over hard and yelped in surprise at the sudden attack. Not one to back down, though, he quickly gained his feet and spun to growl at Malachi.

Glancing over his shoulder and noting Chuck now staring in alarm, Malachi made sure his back was to her. His lips peeled back in a display of fangs, and his eyes glowed red with Hellfire as he glared at the other dog. With a yelp and tail tucking whimper, the Doberman spun and hurried away, crying. *Just like the little bitch you are!* Malachi taunted him. Chuckling, he turned to Reena, who was mourning the status of her leaf, which was now crushed beyond repair. *C'mon, Re-re, Chuck has a new one for you,* he reassured her while also relaying the message to Chuck.

Escorting Reena over to Chuck, where she received her new leaf with a piggy snort of happiness, Malachi rolled his eyes at his companion. She would indeed be a fantastic demon, but she needed to learn to stand up for herself. He would need to teach her a few things.

"Hey!" came a loud, aggressive hail from behind him. Turning, Malachi spotted a blond muscle-bound man who spent too much time in the tanning bed and probably peaked in high school. He glanced around and sure enough, spotted an IROC Z-28 Camaro with peeling paint in the parking lot nearby. "Your dog attacked my dog, lady! I'm reporting that!" he waggled a giant meaty finger at her.

Slowly, Chuck stood, dusting off her pants and regarded the man with a mild smile. "Is that so? I assume you missed the part where your dog was attacking my other dog first?" She lazily gestured at Reena, who was happily trotting in circles, leaf held high in her underbite.

The man squinted at Reena and sneered. "That's a dog? I thought that was a river rat!" A booming laugh erupted from his chest as if he'd just told the world's funniest joke. "C'mon now, Spike wasn't going to hurt it, he was just saying hello. But your other dog actually did attack my boy!" his gaze turned on Malachi and glared, baring his teeth.

Malachi glared right back and bared his own fangs in response.

"See!" the man shouted, pointing his other meaty finger at Malachi now. "He's vicious! He needs to be reported!"

"You're right." Chuck nodded seriously, widening her eyes. "He *is* vicious. You know why?" She leaned in with a sly smile. "I'll let you in on a secret. Malachi is trained to be vicious. His favorite treat is balls. But he's not a fan of those filled with steroids. Those little shriveled sacks just don't hold that juicy squish he's so fond of."

The man blinked in confusion, trying to understand her reference while Malachi wheezed with laughter. He counted down until the meathead got it. *Three... two... one...*

"Fuck you bitch!" he screamed, spit spraying from his lips as his face turned so red he might have been suffering a stroke. He took one step

forward, and before he could lift his other foot, Chuck closed the distance. Now the man stared at her in confusion as she shoved her badge in his face.

"Here's my problem, Bobby. Or Larry. Or Daryl. Whatever your name is. I'm a police officer, and that dog right there? Malachi? He's my partner. My K-9 partner. So, ask yourself, Jimbo. Do you know what the charges are for assaulting an officer? Human or canine? Because I'm happy to explain them both." She arched an eyebrow and waited while the large muppet of a man slowly processed her words.

Fortunately for Timmy, or whatever his name was, he stepped back. "S-sorry," he stuttered. "I didn't know."

Shaking her head, Chuck snorted in disgust. "Does it make a difference? When you didn't know I could shoot your ass or set my K-9 on you, it was all fun and games. You were ready to pound on what you thought was a defenseless woman. Or intimidate me. Now that you know better, I bet it was all just a great joke, wasn't it?" Nodding at his terrified expression, she huffed a wry laugh. "What I thought. So, here's the deal. You're going to turn around, walk away, and I won't write this up. Or stick around, and I'll show you just how tight I can get my cuffs. After Malachi *retrieves* you, of course."

Malachi lifted his lip and curled it slightly, a low warning rumble in his throat.

"My apologies for disturbing you, officer. Have a lovely evening." Beefcake turned on his heel and marched away with what little dignity he had left. His dog hurried after him, tail still between his legs.

Malachi punched a little darkness towards him and was rewarded by watching the Doberman haul ass to the car, sprinkling pee the whole way. *Poor Spike,* Malachi laughed.

Bright bubbling laughter echoed his as Chuck plopped back on the grass and scratched Reena's wiggling behind. "Alright, Malachi. What do you say we go see a witch?"

11

Witches be Trippin'

Watching the street signs pass in the late afternoon sun, Malachi grew even more uneasy. When Chuck said they were going to see a witch, he assumed she was kidding. Surely, she didn't believe in that stuff. Then he recalled how easily she had accepted that he wasn't just a normal dog without freaking out. He glanced over and studied her. She was calm, her aura a steady, even glow. She was humming along with the radio and tapping her fingers to the beat. Reena's snores were muffled from the backseat where she was snuggled into a jacket.

During the altercation with the past his prime jock at the park, Chuck's glow had been the steady purple of justice. She'd never wavered, and he was proud of her for that. But now he was worried about what her aura would look like once she learned the truth. If she actually knew a real witch, they might be able to detect his demonic heritage and out him.

"It's okay, Malachi, Glenda is a good witch." She snickered. "And no, it's not Glenda from the movie. Her name really is Glenda, and she's Wiccan. I figured she might be able to give us an idea of where we could start. She doesn't put spells on people and certainly would never put a man

in a dog's body." She glanced over and frowned, her glow streaking with blue, indicating sadness. "Don't worry, Mal. I would never subject you to someone who means to harm you. I promise."

Slightly reassured, he turned and licked her hand, releasing a soft woof. It didn't mean anything in particular. He just wanted to acknowledge her words, but he didn't want to let her in on his thoughts at the moment.

Pulling to the curb, Chuck put her car in park and glanced through the windshield, pointing at a row of townhomes. "That's her, 242B." She unbuckled her seat belt and smiled softly. "You ready?"

After his nervous nod, he waited for her to open his door and stood quietly on the sidewalk while she woke Reena. Meekly, he followed them both to the door, his steps dragging. As she rang the bell, he tucked his head into her hand, needing comfort. It was a strange sensation, seeking solace from another being. Demons usually only relied on themselves, and no one had ever indicated they would be willing to provide him with anything close to what Chuck offered, without question or quid pro quo.

The door opened almost immediately, and a shrill squeal rent the air with a high-pitched, "Kelly!" This was followed by a boisterous woman swirling out in a flurry of rainbow colors and laughter. The smell of earthy incense wafted around them as Chuck was enveloped in a cloud of scarves and riotous curls.

Stepping back after her enthusiastic embrace of Chuck, Glenda the good witch glanced down and squealed again. "Oh, this must be Reena! What a doll baby you are!" The short, curvy woman leaned down and swooped Reena up in her dark brown arms, hugging her tightly against her ample bosom, rubbing her rosy cheeks against the little dog's fur.

Reena, for her part, welcomed the embrace and excitedly began licking Glenda's face with her now trademark piggy snorts.

Happy laughter boomed again as the woman squeezed her close before transferring her into the cradle of her arms like a baby. Now her eyes turned to Malachi, where he was hiding behind Chuck. Her expression turned serious, and she frowned slightly as her eyebrows drew together. "Oh my stars. You poor dear. You must be Malachi! I can see why Kelly is so in love with you. What a handsome, strong fellow you are!"

Malachi's ears perked up, and his tongue flopped out in surprise. He liked Glenda suddenly. She thought he was handsome and strong. That's why he liked her. It had nothing to do with her saying Chuck loved him, of course. He knew that was just an expression humans used frequently and tossed it about without consequence. The warmth filling him was from the setting sun shining on his glossy black coat. And that rosy red color spreading fetchingly over Chuck's neck as she hissed, "Glenda!" meant absolutely nothing.

"Well, let's go inside. Time's wasting!" Glenda declared and spun, her scarves fluttering behind her and her many bangle bracelets jangling while her hips swayed. Marching back into the bright space of her home, she snapped her fingers. "Come on! Let's go!" she ordered Chuck and Malachi.

Brushing past Chuck quickly, Malachi followed Glenda inside, where he found her seated in a large, fluffy, oversized chair that looked like they could all fit comfortably in it. The room was stuffed floor to ceiling in white bookcases overflowing with books on everything from religion to alien smut. Grinning, Malachi studied that section with interest. He especially enjoyed books with women who wanted to make it with demons. Those were some thirsty bitches, and he was here for it. In addition to the books, every inch of space was filled with crystals, candles, and plants. He dropped his tail low, anxious about accidentally sweeping something over and angering the witch.

"Glenda," Chuck called with a tired complaint. "Please don't spoil her!" she begged.

Turning, Malachi noted Glenda was rubbing Reena's belly while stuffing her with treats. His mouth watered as he caught the smell of bacon, and his stomach rumbled.

"Oh, there's a man for you! Thinking with his tum-tum!" Glenda cheered in a sing-song tone. "Come on then, Malachi, there's plenty for you too!" She held one out towards him.

Easing over, he gingerly took the treat from her outstretched hand and winked at her.

A large grin spread over her face. "Holy shit, Kelly! It's true!"

Malachi swiveled his head towards Chuck and tilted it in confusion. *What's true?*

Chuck smiled again, this time sheepishly. "I told her about you, Mal. I hope you don't mind, but I didn't want to show up and spring this on her without warning. She did laugh herself silly, but she was willing to listen." She shrugged.

Tapping her finger on her lips in contemplation, Glenda narrowed her eyes while a small snore erupted from Reena, who had fallen asleep again. "Well, one wink does not a human make. Kelly said she can hear you telepathically?"

Malachi shrugged, then nodded. He saw no reason to stick to doglike responses when Glenda obviously knew better.

Her eyes growing wide, Glenda nodded automatically in return. Suspecting it was one thing. Seeing it with your own eyes was another. "How about a test?" she blurted. "Malachi, if you're willing, my bedroom is down the hall, last door on the right. There's a dress lying on my bed. Go in there and look, then tell Kelly what it is. Then she'll tell me." At his disgusted expression, she chortled, rocking back and forth. "Oh, that

face was enough to convince me there, but humor a woman, would you, handsome?" She batted her eyelashes at him.

Always a sucker for womanly wiles, Malachi huffed in resignation and trotted down the hall to the indicated bedroom, where he surveyed the scene. There were colorful fabrics everywhere. It looked like a herd of rainbow butterflies had been massacred in the messy, cramped space. Wrinkling his nose in distaste, he glanced at the bed and noted the details of the dress in question. He almost laughed out loud at the pattern, but kept himself together as he hurried back to the living room.

A wheeze slipped from his lips as he approached Chuck, glancing over at Glenda as she watched him closely. He was surprised Glenda would want to reveal this, but as he had no shame, he wasn't going to disappoint. *Alright, so I don't know if you're going to believe this, but I got an eyeful of that dress.* He shook his head in amusement. *Also, please let her know her room looks like a herd of unicorns threw up in there. Anyway, the dress is teal with a square neckline, sleeveless, and covered in skeletons riding giant purple dildos.* With that announcement, he sat and stared at her expectantly.

Chuck stared back, her mouth slightly open and her glow wavering in confusion and embarrassment. "That's not funny, Mal," she scolded as she narrowed her eyes.

Huffing a laugh, he shook his head. *I'm telling you the truth. That's really what it was!*

Turning to Glenda with an expression of pure disbelief, Chuck straightened her shoulders. "Um, Malachi said your room looks like a herd of unicorns threw up in there."

Glenda burst into bright laughter so loud it woke Reena up with an irritated grumble. "Sorry, Princess," Glenda told her, wiping tears from her eyes. "Go on!" she encouraged Chuck. Her eyes were sparkling with mischief.

Malachi realized now the woman had set this up on purpose.

"Sleeveless square-necked teal dress with skeletons riding purple dildos," Chuck blurted out.

Malachi narrowed his eyes. *Giant!* he corrected with a small growl.

Rolling her eyes, Chuck stared at the ceiling. "Sorry. *Giant* purple dildos."

Glenda shrieked in laughter, squeezing Reena tightly as she rocked back and forth. "Oh my stars, that is incredible! Malachi, you are a treasure! Now, my darling. Let's figure out what's going on with you. Sorry, Princess, I need to set you down and take a look at your brother for a moment." She gently set Reena on the floor and smiled indulgently as the small dog stretched and trotted over to Chuck before circling and settling by her feet, watching the proceedings with wide eyes.

Nervous again, Malachi made his way slowly to Glenda, sitting politely at her feet, and cocked one ear. *Now what?*

"Hmm," Glenda murmured in interest as she gently took his head in her soft hands. She turned it side to side, lifting his lips and staring at his teeth. She ran her hands over his ears and stroked down his back. Low mutters and curious humming noises occasionally came from her while she inspected him. Finally, she clicked her tongue in satisfaction. "Okay, well, there's good news and bad news," she announced firmly. Her lips were pursed in slight distress now as she glanced over at Chuck.

"What?" Chuck breathed, leaning forward, her hands clasped anxiously. Her fingers were clenched so tightly that they were turning white.

Malachi's heart bumped and skipped a small beat at the sight of Chuck, so worried on his behalf. He shook his head, startled by the onset of some feeling. He couldn't name it, but it was soft and warm in his stomach. A chuckle caught his attention, and he noticed Glenda was watching him closely.

"You wouldn't know, would you?" she murmured. Turning back to Chuck without explaining her cryptic comment, she pointed at Malachi. "First, bad news. He is cursed by a demon."

Chuck and Malachi both gasped, but for different reasons.

I am well and truly fucked, he bemoaned to himself. *Here's where I get outed.*

"What's the good news?" Chuck asked, her voice tight with an emotion Malachi didn't recognize.

A long pause stretched out before Glenda smiled like a mischievous cat. "I think I can help him."

12

No Fur Equals Naked

Malachi held his breath as Glenda grabbed some crystals and foul-smelling herbs from one of her shelves. She'd claimed she could help him but hadn't yet elaborated on what that meant. He watched as she muttered to herself, collecting more ingredients for whatever ritual she was about to perform. Chancing a glance at Chuck, he noted she was watching Glenda with just as much anticipation and trepidation as he was.

Chuck, he called quietly, *I just want you to know... no matter what happens... I mean... I...* He sighed, unsure how to put what he was feeling into words. Shaking his head, he pushed his body against her leg. *Thank you,* he finished lamely.

"I know, Mal," she whispered, taking his head in her hands and staring into his eyes. "Me too."

They stared at each other in silence for a while until the loud clearing of a throat had them both turn to look at Glenda.

The cherubic face was now set in stern concentration. "Alright, Mr. Malachi, let's see what we can do. I'm going to try my best, but that spell on you is pretty darn powerful. No guarantees, okay?"

Nodding, Malachi smiled. He was grateful; yet another human was willing to do something nice for him with nothing in return. It was such a strange yet comforting feeling. It was something he could get used to. Well, when it wasn't something that would expose him and ruin the good life he had with his only friend.

Glenda was now muttering to herself as she directed them to her workroom, where she had him stand inside a metal circle hammered into the stone floor. Unlike the rest of her home, this space was ruthlessly organized with not a single object out of place. Neatly labeled jars and boxes lined the shelves, dried herbs hung on nearby racks, and more books covered one wall. These titles were covered in tooled hides and bore no publisher marks. A small cauldron bubbled cheerfully in the corner fireplace.

Eyebrows raising, Malachi realized Glenda was much more than just the casual dabbler Chuck believed her to be. A thought that was confirmed at Chuck's low whistle.

"What is all this, Glenda?" she asked with trepidation in her voice. Her fingers were clenching and unclenching. Her aura was wavering again, yellow streaking through it with her fears.

"It's my workshop," Glenda replied nonchalantly. "I dabble in spells. Teas, herbal remedies, salves, and small blessings. But it's always good to have protection when dealing with forces outside of the norm. Thus, my circle." She waved a hand flippantly at the circle, which Malachi studied with further interest.

Chuck, he called softly, *Glenda is more than she seems. This circle is silver. Hammered silver. That's not just a casual protection thing. She means business.*

"What are you going to do, and will it hurt him?" Chuck demanded. "This isn't some basic protection. I'm not blind. There's something else

going on, and I won't have you harming Malachi!" She was frowning now, her tone combative.

"No." Glenda smiled reassuringly, patting the air between them. "I won't hurt your Malachi. And you're right. It's not a basic circle, and I'm sorry I underestimated your willingness to believe. But don't you worry, Kelly." She rubbed Chuck's shoulder gently, reassuringly. "I'm only trying to help. I dare say you'll like the results." She widened her eyes at Malachi and subtly jutted her chin towards Chuck. "Oh, Kelly, I left my amethyst on the shelf out there. Will you grab it for me? It's on the left side."

As Chuck hurried from the room, Glenda put her hands on her ample hips and raised an eyebrow at him.

Studying Glenda, Malachi came to the conclusion that she knew exactly what he was and what he was supposed to do. But somehow, she seemed okay with it. What did she know he didn't? It was almost like she was going to perform some showy ritual just to give him the chance to turn himself human.

Glenda stared at him intensely, then nodded slowly. Giving him a wink.

What the fuck? What the actual nine levels of Hell and all the hookers in L.A. is going on?

A small chuckle escaped the witch, and she smirked. "Language," she muttered.

Ears flattening, Malachi crouched and whimpered. *Shit, you knew all along, didn't you?*

Nodding again, Glenda smirked. She squatted in front of him and leaned down to his ear. "Don't worry, Malachi, I won't tell. I think Kelly is good for you. It will be fun to watch how this plays out. Girl needs some excitement in her life. And whoever killed her dad? They'll come for her next. They want her grace. I bet you'd protect her with your life, wouldn't you?"

Her low voice sent shivers through his body, and he slowly raised his eyes to hers. *I will,* he growled. *No one is going to hurt my Chuck—Kelly—with me around.*

A small smile graced her full lips. "Then make this look good, boy."

Chuck sauntered back in, waving the crystal. "It was on the right shelf!"

Apologizing and blaming her hopeless sense of direction, Glenda took the crystal and turned to her table to grab some candles. She placed them haphazardly around him as he watched in fascination.

Muttering nonsense and waving her hands theatrically, Glenda continued to 'prep' for her spell that Malachi now knew was just a show so he could turn human for Chuck. He tried to keep his laughter to himself at how dramatic she was being. He didn't want Chuck to catch on that this was just a farce. Silently, he monitored her progress while he continued to turn it over in his head that she not only knew what he was, but she was willing to play along. It went against everything he knew.

Before too long, Glenda motioned Chuck into a corner and began a serious-sounding chant in Latin that Malachi realized was just her grocery list. He wasn't quite sure how she conjugated Nutella into the ancient language, but somehow it worked. As she dropped dramatically to her knees and threw herbs over him, he understood it was his turn to add to the performance. Flopping on his side, he released an anguished whimper and began convulsing.

"Malachi!" yelped Chuck, leaping to her feet. Her aura was now yellow and gray, full of sorrow and fear for allowing harm to befall him.

"Back!" Glenda ordered. "Don't interfere; this is the most dangerous part. Any interference can cause the spell to backfire."

Giving it his all, Malachi stretched his mouth into a grim rictus, writhing in pain and moaning before he fell still. Only the bellowing of his chest indicated he was still alive and breathing. At the sharp intake of breath

from Chuck, he jolted, and his limbs trembled. He allowed them to slowly change, the hair falling out in clumps before dissolving into nothing. First, his legs lengthened and then his arms. His back arched, and he groaned as the change continued to spread over his form, growing in size and shaping into a human. Lastly, his muzzle shortened, and his fur turned into shaggy black hair. The process was actually fairly painful to do this way, versus just dissolving and reappearing. It was so exhausting to do with theatrics. Malachi slumped, gasping on the floor, curled in on himself.

"Malachi?" came Chuck's quiet whimper.

Opening his eyes, Malachi sought out her stunned gaze with his human eyes and took a deep breath. Limbs trembling with the effort, he pushed himself back to his hands and knees, then slowly rose to his feet. Something silvery, a wave of unfamiliar magic wrapped around him, making him dizzy. Swaying, he opened his mouth to speak, but nothing came out. Clearing his throat, he tried again and choked out one word. "Chuck..." before his eyes rolled up and he collapsed.

Malachi came to, his head feeling stuffed with cotton, a throbbing ache brewing behind his eyes. Groaning he ground the heel of his hand against one temple, then flinched. A hand? "What the fuck?" he shouted and jerked upright before moaning again and flopping back down as a wave of dizziness washed over him.

"Easy there, Malachi, that was a hard transition, and I'm sure you're exhausted," came a reassuring voice. "I knocked you out so you could get some rest."

Blinking blearily, he focused on the source of the words. His eyes found the soft, kind brown face of Glenda the good witch as she studied him in curiosity. "Glenda?" he croaked.

"Yep, it's me. Look a little different in color, don't I? Or maybe I look the same. By the way, dogs are colorblind, so you shouldn't have been able to tell what color that dress was, you know?" She winked and smirked at him.

"Right," he muttered and rubbed the bridge of his nose. NOSE! Not a muzzle! Excitedly, he ran his hands over his face and sighed in relief.

A confused hum had him glancing back at Glenda. "You really were stuck as a dog, weren't you?" she asked.

Sheepishly, he glanced down. "I really was cursed by another demon. I only got some of my abilities back last night, but I didn't want to leave Chuck. I wasn't sure how to turn human for her." He shook his head slowly. "But... I'm protecting her," he added quietly. "You know what she is, what her father was, and why he's dead. She needs me."

"That she does, Malachi. But I'm going to keep a close eye on you." She shook a finger at him in warning.

Glancing around, he realized Chuck was nowhere to be seen. "Chuck?" he inquired in a voice shaking slightly with nerves.

Laughing in a lascivious manner, Glenda waggled her eyebrows. "Yes, well, Officer Charles got quite the eyeful of her canine partner when he stood up. Good gracious, Malachi, you are quite the looker!" she crowed gleefully. "I didn't realize you didn't have clothes on. Standing there all naked as a jaybird, black hair, flashing eyes, muscles, and mmm... gifted. You are definitely a demon plus. I've never seen such a good-looking specimen. There's more to you than just your dark gifts, isn't there?" She chuckled at his owlish stare.

"My father was an incubus. So yeah, I'm part sex demon." He grinned as her smile ratcheted even wider.

"That I believe. Well, our innocent little thing went to get you some clothes. So now what, Malachi? Are you going to keep protecting our angel girl? Or are you going to try to subvert her soul for Hell?" Glenda asked him seriously. Her eyebrows bunched tightly together, and her lips turned down into a sharp frown that seemed very foreign on her bright face.

"I'm going to find out who killed her father and stop them from hurting her. They can't have my Chuck!" he growled, clenching his fingers on the blanket covering him.

Glenda's lips turned up into a soft smile, and her brow relaxed. An expression much more at home on her features. "I'm glad to hear that. Now, can you turn back into a dog? Or do we need to come up with a story to retire Officer Malachi? And probably need a different name for you when you're human. But I will make one thing clear: you do not take her soul to Hell. Hear me, demon? You can smudge her, heck, that girl needs a little fun in her life, but do *not* claim her soul. Or we will have words. Understood?"

Smirking, Malachi nodded. "I hear you," he answered, but not actually agreeing. A fact that did not escape Glenda, if her glare was any indication.

A door slammed. "I'm back!" called Chuck breathlessly from the other room. "Is he awake?"

13

Let's Make This Awkward

Malachi fidgeted with his seatbelt as he glanced out the window, looking at everything except Chuck. It felt oddly familiar. Except the ride back to her house was much more fraught with tension and nerves. He twitched in his seat; the sleeves of the shirt Chuck brought him dug into his biceps. Without realizing it, his fingers were in the hem now, trying to stretch it around the muscle.

"Sorry, I guess I underestimated your size," came Chuck's soft comment.

Whipping his gaze to his arm, he dropped his hand as if he'd been scalded. "It's fine!" he snapped, then winced. "I'm sorry, Chuck, I'm sure this is just as awkward for you as it is for me," he murmured. The amusing part was that he meant it. He felt bad for putting her through this and was unsure how to act around her now. "It really is fine. I appreciate that you got me something to wear. I didn't expect that to work, much less show up... naked." He couldn't help it. His demon heritage made his voice drop on the last word, and he had to bite his lip to hide his smile.

Feeling the heat from her blush across the car, Malachi snuck a glance at Chuck. The tips of her ears were pink, and her fingers were gripped tightly around the wheel, nearly white. He cleared his throat, the sound making her jump.

Suddenly, she laughed. "Oh, this is stupid. We've been living together for months. Granted, you were four-legged and hairy, but still. We're friends, right? No need to be awkward." She made a concerted show of relaxing her shoulders.

"Yeah," he agreed quietly. "Friends." He couldn't help but feel a strong sense of sadness at that word. He didn't have any real friends, and now that he had one, he was deceiving her. Firming his lips, he scolded himself. *I'm a demon, I need to act like one.* Picturing Hyacinth's threats, he squared his shoulders and inhaled deeply, not missing the way her eyes latched onto his chest as it stretched the material to near bursting. "I'm glad, Chuck. I appreciate you still wanting to help me. I... I don't really know who I am anymore. I don't think I have anywhere to go." He kept his voice soft and scared, but not whiny.

As expected, she immediately went into protective mode. "Of course, Malachi. I said I'd help you. And I will. We will figure this out. In the meantime, I finally have a use for that guest room." She smiled at him, which grew bigger when he smiled back.

"Thanks, Chuck."

Malachi stood in the middle of the guest room, glancing around forlornly. After a quick dinner of take-out, Chuck showed him the room, pointed

out towels, and gave him a few toiletries he might need, promising they could go shopping the next day for essentials. She'd stood there awkwardly staring at him for a moment before planting a quick kiss on his cheek. Something she'd had to stand on tiptoes to do, then hurried away.

Now he stared at the floor, at a loss for what to do next. She had gone to her room, and he could sense her going about her usual nightly routine. He turned to the bed and grimaced. It looked comfortable, and he had no doubt it would be fine, but he would miss sleeping with Chuck.

Wandering to the mattress, he pressed on it with his knuckles and tested it. Sure enough, it was soft and cool. Spinning around, he plopped on the edge and dropped his head in his hands.

In the car, he'd vowed to be more demon-like. That meant he should be trying to seduce her and besmirch her soul. Claim her for Hell. He sat there a few more minutes, wondering how he was going to do that, when he didn't want to hurt her. With a disgusted sigh, he threw himself back on the bed and tucked his arms behind his head. He stared at the ceiling until the shadows grew longer, and he fell asleep.

He dreamed. Nasty, vicious dreams of Hellfire and torture. Of being beaten and demoted to a first-level demon. His skin and powers flayed from him before being scoured with acid and trampled mercilessly by the upper demons. It was a nauseating whirlwind of depravity and torment. One he used to enjoy.

Jolting upright, Malachi stifled a moan and ran his fingers through his long, tangled hair. He couldn't remember ever being scared awake from a nightmare before. He focused on his breathing and tried to slow it down, wishing Chuck were there to reassure him. As he sat trying to get himself under control, he heard a tap on the door frame. Jerking his head up, he stared wide-eyed at Chuck as she stood there, her aura flickering wildly with indecision.

"Malachi, are you okay? I heard you yelling. I guess it was a bad dream. Honestly, you look a little lost," she called softly.

"I don't know." He sighed wearily. "I was having a nightmare, but I just feel kind of restless and on edge. Like, I don't know what to do with myself. I don't think all of me came back when I changed. I just..." he dropped his head in his hands and let his shoulders tremble slightly.

Chuck rushed to his side, sitting on the mattress next to him, putting her hand on his arm. "Malachi," she whispered as he glanced up at her.

Demon. Incubus. You got this, he scolded himself. He let the barest hint of fear come to his eyes. "Chuck," he murmured back. "I don't know *who* I am anymore. I'm scared." His hands crept to her waist. "I... Chuck..." his voice quavered, and she threw her arms around him.

"Shh, Malachi, it's okay. You've been through a lot. I'm here. You have me," she reassured him, stroking his back just the way he hoped she would.

Burying his face in her hair, he pulled her close against him, relishing the feel of her slender form against him. He sighed happily. "This. I needed this," he murmured and held her tighter.

A pink glow surrounded him as her aura brightened. She sighed happily, too. "You know I'm going to miss our nightly argument about you sleeping on my bed." She laughed.

"We could still do that. I would be glad to come curl up with you."

Her arms dropped like stones, and she leaned back, her mouth open wide. "Malachi..."

"Sorry!" he blurted, his eyes widening for good measure. "I didn't mean like *that.*" He let color creep into his cheeks. "I just meant that I'm used to being with you, so being in here by myself..." his gaze wandered the sparsely decorated room before he shivered slightly. "It's a little lonely."

Biting her lip, Chuck stared at him before taking his large hand in hers. "Just this one night, then you're sleeping in your own bed." She rose and tugged on his arm, pulling him with her.

Wordlessly, he followed as she led him to her room. The familiar warmth and the soft scent of lavender instantly loosened the knot in his chest. He stood at the end of the bed, watching her as she crawled under her blanket.

She pulled the other side of the large comforter down and patted the sheet. "Come on." The corners of her eyes crinkled as she smiled invitingly, reassuring him.

Slowly, uncertainly, he crept to the other side and stood there. "Do you um... mind if I take the shirt off? It's a little... small." His lips quirked the tiniest bit.

When her lips curved up higher, he yanked the offending item over his head, then flung it down. "Oh man," he groaned, stretching. He rubbed his arms where the material had dug in and sighed in relief. "Much better." When he looked back at Chuck, her mouth was just slightly open, and he chuckled in his head. Her aura was again tinged with pink streaks. Outwardly, he gave a shy smile and slipped under the blanket with her. He kept to the far side of the bed and folded his arms behind his head, flexing his biceps innocently.

Chuck swallowed hard and quickly flicked off the lamp. "Night, Mal," she whispered.

"Night," he whispered back. Then, "Thank you, Chuck. I feel a lot better already. Just knowing you're close in case... well, I don't know in case of what. But you make me feel safe."

A rustling noise and a shimmy of the mattress were followed by a heartbeat of silence before Chuck's hand patted his arm. "Me too, Mal."

Feeling relaxed, truly, Malachi turned on his side to face Chuck and could just barely make out her eyes in the soft light coming from outside.

She was facing him and watching him closely. He took her hand in his and entwined their fingers, then closed his eyes.

The chirping of birds the next morning woke Malachi, and he blinked groggily at the ceiling, trying to clear his vision. He realized something soft and warm was lying across him, stirring a deep need in his body. Glancing down, he found Chuck had moved over to his side of the bed and wrapped herself around him in her sleep. One arm and leg were thrown over him, and her head was on his chest. Equal parts amused and turned on, he lay still, not wanting to wake her and embarrass her.

He studied the way her dark lashes lay on her smooth cheeks and how her sleep softened lips were parted just the smallest amount. Unable to resist, he traced a finger over her jawline, inching closer to that full bottom lip he desperately wanted to bite. She stirred, and his hand froze before dropping quickly to his side. He saw her eyelids flutter and quickly closed his eyes to see how she would react when she realized where she was sleeping.

A quiet gasp filled the room as Chuck woke fully with a start. He felt her twitch against him as her head lifted. He could almost feel her gaze on him, so he kept his breathing shallow and steady, willing his heart not to pound out of his ribcage. Figuring she was about to pull away, he started to mourn the loss of her warmth, but she surprised him and lay back down. Her head snuggled back into his chest, and her hand spread over his stomach, fingers trailing over his abs, pressing slightly for more contact.

Malachi was in agony. Split between trying to seduce her or working further to gain her trust. He thought hard and decided he would do

both. Giving her time to decide how she wanted to act, he stirred slightly, pretending he was just waking up. She began to pull away from him, and his arms wrapped around her, a low murmur from his throat.

A stifled squeak slipped from her lips as he pulled her closer and turned, pressing himself firmly against her. Trapped against him the way she was, there was no mistaking what his body thought of the contact. He sighed happily but kept his eyes closed, nuzzling her hair and settling further into the pillow.

“Um... Malachi?” came her fervent attempt to wake him. She tapped him on the chest. “Why did I get gray sweatpants...”

“Hmm?” he mumbled sleepily.

“Malachi!” she called a little louder.

Quelling the huge grin that wanted to spread over his face, he blinked at her a few times, then dramatically widened his eyes as he glanced down to see how wrapped up in each other they were. “Oh shit, Chuck, I’m sorry! I didn’t realize!” He quickly let go of her and tried to scoot back, only to realize they were on his side of the bed, and there was nowhere for him to go. A fact that did not escape her notice.

“No, Malachi, it’s um... my fault. I think I got cold, and I woke up lying on you. I tried to move but you ah... um... You turned over and pulled me back. You were asleep and didn’t know you were doing it. Just like I didn’t know. So, yeah, no harm done, right? Anyway, we should get moving so we can get you some better-fitting clothes and things today. I’ll uh take a shower, and if you want to use the guest bathroom, you can. And then we should uh...” her frantic explanations trailed off as he placed a tentative hand on her waist.

“Chuck?” he called softly. “It’s okay. I don’t mind you curling up with me if you’re cold. I liked it. I mean, I must have if I didn’t want you to

leave." He studied her eyes, watching them cloud with indecision. "Come back," he whispered, tugging gently on her hip.

"I don't think that's a good idea," she responded and leapt from the bed. She stared at him a little wild-eyed.

Slowly, he got out of bed and stood on the other side. He watched her eyes tracking him as he rose to his full height. Raking a hand through his wavy black hair, he sighed. "I'm sorry, Chuck. I just still feel a little lost, and I had no right to put that on you. I get it. I'm your dog. Your K-9 partner. That's weird. I'll uh, go use the other bathroom." He glanced around, looking for the too-small shirt, grimacing as he stretched it over his chest. Smoothing the fabric over his stomach, he saw her greedily covering every inch of it with her gaze. He kept his smile inside as she returned her eyes to his. "Maybe it would be easier if I just turned back into a dog." He gave her a lopsided smile, flashing his dimple, and hurried off to the other bedroom.

After he slowly closed the door, he let the large grin curve his lips in triumph. He hadn't missed her guilt-stricken look or the gray and red streaks through her aura as the barb hit home. The grin slowly dissolved, though, as he realized just how much he had manipulated her. It made him feel gross and dirty, something he didn't normally mind. He stared at the floor and closed his eyes, picturing the bulbous form of Hyacinth squinting at him, pointing a dirty claw and threatening to demote him to the base level of demons. He shuddered, and it strengthened his resolve. He had to make some progress soon, or it wouldn't matter anyway.

14

Shopping for Jealousy

At the store, Malachi half-heartedly tossed a handful of essentials into a shopping bag handed to him by the overly exuberant attendant who greeted him. He knew her excitement was not so much the prospect of a sale by the way her eyes traced his body. The tight shirt really left nothing to the imagination, and—being part incubus—it was a very pleasing form. Sighing, Malachi stared at the socks and grabbed a package of black basic ones, adding them to the small pile.

"I got you some things," Chuck mumbled as she dropped another handful of toiletries in the bag. "I wasn't sure what kind of hair care you would use. I just made a guess." She shrugged as her cheeks blushed a slight pink color, echoed by the rose flush of her aura.

Shaking his head slightly, he muttered, "I'm sure it's fine. I don't need a lot. I appreciate the help. You can wait up front, Chuck. You don't have to follow me around. You've done so much already." Sighing, he strode forcefully away to a different section to put some space between them. He didn't want to do it; he wanted to be so close he could feel the heat from her body. But he needed to provoke that desire in her to be near him.

Glancing dubiously at a mannequin dressed in khakis and a popped collar, polo-style shirt, he shuddered and let his eyes roam the racks. Smiling with relief as he saw a small stack of black jeans, he hurried over and snatched a couple of pairs in his size.

"All black," came Chuck's quiet voice.

Spinning to face her, Malachi kept his victory cheer in his head. "Hmm?" he inquired.

"All the clothing you've picked out. It's all black. Is that on purpose? Did you realize you were doing that? Planning on some cat burglarizing later?" She smirked slightly at her joke.

"Yeah, maybe," he replied in a flat tone before turning away again.

A heavy sigh from behind him had his lips curving in glee before he schooled his features. Turning back to her, he arched an eyebrow in question.

"Mal, I'm sorry about this morning. I didn't mean to make you feel bad. It... It's awkward being around you this way. And that's not fair to you. You're the victim in all this. I shouldn't be treating you differently just because you're a man now. I mean, you already were, but then you were a dog, now a man, and... good grief, I'm making a mess out of this." She placed a hand on his arm, and her eyes implored him for forgiveness. "Malachi, I don't want things to change with us. I've... I mean... I care about you. In any form, and I don't want you to leave." Her lower lip was pulled between her teeth in a nervous gesture he'd never seen before from her.

Slowly, giving her a chance to move, flinch, lean back, whatever she wanted, he lifted a hand to her cheek and gently stroked his thumb over it. "Chuck," he said quietly, "thank you. That means a lot to me. More than you know." He took a small step towards her, his tall frame quickly closing the gap between them. "I care about you, too, and I don't want to leave.

But I don't want to make things harder for you. I just don't know where I go from here."

Staring into his eyes, leaning into his hand on her cheek, she said, "Nowhere, Mal. You'll stay with me until you don't want to. Whatever you need. And I promise I will keep working to find out who did this to you and why." Nodding with reassurance, she moved closer.

Malachi wasn't sure if she realized she'd done that, but he wasn't going to point it out and make her regret it. Slowly, he lowered his head towards hers and smiled when her lips parted slightly. "Thanks, Chuck. Blue?"

Blinking in confusion, she shook her head. "Blue?" she repeated.

He held up the shirt in his other hand. "You said I was picking all black, so I grabbed blue. Is that better?" Tilting his head, he let a small smirk creep over his lips as she leaned back, staring at the shirt like it was a foreign object she'd never seen before.

"Uh..." she shook her head as if waking up. "Yeah, blue. That's nice. Go with that!" Her cheeks colored again as her aura brightened with embarrassment and other emotions. "I'm going to uh... go get some more dog food. For Reena. I'm worried Glenda is spoiling her rotten, and she won't want to come back home."

Watching her retreat quickly, Malachi shook his head in amusement. He was sure Glenda had spoiled Reena, but he was also sure Reena would want to return to Chuck. The good witch had volunteered to keep Reena overnight so they could adjust to things now that he was back in human form. But Reena adored Chuck, and she'd sworn allegiance to Malachi.

Grabbing a few more items, Malachi made his way to the front. He scanned the counters, looking for Chuck. He didn't see her yet, so he leaned against a column and waited. Shortly, he became aware of a pair of green eyes firmly latched onto him. It was the attendant from earlier who had been so eager to assist him. She was undressing him with her gaze in a

way that would normally have resulted in an invitation to go somewhere private so he could mark her soul. Today, though, it just made him weary, and he didn't want to examine it too closely to determine why that was.

Seeing Chuck wandering over, he suddenly realized there was an opportunity to be had, and his lips parted in a wide smile for the perky store clerk. At first, she seemed astonished that he'd acknowledged her interest, but she quickly recovered and hurried from behind the counter. She sashayed over to his side, offering him a sultry smile. Knowing how tight the shirt was, he raised one arm and propped it casually on the column, leaning and stretching the material to its limits. "Hello there," he practically purred.

"Hi, handsome," she replied breathlessly. "I'm Keely!" She inhaled in an attempt to lift her breasts higher. Her hands nervously smoothed her hair and her skirt.

Letting some of his incubus power seep over her, he inclined his head. "Keely," he rolled the name over his tongue as if tasting some exquisite delicacy or rich wine. "Such a beautiful name for an incredibly lovely woman. I'm Malachi."

"Malachi..." she moaned, squeezing her thighs together and leaning closer. "Wow, that's not a name I hear a lot! Is it a family name?"

Surprised there wasn't a dribble of drool hanging from her lips, he closed the distance to her ear and murmured, "Well, my father named me after an archdemon, so I guess you could say that."

She giggled and laid her fingers teasingly on his chest, his power overcoming her inhibitions, "Oh, that's so funny!" She moved so close that her breasts were now covering his arm.

The warm weight of her chest on his skin would have sent a strong bolt of lust through him any other time. As it was, he fought back a grimace since he found it revolting. He was keenly aware now of Chuck staring holes into his back while he flirted with Keely. He smoldered at the woman

as she breathed heavily, ready to climb him like a tree. "Hey, Keely, I think Chuck and I are ready to check out now. It's been a *thrill* speaking with you." He let his gaze roam her figure in a completely lascivious way, indicating he would love to see what she looked like under her clothes.

"Chuck?" Keely blurted, confusion clouding her eyes. She took a step back as he released her from his power, snatching her hand off his body as she quickly realized how inappropriate she was being with a customer.

Nodding, he turned and gestured. "Yeah, Chuck. My... partner." His gaze softened, and he flashed a hint of a smile at the irate half angel innocently. As if nothing untoward had occurred and he wasn't baiting her.

Chuck's lips were drawn tight in a thin line, and she was studying Keely with an air of open disdain. "Keely, is it?" When the clerk nodded quickly, her cheeks on fire, Chuck snorted. "Well, if you're quite done manhandling my partner, we'd like to pay and leave. We need to get back home."

Sucking in a sharp breath, Keely hurried behind the counter to log into her register and began ringing them up with a speed that was haphazard and sloppy. Malachi was fairly certain she didn't even scan some items. When she grabbed the packages of underwear, she almost dropped them with a choked sound. Quickly, they were scooped into plastic bags with the store's logo emblazoned across the front. After she scanned the last item, she rattled off a total so fast that it was nearly gibberish. Fortunately, the large display screen showed the amount owed, so Chuck wordlessly swiped a credit card and continued her steady, unblinking perusal of the clerk.

Gathering up all the bags, Malachi hoisted the large sack of dog food over his shoulder as if it weighed nothing. He winked at Keely, whose mouth had dropped at his show of strength. Chuck, however, was not so impressed.

“Seriously, Malachi, I can carry some of that! I’m not helpless. You of all people know that.” Her tone was pointed and sharp, clearly offended by something as she stomped away.

“I absolutely know that, Chuck, but now that I can shoulder more of the burden, I want to help however I can since you’re taking care of me,” came his soft reply as he followed her angry stride to the door.

Coming to a sudden stop, Chuck’s shoulders drooped. She grunted in surprise as Malachi ran into her.

“Sorry! Sorry,” he called anxiously, trying to steady her. “I uh, didn’t realize you were going to stop.”

“You can let me go now.”

Malachi glanced down and realized he had his arm around her waist, holding her to him. He’d been worried she was going to fall, so he’d quickly dropped the dog food and grabbed her in his panic. Slowly, he unwound his arm, letting her straighten up.

“Thanks.”

“Welcome,” he murmured as he leaned down to lift the food again. He hurried out past her and waited by the back of the car to load the purchases when she opened the trunk. Standing there in the parking lot, he stripped off the too-small shirt and rummaged through the bags until he found a new one, then ripped the tag off. He heard a small, choked noise and noticed Chuck was staring at his upper body again, heat filling her expression as she took him all in with the sun shining on his skin.

He was about to call her out on it when they both turned at an incredulous voice.

“Chuck?”

15

Evan's Half-Naked

Great, Detective Dumbfuck has to show up and ruin it all, Malachi thought uncharitably. He rolled his eyes in exasperation as he stretched the shirt a bit before pulling it over his head. Snugging it down over his chest and arms, he nearly moaned in satisfaction at the way it hugged his body without strangling him. Now he refocused on Chuck and Jaxon's discussion.

"I mean, I guess I just wasn't expecting to see you here with a half-naked guy in the parking lot," Jaxon declared hotly, raking his gaze over Malachi in what was assuredly meant to be intimidating. Instead, it merely came across as possessive, and Malachi suddenly realized Jaxon now saw him as competition for Chuck.

"Not half-naked, more like quarter-naked," Malachi interjected with a friendly smile full of innoncence he certainly didn't have. "Just exchanging my shirt since Chuck here was kind enough to buy me a new one."

Staring at him through narrowed eyes, Jaxon snorted in disdain as he raked his gaze disparagingly over his perceived rival. "I guess I missed it, but who are you, and why is Chuck buying you a shirt?"

"I'm Malachi—" he started, but Chuck cut him off.

"Malachi's former owner!" she blurted. "This is Evan. He saw the story about Malachi on the news and realized it was his missing dog. He reached out to talk about it. Turns out, Malachi went missing while he was visiting the area, and he's been looking for him since. But anyway, he agreed that Malachi is happy with me and thought it was cool that he's a K-9 now, so we started talking and anyway..." she trailed off. The flurry of lies she had told was dwindling down as she ran out of ideas.

Grinning at her adorable attempt at lying, Malachi held out his hand, trying not to stare at her wildly flickering aura. "Nice to meet you. Like Chuck said, I'm Evan. And I was overwhelmed by how amazing she is and how happy Malachi is with her. He's the happiest I've ever seen him. I can tell he really enjoys the work and adores Chuck. It was so fascinating, I couldn't help but want to know more about this incredible woman who captured Malachi's heart." He ignored Chuck's startled expression as she tried to figure out what he meant by that. "Anyway, we went out to eat, and Miss Butterfingers here dumped pasta sauce all over my shirt. So, she kindly offered to get me a new one. Since the airline lost my luggage, I took her up on it." He continued to grin at Jaxon as the other man stared at them with an open mouth, leaving Malachi's hand up in between them. Ignored.

"You went on a date? With a stranger?" Jaxon exclaimed, staring at Chuck as if she'd grown three heads.

"Not a date!" Chuck snapped indignantly, her eyes narrowed dangerously. "Even if I did, that's the point of a date, to get to know the other person."

Chuckling uneasily, Malachi held up his hands. "Look, buddy, I didn't know she had a boyfriend, okay? I wasn't trying to move in on your territory. I just wanted to make sure Malachi was alright. He's a great dog. Very

loyal. I'm glad she's looking after him. It wasn't a date, just a friendly meal. And I'm under no delusions that Officer Charles here couldn't swiftly kick my ass if I stepped out of line. She's an amazing person. You're lucky!"

Not missing the look of horror on Chuck's face and the shock on Jaxon's, Malachi tilted his head. "I'm sorry, did I misread this?" He gestured between the two of them.

"We aren't dating!" Chuck hissed.

"Just friends!" Jaxon added quickly, although he glanced at Chuck with sadness pinching his eyes.

"Oh, well, in that case, my further apologies," Malachi offered sheepishly. He turned to Chuck and eyed her speculatively. "But I'm glad to hear that." He gave her a soft smile, just the slightest curve of his lips, that she returned without seeming to think about it. It was an instant response, letting him know it was genuine.

Jaxon cleared his throat, clearly uncomfortable as he shifted on his feet. "Well, good to see you, Chuck. Glad everything's okay. See you tomorrow?" At her distracted nod, he huffed and turned to Malachi. "Nice to meet you, Eric." He held out his hand with a slight smirk.

"Evan," Malachi corrected and took Jaxon's hand. He squeezed harder than necessary, adding some of his demon strength to the grip. As Jaxon winced, Malachi leaned forward and whispered in low warning, "But you knew that... didn't you, Jaxon?" Straightening, he gave a mild smile. "Nice to meet you, too. I hope we can all get together again soon. I would love to meet more people who are important to Chuck." He glanced over at her and was pleased to find she was still smiling at him as if he were the only one there.

Backing away, nodding like a sycophant, Jaxon tried to discreetly shake out his hand without letting on it had hurt. "Yeah, absolutely." Turning, he hurried off to his own vehicle.

Malachi bit the inside of his cheek to keep from bursting into laughter. He heard a soft chuckle and turned to face Chuck again.

"Malachi, thanks."

He arched an eyebrow and popped his hands on his hips, adopting a devilish smirk. "Oh, I'm back to being Malachi now, am I?" He shook his head. "Evan? Really? Of all the names in the world, you come up with Evan?"

"I couldn't well call you Malachi and expect Jax to believe you just happen to have the same name as my K-9 partner!" Chuck exclaimed, throwing her hands in the air. "I mean, fuck, Mal, I did the best I could on the spot like that."

Without thinking, Malachi snatched her by the waist and yanked her against his body. She let out a soft oof as she slammed into him, her fingers landing on his chest. "Chuck," he moaned in a strained voice, "do you know what that bad word coming from your sweet lips does to me?" At her choked gasp, he realized what he'd done and said. Letting her go like she'd scalded him, he backed away with eyes wide and lips parted slightly. He knew his normally tan face must be pale as he felt the blood drain from it. Her aura was flickering wildly in her confusion. "I… I'm sorry. Forget I said that. I shouldn't have crossed that line." He jammed his hands in his pockets and hurried away to the passenger side of the car, waiting for her to unlock it.

After a moment, the locks disengaging chirped, and he shuddered out a shaky breath. He cursed himself for a fool, letting his desire slip through. Quickly, he climbed into the passenger seat, clicking his seatbelt and gluing his eyes to the horizon through the windshield.

After a moment, the driver's door opened, and Chuck slipped into her seat. She sat for a minute, not saying anything, then buckled her seatbelt and started the car. Clearing her throat, she put it in drive, then spoke

casually, as if the episode in the parking lot had never happened. "So, I figure we should go pick up Reena, grab some lunch, then head back to the house. We need to figure out how we're going to explain Malachi's disappearance."

He glanced at her, noting the small content smile curving her lips, and smiled back gratefully at her willingness to move past his fuck up. "Thanks," he mumbled.

At Glenda's house, Malachi stayed in the car. He didn't want to face the knowing glances of the witch and needed a moment without Chuck's presence and glowing aura to reset himself. Groaning, he scrubbed his hands over his face in frustration, then pinched the bridge of his nose. "What the hell, Malachi? Don't fuck this up!"

"That's right, Malachi, don't fuck this up." A low chuckle on a waft of decaying flowery scent washed over him, chilling him to his bones.

"Hey, Hyacinth, how's it going, boss man?" Malachi asked lightly.

Snorting, Hyacinth leaned forward from the back seat and rested his filthy, dirt-encrusted claws on Malachi's shoulder.

"I'm just checking in on you. I was hoping to see some progress by now," the lumpy demon hissed.

"I have progress," Malachi insisted. "I made her think she helped me, she wants me to live with her, and we slept in the same bed last night. She almost kissed me earlier, and I made her jealous by flirting with another woman. It won't be long. She'll melt in my hands before you know it, and that angel grace will be pitch black!" The lecherous sneer that accompanied these words was false, but he was adept at showing what he wanted people to see. He radiated confidence and conceit.

Huffing a breath scented with an earthy swampish undertone, Hyacinth nodded slowly. "Well, that's good news. See that it stays that way." He chuckled. "Of course, as much of a coup as this would be, I almost want

to see you fail so I can drop your pain-in-the-ass self down to the pit." His laugh grew more malignant and shiver-inducing. "I'll be going. Get that angel corrupted soon, Malachi." With a squelching sound, Hyacinth sank back down into Hell, laughing low under his breath.

Moments later, Chuck appeared at the door and plunked a slightly pudgier Reena into the backseat. Getting into the driver's seat, she grumbled under her breath about not needing enemies with friends like Glenda. She leaned forward and waved toward the door at the witch, muttering about overfeeding Reena and needing to mind her own damn business.

Malachi simply sat quietly until they reached a red light. He glanced at Chuck, who glanced at him, and they both burst into laughter as Reena snored in her treat-induced stupor.

When Chuck was finally able to get herself under control, just as the light turned green, she smiled in genuine amusement at Malachi. "I have a feeling Reena is going to have a stomach-ache. Can you still talk to her?"

"Yeah, I can send her my thoughts still. The same way I can send them to you," he answered, slouching slightly in the seat. He felt much more at ease, as if their earlier tension were behind them.

Chuck sniffed then and glanced over again. "Hey, do you smell... flowers?"

16

Now He's Fully Naked

After a casual dinner in which Malachi let Chuck teach him how to cook pasta, they were sitting on the couch watching the evening news as usual. The big difference now was that he wasn't lying on the sofa with his head on her lap while she scratched behind his ears. He sat upright on his own cushion, sneaking glances when she wasn't looking and pretending he didn't notice when she did the same.

Sighing, Chuck lifted the remote and clicked the TV off. "Mal," she started, a sad weariness weaved into her voice and crinkling her eyes. "We've been putting this off, but I need to be able to explain why you—K-9 you—isn't around anymore. I'm not good at lying. I used my maximum effort today with Jax, and you saw how that ended." She wrinkled her nose in disgust, no doubt remembering her blurted excuses with chagrin.

Releasing a weary sigh of his own, Malachi rose to his feet. "I think I have a solution. Wait here," he instructed.

A silent nod was her only response as she watched him hurry to the spare bedroom now considered his. Pushing the door almost closed, he hurriedly stripped off his clothes and concentrated, turning himself back

into the silky Malinois form he'd had when he first met Chuck. Once the transformation was complete, he stretched, acclimating himself to four legs again. Shaking out his coat, he glanced at his collar, laughing silently at how he'd woken up from his initial change wearing only that. He idly wondered if that had given Chuck any fantasies.

Nudging the door open with his snout, he trotted back into the living room. His claws clicking on the hardwood floors alerted Chuck, and she was already on her feet when he rounded the corner.

"No! No, no, no, Malachi! Please tell me you didn't trap yourself in that body again just to avoid the issue at work." She dropped to her knees and wrapped her arms around him, burying her face in his scruff. Her hot tears dripped into his fur. "M-Malachi," she sobbed, her aura solid gray with anguish.

Hurrying to reassure her, he woofed happily. *Chuck, it's okay, really. I figured out I could still change into the dog and back. Whatever the spell was, it's still sort of there, but Glenda made it so that I don't have to stay that way. I'll be fine. I can be your K-9 during the day and your human friend at night while we figure this out. Please don't be sad, Chuck. I want to help you the way you've been helping me. Let me earn my keep this way. I promise, I'll be alright.*

Leaning back, Chuck studied him through red-rimmed eyes, sniffling back further tears. "Truly?" she whispered, the question holding a quiet desperation he decided not to point out. "You're not just making that up because you think it's what I want to hear?" Her aura flickered with hope.

Rising on his hind legs, he placed his paws on her shoulders and licked the tears from her face, making her laugh.

"Gross, Mal." She chuckled, swiping away the slobber with her sleeve. "Be serious, you bad dog."

Sitting back on his haunches, Malachi wheezed out a laughing bark. Closing his eyes, he shifted back to man form. When he opened them again, he was kneeling before her, naked. “Shit,” he muttered, grabbing a pillow to cover his nether region. “Forgot about the clothes part. Uh, sorry.” Even though it had been calculated, and he wasn’t the least embarrassed, he put on a good show of blushing. Scrambling to cover himself further with a throw pulled from the sofa, he groaned in what he knew was a convincing manner. Although his motions seemed panicked and quick, he’d actually dawdled some, giving her a slight nudge of his incubus power to enhance her desire for him before he finally got the blanket in place.

Chuck swallowed hard, the sound as loud as an explosion in the silence surrounding them like a heavy cocoon. Neither moved.

Finally, Malachi gave her a sheepish grin. “I’ll just, uh, change back now. If you’re sure you’re comfortable that I can change at will now. I don’t want to worry you, Chuck.”

“Yep, changing is good. Fur or clothes, you pick,” she blurted, her aura turning bright orange with her embarrassment, but he didn’t miss the dark red streaks of lust swirling amongst it.

“Which makes you happier, Chuck?” he asked softly, lifting one hand as if he would touch her, then bit his lip as if he’d thought better of it and lowered it. “I think my human form makes you uncomfortable. Maybe it’s better if I stay fluffy.” His tone was gentle, conveying no judgment for her answer. He smiled slightly, just a small quirk of his lips, but it was the sadness in his eyes that he couldn’t hide that had her moving closer.

Gently, she ran her fingers over his cheek. “Malachi, I’m sorry. I’m a shit friend.” She shook her head and huffed out a rueful laugh when he started to speak. “No, I am. I shouldn’t be making you doubt something like that. Of course I want you to be in your human form as much as you want to. I appreciate that you’re willing to play K-9 for a little while until we figure

this out. Please don't ever think you need to be something or someone else for me. I… care about you a lot, and I just want you to be happy. So, I mean it, Mal, you pick."

Slowly, he leaned against her palm. "Thanks for that. For what it's worth, I think that makes you a great friend, Kelly."

Her eyes widened slightly as he used her actual name instead of the masculine nickname her squad gave her.

Rising to his feet, adjusting the blanket around his waist, he held out a hand to help her stand as well. She reached her shaking hand to grip his, then grunted in surprise when he pulled her up so fast she stumbled into him.

"Sorry." He grimaced. "I forget my strength in this form. It's a whole mindset change." Glancing down into her shocked face, he studied her parted lips. "Kelly?" He smirked slightly, lifting one corner of his lips, his dimple flashing.

"Yeah?"

"If you'll let go of the blanket, I'll go get dressed again. Unless you want to keep it in here, in which case I guess I can walk back naked." He grinned this time, a devilish gleam in his eyes and an exaggerated wiggle of his eyebrows.

Snorting, she smacked him on the chest and laughed. "You're awful! Bad dog!" she chastised teasingly. Leaning back, she let go of the blanket and waved him away. "Go, get dressed. I'm going to get ready for bed. This day has worn me out, and we've got an early shift tomorrow."

Saluting her mockingly, he spun on his heel and marched to his room again, chuckling the whole way.

Hours after they'd all gone to their rooms, Malachi lay in his bed staring at the dark ceiling. Beside him, Reena snored with her raspy little wheeze. She'd dragged her doggie bed into his room with determination, growling at the stubborn material when it caught on the door frame.

Laughing, he'd picked it up and set it at the foot of his bed, shrugging sheepishly at Chuck's wry smile as she watched.

Arms crossed under her breasts; she'd looked a little lonely. She studied the two of them sitting together, then glanced across the hall at her now quieter room. With a sigh and a small shake of her head, she called a soft good night before she hurried to her door, closing it gently behind her. It was quick, but Malachi had seen a flash of sadness cross her features. The slight pinch to her eyes, the downward turn of her lips, spoke volumes even though it was gone as quickly as it appeared.

Groaning, Malachi scrubbed his hands over his face. He couldn't sleep. It was as elusive as a virgin in Hell. Turning on his side, he stared through his open door at Chuck's. He frowned, recalling yet again the war of emotions surging through her as she went to bed. What her face didn't show, her aura revealed clearly. A heavy sigh escaped his lips. He didn't want to push her too hard, but he hated leaving her this conflicted. Now, he felt like a first-class asshole, something he'd never experienced before. He wanted to help her—just one more first.

Sitting up and staring harder at her door, he came to a decision. He gently gathered Reena's bed in his arms to avoid waking her. Muffling his footsteps, he crept to Chuck's door and eased it open, wincing at the slight squeak of the hinges. He glared at them for their audacity and

silently vowed to end the rust's existence by drowning it in oil first thing tomorrow.

Moving nearer to the bed, he noted with relief that she was still asleep. It sent a pang through his chest when he reached the edge and saw how the sheet was twisted around her legs. She was frowning, and he could tell she was not sleeping peacefully. With painstaking slowness, he eased Reena's bed to the floor and straightened, watching Chuck roll to her back with a groan and grimace.

Cursing himself for wanting to kiss away that frown, he began slipping off his clothes before he shimmered into dog form. With a light leap, he landed on the bed like a cloud and gently crept to her side. He froze when a flailing hand smacked into his fur, and she jolted. Then she sighed and murmured, "Malachi," with a curve of her lips before peacefully dropping back into deeper sleep.

Watching to see if she would stir again, he quietly lay next to her and nuzzled her shoulder. A soft arm crept over his back as she turned and snuggled against him. A definite smile now lifted her mouth, and the crease between her eyebrows smoothed out. With a contented deep breath, he closed his eyes and let sleep overtake him. He knew his dreams would be better this night because Chuck was here to keep him safe.

17

It's Not Theft, It's Borrowing

"Malachi!" came a deafening screech that jolted him awake, heart thundering, instincts on high alert, ready to tear apart whoever had dared to threaten Chuck. Sitting bolt upright, he glared around the room, prepared to sink his fangs into the intruder. Seeing no one, he paused in confusion and ran a hand through his thick, wavy hair. As his fingers tangled, his entire body froze, and sick dread churned his stomach. Hand. Hair. It should have been paw. Fur.

Glancing down at the sheet pooled around his waist, Malachi slowly turned his head towards Chuck. He was pretty sure he knew now why she'd shrieked. "Um..." He curved his lips slightly, flashing his dimple, hoping it would help. "Good morning?"

A wheezy laugh from Reena was the only sound that followed his greeting.

Clearing his throat, he scooted away from Chuck slightly. "This is *not* what it looks like," he pleaded, holding his hands up defensively.

Chuck stared at him with wide eyes before her lips curled up into a wicked grin. "Really? Malachi? Really? Because I'm pretty sure it looks like

I went to bed alone and just woke up to you in bed with me. Naked. So, if not that, then what?"

Raking both hands through his hair, then rubbing them over his chin, he chuckled low. "Okay, fair, it is what it looks like. But not why!"

She started to speak, but he clapped a hand over her mouth. A move that had them both staring in surprise.

Lowering his palm slowly, he laughed again, nervously this time. "Sorry. But I wanted to explain. Last night, you looked sad, and I couldn't get that expression out of my mind. And I couldn't sleep. I had more nightmares." At her sympathetic noise and nod, he pressed on. "So, I was just bringing Reena in here to keep you company. Anyway, I noticed you were tossing and turning. It seemed like you were having a nightmare, too. And I've never seen that happen to you. So, I got in bed with you."

Chuck coughed slightly and raised an eyebrow as she drawled, "Clearly."

"As the dog," he clarified dryly. "I changed into the dog and let you hold on to me that way. You relaxed then. You even smiled. So, I slept here. I swear, though, Chuck, I was the dog when I fell asleep. I must have changed back subconsciously. I didn't mean to scare you." He shrugged his shoulders lamely and gave her an apologetic glance from under his dark eyelashes. He had used that same glance countless times to seduce other women, but his intention this time was to get her to believe him.

"I believe you," she replied. "I thought I dreamt it, though." Running a hand over her own hair, she shook her head. "I *was* having a bad dream before about my dad and his murder. The day I heard the news. You expect that as a police officer's family. You expect that one day you'll get that call, but you pray hard it won't be you. I don't know, my dad just always seemed indestructible."

Shaking his head, Malachi murmured, "You have no idea."

"What?"

"I said, I have no idea. I can't imagine what that was like. How hard that must have been for you. Your dad sounds like a great guy, and I'm so sorry you lost him like that." To his eternally damned surprise, it was true. Although he guessed he shouldn't be surprised anymore, everything he thought he knew about himself was being turned upside down by Chuck—a half angel in form-fitting polyester.

Nodding slowly, she continued, "And then, in my dream, when I was crying, you showed up and hugged me. I guess that must have been when you got in bed with me. I knew you were there, so you appeared in my dream. Thanks, Malachi. It's nice that you care." She gave him a warm smile before her eyes widened in alarm. "Shit! Look at the time! Gonna be late if we don't get moving!"

Malachi was on the verge of asking her which version of him had comforted her in the dream, human or dog, but her panic had him jumping from the bed.

"Mal!" she squealed, covering her eyes.

Glancing down, he realized he'd forgotten, truly this time, that he was naked. He quickly shimmered into dog form and barked, letting her know it was safe to look.

Muttering to herself about illegal bodies, she hurried to the bathroom to shower and dress.

Grinning, Malachi flopped next to Reena. *Hey, kiddo, doing okay with all of this?*

Reena sneezed so hard her tail straightened, then she panted after the happiest little woof ever.

Good to know. So, you know what's going on now with the demons and stuff, right? He studied her closely and sighed in relief at her grumble of understanding. *Alright, just... don't tip Chuck off, okay? I don't want to hurt her. I promise I don't. I'm going to help her figure out who killed her dad.*

Reena stood and barked happily before spinning around in crazy circles, making her piggy snorts of approval. It would seem she liked this plan.

Slow down, turbo tailgate, he chuckled, amused at her antics. *I don't want Chuck to know for a bit. I don't want to get her hopes up if I can't find anything.* He glanced over his shoulder at the bathroom door and calculated how much longer Chuck would be. Hurrying to his room, he shifted back and quickly grabbed a change of clothes. Nothing fancy, just light enough that if he needed to be human, he wouldn't have to scramble for a hiding spot due to nudity. A police station was the last place he wanted to explain being naked.

Running out to the living room, he piled it on the couch and shifted back to dog form, collar around his neck already. He'd damn near giggled putting it on in human form, and he'd never giggled before in his life.

Chuck hurried into the room, tightening her belt, pausing when she saw Malachi waiting. "How did you get your own collar on?" Then her cheeks flushed a bright pink as she realized how he might accomplish it. Her embarrassed gaze became a murderous squint as he laughed at her. The wheezing huff recognizable even in his canine form. "Yeah, yeah, laugh it up, mister. What's with the clothes?"

I want to put them in a bag and take them with us. Just in case, he sent to her. *Never know when I may need to be... Evan, ugh... again.* His tone was nonchalant, and he managed not to vomit when he thought of the name. It was close, though.

Chuck tapped her pointer finger on her lips thoughtfully before nodding slowly. She held up her finger in a wait gesture, then hurried to her bedroom.

Malachi could hear her rummaging around before she ran back in, a drawstring sack held triumphantly in her fist. "Just the thing! I can put your clothes in here, and either one of us can carry them easily." Quickly,

she suited action to words and had his clothes, shoes, and even a hairbrush in the bag. "Because when you change, sometimes your hair is a little wild," she explained.

Why are you so obsessed with my hair? he teased.

"I'm not!" she snapped, then shook her head with chagrin. "Okay, maybe a little. It's such a pretty color. I've never seen someone naturally have hair that black before. I mean, lots of people have black hair, but yours is so vibrant. Which doesn't really make sense about that color. But it's almost iridescent like a raven's wings. It's beautiful, really. And you have so much of it." She stopped rambling, and her cheeks heated again. Standing taller, she smirked. "Well, enough about you. Wouldn't want your ego to get any bigger than it already is."

Bursting into laughter, Malachi let the insult go because he was too busy thinking about how much she truly paid attention to his appearance. That she had studied his hair that closely, it warmed him from the inside in a much more comforting way than the time his cousin Flick had dared him to eat a piece of brimstone when they were children. This reminder of his demonhood had him shaking off the warm feeling, picturing Hyacinth's threats. He sobered and fell in line, trotting next to her so they could get to work, and he could keep corrupting her. If there was a small voice in the back of his mind, jeering, it was the other way around; he ignored it.

When they arrived at the station, they were both heartily greeted by the rest of the squad as they settled in for the day. At her desk, Chuck reviewed some reports and checked her messages. Sighing heavily, she ab-

sently rubbed between his ears. "This is the non-glamorous part you don't see on television," she confided. "But... alas... paperwork makes the world go round."

Yeah, about that. I uh... I want to check on a couple of things. Do you mind? He sent his thoughts carefully and innocently, as if his only goal was to go potty and sucker the guys into some bacon.

"Sure, that's fine, just be back in thirty, we have to head over to a school for a demonstration." Negligently, she shooed him away without watching to see where he went.

Silently, he grabbed his change of clothes and trotted off to the back room where he knew records were kept. He muffled his collar—so nothing jingled—and slipped some shadows over his body to deflect attention. He wasn't truly invisible, but it made him unmemorable if someone asked if he'd been seen.

Slinking low past the counter, he located a darkened corner just on the edge of the camera range. He concentrated, sending a quick burst of power into it. Just enough to give it wavy static and blur the image. Then he rapidly shifted to human form and slipped on his clothes. Once dressed, he hurried down the aisles until he came to where he smelled the stronger scent of angelic grace. Grabbing the container, he snuck back to the corner with his prize.

Opening the evidence box gave him a blast of scent that nearly blew back his hair. The smell was undeniably angelic; this had to be Chuck's father's case. Sure enough, he found the surname Charles and dug into the files within. Glancing around to double-check no one was watching, he stuffed some of the files in his bag. He took some heavy sniffs of the rest, committing those other milder scents to memory.

A scuffling noise had him cursing in his head, worried he was going to get caught. Quickly, he began cramming the remaining things back into

the box haphazardly before slapping the lid on. He lurched to his feet and crept down the aisle, shoving the container on the shelf with a scraping sound that had him wincing.

"Hello?" called a wavering female voice.

Fuck, Janice, he nearly panicked and shucked his clothes, squashing them in the bag with the files. Frantically, he shifted back into dog form before snatching the sack in his mouth and rushing out. He remembered to quiet his sounds, so Janice didn't hear him trotting towards her. His shadows still clung to his fur, so he was able to slip past her undetected. He still held his breath as he slunk lower, forcing himself into the dark baseboards in the neglected hallway.

"Huh," Janice murmured as he rounded the corner, her voice fading with the distance. "I could have sworn I heard something."

Hurrying back to the squad room where Chuck waited, Malachi almost ran into Jaxon. He hadn't been looking too closely where he was going; he was so focused on making sure he wasn't followed.

"Hey, Malachi! Hey, buddy!" called Jaxon with exaggerated cheerfulness. The smarmy bastard eyed him carefully, then took a step back. "Shouldn't you be with Chuck?" he laughed in a false tone that set Malachi's teeth on edge. "Where have you been, huh?"

Not having the patience for any of Jaxon's fake bullshit, he merely loosed a short growl and swerved around the douchecanoe so he could hurry back to Chuck.

Despite his usual lack of brains, Jaxon had enough sense to realize Malachi didn't like him and jumped back with alacrity. "Good to see you, Malachi; good doggie!" he called after the retreating form of the canine who would gladly piss on him even if he wasn't on fire unless Chuck asked him not to, of course. Well, maybe.

Catching sight of Chuck, he romped the last few feet to her and woofed excitedly, shoving the bag into her hands.

Her expression changed from happiness at seeing him to puzzlement as she took the bag. No doubt she'd noticed it being heavier than it should be. "Mal... what..." she started, a small crease between her eyebrows the only outward sign an onlooker would notice that something wasn't quite right.

Shhh, he cautioned.

To her credit, Chuck immediately went into a joyful-to-see-him mode and ruffled his ears. "Who's a good boy? That's you! That's my Mal-Mal," she gushed.

Don't make me puke on you, he warned. He tried to hide his laugh with a cough, but she wasn't fooled.

A large grin curved her full lips into a beautiful smile that felt like a ray of warm sunshine on his fur.

Fuck me, he kept to himself. *I'm in so much deep shit here.*

"What did you do?" Chuck whispered in his ear while stroking his back like she would do if nothing were amiss. "Were you a bad dog?"

Hide that bag, he instructed. *Take it to the car, and I'll explain everything in a bit, okay? Please trust me. Kelly, please.*

"Of course I trust you, Malachi."

18

Stay! Good Girl

True to her word, Chuck locked the bag up in his compartment where he could keep an eye on it. They completed their outreach program at the school, both declaring it a success, though they had different definitions of that term. Chuck signed up a higher-than-usual number of students for the junior ride-along program, and Malachi corrupted several teachers and the principal. The librarian was the easiest one to convince. He was a sucker for a woman in sensible glasses and no-nonsense heels. She'd practically begged to have her soul smudged. He knew just the demon to seduce her and made a mental note to call Mephistopheles later.

Chuck was quiet in the driver's seat, studying him curiously in the mirror. Finally, she groaned. "Okay, fine. You're going to make me ask. What was that all about, Malachi? Where did you go? I have a feeling that wasn't an innocent bacon run back at the station. You were up to something. I'm sure it was inappropriate, or you wouldn't be hiding things. Are you going to tell me?" She was shaking her head now with a bemused smile, the corners of her eyes crinkling.

Can we wait until we get home tonight? I don't want to distract you from your work. He tilted his head and scrunched his fluffy eyebrows in a way he was sure would melt her.

Snorting, she pulled over and parked, then turned to face him. "Don't. Don't give me literal puppy dog eyes. You know I can't resist that, you handsome lump of fur!"

You think I'm handsome? he teased. *Like... are we talking Johnny Depp handsome in a dark, brooding way? Or Chris Hemsworth in a ripped god kind of way? Ohhh... Alan Ritchson. Now that guy could have me on my knees.* He smirked as her mouth worked in stunned silence, taking in what he'd just said. He knew she meant handsome as a dog, but he'd also seen the way her eyes drank him in as a human as well. Still high on the glee from his success in liberating the files, he couldn't resist teasing Chuck.

Finally, she shook her head. "You're too much, Mal. Anyway... quit deflecting. Are you going to tell me or not?"

Just then, her radio came to life, and the squawking had him wheezing out a corny laugh. *Saved by the radio,* he sent, repeating her phrase from before.

Glaring at him, she pointed one finger menacingly as she responded to the dispatcher. Once she logged the details, her expression changed to all business. "Hang on, buddy, we've got a kidnapping."

Arriving on scene with a screech of tires, Chuck and Malachi took in the scene of chaos around them. His ears flattened as he caught a whiff of demon when Chuck opened her door. A high keening whine slipped from his throat before he could stop it.

"Mal?" Chuck paused at the door of the vehicle.

Turning his eyes to her, he pressed his nose against the grate. *Be careful, there's something bad out there. Something that wants to hurt everyone. I can smell it.*

Wrinkling her nose, trying to detect whatever he was sensing, she shook her head firmly. "Got it. Come on out with me so you can watch my back." She hit the release and clipped his leash quickly. "Let's go," she murmured.

Sticking close to her side, Malachi pressed his body as near to her as he could without tripping her.

"Chuck!" came a call as the scene lieutenant from their first mission waved them over. "Malachi, hey, buddy!" the officer greeted excitedly, this time with an eager smile. "Sorry to pull you from so far, but we're gonna need Malachi on this one. His nose is incredible, and time is of the essence. We've got a carjacking, but there was a pretty sick kiddo inside. The mother was shoved out of the car, and the suspect took off out there." He gestured towards a large field surrounded by a dense forest. "Abandoned the car, but no sign of the child. Mother is en route with the officers who initially responded. The little girl needs medicine; she has a heart condition of some kind. We think he took off that way." He pointed towards the left side of the field, then glanced back at Malachi. "But I'm open to whatever this guy thinks."

Malachi hurriedly approached the vehicle. He took a good, thorough whiff and caught the underlying scent of the little girl's sickness. His heart sank; this didn't seem good. She was very ill, and they needed to hurry. Dancing uneasily on his paws, he whimpered slightly as he moved to the driver's seat. He smelled the mother, a clean, wholesome scent, and then he honed in on the suspect. The scent dropped his stomach to his toes. It was demonic. The one he'd caught wind of when they first arrived. And it was no run-of-the-mill lower demon. This was someone on Hyacinth's level. They didn't usually stoop to petty crime or kidnapping. Something else was going on here.

Shit, he thought frantically, then turned, sniffing the air and closing his eyes, letting his senses roam. The smell of brimstone was everywhere, and

he was surprised the humans couldn't smell it. Although the way they kept shifting their weight and glancing around warily let him know they weren't entirely immune to it either.

He homed in on the direction the scent took him, and it was indeed the field. Alerting, he pulled Chuck towards the tall, yellowed grass and urged her to hurry.

"Okay, Mal, retrieve!" She unclipped him, and he took off like a shot.

Chuck made a surprised noise in her throat at the speed at which he launched. His natural Malinois speed was enhanced by his demon powers, and he flew through the field. He continued, knowing she'd never keep up, but he had to hurry if they wanted this little girl alive. Loping through the grass, he reached the edge quickly and disappeared just inside the tree line. He approached a small stone hut with a historical marker outside indicating it had stood for a long time. The desolate air of abandonment surrounding the area made it an ideal creepy place for a demon to spirit away a child and steal their soul. The tall, heavy stand of trees kept the ground dappled in shade dark enough that it seemed like early evening, although it was just after noon.

Pausing outside, Malachi crouched low and listened intently, trying to get a sense of where everyone was positioned. He could hear the ragged breathing of the small child, but no other sounds or movement. That didn't mean anything; he had muffled his own sounds, but he also didn't sense the other demon inside. Slowly, he crept closer, nearly dragging his belly across the ground, and peered through the open doorway. The little girl was curled in on herself, clutching a small, bedraggled stuffed giraffe, her eyes wide in fright as she lay on the packed dirt floor, surrounded by dead leaves and other detritus.

After a quick survey of the interior, Malachi was certain the demon had left the child alone. He slunk in warily, senses on high alert, expecting a

trap. When he reached the tiny girl, he peered into her frightened eyes and sent a wave of calm to her. She immediately stopped trembling and stretched her tiny fingers out to pet him.

"Puppy!" she squealed in relief. "Are you... Mawachi?" she asked in a thin, breathy little voice.

Nodding, he focused sharply on her, confused how she would know to ask.

"The other man said you gonna find me, but you gotta watch out." Her lips trembled as she relayed the message. "He said... I haff to tell you... Hi... Hiya... Hiya-since is twying to twick you." She nodded solemnly, and her eyes filled with tears. "Puppy... I want my mommy!" she wailed. Her tiny body shook with her fear again, and he could hear her heart beating irregularly, stressed by her ordeal.

Spinning to the door, Malachi barked sharply, alerting Chuck of his location, and went back to the child, leaning against her in comfort while contemplating her words. Another demon was trying to send him a message. Apparently, Hyacinth was messing with him. *What else is new?* he thought in disgust. But why go through such lengths to get the word to him?

"Mal?" came Chuck's quiet call.

He could hear her hesitant footsteps and the jaggedness in her breathing. A soft woof meant to guide was rewarded with a quickening of her pace and a soft sigh of relief. Appearing in the doorway, Chuck cleared the room before holstering her weapon. "Good job, Mal." She briefly patted him before crouching by the little girl. "Hi, Analisa? My name is Officer Charles, but my friends call me Chuck. You're safe now, okay? Your mommy is on her way, and we're going to take you to her, alright?" Her tone was soft and light, designed to soothe and comfort.

Malachi noticed that when she used it, her aura glowed gold. Pure heart and grace washed through Chuck in these moments, and Malachi couldn't help the awe that filled him. Normally, an expression of grace would have him cowering or vomiting, but now he wanted to stare at it all day, drinking in the beauty of it. Realizing Chuck was rising and scooping the little girl in her arms, Malachi stood quickly, pressing to her side, warily conveying the importance of getting out of there. The demon may have left the child alone, but he didn't trust that it wasn't still waiting somewhere out there.

As they hurried back to the rendezvous point, a team of medical personnel met them in the field and took over care of the child. A shrill cry and blur of color announced the arrival of the little girl's mother. She rushed forward, medication in hand, waving frantically.

Squatting in the grass, Chuck scratched Malachi's ears. "That was awesome, Mal, I'm really impressed how quickly you found her." She leaned closer. "What about that bad smell you detected earlier? The suspect? Any sign?"

Malachi was about to tell her the suspect had fled when a sharp cracking came from deep in the trees. His head turned quickly towards the sound, and his nostrils flared as the breeze carried the scent of brimstone to him. The demon was back, hiding somewhere in the woods. He crouched low, telling her, *he's there, in the trees. Stay back, Chuck, this guy is super dangerous.* Slinking across the ground, he wove through the grass towards the edge of the trees and peered into the shadows.

"Mal," came Chuck's fierce call from over his shoulder.

Fuck, he cursed to himself. He was so focused on tracking the demon that he didn't realize Chuck was following him. His head whipped around, and he glared. *Stay. Put.* He growled for emphasis, and a pang of sorrow coursed through him at her startled and uncertain expression. *Sorry... Chuck, I... this guy is really dangerous. I don't want you to get hurt.*

With a wry smile, the flickering yellow in her aura solidified into streaks of pink and gold. “Mal, I’m a trained police officer, and I have a gun. You’re in more danger than I am. I’m not letting you get hurt either.” She crouched next to him.

Trust me on this, Chuck, I promise I’m better prepared to deal with him. He’s not quite... human. He swallowed heavily, afraid to get too close to the truth.

Chuck’s eyes widened, and her mouth parted slightly as she rocked back on her heels. “Not... human?”

Stay, he warned again as he crept into the shadows. He didn’t pray, but if he could, he would be begging every god out there that she listened. Pausing next to a particularly wide tree with low-hanging branches, he cautiously sniffed and angled himself towards the demon. As he moved closer, he knew it had him in its sight, but it wasn’t moving. Away or towards him. He paused, puzzled. Did the demon want to be found? Was this the trap?

A flicker of movement caught his eye, and he focused in on the form of the man crouching behind a large clump of twisting vines.

The man was gesturing for Malachi to come closer. He glanced nervously over his shoulder and gestured again, more impatiently this time.

Inching nearer, Malachi suddenly relaxed as he realized who was waving at him. Rising to normal height, he trotted closer. *Rikael, you ass. What the hell are you doing? Damn, I haven’t seen you in at least a decade! What’s with the stunt with that kid?*

“Malachi, sorry, but no time for small talk. Look, you gotta be careful. Hyacinth has it out for you. Bad,” Rikael whispered furiously.

Yeah, no shit. I’m a fucking dog, Rik. He rolled his eyes. Although the closest thing to a friend he’d had, Rikael was not known for being the brightest crayon in the carton.

The demon shook his head quickly. "No, it's more than that. He's sabotaging you! He already knew about the angel cop, that's why he put you in the dog body in the first place. He wanted you to get close to her so he could have you corrupt her and take her grace. He's got no intention of giving her to Lucifer; he's making a power play."

Squinting his eyes and staring at him in concern, Malachi slowly shook his head side to side. *Rik, he's always doing that. Power plays are part of our makeup. We're demons. I don't understand what you're so worried about.*

Grabbing his hair and pulling hard, Rikael groaned in exasperation. "No, Malachi, it's not just that. He has to sacrifice a demon *and* an angel together. He's going to kill you! He sent Bakeeron to snatch the kid so he could get you two out here. I distracted him so he'd leave her in that building, then gave her a message to warn you. But he'll be back any second! You need to watch your..." A wet gurgle interrupted his speech as a razor-sharp talon erupted from his throat with a spray of blood.

Malachi leapt back in surprise as demon ichor arced towards him. *What the...* His thoughts scrambled into a jumbled mess, bouncing around his skull like ping pong balls as a large form rose in front of him, grinning with sadistic glee. *Fuck! CHUCK! RUN! RUN AS FAST AS YOU CAN! GET OUT OF HERE NOW!*

19

Hitting Trees Hurts

Laughing evilly, the demon—Malachi presumed this was Bakeeron—launched itself towards his smaller canine form and tried to grab his head between its massive paws. Quickly, Malachi twisted away, his lithe body slipping through the demon's claws. Roaring in frustration, the large, ungainly beast lunged again. It towered at least eight feet in height and sported talons nearly six inches long. Fangs that would be at home on a sabertoothed tiger hung from its heavy muzzle. Yellow eyes with slit pupils like a snake narrowed on him as the demon growled, missing its prey yet again. Its large size was a detriment as it kept trying to grab the much smaller dog's body, and Malachi planned to keep using it to his advantage.

Snarling, Malachi spun and latched his teeth onto the demon's calf, biting as hard as he could. He shook his head, worrying his fangs deeper into muscle, and yanked the demon to the ground. It flailed at him but howled in anger when it couldn't reach. It started to get up again, then froze as it whipped its head towards the tree line.

"Malachi!" yelled Chuck, her voice strained with worry over the sounds of the demons fighting.

Lucifer's saggy tits! Malachi groaned. *Stubborn-ass woman.*

The demon used his moment of distraction to fling him off its leg and into a tree. The impact shook the giant pine, raining needles all over him and forcing a pained moan from his throat.

"Malachi!" Chuck screamed at the sound.

He heard her charging forward recklessly. Trying to stand, his legs wobbled and gave out, sending him crashing back to the ground. His vision wavered, and he had a very real fear that something was broken inside of him. A whine hissed through his teeth as he tried again to stand.

The other demon had shifted into human form and smiled menacingly before it turned towards Chuck, hands up. "Help!" Bakeeron called, "Someone attacked that dog! Help!" Now in man form, his tone was frantic and pleading, his face scrunched up in innocent worry.

Chuck paused, taking in the scene, the scuff marks, Malachi, the blood on the ground.

"What did you do to Malachi?" she demanded.

The demon reeled back in shock. "Me? I didn't do anything! I heard the fight and came running. I found him like that." He gestured at Malachi's limp form. "The guy went that way!" He pointed behind him with a feigned smile.

Staring at the man with uncertainty, Chuck kept her eyes trained on her suspect while speaking to her partner. "Mal?" she called softly.

Don't trust him! He's the one who took the little girl!

"Yeah, nice try, asshole, but there's a dead body behind you. Funny you missed that part," Chuck drawled casually, as she kept her gun trained on him. She smirked, "Turn around with your hands behind your head."

"What?" Bakeeron shrieked, "I didn't do anything! I saw the body, but it was obvious he was dead. I was trying to help Malachi!" His eyes were wide with forced innocence.

"And yet, you knew Malachi was the dog? Not the dead guy?" Chuck declared with clear disbelief in her tone. "Look, I don't know who you are, or rather what you are, but I do know if you don't turn around right now with your hands up, it's going to get a lot messier."

Snarling, the demon clenched his fists and snapped his elongating fangs at Chuck. Then he took one step towards her, and she fired her weapon. The bullet struck his arm, spinning him to the side as the echo of the shot rang through the stillness in the trees. Birds that had been silently watching startled and flew off, scrambling to get away from the mayhem. Pausing as the air filled with the smell of cordite, Bakeeron glanced at the wound and watched sluggish black blood trickle from the hole with an amused expression. Rolling his eyes, he turned back to her. "What a naughty little girl." His mouth stretched in a mocking rictus of insanity, fangs lengthening further before lurching towards her again as he roared.

Head shot! Malachi sent her, before shifting to human form. Curled on the ground, naked except for his collar, he croaked out, "Between the eyes, Chuck!" He groaned, clutching his ribs and wheezing, "It's the only way to take him down!"

Without hesitation, Chuck squeezed the trigger, putting a round right between the demon's surprised wide eyes. A small gasp escaped his lips before he dropped to the ground. His human body simply collapsed in on itself and fell into an ungainly heap, looking for all the world like he'd fallen asleep, except for the neatly placed hole in the middle of his forehead of course.

Running to Malachi, Chuck dropped to her knees and gently pulled him to her. "Oh shit, Malachi, talk to me, how bad is it? Do I need to call an ambulance?" She grabbed her radio and was ready to signal for help. Already, they could hear the shouts as the other officers on scene responded to the sound of shots fired.

"No, no ambulance. Gotta stay with you. Just need ice," he wheezed, shaking his head frantically, his dark hair floating around his face.

"Malachi, you're hurt!" she cried. "You need help!"

Shaking his head again, more vehemently this time, he turned his eyes on her, pleading. "Please, Chuck, no. I just need to lie down. I'll be okay. I can't go to the hospital. How are you going to explain me being here? Or the missing dog? You don't understand. They're after you!"

The crashing of feet trampling the underbrush caught his ears, and he shifted back to his canine form, laying his head on her lap and whining low in his throat, begging her to listen. *Please, Chuck. I need to protect you.*

"Okay, Malachi," she whispered as the others neared. "Only because I trust you, but you're going to explain this when we get home." She glanced at the body. "Shit, I need a better excuse for shooting him than my dog told me to."

Got you, he gasped. He concentrated and formed a long, wicked knife from the ether, then dropped it in the dead demon's hand. It was shaped like one of his nasty talons and should match the wound in the other man's throat. He flopped back, exhausted.

Chuck's astonished gaze flitted between him and the knife. "A lot of explaining," she declared, then turned to face her peers. "I'm okay!" she reassured. "Had to take him down. He hurt Malachi!"

"Son-of-a... Chuck! Are you sure you're okay?" demanded the lieutenant. "Oh damn, what happened to Malachi?" His eyebrows were bunched in concern, and there were deep furrows around his mouth as he frowned hard. "Do we need the vet?"

Malachi made a brave show of standing, trying hard to keep his legs from wobbling. He gave a lighthearted woof to prove he was okay while each breath felt like glass shards slicing through his lungs. It was becoming

clearer he might have a broken rib or three. Not that he would admit as much here. He just needed to sleep, and his demon powers would heal it.

"That's our suspect. Malachi tracked him, but the bastard tossed Mal into a tree after stabbing that other guy in the throat. He came at me, and I tagged him on the shoulder, but he kept going. Had to take him down." Chuck's report was delivered in a flat monotone, no emotions revealed, but her aura was laced with fear, doubt, and regret for having to lie.

The lieutenant studied them both, then nodded. "Get him checked out, then I need a full report. You understand there will be a review of this before you can resume normal duties, but you guys probably need the rest anyway. Good work, Chuck, Malachi. You're quite the team." With a stiff nod, he began barking orders to the rest of the officers and had their forensics team set up to collect evidence.

Leaning down to his ear where no one else could hear, Chuck asked, "Mal, can you make it back to the car? Or do I need to carry you?"

Concern for him was streaking her aura now, overriding her guilt at lying to the others. Malachi knew he should be happy; he was corrupting her as he should be. But it was a hollow victory because he didn't want to hurt her. Or dim those colors. Sighing, he leaned heavily against her legs. *I can make it if we go slow. And I'm going to need to get back to human ASAP.*

One short nod and Chuck rose. "Gonna take Malachi outta here, get him checked," she mumbled to the others.

A distracted, halfhearted wave was the response, so she moved back toward the field, slowly making her way to her vehicle.

"Chuck!" came the lieutenant's voice. "Let me know what the vet says, okay?"

A feeble, "Will do!" slipped from her lips as she glanced at Malachi from the corner of her eye.

He could see she was biting the inside of her cheek, trying not to laugh at the idea of taking him to the vet. *No,* he advised firmly, *we are not going to the fucking vet. Do you know where they'll stick the thermometer?*

20

Handcuffs and Collars Optional

In the car, Malachi winced and let out an involuntary whimper as he jumped into the back. He turned and noticed Chuck's forehead scrunched in concern. Her lips were compressed into a thin line, and she shook her head. Holding up a shaking finger, she ran to the front seat and grabbed a coat and blanket she kept in an emergency pack. She hurried back and created a cushion for him to rest on. With a heavy sigh, he sank onto it gratefully. *Thanks, Chuck. That helps a lot.*

With a silent nod, Chuck closed the compartment and scurried to the driver's door before climbing inside. She started the vehicle, then just sat there, staring through the windshield.

Malachi gazed at the back of her head, puzzled, until he heard a small sniffle. Alarmed, he raised up slightly. *Chuck?* he called softly, *Are you okay? What's wrong?*

Spinning to face him, a tear trailed down her cheek as her eyes trailed over him. "What's wrong? Malachi, you're injured! I let you go in alone because you wanted to protect me, and you got *hurt.* I should have come

with you. I should have protected you! You're my partner, and it's my job to keep you safe. You were injured on my watch. Dammit... Mal... I'm so sorry." Another sniffle and deep breath as she tried to hold back the tears.

She's crying over me? Because I got hurt? Malachi thought with wonder. No one had ever cared about him like this, and he wasn't sure what to do. It didn't make sense. She was a cop, part angel. He was a demon, part incubus. They should be at war, hate each other. But he could see fear and guilt in her aura. Even more wondrous... were the streaks of red now flitting through her glow. He wasn't quite sure what it all meant, but he knew she felt strongly enough about him that it pained her when he'd been injured.

Chuck, he called quietly, *it's not your fault. I knew what I was getting into. I knew that guy was dangerous. Be honest, what would have happened if you'd been thrown into a tree? I have some abilities... like Glenda. I'll be okay. It hurts now, but I just need to rest, and I'll be alright. He would have killed you, Chuck. I... I couldn't live with that.*

She shrugged hard then shook her head vehemently. "But I can't live with you getting hurt either!"

Blinking, Malachi shimmered to human form and stuck his hand through the small window, gently running his fingers over her cheek. His breath caught when she closed her eyes and leaned against his palm. "Chuck... Kelly," he whispered. He opened his mouth to say more, but a sharp rap on the window had him snatching back his hand and shifting to canine rapidly.

Startled, Chuck quickly turned and rolled down the window. "Hey, Jax, what's up?" she called cheerfully, trying to clear her throat discreetly.

"Chuck, I heard you and Malachi had a scuffle with our suspect," Jaxon explained slowly, peering behind her. "Who's in here with you?" His eyes were squinted, trying to see in the dim interior of the vehicle.

"Who's... what do you mean? It's just Malachi and me. He got a little banged up, so I was just making sure he was comfortable before I took him home. He's moving kind of slow, but I think he's going to be okay." She tried to smile convincingly to make her point.

Jaxson smiled back. "Yeah, weird. I could have sworn you were talking to someone."

"I was. I was talking to Malachi, reassuring him and such. It's good to talk to your partner; it helps build that bond. And strengthen the partnership. I mean, that's what the trainer said, not sure how much I buy into that. But it seems to help. We are pretty in tune, you know." Chuck stopped with a slight grimace, realizing she was babbling and overexplaining.

Jaxon simply stared at her in concern, a slight quirk of his lips as he studied her flushed cheeks and bright eyes. "Were you... Crying, Chuck?" came his quiet question. It was filled with soft sincerity, and Malachi narrowed his eyes, thinking that if the dickhead tried to hug her, he would bite him.

Sighing, her shoulders sagged slightly. "A little. I was just so worried about Malachi. I really care about him. He's a great partner, and he means a lot to me. The thought of him being injured hit me a little hard, but I'm alright now. He's okay. I'm going to take him home and give him a steak." She huffed out a little laugh.

Malachi let out a happy-sounding woof at the mention of steak, playing along with the charade. He was careful not to grimace despite the pain the sound caused his ribs.

Smirking now, Jaxon shook his head. "Well, I guess talking to him helps, because he seems to know the S word." He chuckled and ran a hand through his frosted tips like he was in a re-run of Miami Vice.

Yeah, I know lots of S words, douche, Malachi grumped uncharitably, *like stupid simpering smarmy snake and shady slithery shit-head sucker.*

Chuck squeaked out a small choking sound, hearing Malachi's comment. "Yep, he definitely knows S words."

Smiling, thinking she was amused by him, Jaxon leaned one arm on the door and grinned. "So, how's the boyfriend?"

Startled, Chuck jerked back. "Boyfriend?" she blurted.

"Yeah, the guy at the store. Malachi's former owner. What was his name... Evan?"

"Oh, yeah. Evan. Well... I wouldn't say he's my boyfriend. More of a friend who's a boy but um... yeah, he's fine."

Malachi chuckled. *Oh yeah, Evan's just fine. Other than lying in the back of a police car with two or three broken ribs, trying not to laugh and make it worse. Not even any handcuffs to keep me entertained.* He laughed again as Chuck blushed, then groaned, unable to help it as the movement twinged his broken bones.

Chuck sobered quickly, her eyes flying to him in the mirror. "Yeah, Jax, I gotta go. I need to get Malachi home and comfortable. Maybe take him to the vet if he's not better by tomorrow. Catch you later!" She jammed her finger on the window button, Jaxon barely jumping back as the glass rose quickly. A half-hearted wave, and she put the car in gear, taking off with a spray of gravel.

After they were back on the main road, she glared in the mirror. "Dammit, Malachi. Broken ribs? I didn't know it was that bad! I'm taking you to the vet or the hospital. You pick."

Shimmering back to human form, Malachi grabbed the blanket and wrapped it around his waist, wincing at the movement. "No, Chuck, seriously, I'm okay. I mean, yeah, I've got some broken ribs, but there's nothing a hospital or a vet can do for me. I just need to sleep in this form,

and I'll be fine. I promise. Please, Chuck, just let me get in my bed and take a nap, and I swear I'll be so much better."

Meeting his gaze once more, she sighed, her shoulders drooping with resignation. "Fine. I'll trust you again. But if you're lying to me, I swear I will take you to the vet and tell them to use the biggest thermometer they have."

Stifling a smile, he deadpanned, "Don't threaten me with a good time, sweetheart."

Another of her cute, choked squeaks escaped her lips, and she finally shook her head. "Malachi..." She paused, then burst into laughter. "You really are something else, Mal."

"Were you serious about the steak? That sounds really good, you know." He smiled at her innocently and batted his eyes.

Catching his performance in the mirror, she snorted, then her expression softened. "For saving that little girl and for being brave, yeah, I'd say you deserve a steak. How about this, I'll go to the store and get some things for dinner while you take this magical restorative nap. Deal?"

"Deal."

At the house, Malachi shifted back into dog form so the neighbors—especially Muriel—wouldn't wonder why Chuck was escorting a naked man up her sidewalk. At the last second, he twisted to pick up the bag of evidence, then whimpered at the pain the maneuver caused.

"I got it," Chuck called softly. She grabbed the bag, then helped him out of the car and into the house. As he went down the hall towards his room,

she stopped him. “No, Mal, go lie in my bed. It’s more comfortable, and you’re a big guy, so you need the space.”

Surprised, Malachi shifted to human form and looked up at her from his crouched position on the floor. “Thanks, Chuck.” He rose to his full height and smiled, staring down at her now. Still grinning, he slipped on the shorts she was holding out while studiously averting her gaze. Turning, he walked to her room instead, aware of her gaze on his back where large dark purple bruises spread over his skin like a map of his pain. The ugly marks wrapped from his spine around his side and tapered off around his navel.

“Mal.” Her voice shook with concern, then she choked out: “Oh, the collar.”

He reached up to unfasten it but hissed at the movement, dropping his arm and clutching his side.

“Let me,” she offered softly from behind him.

He could feel the heat of her body close to his skin and closed his eyes, enjoying it.

“Damn, you’re tall,” she muttered, stretching on her toes to reach the buckle.

“Hang on,” he said and turned to face her before slowly sitting on the bed, so she was taller than he was. He stared into her eyes, watching her unblinkingly as she raised her trembling hands to the buckle again.

She fumbled with the fastening a few times until she finally got it undone. Slowly, she pulled the material from around his throat before bunching it between her fists. The tension in the air was thick as she stared at him wordlessly, lips rolling in like she wanted to speak but didn’t know what to say.

“Thank you,” he murmured, gently pulling the collar from her fingers and setting it next to him on the comforter. “Chuck, look… I’m sorry again

for snapping at you out there. I didn't want you to get hurt. The world needs more people like you, and I couldn't stand it if that asshole had laid a single claw on you." He took her nearest hand in his and threaded their fingers together. "And thank you for helping me. Once again, I'm in your debt. I don't know why you put up with me, but meeting you has been the best thing that's ever happened to me. I may not know who I truly am or how I ended up there in that rescue center, but these last six months have been amazing."

"You don't have to thank me for that." She smiled softly and ran her free hand gently through his hair. Her fingers got tangled, and she tugged them free with a chagrined wince. "Sorry, I forgot your hair gets so messy after you change forms."

Taking her other hand now, he smirked, a teasing smile, and with a sing-song tone replied, "You are sooooo obsessed with my hair, Chuck. You liiiike it, you looove it." He tilted his head and widened his eyes innocently, batting his lashes.

"Shut up, you idiot." She laughed and yanked her hand from his, shoving his shoulder playfully. At his stifled gasp, her hand flew to her mouth. "Oh shit, Mal, I'm sorry. I didn't mean to hurt you! Dammit, I'm an idiot. Come on, lie down. What do you need? What can I get you?" She hurried to the head of the bed and yanked down the sheet, plumping up the pillows. "Here, Malachi, please. Tell me what to do."

He watched her worrying her lower lip between her teeth and studied her pale cheeks. "It's okay, Chuck, I just need to sleep for a bit, and I think my body will heal itself. Don't worry about me, I'll be alright. Go do whatever you need to do. I'll take care of whatever I need. I've put you out enough."

"No, you haven't. Nothing is too much for you." Seeming to understand the depth of what she'd said, her aura flared red and orange. She

straightened her shoulders and briskly directed, “Let’s get you tucked in, and I’ll run to the store for dinner.”

Silently, Malachi studied her and her aura. The red was getting stronger, and it unnerved him. She was definitely feeling what seemed to be a strong lust for him, and it was wrong. He was all wrong for her. For the first time in his demonic life span, he felt shame and despair. This was what he was trying to accomplish: gaining her trust, her desire, her grace. But it made him feel awful and grimy. Conflicted. Unfamiliar emotions swirled through him like a hurricane, spinning around the center of stillness that was undeniable. He cared for her too much. He wasn’t going to hurt her.

Groaning from the stiffness of his body and the sickening dance of feelings sweeping through him, he lay back onto the pillow. “Fuck,” he murmured as his muscles relaxed on the silky sheets and all the little aches and pains flared up again. His gaze caught Chuck’s worried stare, and he plastered a reassuring fake smile over his lips, trying to let it reach his eyes. He wasn’t sure it was fully successful, but it earned a timid smile from her in response. “I’m good now, go do what you need. I’ll be here. Just going to sleep.”

Closing his eyes, he forced his breathing to even out and listened until he heard her quiet footsteps retreating. When the door closed gently, and the tiniest click from the catch echoed, he truly relaxed. He stifled a groan as every muscle in his body throbbed all at once, as if punishing him for daring to ignore his injuries. Shifting around until he sank further into the mattress, he released a deep sigh as the quivering stopped, and everything warmed. His healing magic had started, and soon the comfort lulled him into sleep.

21

Chickens, Ruffles, and Steak

A frantic howl that sounded like a crazed lunatic had escaped the asylum and was rampaging through the neighborhood woke Malachi from his restorative sleep. He came awake with a jolt and smirked as he heard Chuck shushing Reena. It would seem his brindle-coated sidekick was demanding her share of steak as well. Stretching his arms over his head until his spine popped, he released a deep groan of satisfaction. No pain greeted the gesture, and he chuckled as Reena's insistence became firmer.

"You cut that out right now, young lady. Malachi is sleeping, and I don't want your greedy butt waking him up. Keep up this nonsense, and you won't get *any* steak," came Chuck's sharp retort.

A strangled yip echoed from the kitchen, then the tiny click of nails on the floor as Reena trotted towards the bedroom. A snuffling at the base of the door was followed by disgruntled murmuring and scratching on the wood.

Reena, he sent her, grinning at her low whine. *Be a good girl for Chuck, okay? She's had a long day. I promise I'll share with you. Just chill out ya little psycho, alright?*

A sigh that spoke of suffering and injustice was followed by a piggy snort of agreement before her nails clicked away down the hall.

He grinned, picturing her curly tail held upright in indignation. He wasn't entirely sure where Reena stood on the debate of being righteous or not, but he was sure that whatever her stance, that tail shouted it. His amused thoughts were interrupted by a soft tap on the door frame.

"Hey," Chuck called, opening the door and finding him awake. "Sorry if she woke you. How are you feeling?"

Sitting up on his elbows, he stared at her with half-closed eyes, a lock of his hair falling over his cheek. He stifled the smile that was trying to emerge as he watched her moisten her lips and shuffle nervously in the hall. "Chuck," he mumbled, "come here. Quit hovering."

Her mouth opened slightly, she shuffled forward, almost like a zombie, uncertainty and lust in her gaze.

Oops, gotta tone that down, he thought, easing up on the dark incubus call that was wrapping around her.

With a slight shake of her head, she continued forward under her own power and sat gingerly on the edge of the mattress. Her fingers suddenly grasped the lock of hair in his face and nudged it back, tucking it behind his ear. Eyes wide at her seeming audacity, she stared at her hand like a foreign invader and then back at him in surprise. "I... uh... it was blocking your face. It's soft. Your hair. I mean, I don't know why that surprises me. Your fur is soft. When you're a dog. Umm." She compressed her lips to cut off the flow of words and watched him warily.

Unable to help himself, he laughed out loud and flopped back on the mattress at the bewildered expression on her face.

"Malachi!" she gasped. "Oh no, are you okay? Did that hurt? What do you need? What can I get you?"

Once again, he acted on impulse and snatched her shoulders in his large hands, then threw her down on the bed next to him before flinging his body over hers. She was so shocked by the movement that she didn't even try to twist away or escape. A fact he found interesting, given her police training. Slowly, he lowered himself closer to her, only the tangled sheet between them. His nose nearly touching hers, their lips a scant two inches apart, he murmured, "I'm fine now. No pain. All better." He lifted one of her hands and placed it against his side, pressing her soft fingers against his ribs. "See? Not a twinge. Bruising is all gone."

Taking in her wide eyes, erratic breathing, and shaking hands, he placed a gentle kiss on her forehead then leaned back on his heels. Smiling, he held up his palms. "I'm a new man! Now I believe there was talk of steak? Something tells me we should get in there before Reena stages a mutiny." He leapt off the bed and held out his hand again, this time in an offer to help her up. As she continued to stare at him, mouth still hanging slightly open, he curled his fingers and dropped his arm to his side. "Okay, well, I'll be in there when you're ready."

With that, he turned on his heel and strode into the hall without a backward glance at her. He didn't need one. He knew what she would look like, rumpled and disheveled in those tangled sheets. Cheeks flushed, lips trembling, and her aura streaked with lust and confusion. His own lips quivered as they drew into a devilish smile.

Standing in the kitchen, he glanced around, looking to see if there was something he could do to help. Then he froze, standing like a statue. *Help? I don't help. What am I even supposed to do?*

A cleared throat behind him startled him from his thoughts as he whirled to face Chuck. She had composed herself for the most part, al-

though her cheeks were still flushed. "Any reason you're standing in the middle of the kitchen, right in my way?"

"Would you prefer me on four legs underfoot instead?" he replied, arching an eyebrow and crossing his arms. "I was going to offer to help, but if I'm just in the way, I can go outside and contemplate my fuzzy existence."

"No!" she said quickly, then her eyes narrowed, and she pointed at him. "Not funny!" she griped as he struggled to hide the grin that had formed. Slowly lowering her hand, her lips twitched as she fought her own smile.

Holding up his thumb and pointer finger, he held them slightly apart and tilted his head.

Rolling her eyes, she blew a rude noise through her lips and smirked. "Okay, yeah, it was a little funny. You want to help? Go wash those potatoes." She moved around him to the counter, stepping over Reena, who was staring soulfully at the platter full of red meat. A tiny line of drool connected her lower lip to the floor.

Resisting the urge to crow in victory, Malachi sauntered to the pantry and rummaged around. Finding his prize, he slipped the apron over his head and tied it around his waist. Moving back to the counter, he grabbed the potatoes and carried them to the sink.

"What the hell?" came Chuck's spluttered exclamation.

Turning his head, Malachi glanced over his shoulder and gave her an innocent shrug. "What?"

Chuck's gaze roamed over the sight of him, wearing only a pair of shorts and a pink ruffled apron covered in cartoon chickens and hearts.

Their eyes connected, and a giggle burst from her lips. "Oh, my goodness, Malachi, you really are a mess sometimes."

"I make this look good!" he insisted, flicking one of the ruffles as she continued to laugh harder. Turning to face her fully, he plopped his wet hands on his hips and glared in mock fury. "Hey, this is *your* apron, you

know. Sorry, I didn't want to get anything on me." He flung his hands out, pretending he was frustrated, chuckling when she squealed as water droplets splattered all over her.

"You ass!" she yelled in between giggles. Suddenly, the most unladylike snort ever came from her, and she gasped. Her eyes went wide, and her hand clapped over her lips while she laughed even louder, a high keening accompanying the sound.

"Holy shit, Chuck!" he bellowed, the sound booming through the room. "You sounded just like Reena!" Laughing even harder as Reena snorted in agreement, he moved closer to Chuck, where she was now leaning against the counter, holding herself up as her face turned fire engine red from trying to gasp for breath. Hands still dripping, he held them up and wiggled his fingers as he stalked her.

Shrieking, she ran from him out the back door onto the patio.

Chasing after her, he glanced around and was blindsided when she swept his feet out from under him, landing him on his back in the grass. "Oof!" he grunted as he hit the ground, and her body landed on his stomach. Before he could blink, she had his hands up over his head and was grinning in his face.

"If I had my cuffs, you'd be in big trouble. Someone forgot I was a police officer, didn't they?"

Grinning in delight, Malachi shimmered into his canine form and slurped his long pink tongue over her cheek. *Someone forgot I am, too!* He chuckled as she groaned and wiped his slobber off her face.

"Ah, gross, Mal, that's cheating!" she huffed and crossed her arms, still sitting in the grass, glaring at him with her eyebrows bunched and her lips pouting in the cutest frown.

Malachi paused in his victory dance and stared. He wanted to kiss those pouty lips more than he'd ever wanted anything in his life. The desire to

do whatever she wanted overwhelmed him. He would bow at the feet of… cough—GOD—cough… if that's what she needed. Crouching down with a frustrated groan, he stared at his paws as conflict roared through him. It expanded each cell to near bursting with the abject need to please her. He was supposed to be corrupting her, not the other way around. Hyacinth was going to kill him. A final death. He was going to be snuffed from existence and never see Chuck again. That thought alone sent tremors across his spine, rippling over his pelt like an earthquake through his very being. If he had a soul, it would be shivering in abject fear.

Tender fingers bunched into the fur on the back of his neck. "I'm sorry, Malachi, I didn't mean to upset you. I was only playing," came Chuck's soft words.

It's not you, he whimpered, aching with pure agony as her sweet concern settled over him like a comforting blanket. *It's just some memories came back reminding me of who I am, and I'm scared, Chuck. I… I don't think I'll be around much longer.*

"Mal, no, what do you mean?" she gasped as her fingers clenched hard in his scruff. Her tone was strained and desperate. Her breathing went shallow and ragged, but smoothed out when he crawled into her lap and lay his muzzle on her shoulder.

Chuck, please, just listen. Let's have that dinner, and then we need to talk. I found information you'll want to know but may find hard to come to terms with. I need a moment to collect myself, and after we talk, if you still want me around, you're going to have to stretch the boundaries of belief.

"Malachi," she called firmly, and gripped both sides of his head in her hands. She stared determinedly into his eyes. "You're a dog that turns into a man… or rather, a man that turns into a dog. My best friend is a witch. You really think I'm not already stretching things?" She tilted her head and stroked her thumbs over his furry cheeks. "I'm not sure what has you so

scared, but you're my partner, and I trust you. With my life. So, we're going to eat dinner, you're going to tell me whatever it is that's bothering you, and we'll figure this out. Together. Okay?"

Nodding silently, not trusting his thoughts, he stared at her adoringly.

"But change back, yeah? No dog hair in the food." She smirked, the wry smile curving her lips as her eyes sparkled.

Shifting into his human form, Malachi stared back as he brushed his fingers across her cheeks now. "I don't deserve you."

"Yeah, you do," she replied even more softly. "Mal..." she shook her head. "You're pretty heavy to be sitting in my lap. And you're naked again."

Glancing down, he realized she was right and blushed. Horrified at the heat and color rushing into his cheeks, he tried to shrug nonchalantly, but it was jerky and stilted. Finally, he just laughed and reached behind him for the apron. Slipping it back over his head, he flung his hair back and propped his hands on his hips as he gave a haughty stare. "Better?" he demanded.

"Whatever, you're still heavy. Get off me!" she chuckled and shoved him backwards.

Windmilling his arms, he tried to catch his balance but instead caught her shoulders and pulled her down with him. "You're making a habit of lying on me, you know," came his groan when they landed.

"Sorry." She laughed, not sounding the least bit apologetic. "I'm really not trying to!"

"Pity," he mumbled.

At his comment, she stilled, and he was pretty sure that she was probably very aware of what was digging into her stomach. And it wasn't his collar.

Clearing her throat, she smacked his chest and stood quickly. "Right. Steaks. Dinner. Then talk." As he stood, she kept her eyes on his face. "You, pants, and a shirt." Whirling around, she marched back into the

kitchen and finished prepping the potatoes. Her eyes caught his through the window, and she jerked her head, gesturing for him to come inside.

Slowly, he slipped through the door and waited.

“You like red wine? Wasn’t sure if you were a beer or wine guy. Or maybe you prefer the blood of your enemies?” She didn’t look at him when she said it, but he could see a small smile playing over her lips.

“Definitely the latter,” he intoned in a deep rumbling voice. “But since we’re short on enemies around here, wine is great.” He pointed towards his room. “I’m gonna...”

“And I’m gonna...” She gestured at the steaks.

Rolling his eyes, he turned and sauntered off towards his room, chuckling at her choked squeak. He had not forgotten he was only wearing the apron. But she had.

22

Trust Me, I've Been Lying

"Should I be concerned about that?" Chuck asked, pointing her fork at Reena. The chuglet menace was sitting at Malachi's feet, growling and grumbling as she gnawed at the chunk of steak he had slipped her.

"Nah," he replied lazily as he cut another bite of the perfectly cooked meat. Slipping it into his mouth, he closed his eyes in bliss while he chewed. Swallowing, he gazed adoringly at Chuck. "Man, I love a woman who knows how to grill a damn good steak. But no, don't worry about Reena. She's just killing her prey, so she doesn't feel as weak about it being given to her."

Reena raised her head and snarled at him lightly, her opinion clear about his words.

He chuckled. "Don't give me that Re-re. You have little dog syndrome, and you know it."

Snorting in amusement, Chuck shook her head. "Weirdos. Both of you. Anyway, time to come clean. You don't need to eat, but you can and seem to enjoy it. And what was with the disappearing act this morning and all

that stuff about them being after me? Who's after me? Do they know I carry a gun?"

Pausing with a bite halfway to his lips, he stared at her. The visual of her in uniform with her gun was always a favorite. At her humming noise, he blinked and shoved the fork in his mouth, chewing slowly as he prepared himself to disclose the shock of her life. Finally, he set the utensils down and crossed his arms over his chest, leaning back in his chair.

"Chuck," he sighed. "I'm going to tell you some things that are going to be hard to believe and are probably going to upset you. Please remember, I'm here for you, and I will help you through this, the same way you helped me."

"You. Dog. Glenda. Witch. I'm good," she replied, reminding him that her suspension of belief was in full effect.

Leaning his head back, he briefly closed his eyes. With an even heavier sigh, he opened them and locked his gaze with hers. "Okay, Chuck. Do you believe in Hell? H-Heaven? Angels and demons?"

"I think it's a little late to be discussing our religious preferences." She smirked. When his expression remained steady, her gaze grew wary, and she lowered her elbows from the table, now gripping the edge of the wooden surface tightly. "You mean like, literal Heaven and Hell? Real angels and demons? As in they exist, not just as a construct or metaphor?"

He nodded silently.

Blowing air steadily between her pursed lips, she dipped her head slowly. "I mean, I guess I didn't before, but these last few months have really thrown a wrench into things. Alright, let's say on the surface I do. What does that have to do with anything?"

"Everything," he murmured. He reached across the table and took her hands, squeezing her fingers lightly. "Chuck, your dad—"

She snatched her hands back before he got any further and stood quickly. Rushing around the table, she crouched next to him, digging her fingers into his thigh. "My dad?" her voice waivered. "What do you know?"

Shaking his head, he stood and pulled her up with him. "You need to sit, Chuck. This isn't going to be easy to hear."

Her head whipped side to side in denial. "No. You tell me!" Her finger stabbed into his chest. "You tell me right now, Malachi! Was my father targeted? Was it premeditated murder?"

Unable to stop himself as her eyes filled with tears, he wrapped her against his body and placed his cheek on hers. Whispering in her ear, his breath hitched as he simply gave her the one word that would change it all. "Yes."

Malachi had expected wails and sobs, harsh crying and pleas to Heaven for answers. He should have known better. Chuck's hands gripped him tightly for a moment, and a shudder rippled over her smaller frame. Then she straightened and met his gaze. Her eyes were liquid pools of chocolate as she stared at him, then she nodded once, blinked away her tears, and, through clenched teeth, demanded, "Tell me the rest."

Leading her to the couch, their dinner forgotten, he motioned for her to sit while he retrieved the bag with the files and then their wine glasses. When he returned, he gently lowered himself next to her with the tote on his lap. "Okay, Chuck, you remember when you were telling me... well, the furry me before you realized I was a man in a... anyway, you were telling me about your father and how you were suspicious of how he died. You mentioned the feathers and the ring of soot. Remember?" He eyed her warily, watching for any signs she'd reached the decision he was crazy. Her gaze remained firmly locked on his.

"I remember," she offered steadily.

"Well, I've seen that before," he admitted, scratching distractedly at the back of his neck. "The feathers were part of him. The ring of soot happens when... well... when grace leaves the body."

"Grace? Part of him how?"

"Part of him... as in..." A small, frustrated groan slipped from his throat. "Look, there's no way to ease into it, so I'm just gonna say it. Chuck, your dad was an angel. The feathers were from his wings." He paused, searching her face and seeing only grim acceptance, and kept going. "You can't kill an angel through ordinary methods. You have to use a special type of weapon. I suspect he was killed with a forsaken blade. That's why there was a ring of ash around him. It charred his grace and pulled it from him, leaving him mortal, and then he died. Forsaken blades aren't just any basic sword. You can't get one at your local pawn shop. Whoever did this knew what they had and knew who—or rather what—your dad was. It was a hit. And Chuck,"—he pulled her limp, cold fingers into his lap—"I'm worried about you. I think they'll come after you next."

Chuck's eyes closed briefly, and she swallowed hard. When she opened them again, she curled her fingers into his, then leaned towards him. "Why me?" she asked, a slight tremor in her voice betraying her steadfast gaze.

"Y-you believe me?" he sputtered incredulously, reeling back the explanations he was prepared to make to gain her understanding. Admiration swirled through him as he stared in awe.

"I always believe you, Malachi. I trust you with my life. You're my partner," was her simple explanation, the gold in her aura lending truth to her words.

Malachi sat in silence, studying her. His gut was churning with anxiety, agonizing about all the ways he had been lying to her. Directly and by omission. He didn't deserve her simple belief. The warmth her words built in his heart was quickly doused by the icy wave of guilt ripping through

him like a tornado. To his horror, his eyes went hot, and he panicked slightly, not understanding why. "Chuck!" he demanded frantically and yanked his hands from hers, touching his face. "What is this?"

Chuck smiled softly and lifted his hands from his cheeks, brushing her thumb under one eye. She showed him the dampness on her thumb. "You're crying, Malachi. Do you not..." she stared at him in quiet contemplation. "Did you not realize that's what you were doing? Have you never cried before?"

He shuddered and sucked in a deep breath, holding it and trying to regain his composure. He was a demon. A lieutenant of the sixth ward. He commanded his own legion and seduced with his incubus power. He was night, he was darkness, he was... so royally fucked.

He was crying, sobbing now.

He was trusted.

Cared for.

Believed.

Grabbing him by the shoulders, Chuck pulled him down to her. His head on her chest, she wrapped her arms tightly around his trembling body and held him. She whispered softly, words of comfort, reassurances. Running her fingers through his hair, she rocked him slowly. "It's okay. Whatever this is, we'll figure it out together."

"I don't deserve your friendship. Your trust," he mumbled against her neck as his tears slowly subsided.

"Shut the fuck up," she insisted, grinning as his eyes snapped up to her in shock. "You do too, Malachi. Whatever you've done in the past, whatever you did to end up as a dog, I know you are a good person deep down in your soul. I see it in your actions every day. The way you care about Reena, the job." She ran her fingers over his cheek. "About me."

Malachi watched as Chuck leaned closer, her lips parting slightly, trembling the smallest amount. Her breath hitched, and he realized she was about to kiss him. He sat up quickly and ground the heels of his hands over his eyes. Both to wipe away the tear-stained evidence of how far he'd strayed from his heritage, and to block the flash of disappointment he knew was covering her face. He could feel it coming from her in waves.

This was why he was here. To seduce her, gain her trust, and besmirch her soul, her grace. He finally had the opportunity, and he was backing away. He couldn't bring himself to let her fall. She deserved better, and warmth filled him as he firmed it in his mind. He'd rather die a final death than let her suffer because of him. Decision made, he knew; he had to tell her all of it.

"Sorry," he murmured. Clearing his throat, he sat up straighter. "Chuck, I need to tell you something else. I..." he sighed miserably. "I haven't been completely honest with you. But you deserve the full truth, and after you know, I understand if you don't want to ever see me again. I promise I'll leave, and I won't make a scene." He lifted his thumb, brushing it over her lower lip, and smiled softly. "Chuck, believe this, I *wanted* you to kiss me. Very much." Chuckling now as her eyes widened and a protest formed on her lips. "No, don't deny it. You can't. You can't deny there's something here between us. But I'm not going to let you fall like this. I won't be the cause."

"I don't understand," she cried softly, shaking her head side to side, no longer hiding her desire for him.

"I know, Chuck. I'll try to explain. Just... hear me out. Okay?" As she silently agreed, he took a deep breath and continued. "I was shocked, I was crying, because I never had before. I didn't know I could. To cry means you need feelings, and I... well, I didn't think I had those. We'll come back to

why in a minute." He chuckled at her cute frowning pout. "So impatient you. Hang in there."

Standing so he could put some distance between them, Malachi began to pace. "Alright, so back to your dad. He was an angel. Full blooded, hundred percent winged host, full of grace angel. Which makes you..." Turning, he stared at her intensely, hoping she would understand.

"Half angel?" she blurted, her words shaking and full of awe. "I'm part angel?" This time her voice cracked on the word, squeaking a high-pitched note.

"Yeah, Chuck. You're half angel. You don't have wings, but you do have a halo." Laughing as her fingers flew to her head, he shook his own side to side. "No, the books are wrong about that. It's not a circle hovering above you, it's your aura. A glow that surrounds your whole body. It reflects your moods and thoughts in patterns and colors. When you're sad, it's gray. Yellow when you get scared, orange when you're embarrassed or irritated. And when you do what you do best, saving lives, it turns gold. Like the last rays of the setting sun. It's the most beautiful thing I've ever seen." He blinked a few times and turned to pace again.

"Why didn't he tell me?" she mused out loud. "We were so close, we talked about everything. Why wouldn't he tell me?" Her eyes were troubled now, a furrow between her eyebrows.

Kneeling, Malachi took her hands in his. "He couldn't, Chuck. I bet your mother didn't know either. It's not the kind of thing he would have wanted spread around. I don't know why he wasn't up there." He pointed above them. "Why was he on Earth? But he didn't tell you... so he could keep you safe, Chuck. If no one knew, no one would come after you."

Nodding slowly, she frowned. "But someone found out, and that's why he's dead. You think they're after me now, don't you? That's why all the

cloak and dagger. The sneaking around." Gripping his hands tighter, she leaned forward, all business now. "Okay, so what did you find?"

Smiling, he lifted one hand and brushed it over her cheek. "There you are. Warrior girl." He rose to his feet and grabbed the bag before retaking a seat next to her. Pulling out the files, he laid them in her lap. "Some of the records from your dad's case. When I opened the box, I could smell the grace and the 'other'." He wrinkled his nose in memory of the bad odor. "I couldn't do a thorough search there; no one would understand why 'Evan' was there or why your K-9 would be looking at reports. So, I uh… I kinda borrowed them. Don't worry! I'll put them back!" he promised quickly.

"Mal." She laughed, waggling a finger at him playfully. "Bad dog." Then she shook her head. "I'm not mad. In a weird way, that's the nicest thing anyone could have done for me." Huffing out another laugh, she leaned closer. "Thank you, Malachi. Wait… is that really your name?"

Chuckling, he bobbed his head sheepishly. "Yeah, it really is Malachi. And I honestly was cursed by a demon into the dog's body. I also truly couldn't change myself back until I got some help. But the rest of it, Chuck, I need to tell you the truth. And you'll probably hate me, so let me just say… that being with you and Reena has been the best part of my life. My very long and decidedly awful life. I'm grateful I got to spend even this small amount of time with you. I hope you'll look back on me fondly one day, and if you ever decide to forgive me, just call my name, and I'll come to you." He stared at the ground, shuddering as he remembered Hyacinth's promise. "Well, if I'm still alive."

Her fingers wrapped around his jaw, lifting his face to hers. "What do you mean if you're alive? Malachi, is someone threatening you?"

Sighing, he pried her fingers from his face and squeezed them. "Yes, I've been threatened with death or worse if I don't corrupt you and collect your angel grace for my dark lord. Kelly…" he groaned and shook his head.

"I'm a demon. Like, eternally damned, brimstone, evil, Satan, Hellspawn. And I was forced into the dog body as a punishment for displeasing my commander." Gazing into her eyes, he was concerned that her expression was carefully neutral, no clues as to how she took the news. Deciding there was nothing for it but to forge ahead, he continued. "But then you showed up, glowing with your angelic grace, and I was terrified. I just knew you were about to smite me." He chuckled at the memory. "I was quaking in my fur. But when you smiled at me, I felt warm all over. Like I'd been granted a reprieve. I thought it was just a chance that we met. But today I learned from one of the demons that took the little girl that it's a long-range plot to capture you."

Groaning in frustration, he rubbed his forehead tiredly. "They want your grace. My commander will stop at nothing to get it. He 'punished' me so I would get close to you. He left me alone for all these months, but then he appeared again. Commanded me to use my demonic influence to seduce you so he could steal your grace. I discovered that I'm to be sacrificed as well. Your power and mine together would give him enough juice to start a major coup of Hell. But I can't do it, Chuck. I've come to... care about you. I didn't know I could. I didn't know it was possible. But I have feelings for the first time in centuries, and I'm so fucking gone over you, I have no idea what to do here. But I can't keep this from you. And I won't let them hurt you. So yeah, he'll kill me one way or the other, but I'd rather die defending you with my last breath than let them take you. I won't. He can't have you, Kelly."

Chest heaving with the force of his declaration, he lifted his eyes to her, terrified of what he would see. He expected scorn, hurt, fright, and disgust. Once again, he should have known better than to underestimate her.

"Malachi, he can't have you. Demon or not, you're my partner." She leaned forward and placed a soft kiss on his cheek.

23

Put Pants on This Time

Stunned silence filled the air as Malachi stared at Chuck, his mouth open wide in shock. He studied the smirk on her face and slowly shook his head side to side. "Chuck. Kelly. Did you hear me? I'm a demon. A literal Hellspawn. My mother is an ash demon, and my father is an incubus. I was a lieutenant of the Sixth Ward Legion of Demons. My sole purpose in existing is to corrupt souls for Hell through whatever means. I'm sin. I'm everything you stand against. Cast me out, Kelly. Send me away."

"Nope!" she grinned so hard her cheeks surely hurt.

"What the fuck, Kelly?" he shouted. His eyebrows bunched together like a stormcloud, and he glared at her, his eyes lighting up with Hellfire. "Don't you have any sense? I'm a fucking demon. A soulless monster here to tarnish your light and steal your grace. I'm supposed to ruin you!" He finally roared in frustration and jumped to his feet. "Fuck!"

Shuffling drew his attention to her as he paced frantically. Chuck strode to him and grabbed his arms, holding him still. "Malachi," she sighed, then smiled. "Shut up."

His jaw dropped, and his eyes flew even wider than he thought possible. He heard Reena snickering as she trotted in and lay next to the couch to watch the drama unfold. She probably liked this better than her daytime TV reruns. Her wheezy little chuckle had him glaring at her. "Stay out of this!" he pointed.

Chuck thumped him on the forehead. "Hey, focus." Her tone was light and full of laughter.

"Dammit, Chuck," he growled, rubbing his skin where she'd flicked him. "I don't understand you at all. Every time I think I know how you're going to react, you surprise me."

"Yeah, I'm used to being underestimated," she replied nonchalantly and shrugged. She pulled him back down to the couch and handed him a folder. "You go through this one, I'll take this other," she instructed as she waved the loose files.

"Kelly. I..." he stared at her as she arched an eyebrow and flashed a mischievous smirk. Finally, he shook his head and laughed. "So, am I to understand you're cool with me being a demon and you're not throwing me out?"

With a deep echoing groan, Chuck leaned back and scrubbed her hands over her face. "Okay, I'll explain. Malachi, I knew you weren't entirely human. Demon—that part I was not expecting—but with everything else, I'm just not surprised. Maybe tonight, maybe tomorrow morning, I'm sure it'll catch up with me and freak me out, but for now..." She shook her head, then took his hand in hers, lacing their fingers together. "Mal... am I angry you weren't honest with me? A little, but I also understand why you wouldn't. My father apparently kept a huge secret from me my whole life. To protect me. I feel like you're doing the same. I refuse to believe that you're purely evil. Yeah, you've probably done some things in your past that were pretty awful. But look at what you're doing now! You've

saved the lives of so many people. You protect Reena. You care about me. Whatever you were before, you're not that same guy now. And who better to protect me from demons than another demon who has switched sides?"

His mouth opened and closed a few times as he pondered her words. "Who says I've switched sides?" he demanded with a small, decidedly feral smile.

"I do." She nodded, a determined expression thinning her lips and narrowing her eyes. "Malachi, I want you in my life. You're staying with me. So that means you're Team Good Guys now. No more corrupting." She hid a smile at his groan. "You might have started out corrupting me, but the tables have turned and you..."—she poked a finger into his chest—"Are going light side!" Her triumphant grin made his mouth go as dry as the Sahara in the peak of summer.

"Fuck, I just don't believe this," he whispered.

Leaning in, Chuck placed one hand on his cheek before gently placing her lips to his. A small tender kiss had his heart exploding with rainbow colors and dancing butterflies, things that would normally make him vomit, but now he wanted more. He moved forward, trying to prolong the kiss. She placed a single finger firmly over his lips and pulled back slightly.

"Malachi, you said you can see my emotional aura or halo, whatever thingy, right?"

Nodding slowly, he focused on the glow surrounding her, in awe of the golden haze now streaked heavily with red.

"So, I think you probably know how I feel about you," her voice wavered, suddenly timid.

Now he shook his head; he didn't understand it at all. "I'm not sure, actually. It's gold like it is when you're doing something you believe in, but it's streaked with red, which I thought was lust... but," he sighed, "I don't know. I kinda suck at this."

"Mal, I think the red is for affection. Because I feel very strongly about you. I care about you a lot. And yes, I'm ready to admit that I want whatever this is between us. But I also think we would be wise to take it slow until we figure out what the threat is and how to end it. How do we keep your commander from dragging you back to Hell? Because you don't belong there, Malachi. You belong here. With me."

"I want that," he breathed, having never been more sure of anything in his life.

"Good," she declared with a decisive nod. "Then let's figure this out." She tapped the evidence folders. "What are we looking for?"

For the next two hours, they delved through the files, talking through each piece of information, making notes, and bouncing ideas off each other. Malachi recounted for her what he'd smelled at the first kidnapping. How he sensed two dark souls that day. He wasn't sure who it was, but it had seemed strongest around the scene lieutenant.

"Bennett?" she mused, tapping a finger on her lips as she stared blindly out the window into the night beyond. "He and my dad were friends." She shook her head. "I don't know. I don't see it, but I don't know who I can trust anymore." Her head turned, and she took his hand in hers. "Except you."

Picking idly at his pants leg with the other hand, he mumbled, "I wish you didn't."

"Why?"

His head snapped up, staring at her as she gazed at him with a curious expression. He realized she truly wanted to know. "Because I don't want to risk hurting you or putting you in more danger than you are already. *I* would never hurt you, Chuck, but there are others who might." He tried to grimace darkly, wanting to throw in some good old-fashioned brooding

for maximum effort, but it was ruined by a yawn. “Sorry,” he groaned as he covered his mouth.

“Bedtime!” she declared with a decisive finality, gathering the folders and jumping to her feet. “We have a long day tomorrow, partner, and your furry ass better be ready.”

Rolling his eyes, he stood as well and towered over her petite frame. “Oh, my ass will be ready. And furry.” He hesitated, then moved a step closer. “I think I should sleep with you tonight. To keep you safe.” Throwing his palms up in a placating gesture, he added, “As the dog! My furry ass will protect you.”

Biting back the retort she was about to deliver, no doubt with painful precision, Chuck laughed. “I don’t want you to be in dog form.”

“But Chuck, I need to be close in case—”

“I didn’t say no,” she interrupted. “I said not in dog form. I agree you need to be on alert. But I’d rather you sleep as a human. I think it’s more comfortable for you.”

He shrugged in agreement as if her words hadn’t lit his skin on fire and sent lava boiling through his veins.

Turning towards her room to begin her nightly bedtime rituals, she glanced over her shoulder. “But wear pants this time, would you?”

Booming laughter followed her as he watched her trot off to her bedroom. Glancing around, Malachi scooped up Reena from where she’d fallen asleep and carried her to Chuck’s room. Softly depositing her in her fur-lined bed, he hurried to his own room, where he got ready faster than he ever had before. Securing the lounge pants around his waist, he nervously sauntered back to Chuck’s room.

He found her already ensconced beneath her large, fluffy comforter, her bedside lamp providing the only light in the room. Clearing his throat and

running a hand nervously through his hair, he gestured at his pajama pants, raising an eyebrow. Silently seeking her approval.

A slight nod was followed by her eyes roving his upper torso, taking in each sculpted plane of his chest. She seemed to catch herself staring, drinking him in, and quickly flipped the blanket down on his side. "Come on then," she called softly.

Timidly, he approached the bed and knelt lightly on the edge before sliding under the sheet with her. He kept firmly to his side and lay there, staring at the ceiling. "Um... night, Chuck," he whispered, keenly aware of the awkward tension between them.

"G'night, Mal," came her sleepy reply before the lamp snicked off and the room was plunged into darkness. Some rustling and shifting around resulted in Chuck lying on her side, facing Malachi. After a few agonizing moments, she sighed and scooted closer. Gingerly, she wrapped her arm around his waist. "Is this okay?"

In response, he reached over and hooked his arm around her middle, then pulled her even closer, wedging her against his side. He kept his smile soft and even as she made a happy little humming noise in her throat before laying her head on his chest and snuggling down.

The scent of her lavender face cream, mixed with the mint of her toothpaste, and the woodsy spicy scent that was just her, clouded his nostrils, drowning him in his favorite smell. Her. Kelly.

Blissfully, Malachi drifted off into a restful sleep.

24

You Know That's Not Real Bacon

Morning dawned, and Malachi stretched, finally feeling fully rested for a change. A happy warmth suffused his limbs as he registered that Chuck was wrapped tightly around him like a barbed-wire tattoo. The peaked in high school dude-bro jock they'd confronted in the park probably had one on each arm. Idly, he wondered how Spike was doing. Chuck snored slightly, and a grin curved his cheeks so hard they almost hurt. He couldn't believe he was here, in her bed this way. She knew who and what he was and still accepted him. Cared for him.

Breathing in her scent, trapping it in his lungs like a core memory, he gently shifted towards her a little more before pulling her in tighter. Her happy mumble had him aching for her. Groaning, his grip clenched around her as his lower body throbbed in response. "Fuck," he hissed through his teeth.

Loathe to wake her but not trusting himself if she pressed any harder against him, he nudged her. "Chuck," he called, shaking her gently.

She mumbled sleepily and snuggled in harder.

"Chuck," he moaned. "Please wake up!" he begged.

"Hmm?" she breathed and blinked at him blearily.

Blowing out a shaky breath, he squeezed her tighter for a moment, then told her, "Chuck, it's not that I don't absolutely love the feeling of your body pressed against mine, but I only have so much control. I'm a demon for Lucifer's sake. Half sex-demon. So, unless you take back what you said about taking it slow, you need to unwrap yourself from me before I let my base nature go."

A low chuckle slipped from her throat. "Is that so? And what would you do?" she teased.

With a growl building in the base of his throat, Malachi hooked his calf around her thigh and flipped them. Her body was now wedged firmly beneath him. Her lips formed a small, surprised o and her breath hitched as she tried in vain to get it under control.

"Well, to start," he murmured, "I would trail my fingers over every inch of your skin until you felt like you were going to erupt into flames." He drew his fingers over her ribs in the lightest caress, feathering just under her breasts. A small smirk lifted his lips as she moaned and arched beneath him.

Leaning down, his warm breath brushed the edge of her ear, and his tongue traced the shell of the delicate pink flesh. "I would let my dark powers spill over your curves, stroking every bit of you until you cried for relief, begged me to let you fall, to release you from my shadow pull." A small tendril of shadow wrapped around her thigh, squeezing gently to demonstrate. His lips moved to hers and stopped millimeters apart, sharing her breath. "Then I would introduce my tongue to every tiny part of you until you scream and pour your release into my mouth. And believe me when I say I will taste... every... inch... of you. Just to start off, of course." By now, his voice was low and husky. Her breathing was jagged and needy.

Without warning, he released her and sat up. Running his fingers through his wavy locks, he shrugged nonchalantly. “But since we’re taking things slow, I won’t do any of that. Until you tell me to.” Standing, he ran a hand over his stomach, chuckling as she swallowed hard in shock. “Dibs on first shower!” he called over his shoulder as he sauntered to the bathroom.

“Damn demon,” came her muffled reply as she buried herself under the blanket.

At the station, Chuck’s eyes darted nervously around, staring at everyone, jumping at every voice. She seemed to be searching for some sign of who would carry an angel-killing blade on their person.

Relax, Malachi sent her as he watched her fretting. *I really doubt anyone would be carrying a sword into a police precinct. If they were stupid enough to do that, you’d have seen it by now. You wouldn’t even have to see it. They give off a low hum of negative energy. You may not hear it with your ears, but I bet even being half angel, you’d sense it.*

“Right, low hum, negative vibes,” she mumbled to herself.

“Who’s humming?” Jaxon asked as he stood next to her.

Jumping slightly, Chuck whirled to face him, plastering a bright fake smile on her face. “Me!” she declared happily. “I’m humming a song.” She proceeded to hum a tune out loud, the last song they’d heard on the radio.

Malachi tried to turn his laugh into a cough, but it didn’t seem to fool anyone as both Chuck and Jaxon glanced at him—Jaxon with mild annoyance, Chuck with murderous intent.

"Humming, huh? Next, you'll tell me you're coming to karaoke with us tonight," Jaxon replied in a teasing tone.

"Us?" Chuck echoed, with a deer-in-the-headlights stare.

"Yeah, me, Bennett, Marchand, Gillespie, and a few of the ladies in dispatch are all meeting up at Frankies for karaoke and beer. You should come!" he exclaimed, warming up to the thought of getting Chuck to meet him somewhere casually.

Malachi could sense that Jaxon was still interested in Chuck and that she was terrified of karaoke. He knew firsthand from her car concerts that singing was not her forte. But one name in particular caught his attention, so he shoved his nose in her hand. *Chuck, he said Bennett will be there. We should go, so I can check him out. As Evan, of course. Ugh, barf, such a douchey name. Still not as bad as Jaxon.*

Fighting the tremble of her lips as she held back a laugh at his words, she blurted, "You know what, Jax, that sounds good. And since I'm on desk duty after the shooting yesterday, I could use some fun."

Blinking his surprise that she'd agreed, Jaxon quickly nodded like a bobblehead mounted to a monster truck dashboard. Malachi was shocked that the fool's head didn't fall right off. *Idiotic douche moron looks like an upside-down hula-girl. Let's shove a stick up his ass and glue him on the dash of your squad car.*

A strangled squeak escaped Chuck's throat, and she slapped her hand over her mouth.

Eying her strangely, Jaxon slowly placed a hand on her shoulder. "Are... are you okay, Chuck?" His voice was full of concern as his eyebrows bunched together so hard it looked like a caterpillar was crawling across his forehead.

"Fine!" she choked out. "Just swallowed funny. Anyway, yeah, see you tonight. Gotta go, reports don't write themselves!" With that, she spun on her heel and scurried to her desk.

Malachi sat next to Jaxon and watched her retreat with amusement. He glanced up at Officer Douchenugget to see that he was staring too. Growling lightly to get his attention, Malachi glared at Jaxon with the slightest hint of Hellfire in his eyes, before panting and holding out a paw to shake.

Jaxon scratched his head in confusion before gingerly leaning over to shake Malachi's paw.

"Mal! Come here!" Chuck shouted, knowing full well Malachi didn't care for Jaxon and was likely up to no good.

Grumbling, he trotted off to her desk, keeping up a running litany of offenses the man deserved to be punished for, *including wearing Axe body spray. I bet he's friends with that guy from the park. Does he have a barbed wire or tribal tattoo on his bicep? A hundred bucks says he does.* Malachi plopped next to her on his butt and let his tongue loll out, looking for all the world like a good boy.

"I don't know, but stop that! He's a good guy, even if he is annoying," she scolded and shook her finger at his muzzle.

"Aw, poor Malachi. Look at him sitting there all sweet and innocent. Is Chuck being mean to you? After what you went through yesterday? He's just a good boy, a hero, and doesn't deserve that, does he? No, sir, here you go, buddy!" Lieutenant Jeffers leaned over and handed Malachi a small bowl of bacon treats.

Oh, fuck yeah! he cheered, *listen to the man, Chuck, he's a genius! I'm a hero! And I got bacon. What did you get? Benched!*

"You know that's not real bacon!" she snapped at him.

Yeah, and it still tastes good with this body. But hey, what do I know, you're the one yelling at a dog in a police station. He glanced up and chuckled as her cheeks flushed a vibrant crimson color, matching the stop sign hanging haphazardly on the wall behind her. He watched her eyes slowly move up the lieutenant's body until she reached his worried gaze.

Jeffers stared at her with concern plain on his rugged face. "Chuck, you okay?" he asked softly, clearly not wanting to upset the crazy person.

"Fine, sir. Malachi was being a little ornery earlier with Jaxon. But you're right, he is a hero for his actions yesterday. He got a big steak for dinner last night, too." Chuck smiled weakly, attempting to reassure the lieutenant.

Nodding slowly while pinching his chin, Jeffers relaxed his shoulders a bit. "Well, I wanted to see how our hero was doing. Word is, Officer Malachi sustained some injuries yesterday. What did the vet say?"

"Oh, he's fine. He was a little shaken, and it seemed worse than it was. He's great!" She nodded quickly, obviously hoping he would drop it.

Pinching his chin again, Jeffers squinted at her. "So, you have a vet report to back that up?" At her reluctant head shake, he sighed. "Chuck, you know the protocol. Take him in. That's an order! I'll expect the report by end of shift."

Groaning, Chuck wearily waved him off. "I'll take him; he just has a thing about thermometers." She turned back to Malachi as Jeffers left and studied him. "Don't look at me like that. You know I tried to avoid it."

What. The. Fuck. Chuck? How could you betray me like this? I thought we had an understanding. Is this about the hero comment? I take it back! He was staring at her in abject horror now. *I swear on Lucifer's saggy tits if anyone comes near my ass with anything other than a friendly sniff, I WILL bite them.*

Chuck leaned forward and propped her chin in one hand, resting her elbow on her knees. "Mal," she groaned. "I have to. It's protocol. A direct

order. You heard it." With her other hand, she reached out and ruffled his ears. "C'mon, Mal, I'll tell them no temperature. Remember, you're the one who wanted to stay my canine partner."

Betrayal. Utter betrayal.

"Come *on,* Malachi. At least they agreed to not stick the thermometer up your behind," Chuck wheedled as he glared at her from across the living room. She smirked as Reena stood next to her, wheezing in laughter at the defiant expression on his face. Frowning, he crossed his arms even tighter across his chest while he glared at Reena for ganging up on him.

"Traitor," he whispered fiercely at the small chuglet. She simply snorted and trotted over before she curled up on his feet. Turning his eyes back to Chuck, who was still grinning, he sneered at her and angled his shoulders so he was staring at the TV instead.

"Mal," she sighed, "I know it was a blow to your dignity, but you know I had no choice."

"I get it," he rumbled. "But did you have to laugh so hard when the tech called me her fluffy spookums woofums?" He shuddered. "Gah, that was so embarrassing."

Ruffling his hair as she dropped by his side, she snickered. "You have to admit, that was pretty funny. You are a spooky woofums, though, aren't you? Who's a good boy?" she teased.

With aching slowness, he turned to face her, then shoved a wave of his incubus power towards her as he leaned close. "Me," he drawled in a sultry voice dripping with lust and desire. "I am a *very*... good... boy." He lightly

ran his nose over her throat and nipped her jaw as she moaned softly. Sitting back, grinning, he released her from his power. "Such a good boy, you'll never forget it again, will you?"

Shaking her head mechanically side to side, Chuck licked her lips and squirmed on the cushion next to him. Clearing her throat, she blinked a few times, then sighed. "You told me you were part incubus. I almost want to ask if what I feel for you is part of your demon powers, but I don't think there's any mistaking that. Malachi, please don't do that to me again."

Winking, he curled his lips and smoldered at her, letting tiny flames flicker in his eyes. "Not even if you beg me?" he asked, his voice still husky.

"Okay, yeah, maybe if I ask nicely." Chuck's face turned a fetching shade of rose as she leapt to her feet. "I'm gonna get ready to go out. I can't believe you're dragging me to this. Just so you know, I can't sing." She turned and escaped to her room as he watched with an amused grin.

"Well aware."

25

Nickelback is Not a Sin

Sitting in his own room, Malachi thought about Chuck's words, that she felt something for him. Something that wasn't just pure lust. He desperately wanted to know what it was, but he was scared to ask. Groaning, he pinched the bridge of his nose, conflicted. All at once, the absurdity of his situation hit him, and he let out a small sound of disgust at himself. A demon. Scared of a tiny woman. Granted, she was half angel and could hold her own in a fight, but she was a human, nonetheless. He was a being made for corruption and darkness. They didn't make sense. They shouldn't work. But he'd never been happier in his life than he was when he was with Chuck. She didn't want him to use his powers on her; he wouldn't. He would do anything for her, the thought curving his lips.

Slowly, the smile left his face as he knew that anything could include dying. Something he would be doing soon. He needed to know how she felt before then. His head snapped up, and his nostrils flared as he caught a whiff of floral rot and decay. As if summoned by his thoughts, Hyacinth climbed through the floor and grinned at Malachi with his rotted, broken stumps of teeth.

"Malachi..." came Hyacinth's rumbly evil hiss. His breath coated Malachi with a film of filthy slime that he felt might never wash free. "Naughty puppy, what are you doing in here? I heard you took out another lieutenant yesterday. That better be part of your plan to seduce our angel. Otherwise, I might get a little—irritated—about it." A knowing smirk crossed his warty face, and he cracked his knuckles. Dirt trickled to the floor from under his nails.

"It was!" Malachi reassured him quickly with a near-frantic nod. He glanced towards Chuck's door, hoping against hope she couldn't hear them. Lowering his voice, he grudgingly moved closer and bowed his head. "I was helping her find a missing child so she would think me a hero. And it worked. The other demon tried to interfere, and she's the one who killed him."

Nodding slowly, Hyacinth squinted then grunted out, "But you told her how."

Shrugging, Malachi spread his palms in a helpless gesture. "Well, I can't seduce her and steal her grace if she dies." He figured he was safe with this stance as he wasn't supposed to know Hyacinth's true plan. "And it's going great! Last night, she wanted me in her bed like this, and she admitted to feelings for me. We're going out on a 'date' tonight," he exclaimed, using air quotes. "I'll have that bitch out of her panties and begging for more really soon."

"Huh," grunted the squat demon, tapping a finger on his jagged wrinkly lips. His eyes were squinted as if he were in deep contemplation. "You know I almost believe you, Malachi. But I've never seen you take so long to bed a female before." He smirked, "What's the hold up?"

Raising his eyes to the ceiling, Malachi sighed as if he were long suffering. "Satan's ass boils, the chick is a bit of a prude. But don't worry, I've got her firmly in my power. She could walk in here right now, and I've made it so

she wouldn't even see you. I'm this close!" He pinched his fingers together, almost touching before clenching his hand tightly as Chuck's door opened and she strolled out.

"Mal, baby, aren't you going to change? I want to show you off on our date tonight." She ran her hands over his chest and moaned seductively. "Oh, wear that black dress shirt, it looks so good on you." Pressing her body against his side, she stared into his eyes with her gaze full of lust. Her fingers curled into the hair at the nape of his neck. "And be a good boy so when we get home, I can show you how... grateful I am," she murmured, pulling his head down to hers and locking their lips in a passionate kiss.

Changing the angle, he gripped her waist with one hand and cupped the back of her head with the other. He licked the seam of her lips and moaned as that sweet mouth parted, allowing him to trace his tongue over hers, her passion and lust kicking into a whirlwind of desire surrounding them both in the eye of their own hurricane.

When the kiss tapered off, he leaned his forehead against hers, breathing hard as they each fought to catch their breath.

"Is he gone?" she whispered against his ear, where she was nibbling on the lobe.

Jolting back to the situation at hand, Malachi peered over her shoulder, then relaxed as he saw Hyacinth had indeed left. He shuddered and sagged against her. Leaning back, he stared into her eyes and gently ran his hand over her hair. "Not that I'm complaining, because I've been wanting to do that for weeks, but what was that for?" he murmured.

Releasing a shaky sigh, Chuck leaned into him and laid her head on his chest. "Keeping sane," she murmured as he wrapped her in his arms. "Mal... who was that? *What* was that? I heard you talking, and the words just didn't make sense. I didn't know why you were saying such disgusting things. Then I peeked out and saw that... *awful* creature, and I realized you

were trying to protect me. Again. You saying you could control me gave me the idea."

Stepping back, Chuck stared at him warily now, and he knew something fragile was about to break or grow stronger depending on how he handled this.

"Could you?" she asked. "Could you really have done those things to me, Mal?"

Slowly nodding, he took one step forward with his palms up in surrender. "I *could*, but I would never. You asked me not to use my power on you. And I promise I won't. Chuck, I would never hurt you. I care about you too much. Please, don't be scared of me, Kelly."

Still studying him with an uneasy gaze, she pursed her lips and raised her chin. "So, what was that creature?"

"That was Hyacinth, my former commander. He's the one who turned me into a dog in the first place. It was supposed to be a punishment because I uh..." he broke off, embarrassed. He rubbed the back of his head and grinned sheepishly. "Well, I had a fling with his daughter. He didn't like that, so he forced me into the canine body and locked my powers down so I couldn't use them. I couldn't turn into this human form. I didn't have any contact with him again until just before Glenda did her thing. He appeared in the middle of the night in the backyard. You were asleep. That's when he told me to corrupt you, and he would give me my powers back as a reward. But he warned me that if I failed, he would punish me with a fate worse than final death. So, that's why I have to leave soon, because I won't go through with it. I won't corrupt you."

Chuck took one step closer. "I see," she said. She gently placed her hands on his arms and gazed into his eyes. "Malachi, I also remember I told you, you belong with me, and he can't have you."

Trembling, he gazed back at her, overcome with whatever this emotion was. "Kelly," he said before his throat closed.

"Shh, Malachi. Thank you. I believe you. I know I shouldn't. Common sense says no." She took his hand and placed it over her heart. "But this... this tells me to take this chance. I was never one to listen to reason. My dad always told me to follow my heart." Leaning forward, she kissed him again. Softer this time and with more emotion than lust.

"Kelly, I have to know something. If I can't find a way to break away from Hyacinth, he will kill me within days. I don't have long. So, I need to know, what is this between us? How do you feel about me?" His breath caught, and he shook inside, his stomach twisting and aching, waiting for her answer.

Shaking her head, she smiled softly. "I don't know what to call it. But I care about you a lot, and I could see being happy with you. I don't want you to leave. I don't want anyone else in your life or anyone else in mine. Is that enough for now?"

Nodding, he closed his eyes in relief. "More than enough. Chuck, no one has ever cared for me before. I've never cared either." He opened his eyes and brushed his fingers over her cheek. "Until now. Until you. So... please. Be patient with me. I guarantee you I'm going to mess up and say something stupid. Do something stupider. But always know, you're it for me."

"I do have one question, though," Chuck asked with a mischievous twinkle in her eyes as she tried but failed to keep the grin from her face. "Do you have another form? A demon form? Like that plant guy? That was horrible, and I don't know if I want to see you like that."

Malachi blinked once in surprise, then threw back his head and laughed heartily. "I do actually have another form. A demon form. It's nothing like his, though. He comes from one of the 'pure' demon lines." He shook his

head as he made sarcastic finger quotes. "There are a lot of demons that believe the uglier you are, the closer to Satan you are, therefore the more powerful you are. I don't subscribe to that, but looking like I do, I had to fight my way up the ladder to get where I was."

"Can I see it?" Chuck asked timidly, a small voice unlike her usual confident tone.

Sighing, Malachi shook his head. "Not yet, please. I'm not ready for that. Soon, though," he reassured her as her lips parted to argue. She looked disappointed and relieved at the same time, and he congratulated himself on making the right choice. His elation was short-lived as she smirked like she was plotting something. "What?" he asked warily.

"Now we have to go hang out with your buddy Jaxon and sing badly in front of other people!" she crowed. Spinning, she hurried back to her room to grab her purse.

It was only then that Malachi realized Chuck, his Chuck, was wearing a dress. A red body-hugging dress with cap sleeves and a flowing skirt that billowed around her legs. He'd seen her in far less clothing than this, but somehow, this felt more intimate. All his blood rushed south to his groin, and he grimaced. He wasn't sure how he was supposed to walk around like this. Shaking his head, he hurried to put on the shirt she mentioned. She may have been play-acting for Hyacinth, but he knew she was serious about liking this outfit.

Entering the bar with Chuck on his arm, watching all the men's heads turn at the sight of her, Malachi wanted to roar in pride. She was gorgeous

and captivating. And she was his. He didn't mind other men looking; he enjoyed eye candy as much as the next guy, or demon. Women were the most amazing and frustrating creatures on the planet. He could find something to appreciate about each and every one, regardless of their size, color, or personality. But Chuck was special, and he wanted to show her off.

"Stop it," she snapped through her teeth as she faked a smile, waving at her friends while they approached the table.

Tilting his head in question, he raised his eyebrows in inquiry.

"Quit strutting like a peacock. It's weird," she hissed, glancing at him.

"Can't help it. I have the prettiest girl in the city on my arm. Every man in here wants you. Some of the women, too. Those who don't want you, want to be you. So yeah, does my ego good." He smirked at her astonished expression as she stumbled and stopped. Leaning down, he brushed a light kiss over her parted lips. "Incubus. Sex demon. I know when people are lusting," he reminded her.

Shaking her head in amusement, her eyes suddenly widened. "Wait," she gasped, her expression now horrified. "You can tell when people are turned on?" she squeaked.

Nodding with a large grin spreading from ear to ear, he moved closer to her. "I can. Including you. Do you have *any* idea how difficult it's been to keep my hands to myself? Lucifer's left butt cheek, Chuck, every time you look at my hair, it gets me hard. Keep your eyes forward unless you want me to embarrass myself here."

With a strangled hum, Chuck's eyes flew to her friends, and she plastered her fake grin over her lips again as she tugged him forward.

A chuckle slipped from his throat as he murmured, "All one hundred of my peacock ass eyes are rolling at you right now. That smile isn't fooling anyone, you know."

Stopping again, she whirled and glared at him, her fake smile disappearing faster than a cat in a rocking chair factory. She poked him in the chest. “Bad dog,” she scolded.

“That’s my sassy girl!” he smirked and stepped against her. “But don’t call me that. It makes me want to prove what a good boy I am. Now get that perky ass over there before your cop friends come arrest me.” He smiled brightly, much better at fake grins than she was.

Taking a moment to arrange her features carefully this time, she turned to resume her journey to her friends. “Hey, guys, sorry, Evan just surprised me by telling me he’s a huge karaoke fan. I had no idea. Shocking really. But now I can’t wait to hear him sing.”

“That’s me, I’m Evan. Apparently, she’s so surprised she forgot to introduce me. Oh, wait, Jaxon, right? I met you in that parking lot.” Malachi smoothly offered his hand as everyone else introduced themselves. He nudged them all to like him instantly. All except Jaxon. He let that one stew in his own irritation.

“Evan,” purred one of the dispatchers. “Where has Chuck been hiding you? I’ve never heard your name from her lips. Of course, I can see why she’s keeping you to herself.” The woman ran a hand over her hair and inhaled deeply, thrusting her leopard print-covered breasts forward, her push-up bra fighting a valiant battle against gravity.

Malachi took a moment to enjoy the display before he turned an adoring gaze on Chuck. “Well, I’m not surprised. I’ve been keeping her to myself as well. There’s just something so incredibly captivating, mesmerizing, and completely irresistible about this stunning woman.” He gently stroked the back of his knuckles over her cheek, rubbing his thumb over her lower lip. Shaking himself as if waking up, he smiled abashedly at them. “Sorry, I just get so caught up in her I tend to forget others are around.” His eyes drifted back to her, like he couldn’t keep them away.

As the others in the group stared in disbelief, Chuck only had eyes for him. Finally, she remembered where she was and smiled at the others. "He's a charmer, isn't he? So, who's singing first?"

Jaxon grunted, "I think I'm up in a few more songs." He glanced over towards the sign-up table, his expression that of someone drinking sour milk.

After some good-natured jokes, the others crowded around the song list and made their selections. Malachi went along with Chuck's announcement and signed up as well. Sitting beside her again, he leaned to her ear, whispering, "I don't detect any darkness here. Just doucheness." He glanced at Jaxon with a leer.

"Stop it," she scolded. "Bennett's the only one missing."

After a few more singers, Jaxon's turn came up, and he sauntered to the stage amid a few cheers from some of the ladies in the bar. He winked at them and grabbed the microphone in a confident manner that screamed he was a regular. It was apparent he felt he was about to command the room.

Malachi settled back in his chair and narrowed his eyes. He hummed and blurted, "Nickelback. He's going to sing a Nickelback song, isn't he?"

Snorting in amusement, Chuck covered her mouth to stifle her giggle. The others held no such restraint, and the whole table burst into laughter.

"Oh, man, he already knows him well, doesn't he!" barked one of the other officers, clapping Malachi on the shoulder.

The laughter grew even louder to the point that everyone in the bar was staring at them. The stares included that of Jaxon, who was so thrown off that he missed the intro to the song and had to scramble to find his place. To his credit, he did sing well, having a pleasant tenor, but it was indeed *Hero,* by Nickelback.

26

Cupid Plays a Wicked Game

Malachi leaned against the table and braced his elbows on the sticky wood, propping his chin in his hands, intently watching Jaxon. It was enough to make the man nervous, and his voice cracked a few times. By the time he finished the song, he was a shaking mess.

"Stop it, Mal," Chuck murmured as she elbowed him in the ribs. "Play nice or you're going home."

"I *am* being nice!" he hissed, glaring as he rubbed his side. "I could have made the hooker in the corner go grab his nuts while he was on the stage. But you didn't consider that, did you?"

She stared at him, eyes wide, lips slightly parted. "You can do that?"

Putting just a little flame in his eyes, he smirked. "Oh, Chuck, I can do just about anything. Since I got my full form back, all my powers are returning." His lips quirked as her mouth opened and closed a few times.

"Can you... nudge two people together without really forcing them?" she asked now with a calculating expression. Her eyes darted between Jaxon and the quiet dispatcher sitting at the other end of the table. "Marla

has a huge crush on Jax, but she's too shy to approach him. And he needs someone like her in his life. Could you, I don't know… help them?"

A strained sigh, then a deeper groan, and finally a hard flop back into his chair had Malachi staring at her with a grimace.

"Too much? It's too much, I'm sorry I asked," she offered quickly and gave him an awkward smile as she tried to lighten the mood.

"No. It's not too much. And I can. I'm just conflicted. The demon in me—the demon I was before you—would do it in a heartbeat just to mess with them. The me now—the me that cares about you and is trying to be… good." He swallowed down some nausea. "Knows I shouldn't toy with people's emotions or interfere in their lives." He squeezed the bridge of his nose. "This is one of those I don't know what to do here things."

A soft, warm hand landed on his arm, and he opened his eyes to find Chuck smiling at him, genuinely this time. "Honestly, that's so sweet. I think the answer here is don't make decisions based on what you think makes you a better person. Do what seems right at the time. I'm not asking you to interfere overly much. I just think she needs help overcoming her inhibitions, her shyness. And he needs to be open to a woman who isn't a supermodel." She tried in vain to tamp down the curve of her lips. "Don't force them together, just give them the nudge they need and let them take it from there."

"Chuck." He snorted. "I'm not fucking Cupid. This better not become a frequent thing." His eyebrow arched sternly as she batted her eyelashes at him.

"It won't!" she promised. "Besides, look at it this way. If Jaxon has a love interest, he'll leave me alone. And it might make him less douchey."

Sitting straight up, with wide, eager eyes, Malachi grinned as he eyed Jaxon sitting halfway down the table. The man was drowning his nerves in a beer after his less-than-perfect performance.

"Alright, I'll do it. But I'm only lowering her inhibitions and raising his awareness of her. I'm not making them fall in love. And no guarantees!" he warned.

Miming zipping her lips, Chuck hugged him quickly.

Turning towards Jaxon, Malachi shuddered briefly and delved into the man's mind. He found Jaxon's desire for Chuck and grimaced at how much the man wanted her. Dialing it back, he smirked as the other man's shoulders drooped, and his expression turned forlorn. Without Chuck to moon over, it seemed he had no reason to pretend to be macho. He nearly shriveled in on himself. Huffing out as near to a righteous laugh as he was able, Malachi then turned his attention to Marla.

Studying the timid, mousy woman, Malachi realized she was actually quite pretty; she just didn't have much confidence or know how to best present herself. "Get her to the bathroom," he murmured to Chuck. "I need to fix a few things first."

Eying him warily, Chuck leapt from her chair. Looping her arm through Marla's, she pulled the woman to her feet and dragged her away. "Marla, honey, come here with me a moment, I want you to meet someone!"

The other woman's bewildered stare as she obediently followed Chuck had Malachi choking back a laugh. He waited a moment for their disappearance to be out of mind, then stood. "Gonna grab another round, be right back," he murmured and headed towards the bar.

Leaning against the scarred surface, he tapped his fingers to the music as he gave his order to the bubbly blonde who had been undressing him with her eyes since they arrived. Winking as she quickly supplied him with a tumbler of scotch, he slipped some cash her way. The money was made from ether, and the bills would dissolve into nothing when he left at the end of the night. He supposed he should feel bad about it, and he was sure Chuck would scold him. But he would worry about that later, if he even

told her. Watching the door, he was finally sure the bathroom was empty except for Chuck and Marla.

Making his way over, he cast his form into the shadows and slipped between the small gap in the frame. Leaning against the inside of the wood panel, he sealed the door closed with his power and moved closer to Chuck. "Hi," he breathed in her ear, chuckling when she jumped. His shadows had concealed him from her view as well. "Sorry, didn't mean to startle you." Lie, he absolutely had.

The expression on her face suggested Chuck didn't believe him, so he moved around her and approached the confused and overwhelmed Marla. "Hello, Marla," he practically purred.

"Y-you c-can't be in here!" she protested nervously, her fingers fluttering and twisting the hem of her blouse. "This is the w-women's room."

"I know. And you are a woman. A beautiful one." He nodded, pleased that she nodded along with him as his influence wrapped around her. "But Marla, do you know what makes me sad?"

She mechanically shook her head side to side, eyes widening, mesmerized by his voice.

Sliding behind her, he placed his hands on her shoulders and turned her to face the mirror. He slipped a finger under her chin and lifted her face towards her reflection. "Look at yourself," he commanded softly. "See that gorgeous creature staring back at you?"

Her eyes filled, and she shook her head again. "I don't," she whimpered.

"That. That's what makes me sad. Such beauty, and you don't even know it. Marla," he breathed on her neck and lifted her hair from her shoulders. "Pull this hair back from your face. Quit hiding behind it." He twisted the hair around and formed a clip from the ether, securing the thick locks of her mahogany tresses in a pretty up-do. "There, now we can see that strong jaw, the pert nose, those gorgeous amber eyes."

Marla stared at herself now, intrigued despite her shyness.

"Now, pull those shoulders back, show the world you are Marla, and you mean business. You are gorgeous, self-assured, and aware of your appeal." He nudged her arms to move behind her, and she transformed before their eyes into a confident, alluring woman. She perked her breasts up and raised her chin. Her eyes filled with a certainty that she was desirable. Malachi tapered off his charm, leaving the confidence he'd been pushing into her. "You won't remember me, but you'll remember Chuck brought you in here and gave you a pep-talk. She encouraged you to talk to Jaxon. He's lonely; he needs someone who wants him. That someone should be you." He pulled a tube of lipstick from the ether and handed it to her, watching with satisfaction as she slicked the deep crimson across her lips.

Chuck stared in awed silence now. Watching the way her co-worker changed, with the right kind of belief in herself. She jerked her gaze to Malachi as he stepped back into the shadows and swirled towards the door, releasing the seal.

"Kelly," Marla called, her voice lacking its usual timid tremble and whispery quality. Now her tone was warm, assured, and confident. "Thank you for the pep-talk and the fashion tips." She patted her hair and preened in the mirror. "I never would have worn this color. I'm grateful you suggested it."

Nodding quickly, Chuck replied, "You're welcome, Marla. It looks great on you. The color really warms up your skin."

Tilting her head to the side and studying her reflection, Marla's mouth curved into a wicked bow. "It does. And now, I'm going to make Jaxon buy me a drink."

"Good for you!" Chuck declared excitedly, squeezing the other woman's shoulder. "Go get him!"

Marla spun on her heel and marched determinedly to the door, flinging it open before continuing her forceful approach towards their table.

Chuck followed quickly, Malachi on her heels. “That was impressive,” she called over her shoulder.

“It didn’t take much. I just made her see what was true about her. She did the rest.” He put a hand on Chuck’s waist and spun her back to him. “Dance with me,” he murmured, pulling her close.

Dancing with Chuck was something he would cherish forever. Well, as long as his forever lasted, considering he expected to be dead in a few days. Another couple joined them, and his smile grew larger at Chuck’s excited squeal, seeing it was Marla and Jaxon.

“I really like what you’ve done with your hair, Marla,” Jaxon shouted over the music.

Chuck leaned her head against Malachi’s chest. “Thank you,” she murmured. “That was a really nice thing you did.”

Grunting, Malachi waggled one hand. “That remains to be seen. Sometimes when there’s smoke, it doesn’t always flash to a fire. Sometimes, those sparks fade out, and there’s nothing but cold, lonely ash in their place.” He glanced down and smiled sheepishly. “Sorry, I know that’s a little morbid.”

“Morbid,” she agreed, “but poetic and accurate.” A gleam filled her eyes, now hearing his fake name being called to the front. “Go on, Evan, it’s your time to shine!” Shoving him forward, she hurried to their table, starting a raucous cheer with her friends, chanting his ‘name’.

Rolling his eyes, Malachi approached the stage, confirmed his song choice with the man running the sound, and stepped up to the microphone. The opening notes sounded, and he let some of his incubus power swirl through the room, enhancing everyone’s desires and awareness into a dream-like state. Everyone except for Chuck. He wrapped her in a protective layer to keep her from feeling his magic. His lips parted, and the first

dark, intriguing line of *Wicked Game,* by Chris Isaak floated through the room.

Women began to fan themselves, men started draining their drinks, and many couples took to the dance floor. Chuck sat, mesmerized by his voice, and it filled him with pride, knowing it wasn't his magic that kept her rapt attention. He continued his skillful yet seductive rendering of the song, letting his voice rise and fall with the intensity of the lyrics to the delight of those in the bar. His vocals tantalized the back of their necks, like fingers teasing just above their skin. Stroking and strumming their awareness of each other into a near frenzy.

As the final outro played, his voice lingered in the smoky room, resting like a physical layer on everyone's bodies. There was silence for a heartbeat. Then another. Then every pair of hands came together with thunderous applause. Shouts, whistles, and marriage proposals followed Malachi back to the table.

Standing in front of Chuck, he said nothing. Simply gazing into her eyes as she stared, unblinking at him. Finally, he pulled his hands from his pockets and held his palms up in question.

"Incredible," she said. "Was that really you? Or magic?"

"That was me." He smiled. "I used my power to enhance how people responded, but not on you. I kept it off you. But the singing, that was all my true voice."

"Your voice is perfect. You know, I just realized, you sound exactly the same out loud as you do in my head when you're... you know."

Laughing, he leaned down. "Woof."

"Right. I know you were using your power on the others, but what I don't know is why. You didn't have to do that to make them like you. They would have anyway."

He tilted his head and smirked. "Because I wanted you to see what I'm capable of, so you're aware. That was barely a hint. But I didn't touch you with it because you asked me not to."

Smiling softly, she tilted her head. "I felt it. I felt you wrap me in... well, I don't know what it was, but it was like a warm blanket. I felt safe. Secure. Cherished."

"I do," he responded immediately, then blinked. "I... ch-ch- cherish you," he stammered. "Sorry, some words are hard to say." He smiled apologetically.

Seeming intrigued by that idea, Chuck traced his jaw with a finger and stared at his lips. "Like what? What other words?"

A small laugh at her question had her squinting at him in annoyance. "Why is that funny?" she demanded in irritation.

"Because you're so cute. I tell you I can't do something, and you immediately want me to try it anyway. I don't know if it's because you're not a quitter and you don't believe in giving up, or you're a sadistic mistress and you like me in pain. Is that it? Do you want to hurt me?" His lips curved so sinfully, his smile would melt the panties off a nun. It nearly melted Chuck's. He could see her aura streaking with lust again.

"The former!" she blurted breathlessly. "Definitely the former."

Shaking his head slightly, he sucked in a deep breath and blew it slowly through his lips. "Alright, anything to do with the guy up there?" He pointed up. "Like the big G dude, and little JC, you know? Can't say their names. Can't do the p thing you guys do in a... um... that building where you w-w- ugh—sounds like war ship—you know sing special songs and talk about that one book."

"God, Jesus Christ, pray, church, worship, hymns, the Bible?" she ticked off on her fingers.

Malachi swayed on his feet before grabbing the back of a chair as his stomach heaved. Choking on bile, he managed to swallow it down and bite back the wave of nausea. He nodded meekly as he stared at her through watery eyes. A shaky thumbs up confirmed it for her, while he wiped a film of cold sweat from his upper lip.

"Oh, good grief, Malachi, I'm so sorry!" she murmured as she shook her head. "I didn't realize it would have that kind of physical effect on you." Studying his obvious discomfort, she shook her head harder. "Damn, I really am sorry!"

He noted her aura was now streaked with gray, lending veracity to her words. Nodding, he waved off her apology. She truly didn't know and hadn't done it on purpose. "It's okay," he croaked. "Just don't do that again." He wiped his clammy hands on his thighs to dry them.

"I keep forgetting. You know? That you're a literal demon from Hell and not just a hot guy with super woo-woo powers like Glenda." She smiled slightly, seeming mollified by his acceptance of her apology.

"Woo-woo powers?" He snorted, wrinkling his nose in mock disgust. "I'm going to forget you said that and focus on the fact that you think I'm hot." Suddenly, he straightened, his senses on high alert, nausea gone. He stood perfectly still and moved only his eyes, searching the crowd.

Chuck noticed the change in his demeanor and also went on high alert. "What is it? What do you see?"

Shaking his head, he slowly raised one hand in a wait gesture before speaking to her with his mind. *Not see, smell. Sense. The dark presence. The one I detected at that kidnapping scene. Is Bennett here? Don't make it obvious, just a casual glance around.*

"You're right, Evan, you should sing another song. Hey, maybe Jax will do another one, too!" She glanced around, ostensibly looking for Jaxon. Spotting him on the dance floor, she waved and gave him an enthusiastic

thumbs-up. “Well, maybe not Jax, he’s busy. How about...” tapping a finger on her lips, she studied the group around the table. “Oh, Bennett! When did you get here? Hey, are you going to sing? I was just telling Evan I want him to sing another song, but I think he needs some encouragement.” Playfully, she patted Malachi on the chest. Turning to the other officer, she smacked her forehead. “Oh, I’m sorry. You haven’t met, have you? Evan, this is Nathan Bennett. I work with him sometimes. Bennett, this is my boyfriend, Evan.”

27

Pointy Elbows and Black Feathers

Malachi leaned forward and shook the hand of the slender man, whose sandy hair was nicely blending into the gray at his temples. An impressive mustache nearly covered his upper lip, but his chin was as bare as a baby's bottom. His stark blue eyes locked onto Malachi with heavy appraisal as he squinted and squeezed back. Fairly harder than was necessary, but Malachi gave as good as he got. "Nice to meet you, Bennett. Or should I call you Nathan? What's the protocol for a civilian here?" He released Bennett's hand and smiled unassumingly.

"Bennett's fine," the older man huffed. He glanced at Chuck, his gaze softening. "Boyfriend, huh? Well, it's about time. But let me know if he steps outta line. Your daddy would want me to keep an eye on things." He chuckled with a crinkle around his eyes that implied he was only partially teasing. Turning a glare at Malachi, the part that wasn't teasing was clearly a warning.

"I've heard a lot of wonderful things about the late Officer Charles. He sounds like an amazing person. I'm sorry I won't get to meet him. Were you partners?" Malachi asked softly.

It was the right thing to say as Bennett's suspicious gaze fell, and his shoulders relaxed. "Yeah, Chuck senior *was* a great man. A damn shame what happened to him. An absolute travesty they never caught the bastards responsible." His cheeks flushed with seeming anger now, and he shook his head. "Well, Evan, I won't be singing with you, but if you're up for a beer, I'm interested in that!"

Grinning, Malachi beamed. "I'd love that, sir!"

Bennett pointed, and his mustache twitched. "Don't call me sir, you don't work for me." He smirked to show he was teasing and slapped Malachi on the shoulder as he waved a waitress over.

Chuck elbowed Malachi in the side again and widened her eyes in question.

Rubbing his side—again—Malachi glared at her. *Damn pointy-elbowed woman. Can't you just tap my arm? Or squeeze my hand? Stroke my thigh? Why do you have to jam your bony ass arm into me like that?*

A fair imitation of a growl escaped her lips, and her aura was streaked with lightning-like bolts zigzagging through it.

Calm down, Chuck. He's clean. Well, not completely clean. There's still a faint haze of darkness around him, but it's not coming from him if that makes any sense. Malachi squinted at the other man, who was ordering beers for the table. *It definitely doesn't originate with him. It's like, it's clinging to him because of extended proximity. You know how, if you're in a bar, when you leave, you'll smell like stale cigarettes, even if you don't smoke?* At her slight nod, he continued, *It's similar to that. I think he spends a lot of time around someone who is dark. That's who we need to find.*

Hesitating for a moment, Malachi slipped his fingers in hers. *Chuck, I meant what I said earlier. I do wish I could have met your dad. He really did sound like a great guy. I mean, if I were human, or he wouldn't smite me. You know, cause I'm a demon.* To his absolute horror, Chuck's fingers clamped on his, and her eyes went shiny. Her lips compressed in a thin line, and her aura turned almost solid black.

"I'm sorry," he blurted, tracing a finger over her cheek. "I didn't mean to make you so sad. Please, don't cry."

Frantically shaking her head, she leaned against his chest and hid her face. "No," she replied. "It's okay. Just sometimes, thoughts of him catch me off guard, and I have to reset. It was sweet, Mal. I think he would have liked you once he got to know you. I know he would. Look, I'm going to go to the bathroom and splash some water on my face. Take a quick breather. Why don't you see if you can learn anything about Bennett?" She squeezed his arm and hurried off before he could answer.

Briefly, he thought of going after her, but Bennett placed a companionable hand on his shoulder. "You really care about her a lot, don't you?"

Not trusting his voice, Malachi simply nodded in response before clearing his throat.

"That's good. Real good. Girl needs someone to look after her."

Malachi snorted. "I'm under no delusions that woman can't look after herself, and I'm not too proud to admit she could probably kick my ass."

Bursting into deep booming laughter, Bennett clapped him hard on the back. "Alright, Evan. Dammit, I like you. You're right, she's more than physically capable. But her heart needs to be watched over. She's always been so stubborn and determined to prove she's capable of anything and everything. Her daddy's death hit her a lot harder than she's willing to admit. So be good to her, but give her some space for a minute."

"Wise words," Malachi murmured. "How'd you get so smart? Is there a Mrs. Bennett who teaches you these things? I may need some lessons."

Chuckling, Bennett smirked. "Nah. I mean, there was. Twice. Both of 'em divorced me. Takes a different kind of woman to be a cop's partner. Long hours, unpredictable nights, cases you can't leave at the office sometimes. It's hard. And with Chuck, you have the added bonus of that dog of hers. Malachi. Man, that is a damn fine officer in his own right."

Chest puffing with pride, Malachi was about to thank the man for the compliment when he felt a burst of panic wash over him. Dizziness assaulted his body, and a blast of angelic grace slammed him against the table. *Kelly!* He screamed in his head.

Out loud, Malachi claimed he was running to the restroom but barreled out the back door instead, following the smell of grace and fear like a shark scenting blood in water. An unearthly roar ripped from his throat as his eyes quickly absorbed the scene.

Chuck lay on the ground, clutching her arm, blood and angelic grace leaking in equal proportions. She was glaring and shouting threats at the man who stood over her, holding a forsaken blade in one hand, a gun in the other. Both weapons were trained on her steadily. Madness swirled in his eyes as he glared at her with undisguised fervor for the perceived right in what he was about to do.

At Malachi's roar, the man looming over Chuck jerked his head up and stared at him in shock. "Stay out of this, man, you don't know what she is! She needs to die!"

Snarling, as his skin began to ripple and roil uncontrollably with his irritation, Malachi clenched his jaws together tightly. His teeth elongated into fangs, and his eyes glowed with Hellfire. "What she is..." he hissed, his voice deepening until the timbre resembled an erupting volcano, "is *mine.* She belongs to me. What you should be more worried about is what *I* am." An evil chuckle bounced off the brick walls enclosing the small space. It rattled across the surface of the old, crumbling mortar, sending sandy particles dancing with fear into the night. The sound was followed by loud cracking as Malachi's bones snapped and reformed. A bit dramatic? Abso-fucking-lutely. But he wanted to scare the soul right out of the man's body.

His skin darkened to a deep swirling dusky gray, similar to that of the sky before an impending storm. Ebony horns that glistened in the streetlight spiraled from his head as they tapered to razor-sharp points reaching for the faint moonlight above them. A roiling fog of sickly green mist swept around his body as it grew upwards, his height expanding to a little over nine feet. Massive feathery wings, black as a raven, sprouted from his back and spread behind him, blocking the feeble light and throwing their tableau into further shadows.

Reaching the final stage of his true demon form, Malachi roared again. This time, fire shot from his hands, scorching the man's fingers, forcing him to drop the gun. "You will release that blade and step back. I'm giving you this one warning only, then I'll end you. It *will* be messy, and I *will* enjoy it." An echoing growl emanated from deep in his throat, rattling the nearby dumpsters, punctuating his fury with their metallic shivers. He didn't dare look at Chuck; he couldn't bear to see the disgust on her face at his monstrous form.

An unhinged laugh from the man echoed throughout the alley. "You're a demon? And you're *protecting her?*" he demanded incredulously. "We're

working toward the same goal!" he shouted, tightly gripping his hair with his free hand. "This doesn't make sense! All her kind must die! Why would you stop me?"

Shrugging his massive shoulders, Malachi grinned obnoxiously, showing all his fangs. "Dibs," he replied casually. Leaning down, he studied the man closely. He was an average nobody—sandy hair, pale washed-out skin, like he'd been inside too long, and faded blue eyes the color of worn-out denim. Ultimately, he was utterly forgettable. Someone you passed on the street and promptly forgot. Slumped shoulders, frumpy clothes the color of mud, and ratty shoes with one lace untied. Hardly the portrait of a crazed zealot, hellbent on destroying the host of Heaven.

But there was no mistaking the burning determination in his gaze. He truly believed Chuck to be an enemy and that she deserved to die. Too bad for him, his belief was wrong.

Snorting, Malachi whipped his claws out fast as a snake and wrapped them around the man's ankles. Snatching him into the air, he dangled the attacker upside down and peered into his eyes again. "So, this is the part where you drop that blade." A wordless denial from the inverted man, made Malachi growl and shake him like a rag doll. The metallic clang as the sword hit the asphalt below drew a satisfied hum from his throat. "There we go, now you're being more reasonable." He bobbed his chin encouragingly.

"Put me down! Let me go!" the man screamed, terror causing his voice to crack and shake now.

"No, I think I'll turn you into a chew toy for my friend Reena. She's a little bit psycho and needs to taste human flesh before she becomes a fully-fledged Hellhound." Malachi raised his arm up and down a few times, bouncing the man like a yo-yo, chuckling as the captive screamed.

The smell of his fear was delicious. “Hey, do you think you’re gonna piss yourself? It makes this a lot more fun,” he confided wistfully.

A soft hand on his leg drew his attention to Chuck, standing beside him. He blinked, suddenly highly aware that she was seeing the real him. Waiting for her to shudder and withdraw, or maybe scream and run, he held his breath.

“Put him down, Mal, let me arrest him. We need to know if he killed my father,” came her soft admonishment.

Startled, he exhaled on a heavy gust before he slowly lowered the man to the ground and placed one massive taloned foot on top of him, pinning him in place. “Yeah, if that’s what you want,” he mumbled. “I was kidding about the Hellhound thing. Reena’s too small to be a real one.” He shrugged apologetically, waiting for her next reaction.

“This is your true demon form, isn’t it?” came her quiet, but not timid question. Her voice was steady and low.

Nodding reluctantly, he stared at his toes, watching her attacker squirm, trying to get away.

“Bend down so I can see you better,” she instructed, her tone brooking no argument.

Perplexed now, he slowly crouched, sitting back on his heels so his eyes were level with hers. He held perfectly still as she studied his body. Reaching up tentatively, she traced her fingers over one of his horns, marveling at the complexity of the swirling spire. She ran her fingers through his hair, still black like his human form, but trailing down almost to his waist. Squatting as he was, it nearly brushed the concrete beneath him. A smile crept over her lips as she wrapped his hair around her wrist, then let it fall like a curtain around him. He finally smirked at that. He knew she was obsessed with his hair, but she hadn’t finished her study of him yet.

Finished with her perusal of his front, she began a slow, torturous circuit around him. Standing behind him now, she made an inquisitive hum, which he understood was her asking permission to touch his wings. "Yes," came his quiet reply. Soft fingers traced the scarred patterns on his back before they finally tangled in the feathers and stroked them. He shuddered and moaned at the touch, overcome by how sensitive they were.

"Sorry!" she yelped, snatching her hands back. "I didn't mean to—"

"No," he reassured her quickly. "It didn't hurt. In fact, it felt good. Really good. I've never had anyone touch my wings before. Chuck..." He trailed off, not wanting to ask her what she was thinking, but slowly dying inside, not knowing.

Her footsteps sounded as she finished her circuit and stood in front of him again. "Malachi, you're beautiful."

Mouth dropping open in a near comical fashion, he stared, unable to formulate any words. "Uh... I... um..." he sputtered. Taking a deep breath, he shook his large head and smiled ruefully at the tiny woman staring at him defiantly now, hands on her hips, ready to take him down with the slightest provocation. "Wow, that was intelligent. Chuck, I think you need your eyes checked. I'm not beautiful." He snorted as she started to disagree. "I'm Hellspawn. A demon. Dark and brooding. Monstrous. You should be terrified."

Shaking her head fiercely, refuting his words, she threw her hands in the air. "Yeah, okay, maybe. To be honest, I probably would be if I didn't know you. But I'm not, Mal. Because I *do* know you, and I know I trust you with my life. You saved me again tonight. And you are beautiful. Your wings are gorgeous! You look like an oncoming storm, a harbinger of the fury within. But you're still you, just... bigger. And darker." Stepping closer, she whispered, "Malachi, you're my storm." Her hands landed on

his shoulders, and she leaned in, placing her small lips to his while carefully avoiding his fangs as she kissed him gently.

When she backed up, he couldn't find the words to say what he wanted. He didn't understand the emotions coursing through him. They were new, shiny, and warm. She wasn't scared of him! She *liked* his demon form. Tilting his head, he studied her smile for any sign of duplicity but only found straightforward acceptance and trust. Finally, he smiled at her. "Thank you, Kelly. You might be crazy, but I'm glad you are. I... I feel... shit. I don't know how to say those words and mean them. I never have before, and I don't know if I'm able. I feel... I'm..." He stared forlornly into her eyes. Raising a claw, he gently rubbed it down her cheek.

Chuck smiled softly, and he hoped it meant she understood what he couldn't say. She closed her eyes and leaned into his touch, rubbing her face against his massive palm. "Mal..." she breathed.

A choked, sputtering cough broke the spell they held over each other as they glanced down at the man under Malachi's foot. He'd been suffocating as the demon subconsciously leaned towards Chuck. They both studied him disinterestedly until the man's lips turned blue.

"So, what do I do with this?" Malachi inquired as he pulled the man to his feet, chuckling at his ragged gasps. Shrinking back into human form, he shook the captive again, still strong enough to lift him off the ground.

"First, I want to know his name," Chuck declared darkly, her cheeks flushing and her eyebrows bunching together like thunderclouds. "And why he killed my father!" Her eyelashes fluttered at this, as if trying to hold back angry tears that were no doubt boiling hot.

"I'm not telling you anything!" the captive shouted. "You'll kill me!"

Malachi shook him. "She won't, but I will if you don't start talking."

The man cackled, a crazed braying. "A demon in love with an angel. What world am I living in?"

"You heard the lady, you miserable piece of shit. Answer her before I make you taste pain," Malachi growled. He picked up the forsaken blade and waved it under the man's nose threateningly. When the man merely clenched his lips together tighter, Malachi flashed Hellfire in his eyes and shook the creep so hard his neck nearly snapped. "Or I'll just take your soul now and find out everything I need to know." He inhaled hard and tugged lightly at the edge of the dark, tainted soul, just enough so his prisoner could feel the searing pain of it.

"B-B-Blake!" the would-be assassin shouted. "Please! Stop! My name's Blake. Blake Bennett."

Chuck froze, and all color drained from her face, leaving her pale and sickly appearing. She swayed on her feet, then grabbed the wall for support as her knees almost gave out. "No," she cried. "Not Nathan's son."

28

Demons Drive Offensively

Red and blue lights bounced dizzily off the brick behind the bar like some disco circus that was high on LSD. Malachi studied the strobing pulses of color with detached interest as he remained crouched next to Chuck, refusing to leave her side. He steadily rubbed his hand in circles over her back, offering comfort, trying to soothe her. The revelation that her attacker was her co-worker's son had rocked her world. She was staring blindly at the ground, occasionally a ripple of something shook her small frame as some memory or recollection made her shudder.

"Chuck," he whispered, pulling the blanket tighter around her shoulders. "I know this is a bad time to think about it, and I know they need to take the sword into evidence, but we must get it back. I need to know where it came from so I can figure out who's behind this." She nodded stiffly, almost mechanically, at his words, and he was unsure if she truly comprehended him.

Glancing over toward the sound of a car door opening, he watched as an officer shoved a meek, compliant, and now handcuffed Blake into the back of the squad car. His father stood by, expressionless and motionless,

his hands tightly clenched in front of him. His fingers were turning white from how hard they were clenched. If not for the occasional rise and fall of his chest, one might think he was a statue. His eyes were blazing with fury and disgust as he watched his son being driven away.

Once the taillights were out of sight, Bennett's hands abruptly dropped to his sides. He flexed his fingers, stretching them to return blood flow, and turned slowly towards Chuck. His steps wooden and dragging, he made his way to her side before squatting in front of her. "Kelly," he called softly.

Her eyes jerked up to his.

"I'm so sorry," Bennett blurted, his voice thick with emotion. Betrayal, fear, sadness, so many different feelings were wrapped up in his words. He shook his head. "I... I don't know what else to say. I didn't even know he was in town, much less..." Blowing out a sharp breath, he stared over her head. His eyes were fixed on the brick wall behind her, as if the consistency of the mortar was of the utmost importance.

Finally, his gaze snapped back to hers. "Chuck, I didn't know Blake was here. I haven't seen him for months. He hasn't forgiven me for his mother leaving me, so we aren't that close. I promise, if I had known he was—sick—like that..." he sighed heavily. "Please, believe me. I never would have let him out of my sight."

"Nathan," she responded tiredly. "He's a grown adult. There's nothing you could have done. I just... I need to know Nathan. I need to know if he killed my father. He seemed to think I was evil."

"I promise you, Kelly. We will find out. If he killed your dad..." he choked up. Clearing his throat and shaking his head, he started again. "If he did it, I promise, I will stand with you and make sure he's punished to the full extent of the law." He squeezed her hands tightly for a moment before turning to Malachi. "Evan, thank you. Thank you for being there for her."

Nodding, not trusting himself to speak without giving his opinion on Nathan's parenting skills, Malachi pulled Chuck to her feet. "C'mon, sweetheart, let's get you home and tucked in bed. I'm sure Malachi will cuddle up with you if you want."

At this, Chuck clapped a hand over her mouth and burst into giggles. She leaned against him, her shoulders shaking with laughter as she tried to rein in her hysteria. Finally, the laughing turned to sobbing, and Malachi scooped her up in his arms, cradling her against his chest.

Turning to the others, he gave an apologetic smile. "Gonna take her home. Been a long day. Nice meeting you all, see you 'round I hope." He tilted his chin up in what he hoped was a convincing and reassuring manner before turning swiftly and carrying her to the car. Fishing the keys from her purse, he unlocked it and then settled her gently into the passenger seat. Fastening her seatbelt, he pressed a soft kiss on her forehead. "I've got you," he whispered.

Hurrying around to the driver's side, he slid behind the wheel and huffed softly before starting the vehicle. "Here's hoping I can figure out how to drive between here and your house."

Chuck sat up quickly and stared at him with wide, horrified eyes as he put the car into gear and pressed the gas. "Malachi!" she squeaked.

"Kidding! I know how to drive!" he smirked. "Just wanted to distract you. But I meant it, Chuck. I'm here. I've got you."

"Jerk," she murmured softly. "Thank you, Malachi. Sorry, I spaced out there. I appreciate you being there for me." Lightly stroking her fingers over his forearm, she frowned. "Do... do you think Bennett knew? Was he acting? Or was he just as shocked as I was?"

Absently patting her hand, Malachi shared his thoughts. "I think he's lying. He may not have known what his son intended, but he knew he was around. It's why I was sensing darkness on him. The darkness that's on

Nathan—that faint haze—is the same as what's cloaking Blake. So, he's definitely been around him. Had to be for it to rub off on him like that. I don't know *why* he's lying, or to what extent." Glancing over through the darkened car, he watched lights from the passing streetlamps play across her face, her expression turning troubled.

He had to fight the urge to pull over and take her in his arms. The best thing now would be to get her home and tend to her wound further. Then he could wrap her up with him and never let go. His stomach churned, sour with acid as he thought about how close he came to losing her. If she weren't such a fighter in her own right, Blake might have succeeded in his mission.

"I'm impressed by you, Chuck," he murmured, the corners of his lips twitching at her startled gaze. "Don't act so surprised, I am capable of that, you know. I just... well, I've been around for a while, and most women I've known would either be dead or have fallen completely apart by now. You not only escaped, but you're also working through the facts and trying to figure this out. For the love of Satan, you're fucking bleeding and still trying to solve the mystery." He shook his head. "Anyone else, I'd think they're crazy. But it's you, so I know it's because you're so strong. And relentless. It's impressive."

"Thanks, Mal, that means a lot to me." She grimaced and glanced at her arm. "Speaking of bleeding, how did you even know to come out there?"

Tightening his grip on the wheel, he eased the car to a smooth stop at a red light. Turning to gaze at her fully, he explained, "I felt you. I felt your fear. Your pain. I thought my heart was going to burst right out of my chest. I knew something was wrong, and then I was hit with this... I don't know... tsunami I guess, of your grace. The only reason I would feel that is if you had either performed a miracle, you smote someone, or your blood was

spilled with a forsaken blade. I knew the first two were unlikely, so I had to get to you."

A honk came behind them as the light turned green, and he didn't immediately move the car. Malachi glanced in the mirror and gave a small apologetic wave, turning back to leave when the person behind them laid on the horn and began gesturing rudely. Growling, Malachi's eyes flashed with Hellfire, and he raised one hand. Snapping his fingers, flames suddenly billowed from under the hood of the offending driver's vehicle. Dismayed cries and bellows filled the air as Malachi slowly pulled away from the light and continued on his way.

"Malachi!" Chuck scolded. "You can't do things like that!" She watched behind them as the driver frantically ran around waving his arms for help.

"Pretty sure I just did, Chuck," he retorted dryly.

Snorting and shaking her head, she rolled her eyes. "You know what I mean. Yeah, you *can,* but that doesn't mean you *should.*"

"Well, just because he could honk at me, doesn't mean he should have!" Malachi protested. "He was a dickhead, he deserved it!" He smiled innocently at her. "At least I didn't take his soul," he offered, batting his eyelashes.

Blinking several times, Chuck finally barked out a short laugh. "Demon. Right." She sighed, "I guess you're getting more comfortable being your true self around me, aren't you?"

Shrugging, he hummed, "Eehhh. I've always been like this. You just couldn't always hear me."

"You heard me, though," she murmured, frowning now. "You heard that I was scared. I guess maybe heard isn't right. You felt it. You somehow sensed I needed you. Why is that, do you think?"

"I guess it was just all that grace coming through. It was like an instant sunburn. My skin suddenly felt like it was on fire, prickling and tingling all

over. I was filled with this sick sense of dread. I knew. I just *knew* something bad was happening to you. And I couldn't stand it, Chuck. The thought of you being hurt." He shook his head as he pulled into her driveway and parked. Turning to face her in the dark shadow of her house, he reached for her, cupping her cheek in his hand. "No one... better lay a fucking finger on you, Chuck."

Smiling and laying her hand over his own, she replied. "Careful there, demon-boy. If I didn't know you weren't capable of it, I'd think you were developing *real* feelings for me."

Pulling her slowly to him until her nose was touching his, Malachi whispered, "But I am capable, and I've got all kinds of interesting feelings for you."

Swallowing hard, Chuck shrugged. "Yeah, I'm sure you think you are. Well, let's feel what it would be like to go inside and re-bandage this cut."

Letting go quickly as if her skin had scalded him, Malachi snatched his hands back. Chuck lurched forward slightly, no longer being supported. She frowned, perhaps realizing her words had caused his reaction. Nodding in silence, he turned off the car and exited, hurrying to her door to offer a hand she didn't need but accepted anyway. He wasn't even sure she would take his hand, knowing how poorly he had misread her. He'd begun to think she wanted him in more than a sexual way before tonight, that she cared for him and wanted his feelings in return. But the way she'd pulled back from him, he figured seeing his demon form earlier must have changed her mind. Maybe she was trying to let him down gently.

Confusion swirled through him, causing a deep ache in the pit of his stomach. *I completely suck at reading women,* he thought in disgust. His inner voice quietly corrected him, *not all women, just this one.* Shushing his reasonable side, he steadied her and helped her into the house. When she didn't move fast enough for his liking, he simply scooped her in his arms

and carried her to the bathroom, ignoring her protests. Dodging Reena and her worried yips as she trotted underfoot, he deposited Chuck on the edge of the counter by the sink.

"Mal," she started, huffing out an irritated breath and shoving a hand through her soft brown hair. "I can clean up a simple cut." She insisted in exasperation, making him feel like he must be nagging her.

"Not this one," he snapped, his embarrassment and irritation about having rejected feelings causing him to be shorter than necessary. Her expression almost mirrored his own frustration.

Teeth grinding and eyes narrowed, a grimace stretched her lips as she poked him in the chest. "I've had more cuts than I care to admit. What's so special about this one?" she demanded.

"The blade," he explained, trying to remain patient. "It's designed to bypass your angelic defenses and wound the way an Earthbound blade couldn't. The bleeding may have stopped, but your grace is still escaping." His voice was flat and cold. Detached as he tried to create distance between himself and the nearly overwhelming urge to hold her tightly.

"How do you know?" she retorted, her voice full of irritation as well. "I don't see anything."

Slamming his hands to the counter on each side of her, his eyes flared with flames, and he growled. "Because I can fucking see it. Demon, remember? Not of this world. Different, ugly, scary. I may not be capable of saying some words, but I can see fucking angel grace when it's smearing around like a slaughterhouse."

"What the hell, Mal?" she shook her head. "So, bandage it up and let's move on with it. Why are you so wound up?"

Trying to keep from yelling, he closed his eyes, focusing his power until his hands started glowing. Gently laying them on her skin, he kept his thoughts trained on closing the metaphysical wound and not on how soft

she was. When he finished closing the laceration, his hands dropped to his side like lead weights, and he stared at her. "All healed. Now it's just an ordinary cut so you can clean it and put as many bandages as you want on it. And you may think I don't have *real* feelings or that I know what it means to give up your life for another person, but reality check, Officer Charles. I do have real feelings. Very strong ones when it comes to you. I'm sorry if that's inconvenient for your plans in life. I can fix that burden easily enough. I'll just go back to being the creature you think of me as."

Stepping back, ignoring her wide-eyed stare, he shimmered and shifted into his canine form. Shrugging off the clothing still clinging to his body, he picked it up in his jaws and carried it off to his room, where he nudged the door shut with his snout.

"Malachi!" she called after him, her voice thick, full of shock. "No, Mal, that's not what I meant!"

Shifting back to lock the door, he leaned his head on the wood and squeezed his eyes closed. He hated the sound of pain in her tone, but he couldn't risk himself or even her this way. It was better that she only thought of him as an animal until Hyacinth called him back to kill him. Was it easier to bury a pet than a friend or lover? He wasn't sure. He'd never had either before.

Maybe he could fake his death, like a sudden seizure, so Chuck wouldn't have to explain the disappearance of her partner. Then they could have a clean break. In fact, he would do that at the station the next day. With witnesses, it was no fault of hers. He banged his head on the door once and groaned. Turning to the bed, he stumbled towards it and threw himself down face-first.

After a few minutes, he heard whimpering and scratching at the door. Reena wanted in; she was worried about him. But he didn't have the energy to drag himself over, and truthfully, he wanted to be alone to wallow in his

despair. He hadn't finished criticizing himself and calling himself names for being stupid enough to believe he had a chance at something real with a human. Not just any human, a half-angel. Someone like Chuck. A police officer, for Hell's sake. Someone who stood for truth and justice. Someone who believes right should triumph over wrong and punish evildoers. Like him.

Rolling on his back, he covered his face with his hands and ground the heels of them into his eyes hard to stop the tears that wanted to fall. *Stupid fucking idiot. Abysmal pimple on Satan's ass. Mud between Lucifer's hooves. Wart on Asmodeus' ball sack. Worse. So much worse. I deserve everything Hyacinth is going to do to me. And more.*

On and on his self-flagellation went until Reena gave up and moved to Chuck's room. He heard her soft murmur and sniffling as she closed her door again. Heaving out a sigh, he strained his ears, tormenting himself, listening to the sounds of her tears. *She's crying; maybe that means she does still care about me.* Groaning in disgust at how weak and desperate he sounded even to himself, he burrowed under the blanket and put a pillow over his head to muffle the sound. *Stop, she's crying because you yelled at her, and she didn't get the last word. You heard her; she doesn't think you're capable of having real feelings. She's certainly not worried about that.*

Finally, he fell into a fitful, restless sleep.

29

Of Angels and Unicorn Farts

What felt like days later, but was in actuality only two hours, Malachi heard a tap at the door. It was hesitant and so light, he almost thought he'd imagined it. Listening hard, it came again, faintly. He could hear her breathing, now. Ignoring it, he flopped to his other side and ground his jaw. His eyes burned, gritty and rough from his stupid emotions. He couldn't even pretend it was a lack of sleep; it was just raw gut-wrenching feelings that he didn't ask for and couldn't get rid of. The worst part was that no matter how bad this felt, he wouldn't trade it for anything.

"Malachi," came a soft, tearful plea. "Please, talk to me."

Gritting his teeth, he strengthened his resolve to stay silent. He crossed his arms over his chest and hugged himself tightly.

"Please," she sobbed. "Mal, don't ice me out like this."

Groaning, he sat up and slid off the bed. Making his way towards the door, he slowly unlocked it and immediately shifted back to canine form, nudging the door wider. He stared at her, tilting his head to the side.

Dropping to her knees, Chuck took his head in her hands, ruffling his ears with her fingers. “Malachi, please don’t do this. You don’t need to be a dog around me. I like your human form. Even your demon form. I’m sorry, I’m not sure what I said. But please, let’s talk this out.”

Hanging his head low, he studied the grain in the hardwood, debating how to respond. *Chuck, I think it’s better this way. We need distance. I’m going to die soon, and it will be awkward for you. My human form is too complicated. This is easier.*

“Fuck easy,” she shouted. “Malachi, I don’t want you to die. I don’t want to live without you. What did I say? What did I do? Please… tell me so I can fix this.” Her eyes drowned in sorrow, and her aura was the solid black of mourning.

The color was the final straw. He knew then he needed to make this break. *No, Chuck. There’s nothing else to discuss; I’ll be dead in a few days. There’s no ‘fixing’ this.* He brushed past her and headed to the back door. Slinking through the dog flap, he crept into the backyard. Taking a deep breath of the close air, he whimpered slightly at the thought of what he left behind in that room. The image of Chuck on her knees, her eyes swollen, desolate, burning pits of despair flashed helpfully through his mind.

Staring at the sky, desperate for relief of this torment, Malachi sent out: *I don’t know if anyone is listening, or if you even care to hear from someone like me, but if you are, help Chuck. Keep her safe. Protect her when I can’t. And… please don’t let her hurt too long after I die. If she even cares. Maybe she doesn’t, but if she does…* Dropping his head and shaking it, he huffed. *No one’s listening to me.*

Gathering himself, Malachi turned towards the gate, intending to roam the neighborhood for a while. Maybe run and clear his head. A sharp burning sensation coated his skin like he was caught inside an oven. Nothing had touched him, but he was encased in a tingling wash of pain so

strong, even his fur hurt. Dropping to the ground, Malachi panted hard and whined low in his throat. Whatever was attacking him was rendering him helpless. He couldn't remember anything ever hurting this much.

"I'm listening," came a ringing voice, the force of it shoving Malachi further into the grass as it rolled over him like a peal of thunder.

Thanks, but can you dial down the grace there, wing boy? You're melting me, Malachi panted as he blinked blearily at the angel towering over him. This was the source of his agony.

"Oh, my apologies," the angel offered as he bowed with a slight grin, not looking the least bit sorry. He did, however, turn down the wattage of his glow, granting Malachi a slight reprieve. "It's not every day a demon prays to Heaven—at least not authentically, especially on someone else's behalf. So, I was sent personally to check this out. Tell me." The angel smiled serenely now as he settled himself cross-legged on the grass, adjusting his wings behind him to get more comfortable. "Why on Earth is a *demon* praying?"

Huffing a sigh, Malachi shook his head as he dragged himself to his feet, unsure how he ended up in these kinds of situations. *I didn't realize that's what I was doing. I thought I was just asking for help for Chuck.* He glanced up at the angel again, and seeing only quiet contemplation, he forged ahead. *Look, this is awkward, so I'm just going to put it out there. Chuck, well, Kelly Charles, is half-angel. Her father was a full angel. He died and never told her. Demons are after her now, and I was sent here undercover to corrupt her for Hell. I didn't know it at first, but my former commander came and told me to do it, or I would be killed. I was on board with it, I mean... demon, you know?* He snuck a peek and saw the angel nodding along, indicating he understood.

Anyway, thing is, I got to know her, Chuck. And well, I can't do it. I care about her too much. I didn't know it was possible, but... dammit, I developed

feelings for her, and I think I... l-love her. Never knew I could feel that way, much less for someone on your side, but here we are. I do. I love her. I won't hurt her, and I'm going to die because of it. I don't want her to suffer because of it either. She needs protection. And maybe, can you like... erase her memories of me? Make it so she doesn't remember any of it? She deserves better.

Sighing heavily, the angel dropped his head and steepled his fingers against his lips. "It's a very noble thing you ask, demon Malachi." He glanced up and winked as Malachi jumped at his name. "Yes, I know who you are. I'm very interested in what's going on with Kelly Charles. She's my niece."

Sitting back, Malachi huffed. *Well, I'll be damned even more than I already am. Any other feathery family lurking out there?*

"Quite a few of us, actually. But here's the thing. I won't do it. Grief and pain are part of the human experience. She has to go through this to grow."

Fuck that! Malachi shouted. *Human experience my furry ass, she doesn't deserve that. She didn't ask for this. She's an innocent pawn in this sick fucking game. You have the ability, do it! Help her, she's your family. You know it's not fair.*

Shaking his head, his expression sorrowful now, the angel gave a sad smile. The corners of his eyes crinkled as he studied Malachi. "I know, it sucks. What's the cliché? Life isn't fair? Well, it's true. Life isn't fair. She has free will, and we will not manipulate her mind or her life just because of a setback. Maybe you—"

Malachi was vibrating with fury and transitioned to his full demon form, hulking over the annoying angel seated before him. "*I AM NOT A SETBACK*!" he roared, heedless of who could hear him now. "She doesn't deserve to be a pawn while you monitor some stupid little game. I thought you were family, you winged freak! Don't you care?"

Rising to his own considerable but in comparison still shorter height, the angel tilted his face up to meet his flaming gaze. "Nick. My name is Nick. And yes, I care. The real question, Malachi, is do *you?*"

Taking a startled step back, Malachi stared uneasily at the angel, then recovered his demonic bravado. "Nick?" he repeated incredulously. "Seriously? Whoever heard of an angel named Nick? Is that short for Nicholai? Nicaroni?" He grinned cheekily and wafted his much larger wings.

Sighing, as his hair fluttered back, the angel rolled his eyes heavenward. "Puppy's got jokes. Look, milk-bone breath, I asked you a simple question. Do you care about Kelly?"

Holding back surprised laughter at the angel's witty comeback, Malachi studied the glowing jerk. Slowly, his grin fell, and his eyes heated with the seriousness of the answer. "I do, Nicky. I love her."

"There you go!" Nick applauded. The clapping was obnoxiously loud and seemed a bit sarcastic if Malachi was allowed to judge. It stopped as abruptly as it started. "Well, if you love her, *you* take care of her. Don't break her heart."

Now, Malachi was shocked, taken aback that Nick apparently *wanted* him to stay with Chuck. "I don't get it." He shook his head as confusion filled him, making his skin tingle. "Why are you encouraging me—a demon—to stay with her? With Chuck? She's half-angel, shouldn't you be smiting me? Warning me away from her?"

Nick waved a palm negligently, blowing a rude noise through his lips. "But don't you see, Malachi, that's exactly why! Because you aren't just any demon, are you? You've developed feelings. You *care.* You prayed to us to watch over her. Which means you're coming to the light side. We believe everyone can be redeemed if they just ask forgiveness, even demons. You were born into this life, but you have the capacity to change. So, who better to protect her than someone who will sense supernatural dangers and act

on her behalf? Added bonus, if you continue to help her with upholding their human laws, you're doing the work of Heaven as well!" Nick beamed from ear to ear in a way that faintly reminded Malachi of paintings he'd defaced in a museum once.

"So..." Malachi furrowed his eyebrows and shrank back to human form. "You want me to stay with Chuck because you want me to protect her and keep being her K-9 partner. And you think it's a win for Hea... Hea..." He rolled his eyes as he grunted and pointed up. "Your people, because I—a demon—would be doing good deeds, is that what I heard, Nicholas?"

"In a nutshell," agreed Nick happily. His icy blue eyes were twinkling, and Malachi was certain his hair was now glittering as a silver halo formed around his head.

"Cut that shit out," Malachi grumbled in disgust, narrowing his eyes. "You look like a cross between *Twilight* and a Hallmark movie."

Chuckling, Nick waved a hand in front of his face, and his visage returned to normal. "You're no fun," he snorted. Then he straightened and clasped his hands. "So, do we have an accord? You'll protect Chuck, take care of her, and I won't smite you?"

Grunting in disbelief, Malachi propped his hands on his hips. "One little problem there, Nicodemus."

"It's not... never mind," Nick groaned and shook his head, accepting defeat. "What?"

"Hyacinth, my commander. He's going to kill me sometime between now and probably Friday. Gonna make Operation Chuck Watch a tiny bit harder." Malachi held his thumb and pointer about half an inch apart, squinting at the angel through the scant space between his fingers.

"Not a problem."

A growl slipped out in exasperation. "I find it to be a problem. A big fucking problem, Nicco. So, what do you know that I don't?" Malachi demanded, then held up a hand. "About this specific problem, smart ass."

Grumbling under his breath, Nick finally narrowed his eyes and repeated, "No fun!" Then he heaved a sigh and waved his hands, chanting muffled words that sounded like a cross between a Gregorian chant and something from a Monty Python skit. A sparkling, hazy purple cloud flew from his fingers and wrapped around Malachi like a shroud, encasing him in suffocating lilac smoke.

"Ow!" Malachi snapped as the shimmering cloak closed in on him, squeezing firmly until it popped and sank into his skin. "What the actual fuck, Nicorette?" he shouted, dancing around, shaking his limbs, trying to get the heavenly unicorn fart out of his body.

"Nick!" the angel snapped. "It's Nick!" Then he stopped and leaned back, a chagrined smile over his lips as he realized Malachi had finally succeeded in getting to him. "But you knew that."

Malachi winked conspiratorially, then sobered. "Seriously, though, what was that?"

The ground under their feet shook and trembled, bubbling like a tar pit, and smelling like the lower depths of a peat bog on fire. From the ground rose the bulbous and wrinkled form of Hyacinth the Destroyer. His arms were crossed, his claws clenched, and he looked downright pissed.

30

Angels are Kind of Jerks

Tapping his wrinkled toes, which looked for all the world like wriggling worms trying to escape, Hyacinth glared in equal parts disgust and distrust at Malachi and Nick. His shoulders shook with anger, causing dirt to patter on the ground where it sank into the still bubbling mud pit at his feet. The strong smell of floral decay wafted through the air, displaying Hyacinth's displeasure at the situation. "Malachi," came his gravelly rumble as his yellow eyes darted suspiciously between the pair. "Care to explain how in Lucifer's saggy ass cheeks you came to be consorting with a whole damn angel and are now marked as an upper H-town sacred guardian?"

"I'm not entirely sure, oh awful one." Malachi bowed to the ground before the filthy demon. "I was coming outside to call on you, report progress, and this winged freak appeared, threatening to smite me. I was prepared to fight ferociously, but he cast some spell over me. It burned like Hellfire within my veins, and then you appeared. I haven't had time to properly curse this foul fiend for what it has wrought upon me. No doubt, I should rip him to shreds for this vile abuse."

Nick, for his part, bowed sarcastically during Malachi's exaggerated protests but kept quiet, simply nodding when Hyacinth turned towards him. When it was clear Malachi's mock outrage was spent, he began his own flowery rant. "It is true, damned abhorrent beasts! I caught this one sneaking about in the garden and demanded to know his dastardly plot. I was preparing to smite him fully when I learned of an even fouler plan involving the child of grace and light inside, and this demonic smirch upon the world. He is not aware, it seems, that you were planning to sacrifice him and the angel child both in a bid to wrest power from our fallen brother." His eyes blazed with Holy righteousness then, daring Hyacinth to contradict him.

Malachi gasped dramatically, feigning surprise at this revelation.

Hyacinth took a faltering step back. "What?" he thundered dramatically. "I know of no such... oh fuck it." His shoulders relaxed, and he shook his head. "Fine. Yeah, I was gonna kill that whelp and the angel bitch." Ignoring Malachi's sputtering indignation, he waved his grimy claws in a shooing motion. "I mean, you have to take opportunities when they come. I get you interfering, but what's with the guardian cloak?" He squinted suspiciously at Malachi again; clearly, he thought the demon had requested it.

Shaking his head with a bewildered expression, Malachi held his palms out as innocently as a demon could and turned to Nick. "I was just trying to find that out myself. What gives?" he demanded, trying not to laugh as he finally realized what the angel had done.

"We have declared that woman to be sacred property of Heaven and assigned this demon to be her guardian. He must protect her from all foes, holy or damned." Nick nodded with pious righteousness.

"What?" screeched Malachi in his best impression of indignation, just as Hyacinth also growled his displeasure.

"You cannot co-opt one of my troops that way!" Hyacinth howled, shaking his fists, flinging dirt around, pelting the angel's white robes with gobs of foul-smelling mud.

Nick scowled as he flicked his hand at the stains, making them disappear before admiring the pearly shine of the material. Satisfied he was clean, he raised his gaze to Hyacinth and frowned as he tilted his head. "Oh, now he's one of your troops? I understood you to be punishing him and ready to sacrifice his life for power. I figured tying his fate to that of the angel would be an even more preferable torment to you. Now you want him back?"

Caught in the lie, Hyacinth rubbed his stubby fingers over his chin, the rasping of the leathery skin loud in the stillness of the dark yard. "I see your point." Moaning in disgust, he waved his fingers in dismissal, then began sinking again. "Fine, he's yours. I'm better off without him anyway." With a sickening squelch and gurgle, the mud pit closed slowly over the demon's head until it was gone, and the grass resumed its normal spread.

"Huh," Nick mused. "That was anticlimactic." He glanced at Malachi and shrugged. "I thought I was going to have to get all high and mighty. Maybe even smitey. Hehe... rhymes." He straightened suddenly and bowed his head. "Now, where were we, before we were so rudely interrupted by that aberration?"

"What the fuck, Nickles?" Malachi blurted, throwing his hands out to his sides. "I thought angels couldn't lie?"

Grinning in a mischievous way, Nick raised his eyebrows before he innocently asked, "What did I lie about?"

"I don't know, all of it?"

Blowing air through his lips in a low whistle, Nick swatted Malachi on the side of the head, leaving the demon stunned and quiet. "Nothing," Nick insisted. "I did learn about the plot. I did plan on smiting you before

I learned all of that, and I have now assigned you as her guardian. You're on Heaven's payroll now, buddy."

"Why?" Malachi asked quietly.

"Simple." Nick smiled beatifically now, a serene, wholesome glow surrounding him. He folded his hands together as if praying and bowed his head. "Malachi, you—a demon—prayed to the Holy host for someone to care for and watch over Kelly. You admitted to me that you care about her and were upset when I refused to remove her memory of you. You were ready to take on a full-powered angel for such a little thing in the grand scheme of the universe. *That* is why, Malachi. Never before has a demon prayed for someone else, and never before has a demon cared enough to give up their life for a human. So, as a reward for your loyalty—and to encourage it further—I granted you safe harbor from those who would harm you. But know this, if you leave her, or fail in your duties, I will personally smite your ass right back to the pits of Hell." He bowed. "Have fun!"

With those parting words, Nick the angel blinked out of sight.

Spluttering, Malachi threw his hands in the air and spun around, looking behind him for a camera crew, sure he was on some supernatural version of a prank show. He didn't find a camera, but he did find Chuck. She was leaning against the door frame, arms crossed tightly over her midsection. Her eyes were swollen and puffy from crying, her nose as red as a Christmas reindeer. She was holding herself guardedly and slowly shook her head.

"Chuck," he moaned in a pained voice, unsure of how much she had witnessed, overheard.

"Malachi, I was wrong, and I'm sorry," she croaked, her voice thick with tears and emotion.

Tilting his head, he narrowed his eyes, confused, and slowly asked, "About what?"

"Feelings... emotions," she blurted. "Y-you do have feelings. And you have them about me." She rubbed her hands up and down her arms now, as if she were cold, and shook her head ruefully. "I'm such an idiot. You tried to tell me, and I blew it off. I thought it was just lust, sex. That's all that you wanted from me. And I basically laughed in your face. No wonder you were so hurt. Malachi, you prayed? You challenged an angel for me? After what I did to you? Why?"

Dropping his head and staring at his feet, he realized now Nick's words weren't for his benefit. They were for hers. The angel was trying to help him. He didn't understand it, but he was still demon enough to take this gift and run with it. "You heard why." He moved until he was standing directly in front of her. "Kelly, I don't know how it happened, why it happened, but it did. If I couldn't be with you, I didn't want you to be in pain or suffer because of me. I asked *them* to take care of you. To help you. And they answered." His voice filled with awe.

Taking her face in his hands, he ran his thumbs over her cheeks, wiping away the remnants of her tears. "Kelly, H-H-Heaven answered me," he choked out. "They heard my p-prayer and answered me. Granted, the angel was kind of a dick and jerked me around a bit. But he made me your official holy guardian. To protect you from all supernatural threats. It trumps Hyacinth's command. He can't take me from you." He smiled and pulled her to him, his lips slowly turning down into a frown when she resisted his embrace.

"If you'll still have me," he murmured, dropping his forehead to hers.

"Of course I will, that's not the problem. I guess I need to know if you'll forgive me first for how I treated you. I'm surprised *you* still want *me*."

He jerked his head back in shock. "I will always forgive you! I'm so sorry, Kelly. I thought it would be better for you if you didn't have to see me die. I thought it might hurt you, and I didn't want that, so I was trying to make it easier. It was stupid."

"It was stupid, but sweet, Mal." She smiled gently and with one finger, raised his chin to stare into his eyes. "I don't think anything could ever top that kind of gesture. A literal demon from Hell prayed to Heaven for me and was ready to fight an angel on my behalf. Malachi, you truly care about me." Her voice was full of wonder, and something he couldn't identify that warmed his insides and fluttered like a horde of rampaging butterflies.

Momentarily distracted by the thought of exactly how a butterfly could rampage, he turned his attention back to her waiting stare. Nodding, his lips quivered. "I do."

"Dummy." She laughed and gently kissed him. "I hope you know I care about you, too. Now please, come inside and just hold me for a while."

Reeling from her acceptance of his feelings, the knowledge they could be together, and the fact that Heaven had actually answered his prayer, Malachi simply nodded and followed her quietly into the house. In the living room, she threaded her fingers through his and tugged him towards the bedroom. Pausing by her side of the mattress, she pulled down the comforter before crawling under it, patting the pillow next to hers.

"C'mere, you, get in bed." Chuck grinned at him, her eyes alight with mischief.

Thinking he should change into pajama pants, it was only then that Malachi realized he was stark naked. He remembered he'd gone outside as a canine, then turned full demon before going human, thus no clothes. Bursting into laughter, he quickly leapt over her and hurriedly yanked the blanket up to his waist. "I cannot believe that asshole angel let me stand there and argue with him naked." Shaking his head, he smirked. "Probably

because I kept getting his name wrong on purpose." Chuckling, he pulled her over so she could lay her head on his chest while he wrapped his arms around her and recounted for her the different variations he'd come up with.

After she laughed and gently chastised him for it, she snuggled in deeper, her breathing evening out. Soon, she was asleep, and he lay there, listening to her quiet sounds. Savoring each one, knowing they should have been the last. By some miracle, he was safe from Hyacinth's threats and now had the opportunity to find out who was after his Chuck and keep her safe. No, not just some miracle. His own miracle, courtesy of an angel named Nick.

"Thank you," he said, casting his gaze up to the ceiling, knowing now that someone *was* listening.

31

Glenda Must Die

Gentle fingers tracing his jaw woke Malachi the next morning. The scraping of Kelly's nails on his stubble tickled as the rasping noise filled his ears. Yawning, he mumbled, "Morning," before grinning sleepily at the gorgeous woman wrapped around him.

"You need to shave," she teased with an amused smile. "You're starting to look more like your canine form." A small laugh seeped from her throat as she tried to swallow it down.

Pretending he was affronted, Malachi shook his shaggy black hair around, whacking her in the face and laughing as she sputtered over a mouthful of it. "Woof," he responded playfully.

"Rude," she declared and started to push up from the bed.

Grabbing her wrist and yanking her back down with one arm, he waved his other hand over his jaw and removed the stubble with a small burst of his magic. "Better?" he asked, arching an eyebrow as his lips quirked into a sarcastic twist.

Her mouth fell open as she gasped. "Wait, you can do that? Change your appearance? So, is this?" She waved her free hand at his body. "What you even really look like?"

"It is," he reassured her. "My demon form is my truest form. My human form matches it pretty closely. I can do minor things like that. I can shorten or lengthen my hair some, but the overall features, I can't change. Like I can't make my nose smaller or my arms longer. Does that make sense?"

She nodded quickly, seeming relieved as her shoulders sagged and she blew a pent-up breath between her lips.

"Were you worried about that?" he asked, confused.

Tracing small circles on his skin, she mumbled something into his chest that he couldn't hear. Lifting her chin with a finger, he stared at her until she repeated it. "I like the way you look; I don't want you to change it."

Humming happily, he pulled her close again. "I was worried, you know," he admitted. At her inquiring noise, he continued. "After I turned full demon in that alley. I just... reacted when that man hurt you. It freaked me out to see your blood and grace spilled. When I realized you were seeing the real me, I thought you would turn away. I figured you would be disgusted and not want anything else to do with me." His voice turned small and quiet with his words. He wouldn't normally admit a weakness, a way to defeat him, but this was Chuck. He couldn't hide anything from her.

"No, I'm glad you showed me. Honestly, your demon form did scare me at first. Hey!" she added soothingly as his arms clenched around her. "At first," she emphasized, "but then I recognized it was you. And you were so beautiful to me. Truly, Malachi, you're magnificent. I love your wings. Can you fly?"

"I can," he answered, his voice gone low and husky with her words. She thought he was beautiful. She'd said it that night, but that was the heat of

the moment. Now, there was only the truth between them. "Kelly, do you mean it? You're not scared of me?"

Nodding, then shaking her head, she smirked. "Yes, I mean it, no, I'm not scared of you." She laughed then at his expression as he scrunched his nose, realizing the contradictory questions he'd asked. "Malachi, you've only ever done things to protect me and keep me safe. Why would I be scared of you?"

Bobbing his head a little, embarrassed, he admitted, "Well, I was doing some things you probably wouldn't approve of. I maaaay have corrupted a few souls along the way." He smirked at her wide eyes before they narrowed, and he had a second to be concerned. "Ow!" He grimaced and glared fiercely after she dug her fingers into his ribs. "Demon, remember? It's in my nature. Besides, all I did was give them some dark fantasies and desires. Probably the most fun some of them have had in a long time. But not you. Never you." He trailed his fingers along her cheek, then traced his thumb over her bottom lip.

"Malachi." Her voice trembled with nerves suddenly as her fingers whorled listlessly in the light sprinkle of hair on his chest. "I was wondering..."

"What do you want to know?" His own tone was low and quiet as he watched the red streaks swirl through her glowing aura. He had an idea about what she wanted. And if he was right, she was going to see a side of him she'd never forget.

Dropping her gaze from his, she sucked in a deep breath, seeming to fortify herself. "I was wondering since you're a demon, and I'm half angel, if we were to... um... you know... uh..." A stifled squeak escaped from her throat when he lifted her chin to lock his gaze with hers.

"Kelly, I'm part incubus. There's nothing you could ask me that would surprise me or turn me away. But let me help you. You want to know if

it's possible for us to have sex? Physically? Or is there some other concern? Because I can assure you, if you're worried about the physical part, I am one-hundred percent able and more than willing to accommodate any desire you have."

Her breath whooshing out in a hard gust, she replied, "Okay, yeah, good to know. Umm. Yeah, that was part of it. I was also uh... wondering about my soul."

Blinking, Malachi leaned back. "Your soul?" he repeated, confused.

"My soul," she agreed. "If you and I—go there—will it darken my soul? Will it corrupt me?"

"Oh, Kelly," he breathed and flipped her on her back, lowering his body over hers. "It's the other way around. You're putting your light into me. You've altered me, and there's no going back. I can't corrupt you anymore. The angel's spell made sure of that. So, tell me," he continued in a sultry whisper as he brushed her hair from her face, lowering his lips an inch from hers. "Is this what you want? Do you want me?"

A shiver rippled over her body as she moaned. "More than anything," she whispered back before wrapping her trembling arms around his neck.

Taking her invitation, he lowered his lips to her and captured them in a kiss that should have set the bed on fire. He ground his hips against hers, letting her feel the hard length of him that left no doubt how much he wanted her in return.

The throaty moan that left her nearly undid him then. "Kelly," he groaned, "you have on entirely too many clothes. I can fix that."

He had just grasped the hem of her tank top when a frantic pounding sounded at her front door. Lying his forehead on hers in frustration, he groaned. "Ignore it. Please, I'm begging you. Let them think you aren't home, and they'll go away."

Chuckling, she arched her back and tangled her fingers in his hair. "Agreed," she murmured, licking up the line of his throat before biting his jaw.

Talons sprouted from his fingers, ready to shred her clothing from her body when the knocking came again. Even louder this time, accompanied by shouts of her name. It was a woman's voice, and it set Reena off into a cacophony of howls and yips.

"Fuck," Malachi growled and sagged against her. "It's Glenda. She's worried." He rolled over and stared at the ceiling. "Go ahead. See what she needs. I'm going to drown myself in the coldest shower I can manage. If you come into your bathroom and find icicles, mind your own business," he muttered grumpily. Crossing his arms over his chest, he frowned at his groin where the tented sheet displayed exactly why he was upset.

Clearing her throat, eyes wide, Chuck stared openly at this display. "You know, I've seen you naked, but never when you were... ahem... I'm going to go answer that before she breaks down the door." Indeed, it now sounded as if Glenda were kicking the wood. She leapt from the bed but got one foot tangled in the sheet. Hopping on one leg, she tried to free the other. The banging intensified, and Reena howled even louder, so Chuck hollered, "Coming!" over her shoulder.

"You were about to," Malachi grumbled before leaning over to yank the sheet away from her foot.

Flashing him a grateful smile with an embarrassed flush creeping over her cheeks, she raked her hands over the short cap of her silky hair. No doubt trying to flatten it so it didn't look like she'd been doing exactly what they were about to do.

Stumbling over her shoes, Chuck snatched her robe from the closet and ran towards the entryway to answer the door. Thankfully, Glenda seemed to recognize that they were indeed alive and was now waiting patiently.

Groaning, Malachi dragged himself from the warm bed, staring down regretfully at the mussed sheets. His cock was throbbing painfully now with the demand for the release it had been promised. Palming himself, he squeezed and willed his body to calm down. It did not work. Grumbling about fucking nosy witches, he hurried to the shower and set it as cold as it would go. Hissing under the icy spray, he thought of several inventive ways he could justify dragging Glenda to Hell for her intrusion. Surely interrupting the multiple orgasms he'd planned to give Kelly would count as harm. He wasn't sure Nick the winged freak would see it that way, but he could be fairly persuasive when he wanted to.

Finally calming down, at least he was only semi-hard, he stepped out and toweled himself dry. Grinning, he shifted to dog form and trotted out to the living room. He woofed a greeting to Glenda and Chuck before leaping to the sofa next to them. Curling up beside Chuck, he lay his head in her lap and grumbled his displeasure.

"Hey, Mal," Chuck offered softly, absently rubbing between his ears.

"Don't play me, demon boy," Glenda snapped, pointing an accusing finger at him. "I know you can be in your other form when you want. Change. Face me like the demon you are!"

Pleased to be able to partake in some malicious compliance, Malachi jumped down from the couch and stood before her. In a blink, he morphed into his full demon form. Towering over the women, he fanned his wings lightly and bent his head so his horns wouldn't scrape the ceiling. Bowing, he winked and asked, "Better?" in a tone that was only slightly snarky. He

grinned, showing his fangs as Glenda's dark brown face paled to an ashen gray that closely matched his own skin.

Reena happily trotted into the room and paused. She took in his hulking demon form and barked once in excitement before running to him and rubbing on his ankles. She reared up on her hind legs, pawing the air and prancing in excitement.

Indulging her, Malachi bent and picked up the Chuglet, then cradled her like a baby. He tickled her tummy with his talons and cooed at her. She sighed in contentment and gazed at him adoringly. Rocking her slightly, Malachi raised his gaze to the women on the couch, studying them as they did the same. Chuck was grinning at his display, no doubt aware he was retaliating for being interrupted. Glenda's mouth was opening and closing like a fish, trying to gather her wits.

Folding his legs underneath him, Malachi settled to the floor and tucked his wings behind him. Smiling innocently, well, as innocently as a sex demon could smile, he tossed his long black hair over his shoulder. "What can we help you with, Glenda?" he inquired politely.

32

Demons are NOT Precious

After Glenda had regained her composure and Chuck had made them all coffee, they settled down to discuss why she was there. Malachi had already grudgingly gone to get clothes and change back to human form. Still feeling spiteful, he shifted first, then went to his room, giving both ladies a whole eyeful of what he had to offer. He heard Chuck cackling gleefully and Glenda scolding her for encouraging him.

Sitting at the dining table now, Malachi held the coffee cup between his palms. He didn't plan to drink it but was intrigued by the way humans seemed to be fueled by their daily ritual of consuming the bitter bean water simply to get by. As the cup warmed his palms, he tuned back into the conversation about why Glenda had appeared that morning, banging on the door like she was serving a warrant.

"So, this whole time you knew Malachi was a demon?" Chuck demanded of her friend.

Waving her fingers, sending her bracelets jangling, Glenda waggled her head quickly. "Yeah, yeah, I knew. But I also knew how protective of you he was and that he would watch out for you. And yes, before you ask, I

know what you are and what your daddy was. It's why I'm always in your business, honey. I love you, and you need extra lookin' out for!"

Shaking her head in disbelief, Chuck leaned back in her chair, a stunned expression on her face as she processed this news.

"I didn't know what the boy looked like with his wings, though, damn near made my heart fall out of my chest." Glenda tapped her finger on her lips and studied Malachi through narrowed eyes. "And you didn't seem surprised to see it, so I'm guessing you two know all about each other now?"

Nodding with a soft smile, Chuck threaded her fingers through Malachi's and leaned forward. "We do. He shared his background with me, and well, we've come to care about each other. A lot. But that still doesn't explain why you're here."

"I don't know what in the name of the goddess you were doing, but every protective ward I have set for you was going off. I wasn't home last night; I went to help deliver a baby with a coven member. So, imagine my surprise when I walk in, and my workroom is in total disarray with all my alarms going batshit crazy!" Glenda explained.

"Hmm," Malachi hummed, and at their inquiring looks explained. "I've always wondered about that phrase. Batshit crazy. I mean... who decided batshit was the craziest shit? Yeah, high concentrations will kill you with the insane nitrogen levels, and histoplasmosis is always a risk, but still, have you ever seen giraffe shit? It's like little balls of cocoa. Oversized cocoa pebbles. How does a huge animal like that have such tiny little poos? Elephants, now there's a respectable pile of shit. They just let it all go. And don't get me started on hippos. Whew! But bats? A tiny flying mammal that shits where it sleeps? No, thank you." He glanced up from where he was gazing into his coffee cup to see both of them staring at him, jaws hanging open. "What?" he demanded.

Chuck slowly shook her head and chuckled. “I guess I shouldn’t be surprised, but you are a wealth of weird knowledge, Malachi.” Turning to Glenda, she smiled. “Anyway, as you can see, I’m perfectly fine. So is Malachi. It seems whatever alarms you have tuned to me—which by the way, stalker much?—were a little premature.”

“No,” Glenda insisted. “They weren’t, I was just delayed in receiving them. Now start from the beginning.”

Sighing, Chuck told the story of Malachi revealing her heritage and warning her of the threat against her. Then, their trip to the bar, and the subsequent attack on her. His revealing his demon form and capturing her would be assassin. Describing how Blake had grabbed her, then cut her. She showed Glenda the angry red cut and pointed at Malachi, explaining how he’d healed it from oozing grace.

He took up the narrative then. Leaving out their fight, he went to the backyard, thinking to spare Chuck the pain of his death and the angel confronting him. As they’d gone to sleep shortly after, Chuck hadn’t heard some of this. She gasped when he revealed that the angel Nick was actually her uncle. Tears filled her eyes, turning the brown irises into pools of melted chocolate he would gladly drown in to remove the sadness from her expression.

“I have other family?” she said, her voice cracking with emotion.

Nodding slowly, Malachi met her gaze. “You do. Nick, who answered my p-prayer, was an angel. He said he was your uncle from H-Heaven. I think he’s been watching you and took advantage of my feelings for you to find a guardian.” He snorted. “As if I wouldn’t have watched you anyway.” He arched an eyebrow, daring either of them to contradict him.

“But you weren’t leaving for real, right?” Glenda demanded, pointing at him.

Squirming uncomfortably, Malachi glared at her. "I was thinking about it, I won't lie." At the witch's disbelieving snort, he growled. "I won't. When it comes to Kelly, I would never lie. She's everything to me. That's why I was trying to create distance. I thought if I forfeited my life, they couldn't use me to hurt her. I p-prayed, asking H-Heaven to help her. Me. A demon. And they answered me because they knew I meant it. There's nothing I won't do to protect her, keep her safe."

Nodding, Glenda crossed her arms over her ample bosom. "Good," she declared and sniffed. "As it should be. You care about her; she cares about you. You can protect her from the forces against her. Just make sure you don't hurt her, or angels be damned, *I'll* be on your ass."

Grinning now, Malachi bowed his head. "Noted and agreed. I'm so incredibly attached to her ass. No one will touch it but me."

"Ugh," the witch groaned, clapping a hand over her forehead dramatically. "Yeah, I understand, please, nothing more." She waved her other hand and dismissed him. "Anyway, so you're alive." She pointed at Chuck. "Meaning I don't need to worry about you dying, and he's still here, so it wasn't him." Sighing, Glenda rolled her eyes theatrically, not done being extra. "I guess this Nick fellow made it all safe with his spell. That leads me to now. You're both safe, but you seemed really irritated this morning. I take that to mean I interrupted something exciting? Have you seriously not done it yet? There's enough tension between you two to strangle a saint," her tone rose in incredulity.

"No," Malachi growled. "We *were* getting there, but *someone* interrupted." He glanced at Reena, chuckling as she wheezed her amused laughter about the situation.

Grinning, unashamed, Glenda shrugged. "Well, I'm sure you'll find other opportunities to get each other naked. Regardless, you need to figure out who is after Kelly."

Sobering, Malachi dropped his gaze, agreeing with Glenda's statement, if not her timing. "We might have a lead."

Chuck cleared her throat and sat up straighter from where she'd been leaning towards Malachi, twirling her fingers in his hair. "Yeah, turns out the lunatic that attacked me last night is the son of one of my dad's friends. A guy I now work with. And Malachi has detected darkness on him before. But he said it's darkness from association, like being around his son. So, I'm not really sure where to go from here, but Mal wants to get another look at the sword. He called it a forsaken blade."

Gasping, Glenda clutched at her throat. "A *forsaken* blade? Of course! Because how else could he have released your grace? Where the hell did he get something like that?"

"From Hell obviously." Malachi snorted and shook his head. He grinned unrepentantly at the witch who was now glaring at him again. "Someone had to have conscripted him from Hell. Those blades aren't just lying around waiting for someone to find. And he knew what it was, what she was. He was absolutely recruited for it. But he didn't strike me as the kind of person who could orchestrate and carry out an attack on two seasoned police officers, especially given one was a full angel."

Glenda settled back into her chair and tapped her long magenta nails repeatedly on the ceramic surface of her coffee cup. The clicking noise was causing a muscle in Malachi's face to twitch to the point he was about to snatch the cup from her. Perhaps sensing his irritation, Glenda's fingers stilled, and she sat up straighter. "You need to inspect that blade." She nodded definitively as if they hadn't just discussed that very thing.

"Agreed," Malachi added dryly as he barely restrained himself from snarling in frustration. "But Chuck is on leave while this is investigated, and I can't just show up to the station as a human or as the K-9 alone without raising suspicion."

"I can still take you up there, and you can sneak into the evidence room again," Chuck offered. "I'll go see the lieutenant and discuss my concerns about this situation. It would be plausible with Nathan's involvement and everything."

Taking her hand in his, Malachi turned and brushed the back of his other hand over her cheek tenderly. "Are you sure? I can find another way. Do you feel up to it?"

"Damn..." Glenda sighed, watching them with a dreamy smile and damp eyes. At their combined stare, she waved a hand. "Don't mind me, I'm just enjoying my front row seat to the romance of the century. The angel and the demon. Not on my bingo card this year I can tell you that. But good goddess, you two are adorable." She rested her chin in her hands, planting her elbows on the table on each side of her coffee cup, and sighed. "Just precious."

Wrinkling his nose, Malachi growled, "I am not fucking precious." His eyes lit with Hellfire, and he allowed his fangs to slip down just a bit.

"Yes... you are!" Glenda stabbed one of her long nails at him. "Look at Kelly," she commanded.

Startled, he did as she directed, and his snarl softened into a genuine smile at the grin on Chuck's stunning face. "Sorry," he said, ducking his head in embarrassment.

"See?" crowed Glenda. "Precious!"

Lowering his lips to Kelly's, he murmured, "Make her leave." Then he captured her mouth and poured all his suppressed longing into the kiss, ensuring she understood exactly what he wanted.

"Okay, Romeo, while I appreciate the show, I'm not a complete voyeur. You need to get your fuzzy behind up to the station so you can snoop. Now let her get dressed so I can drive you up there. I'm going to do some spell casting of my own." Glenda slapped her hand on the table when they

didn't stop kissing. "Hey!" She began snapping her fingers. "I know you didn't suddenly go deaf. Let's get a move on!"

Without acknowledging Glenda—or breaking the kiss—Malachi scooped Kelly in his arms, wrapping her legs around his waist, and started moving towards her bedroom. He fought back a smile against her mouth at her squeal of surprise and Glenda's snort of amusement. Reaching his destination, he kicked the door shut behind them and spun around, putting Kelly's back to the wall.

Pressing against her, he tilted his head and deepened his possession of her lips. When she arched her back and pressed her hips harder against his, he groaned and dropped his forehead against the frame. "Fuck Kelly, it's going to take hours to do what I want to you. I'm going to put you down so you can get dressed. I can't believe I'm going to say this, but Glenda's right. We need to get you to the station so we can find out who's behind all of this."

With a small, pained moan, she unwound her arms and legs from him, sliding down his body. He was fairly certain she had purposely ensured every single curve connected with all of him as she did. "Bad girl," he hissed between clenched teeth. Pointing at himself, he grinned. "Incubus. Sex demon. Don't tease me like that. I can get really dark, really fast."

Nodding, she trailed a finger over his shoulder before scooting around him. "I'm looking forward to that." Hurrying to the bathroom, she whirled and winked at him before shutting the door.

Malachi smirked as he heard the lock click. He decided now was not the time to demonstrate that he could just smoke under the door and get to her anyway. He'd save that particular surprise for another time. Now he pressed his palm to his aching groin again, grimacing that he wasn't getting the happy ending he wanted, again. "Fucking witches," he muttered before turning around and stomping back out to the living room.

33

Fleas, Abominations, and Possession

Scratching at the collar once again around his neck, Malachi sighed as Glenda swung her car into the parking lot. The tires screeched as the vehicle lurched to a halt, and he almost lost his balance. Grumbling, he righted himself and considered peeing on the back seat.

"Don't think I can't hear you cursing me back there, demon-boy!" Glenda scolded as she caught his gaze in the rearview mirror. "And you better not be scratching because of fleas!"

This collar itches. Why don't we put a collar on you, or better yet, a muzzle! He glared right back at her, baring his fangs.

"Malachi." Chuck stifled a laugh. "That's not nice!"

Neither is she. I almost barfed when she took that corner on two wheels. Who let her have a license? She's a fucking menace! I'm a much better driver. Probably even with paws!

Nodding, Chuck winked at him conspiratorially. "I agree, but still, she's helping us so try to think kinder thoughts."

Kind thoughts? I'll kindly think about having you naked under me. Writhing, screaming my name, tangling your fingers in my hair while I lick your—

"Malachi!"

Toes. He chuckled at her narrowed eyes and blinked innocently, letting his tongue loll out like a good dog.

Pointing a finger at him, she grimaced. "Behave!"

Glenda laughed as she opened her door. "You two are a hoot. I don't care that the fuzzy boy is speaking truth, I'm a bad driver, and I accept it." She slammed the door and launched herself onto the sidewalk, storming through the front door of the station like a whirlwind, shaking up the building.

Rolling her eyes, Chuck opened the passenger door and came to the back to let Malachi out. Leaping to the asphalt below, he stretched and sniffed the air, alert for any danger. Finding none, he leaned against her legs. *All clear, let's move.*

"Yes, sir!" She saluted sarcastically with a cheeky grin.

Cut it out, he grumbled, *I'm trying to keep your smartass alive.*

Abruptly sobering, Chuck nodded. "Sorry, I'll behave. Maybe."

You want to be spanked, don't you? He teased, nipping her fingers with his teeth. *Seriously, though, get that ass inside before I bite it. In fact,* he growled and snapped at her bottom, chuckling at her squeal as she darted forward.

"Hey, Chuck," called the familiar voice of Officer Douche. "What are you doing here? I thought you were benched while they figure out this ordeal with Bennett?"

Rolling her eyes, Chuck patted her thigh in the heel signal. Dutifully, Malachi parked his butt right next to her but glared at Jaxon disdainfully. The man may have been sucking face with the now perky brunette from dispatch, but Malachi still didn't like him.

"Came in to talk to Jeffers." She shrugged casually to sell it. "Not used to sitting at home like this, and Malachi was a little on edge. He likes the work, so I figured I'd bring him with me. You know, so he stays sharp." She glanced around. "So," her voice said with a teasing edge, "how's Marla?"

Blushing so hard even his ears turned crimson, Jaxon dragged his toe over the sidewalk, shuffling an acorn around like it was his main priority. Finally, he blurted, "Great, she's great." He heaved a big sigh—a happy one—before he met her eyes. "She's incredible, really. I can't believe I never noticed her before. Her eyes are stunning, and her hair is so soft. Did you know she paints? She's really talented! She showed me some pictures. I'm uh... taking her to dinner tomorrow night." His smile was sheepish and shy, an expression previously foreign to his face but so much sweeter for it.

Malachi woofed happily and held out a paw to shake. Jaxon blinked at him rapidly, caught off guard.

"I think Malachi is congratulating you, Jax. Don't leave him hanging," Chuck murmured. She was biting the inside of her cheek, obviously trying not to laugh.

"Yeah," Jaxon blurted as he squatted. "Thanks, man, I appreciate it. Good boy!" he gushed as he shook Malachi's paw. Tentatively, he reached up and ruffled Malachi's ears the way Chuck frequently did. "Wow." He blinked. "His fur is really soft."

Not into dudes, you douchenugget, Malachi thought furiously, but moaned happily when Jaxon started scratching just the right spot. *Okay, maybe a little... to the right... just a.... oh fuck... that's the spot.* His tongue flopped out, and he panted before leaning against Jaxon's chest just a little.

"Chuck," Jaxon called happily. "Look! Your partner finally likes me!"

Slow your roll there, bucko, you just happened to hit the right scritching spot. We're not about to hit the sauna balls out or anything. There will be no bromance here.

A small laugh slipped from Chuck's lips. As both guys stared at her, she cleared her throat. "Sorry, it's just really cute the way you two are bonding. I guess Malachi warmed up to you after all. What do you know? Miracles do happen!" She smiled so brightly that her cheeks made her eyes squint.

I swear to Satan if he calls me a brochacho, I'm biting YOUR ass really hard. Malachi glanced at Jaxon and gave a short nod before moving back to her side. *C'mon, we need to get in there before the good witch causes a scene.*

As if on cue, a loud crash sounded from the lobby, and piercing screams echoed behind the glass doors. Malachi, Jaxon, and Chuck exchanged panicked glances before they ran towards the cacophony inside.

Throwing the door open, their mouths dropped in unison at the pile of colorful silk on the floor, surrounded by a mound of shattered glass. Glenda was wailing like a horde of banshees had been sent to claim her soul, flailing her arms and moaning. She caught sight of them, giving a quick conspiratorial wink, before resuming her shrieking and caterwauling. "I'm dying!" she screamed. "You've killed me, oh, the end is near! I knew it! I knew this would be the last of me!" She rolled side to side in the glass but somehow managed to keep from sustaining a single cut.

Malachi glanced around and noticed a glass partition, meant to separate the front clerks from those coming in from the street, had seemingly exploded outward, centering its deadly embrace on the woman crying in front of them. Already, dozens of officers and workers were crowding the lobby, twisting their fingers and uttering expressions of disbelief. Glenda

had told them she was going to create a diversion, and he had to hand it to her; it was one hell of a trick.

Sticking his nose in Chuck's hand, he said, *I'm heading to evidence, cover for me.*

Giving a distracted nod, Chuck patted him on the head before hurrying forward to aid the poor woman who had been injured while "trying to report a crime in good faith."

Slinking through the door to the back while casting his stealth spell, Malachi hurried to evidence. Slipping unnoticed past the clerk, he hurried to the processing table, suspecting it hadn't all been catalogued yet. Inhaling deeply, he tried to center in on the smell of Chuck's blood or grace, maybe brimstone, but he found nothing. Closing his eyes, he concentrated his senses on anything supernatural, looking for the slightest flicker of darkness—any sign of Chuck's would-be assassin.

Frowning, a low growl formed in his throat when he realized not only was the blade missing, but the rest of Chuck's father's case files were gone as well. There was no hint of either of the Charles cases in this room. His stomach filled with dread as his heart began a rapid tattoo. Someone was covering up what happened. Trotting closer to the shelf where her dad's case file should be, Malachi found an empty box and the residual dark haze that surrounded the Bennetts.

Closing his eyes once more, he cast his senses even wider, searching for the darkness that surrounded the men who carried it. Finally, he detected a large concentration of it nearby in what he suspected were the holding cells. Scurrying silently from the evidence room, Malachi perked his ears towards the commotion unfolding in the lobby. Glenda was still carrying on and making her scene, so he sent her thoughts of gratitude before hurrying towards the lock-up.

Quietly slipping past the guards, Malachi pressed his nose to the lock, sending a small surge of power pulsing through until it clicked, and the gate swung slightly open. Slithering into the narrow gap, he nudged it nearly closed again before trotting down the hall. The dark haze grew stronger and heavier until it was almost an electric buzz beneath his fur. It rippled over his body as if it were trying to burrow inside of him.

Coming to a halt near a central cell, Malachi shivered as he witnessed Nathan Bennett leaning against the unforgiving cold metal bars, pleading with his son.

"Please, Blake, tell me why?" Nathan begged, his voice thready and weak. "Why did you do this? Our part was done. There was no need for this!" He shook his head and moaned, clutching a hand over his chest. The man was so deep in his despair that he was struggling to even take a breath.

In a flat, emotionless tone, Blake responded, "I had no choice, Father. I had to finish what you started." His eyes were far away, devoid of awareness of his surroundings. He seemed detached, robotic. Completely disassociated from the real world.

"What I..." Nathan reeled back, eyes wide in shock. "I didn't start this! I tried to stop it!"

Nodding solemnly, Blake continued, "Yes, and the abomination still lives. You stopped the will of the Great One. You didn't complete your duty. Now the failures of the father are visited on the son." He swayed slightly, his hands limp at his sides in a dull, lifeless state. "The sins of the father... the sins of the father..." he chanted under his breath.

"No!" Nathan screamed, pounding his fists on the bars.

Chuck, holding cells. Get your ass down here now, we've got a problem. HURRY! Malachi watched with growing concern as Nathan slid to his knees, forehead on the metal barrier, bawling, babbling, and begging for his son's life.

A quiet clang announced Chuck's arrival. Malachi dropped his cloak and appeared in the hallway so she could see him. Which also meant Nathan could now see him.

"Malachi?" he blurted in surprise as he hurriedly wiped his tears. "Are you lost, boy? What are you doing?"

"Demon!" Blake hissed, pointing a shaking finger down the hall. "That's *her* demon, the one who stopped me! Another abomination!" he wailed, his cries growing louder with each word as he gripped the bars tightly.

Whipping his eyes from his son to Malachi, Nathan's expression grew even more troubled. "Blake, that's a dog. Chuck's dog, yes, but he's just a dog." He tried to soothe his son, but Blake grew more agitated and started chanting again about the sins of the father.

Chuck's fingers tangled in the fur behind Malachi's ears as she arrived and faced Nathan. "Bennett," she called softly. "What's going on? You know what happened, don't you? You know about me, about my father. What we are. Did you kill him? Did you murder my father?" Her voice remained low and calm, but Malachi could feel her hand trembling on his head as Nathan stared at her with sorrow in his gaze.

Lifting his snout, he tucked his nose into her hand to reassure her. *I've got you. He won't hurt you. Tell him the truth about me. In fact, take off your jacket.*

Without breaking eye contact, Chuck peeled off her jacket and held it loose at her side. "Nathan, there's something you need to know about Malachi."

Malachi shifted to his human form then, snatching the jacket from Chuck's hand and wrapping it around his waist. "Hey, Nathan," he called casually.

"E-Evan?" Nate stuttered, leaping to his feet and stumbling backwards, trying to distance himself from what he was seeing. "Y-you... you're the dog?"

"Malachi. My name is Malachi. Chuck just gave me that other awful name because she didn't think people would accept the coincidence that she was dating a guy who had the same name as her dog," he explained. "And actually... I'm not really a dog; I can just turn into one. Blake is right about one thing. I am a demon." He turned to Chuck and took her hand in his, kissing the back of her knuckles. "I'm her demon, and Chuck is my reason for being here. I'm her guardian. So last night, when Blake attacked my girl, I subdued him. I'm afraid he did bring out the beast in me; I went full demon mode." He shrugged as Chuck watched in silence.

"So right now, it stands like this. I don't think Nathan killed your dad, but he knows something about it. Also, the evidence from last night is missing, and now the other case files are gone as well. I'm pretty sure Nathan had something to do with it; I could see the dark smear on the shelf where the box had been. And his scent is all over the counter. I think we need to talk with him, but not here." He turned back to the wide-eyed man whose eyes were fluttering rapidly as if he didn't believe what was in front of him. "So the question, Bennett, is, are you coming with us quietly? Willingly? Or do I need to go full Hellfire and fury? Maybe break a hole in the wall, take you forcibly. Because I'm going to make something extra super fucking clear right now." He stepped closer until he was nose to nose with the veteran officer. Growling, he dropped the matter-of-fact tone, adopting a quieter, more lethal voice as he explained, "Kelly is my life, and I will protect her with every cell in my being. The way I see it, you not giving me the information we need to stop the attacks on her life will be treated as a high-level threat. And threats to her make me a little... unhinged."

Malachi grinned, twitching his shoulders, baring his fangs, and flashing Hellfire through his eyes. Waggling his eyebrows, he crooned now in a sing-song tone, "What's it going to be, Bennett? Are you gonna play nice with the good boy puppy? Or does he need to go rabid to protect his partner?" He tapped his talons rhythmically on the buckle of the collar still fastened around his throat. The sharp metallic pings made Blake twitch with each sound, shoulders jerking in time.

Bennett swallowed hard, trembling in his sneakers. He glanced at Chuck and nodded slowly. "I'll come with you, but I want you to know, Chuck." He sighed. "Kelly. I didn't kill your father."

Blake began to laugh, a feral choked sound that shivered across their skin like a physical thing crawling over them with creepy hairy legs. Chuck rubbed her hands over her arms as if she could brush them away, and Nathan shuddered. Malachi turned to Blake and growled, snapping his teeth in the man's face. The laugh cut off as suddenly as it started, and Blake stared at the demon before him with pure terror written over his features. A slight whimper came from his throat.

"Dad?" Blake's voice trembled. "What's going on?" He glanced around him sharply, taking in his surroundings before gripping the bars in his fists. "Why am I here? Who is he? Who is she?" He pointed a shaking finger at Chuck and Malachi.

Stepping back, Malachi studied the seemingly terrified young man with a suspicious gaze before he barked a short laugh. "Oh, come off it. We aren't falling for that shit!" He shook his head. "Oldest trick in the book." He held his fingers up and made sarcastic air quotes. "I didn't know I was possessed," he said, his tone mocking. He chuckled. "You want to be possessed for real? I can make some calls."

Blake's terrified expression relaxed. "It was worth a try." He shook his head in distaste. "Abominations, both of you."

"Blake!" Nathan snapped. "Not another word." He turned to the others. "Let's go. Coffee shop on the corner, you know the one?"

Chuck agreed, her mouth still hanging open slightly. She glanced over as Malachi handed her the jacket a second before he shifted back to dog form. "Cameras," she mumbled, jerking her chin towards the devices mounted to the ceiling.

Rolling his eyes, Malachi sighed. *Way ahead of you, babe. Already zapped 'em.*

34

"The Conjuring" is a Comedy

Settling in at the coffee shop, Malachi rested his chin on Chuck's thigh, leaning against her leg while he stared determinedly at Nathan Bennett. The man was all nerves; his legs jittering, fingers twitching, and jaw moving side to side. Since they didn't have a change of clothes for him, Malachi was staying in canine form for now, relaying his questions directly to Chuck.

"Start at the beginning!" Chuck commanded. Her initial shock had worn off, and her fierce determination was fully in charge. "Don't leave a detail out, or I swear Malachi will go full demon and rip your head off. I will dance in your blood while stomping your balls."

Malachi glanced sideways at her. *I may be rubbing off on you a little too much.*

Her eyes darted down to him briefly, and she smirked. "Now, Bennett. Talk."

"Yeah, fine. The beginning." He blew out a sharp breath and rubbed his hand over his mouth, a distant look in his eyes. "First, again, I did not kill your dad. I know this is going to be hard to hear, but it was Roger."

Throwing herself back in the booth—surprise widening her eyes—Chuck clenched her fingers on the edge of the table until they turned white. "Roger?" she repeated. "But he was Dad's partner. His best friend. And he died too! Why would he? How could he?" Her voice was steadily rising in pitch.

Malachi whimpered slightly and advised, *let him finish. I have a feeling I know where this is going, and you need to hear it all.*

Nodding reluctantly, Chuck quietly threaded the fingers of one hand into his fur and waved for Bennett to continue with the other.

"Sorry, I know that's shocking. But I promise, it's true. Roger and I found out what your dad was about two years ago. I thought we were all okay with it. I mean, it was shocking. Angels? Demons? The mere fact that they existed was crazy enough, but that your dad gave up a life in Heaven to be with your mother. Mind-blowing. I hope you understand how much Gavin loved Carla. She was his entire world, until you came along. Then you both became his reason to live. When she died." He shook his head. "You evolved into the center of his universe. It made him more terrified but prouder than anything when you followed him into the force."

Leaning back, Bennett studied her with his tired, faded denim eyes. "Kelly, you must know that you were his greatest love, but you're also his greatest weakness. You're considered an abomination by Heaven's standards, but he didn't care."

"Abomination?" she repeated, no doubt recalling Blake's heated words.

Technically, yes, Malachi explained with a reluctant sigh. *You're what's known as a Nephilim. Half angel, half human. The winged freaks upstairs don't like that because it dilutes their precious blood. So they say. I don't know*

because I'm not exactly a confidante of theirs, but I know they usually do try to get rid of them. I don't think you are an abomination, though, far from it. To me, you're Kelly Charles, perfection in a tiny ass kicking police officer uniform.

Chuck's lips wobbled as she stared at him, then her eyes flew to Bennett's and met his concerned gaze.

"I guess Malachi told you?" At her slight nod, he continued. "Like I said, Gavin didn't care. He loved you and protected you. Warded you from discovery for years. Roger and I didn't care about that part, the Nephilim thing, but Gavin swore us to secrecy. He warned us what could happen to you if anyone knew. Everything went back to normal until about a month before they died, when Roger started acting really cagey. Talking about prophets and the end of times. But he'd never do it around Gavin. I mentioned it to your dad, but he blew it off. Said being close to an angel could have that effect on people."

Shaking his head, Bennett toyed with the handle of his coffee cup, spinning it one way then the other. Finally, he raised his gaze to hers again. "The day of the raid, Roger was even more jumpy than usual. Something just wasn't sitting right with me. So I cornered him, and he told me another angel had visited him and explained the problem with Gavin forsaking his heritage. He urged me to talk to the angel, but I thought he was having a breakdown. I humored him. Told him why not?" Staring off into the distance, his gaze slightly unfocused, Bennett shook his head then continued. "He dropped to his knees and started praying. I was about to haul him to the psych shack when the angel herself appeared."

Malachi sat up straighter, concern rolling over his shoulders. An *angel* set Roger on Chuck's dad? This was definitely news that chilled him to his very bones. But it didn't make sense. Why would angels assign him to

protect her if they wanted her dead? Someone was lying. He tuned back in to Bennett.

"So there we are, a whole damn angel in my living room. Wings, robes, halo, the whole nine yards." He paused as the server refilled their cups and offered menus. After politely declining, the story resumed. "Uh, angel, living room. She explains all this same stuff Rog was saying and so help me, I believed her." His eyes filled with tears, and he wiped his mouth with a heavy hand. A shaky breath shuddered from him. "I'm so sorry, Kelly, but I believed what she told us. She was hypnotic, convincing, and put the literal fear of God in me. It was all laid out. The raid, the forsaken sword, and Gavin's death. Then we were coming for you."

A vicious snarl erupted from Malachi's throat as he stood between Chuck and Bennett. Alarmed stares and murmurs came from the other customers as they turned to watch the commotion.

"It's okay, Malachi," Chuck soothed. "He's not going to hurt me. I'll shoot him before he gets close enough." Her voice was deadly calm and steady. The barrel of her personal weapon was now trained on Bennett under the table.

Fucking Hell, that's hot, Chuck! Please tell me you'll handcuff me at some point? I'm begging you.

As a small smile toyed with her lips, she glanced at Malachi and winked. "Calm down. Not the time or place."

Oh, yeah, sorry. He glanced back at Bennett, who had both palms flat on the table in a placating manner. *Talk. Now.* Malachi gave a low warning rumble in his throat.

"And I would deserve it, but I swear I don't want to harm you." He nodded quickly, trying to add some credulity to his words. "I know this is a lot to process, but it was overwhelming that day. We got to the raid, and I was there early as planned with the blade. Gavin and Roger burst in, and

I raised that sword behind him... but I couldn't do it. I couldn't kill my friend. I couldn't kill a man whose only sin was loving a good woman and raising a beautiful child. I knew that the other angel was wrong." Bennett buried his face in his palms, shoulders shaking, sobs breaking from deep in his chest.

"Roger..." Chuck started then stopped, swallowing heavily. "Roger took the sword, didn't he? He finished what you couldn't."

Nodding miserably, Bennett raised his red-rimmed eyes to hers, his face splotchy as he reached for a paper napkin to wipe his nose. "He did. Kelly, I held Gavin in my arms as he lay dying. His last words were begging me to protect you." He straightened his shoulders. "So, I did. I killed Roger to keep him from coming after you."

Chuck and Malachi both stared in horrified silence for several long, tense moments as they processed what they'd just heard. "No," she insisted, shaking her head vehemently side to side as if the motion would jar the words from her mind. "No," she repeated, her eyes brimming with tears, looking like her world was ending as she glanced around frantically, trying to find an escape from this reality.

The misery and pain emanating from her washed over Malachi like a physical blow, ruffling his fur, making him shiver. A whimper escaped his throat, and he shoved his head against her chest.

Immediately, she wrapped her arms around him and buried her face in his scruff, stifling the sobs that tried to break free. "Malachi," she cried, pain etched into every syllable as her shoulders quaked.

I'm here, Kelly. I've got you, hold on. He stood on his hind legs and leaned his head on her shoulder so she could better hang on to him. *Shh, it's going to be okay. We'll get through this. This will not break you. It won't, you're too strong. Deep breath, come on. Breathe. One at a time.* As her tears subsided and her shudders lessened, she leaned back and stared at him with a weak,

watery smile. *That's my girl, my badass Chuck. Let's get the rest of what we need to know, then we can go home, and you can have an entire pint of that awful ice cream you like. I'll even watch a chick flick with you. Or two, but that's my limit. Then we have to watch a comedy, like 'The Conjuring.'*

Laughing now, she stroked his ears. "Pistachio ice cream is not awful," she replied gratefully. Lifting her gaze to Bennett, she narrowed her eyes. "You..."—she paused and glanced around to make sure they weren't overheard—"ended Roger?"

A sorrowful nod before he hung his head, Bennett sighed heavily. "I did. It's been hell not telling anyone. You deserved better, Gavin deserved better. I just didn't know what to do. I was worried that if I didn't hide my part, I couldn't keep an eye on you." He shook his head and met her gaze again, his eyebrows furrowed. "The angel came to me that night. She congratulated me on Gavin's death. Then gave me the blade, told me to come after you. I refused." He sat up straighter as determination firmed his lips and brightened his eyes. "I told her flat out I wouldn't take your life, and I would stick to your side to make sure she didn't send another freak after you."

Ask him what the angel's name was, and what she looked like, Malachi relayed to Chuck. As she repeated his question to Bennett, the older man scrubbed a hand over his tired eyes. Malachi watched him intently for any signs of deception. His next questions were going to be harder.

"No name was given. White female, average height, about five six, medium build, around one hundred forty pounds, shoulder-length red hair, slight wave, green eyes, white robe, giant white wings, gold halo." Bennett closed his eyes while reciting the description like a suspect, then whirled his finger over his head in a circle.

Malachi frowned and growled low. He pushed forward and stared deep into Bennett's eyes. *All angels are blond with blue eyes, and their halos aren't*

gold circles on their heads. It's a light around their bodies. They glow, like an aura. Their wings are small, more for visual impact than flying, and the feathers are usually gray.

Just as Chuck started to repeat his words, Bennett shook his head and stared wide-eyed at Malachi. "I heard you," he said. "In my head, I heard you."

Good, saves time. Now we have a serious problem because whoever put a hit on Chuck and her father... was no angel. It sounds like a demon pretending to be an angel. Especially since they had a forsaken blade.

"But if it wasn't an angel..." Chuck trailed off as her expression turned troubled, realizing what the likely person or being was.

"A demon?" Nathan asked, his voice cracking.

Nodding gravely, Malachi tucked his chin to his chest, thinking hard. *I'm almost one-hundred percent certain. Impersonating an angel is not unheard of,* he admitted, *and they probably went with that classic halo-wing visual because that's what most humans would expect.*

"Read me in, what did I miss?" Glenda demanded as she plopped down at the table next to Nathan and flagged down a server for a glass of water, chugging it down as if she'd been in the desert for a month.

35

It's Still Not Real Bacon

After introducing Glenda to Nathan and explaining her role, Chuck updated her on what had been discovered. Now the witch was leaning back in the booth, staring at the ceiling in deep contemplation. She'd punctuated the re-telling with gasps and squeals, drawing more attention to their group than Malachi was comfortable with. His pointed stares and snarky comments went ignored as Glenda fluttered her hands, her bangles clanging like a wind chime in a hurricane.

"Goddess be," Glenda finally gasped. "This is much worse than I imagined." She whirled in a colorful flutter of scarves and grabbed a startled Malachi by the sides of his head, planting a large kiss on his nose. "Thank the Goddess you're here protecting our girl. Never thought I'd be indebted to a demon like this, but I'm so glad you're here, Malachi. Comments on my driving and personal fashion choices aside." She grinned then, ruffling his ears and turning back to the table. Now her eyes narrowed, and she pointed an accusing finger at Bennett. "You."

Malachi used a paw to try to scrape the kiss from his nose, gagging at the smear of bright purple lipstick staining his skin. He glared at Chuck as she worked to stifle her laughter and focused on Bennett instead.

"Yeah. Me." Bennett sighed and ran a hand through his short sandy hair. "Look, I don't know what the best thing to do here would be. So Chuck, however you want to handle it, I'll go with it. If you want me to take the fall for Gavin's death, I will. If you want me to admit it was Roger and I killed him, I will. You've deserved the truth, and I deserve to be punished." He hung his head as he folded his fingers together on the tabletop, patiently awaiting her verdict.

For agonizing moments that seemed like hours, the tension and silence stretched between them. The air was fraught with unease like a palpable miasma. Finally, Chuck shook herself as if waking up and reached slowly across the table. She gently laid her shaking fingers over Bennett's hands and squeezed. "Nathan, no. It wasn't truly Roger, and I know you were trying to do what you thought best in an impossible situation. We need to figure out who is truly behind this, because,"—she swallowed heavily—"I don't want you to lose Blake."

Malachi growled, *fuck that! He stabbed you! He tried to kill you. He deserves to be locked up. No offense, Nathan, I'm sure you're a great guy and all. But Blake tried to KILL Chuck.*

"He's right," Bennett offered quietly. "Blake tried to hurt you, and that's also my fault. I should have stood up more, been there for him when I noticed he seemed different. He started coming around two weeks ago, acting like he wanted to rekindle our relationship. Prior to that, Blake hadn't spoken to me in almost a year. Blamed me for things not ending well with his mother, especially when she died six months ago in a car accident. Which is true to an extent. I was more married to the job than her, but I was so glad to see him, I overlooked the signs." He shook his head and

hunched his shoulders forward as if the weight of the universe was pressing him down to the laminate surface of the table. If he could become part of the wobbly furniture coated with layers of despair and grime, he probably would have.

Dammit, Malachi huffed and flopped to the floor. At Chuck's inquiring glance, he rolled his eyes. *It's hard to be mad at the guy when he's so damn agreeable.* He covered his eyes with his paws. *Gross, you're rubbing off on me and making me... barf... nice.*

Glenda released a booming laugh at his words and offered him a treat. "Good boy, Malachi."

Staring at him in fascination, Bennett opened his mouth and closed it, then opened it again. "Okay, I know it's off topic, but... you're a human. Or human-like, but you like dog treats?"

Peering incredulously at Bennett from beneath his fuzzy eyebrows, Malachi snorted. *Dude... It's bacon.*

"It's not *real* bacon," Chuck muttered under her breath. Before Malachi could voice his retort, she carried on louder, "Look, I know this is a mess, and there's a lot of blame to sort through for years, but I think the most important thing is we figure out who this is and stop them before they kill me."

Barking loudly, Malachi shouted, *NOBODY is killing you. They'll have to kill me first. And that ain't happening, sweetheart.* Hackles on his neck standing up, Malachi ignored the terrified shouts as other customers jumped from their seats at his outburst.

"Ma'am, I'm sorry, but you'll have to take the dog outside if you can't..." their server started to say but was quickly quieted when both Bennett and Chuck flashed their badges and snapped, "K-9," in unison.

The server scurried away as Chuck turned to Malachi. "Calm down, Mal. I only meant that figuratively. Of course no one is going to kill me. Neither you nor I will allow that to happen. I know that."

I don't like it anyway. Don't say things like that. I can't lose you, Kelly, not now. He put a paw on her leg and leaned into her. *I don't care how undemonly that is or how weak it makes me look. Kelly, I'm never leaving you. I... I...*

"It's okay, Malachi," Chuck reassured him. "I don't think it makes you weak at all. If anything, it makes you stronger to go against your nature like this."

A clatter drew their attention as the server dropped the coffee pot on the floor. "Sorry," he squeaked. "I thought you were talking to the dog." He laughed nervously as he squatted to start picking up the larger pieces.

Exchanging glances, the three humans and one dog all nodded, silently agreeing they needed to carry this conversation somewhere else.

Chuck's house, Malachi declared, *I want to be on two legs and in clothes. Well, clothes if you two are coming with us.* He released a wheezing laugh that had the server hurrying to the back, looking over his shoulder like he expected Satan himself to follow in pursuit.

"Bad dog," Chuck sighed.

At Chuck's house, Reena was once again cuddled like a baby in Glenda's arms while Malachi went to get dressed. When he returned, Reena flailed her legs in an effort to get down and yipped at him until he took her from

Glenda and rocked her. The witch laughed good-naturedly about it, while glancing at Nathan from the corner of her eye.

Nathan was staring at Malachi with concern etched deep into his forehead, looking like he'd aged a decade in the last hour. "So, do I call you Malachi or Evan?" he inquired lightly.

"Malachi."

"Evan."

Chuck and Malachi glared at each other. Finally, she looked away, and he smirked before turning to Nathan. "Malachi, if it's just us, but Evan—gross—if we're around others. Is that doable? Because I hate that fake-ass name. I was named for my great-grandfather, who was an archdemon, a major honor. And Evan is a douche name. Not quite as bad as Jaxon, but still, ugh." He tickled Reena under the chin, and she wheezed happily. "Isn't it Re-re?" he cooed and sauntered into the kitchen, the Chuglet tucked in his arm, paws dangling in front of her looking for all the world like a miniature kangaroo with an underbite.

Nathan simply stared after him, mouth hanging slightly open. He turned to Chuck and closed his jaw with an audible snap of his teeth. Then he shook his head and laughed. "I don't know why I'm surprised. I mean... your dad was an angel. You're half an angel. Malachi is a demon. I met another creature pretending to be an angel, and we're pretty sure it's another demon. And you're a witch?" he glanced at Glenda. When she bowed her head regally, he huffed out another short laugh. "What about the other dog?"

"Reena?" Chuck snorted. "She's just a dog, but she does like reality TV." She glanced up as Malachi came back in and handed her a glass of wine. Nodding in thanks, she smiled softly.

Winking, Malachi turned to Glenda and handed her one as well. He gave a slight bow to her blushing thanks and moved over to Nathan, handing

the man a beer before flopping on the couch near him. He had his own beer in one hand and Reena in the other. “So, where were we?” he tilted the bottle back and took a long pull before sighing happily.

“Wait.” Chuck jolted slightly. “Where did that beer come from?” She squinted at him.

“Oh, I ordered a few things to be delivered,” Malachi replied casually.

Narrowing her eyes even further, her voice low, she sweetly inquired, “With what money?”

Grinning, he wedged the bottle between his knees and snapped; a black credit card with flames flickering across the surface appeared between his fingers. “Demon Express, never leave Hell without it.”

Smacking her hand over her face, Chuck shook her head as she laughed quietly. “Seriously, I never know what’s going to come out of your mouth. One of the things I love about you.”

The room went quiet at her words, and she cleared her throat. “Anyway, so do we have any idea who could have been the person pretending to be the angel? Where do we start?”

As they all stared at each other, Malachi sighed. “I got this. Let’s see if it works.” He set Reena down next to him on the sofa and sat up straight. Squaring his shoulders, he put his hands together as if praying and stared at the ceiling. “Hey, Nicorette? You around? C’mon Nicaroni.” Shaking his head, he sighed as Nathan’s eyes bugged, watching him worriedly. After a minute of silence, he tried again. “Don’t be shy, Nicodemus. We know you’re listening. Ugh, seriously, Nicola? You’re gonna make me say it, aren’t you?”

Sitting quietly for a few more moments, the others exchanged a confused glance and shrugged their shoulders.

“Bro,” sighed Malachi. “Don’t be like this, Nicholai.” He glanced around before rolling his eyes. In a monotone voice, he quickly offered,

"Fine, I'm sorry, your name is Nick. Can you *please* come give us a hand? It's about protecting Kelly. You remember, your niece?"

Suddenly, Malachi groaned and slid to the floor, curled in on himself, covering his head. "Fuck!" he shouted. "I said I was sorry, is that really necessary?"

Nick, the angel, sat on the sofa, staring down at Malachi with an amused smile before dialing down his glow. "Oopsie, apologies," he called in a sing-song tone that fooled no one into thinking it was an accident. He glanced around the room and nodded a greeting to the others before his gaze landed on Chuck. "Kelly," he breathed. "You look so much like your father." His fingers briefly covered his lips before his line of sight was broken by Malachi standing in front of him.

The demon's fists were clenched, and his teeth were grinding together. "Hello, *Nick.*" He flopped back on the couch and crossed his arms across his chest. "Thanks for coming. No doubt you're wondering why we invited you to join us." His tone was unmistakably sarcastic and acidic.

"Oh, an invitation? Is that what it was? The purposeful wrong names, the obnoxious tone? The lack of respect? Only using my real name when you knew I wasn't going to respond otherwise?" Nick snapped back, mirroring Malachi's pose with his arms crossed over his robe.

The pair continued bickering and snarking at each other like two kids arguing over a toy until a hail from across the room interrupted them.

"*GIRLS*!" Chuck shouted. "You're both pretty. Now put away the measuring sticks and let's get down to business." Her lips were squirming around suspiciously, and she was biting the inside of her cheek.

Malachi broke first, bursting into booming laughter, which made Chuck let out a laugh, followed quickly by Glenda and, finally, Nick, who merely chuckled ruefully. Nathan simply stared in awe at the scene before him.

Nick sighed, "Alright, fine. I'm sorry, Malachi. I know you're a demon and you probably can't help it."

Nodding graciously, Malachi snorted. "Exactly. Now, let's talk about why we invited you."

Chuck cleared her throat and glared at Malachi, nodding her head towards where Nick sat expectantly, patiently waiting.

Glancing between them, Malachi bunched his eyebrows in confusion and held out his hands in a 'what' gesture.

"Apologize," Chuck urged.

"What?" his tone rose in incredulity. "Apologize for what? Being me? He acknowledged it!" Malachi pointed at Nick with exasperation. "I'm a demon. I might have developed feelings and emotions, but he's still an angel, I'm still a Hellspawn for the love of Lucifer." He sat back with indignation and crossed his arms over his chest again.

Nick held his palms out, patting the air in a calming motion, trying to instill peace. "It's fine, I wasn't truly expecting an apology. He did acknowledge it was on purpose, and he did say please. That's truly a lot for any demon."

Pointing at the angel again in as close to a righteous gesture as he could manage, Malachi beamed before turning to Chuck with a smug smile.

"Hi, human, confused. What's going on here?" Nathan blurted out, his eyes wide and fingers clenched on his knees. His whole frame was tense and on edge, nearly trembling with his anxiety. The question dimmed the lighthearted atmosphere as quickly as a bucket of ice water dumped on a fire. The others deflated in on themselves as they returned to the seriousness of the situation.

"Of course," Nick murmured placatingly. "My name is Nick, regardless of what Malachi tells you. I'm an angel, a real one. Nathan Bennett, it is a pleasure to meet you to some extent. I'm very displeased that you allowed

my brother to be murdered, of course, but…" He leaned back and primly placed his hands on his knees. Taking a deep breath, Nick continued. "I am torn," he admitted. "You allowed my brother to die, but not at your hands. I appreciate that you refused. I'm grateful to you for holding him and offering comfort as his soul was returned to us. And I'm even more grateful that you stopped the other from harming my niece." He blew out a steady breath, shaking his head. "But now your son is consumed by the darkness, and you have hidden this. Your silence in the face of the attempts on Kelly's life, well, I must ruminate upon this."

Malachi growled low as Nick leaned farther back into the cushions, his expression adopting the serene smile he used when he was being pious. "Oh, come *on,* Nicklerama," he moaned. "Quit being dramatic. We aren't here to judge and smite Nathan. He shanked the bad guy; he offered to turn himself in for his crimes. You know you're going to forgive him; your kind always does. So, let's pretend he asked, and you agreed, so we can keep going. Who is masquerading as one of you winged freaks to commit crimes in the name of your head honcho while actually doing it for mine?"

"Malachi," Chuck hissed, clearly horrified at his behavior.

A small, tiny, almost minuscule worm of doubt about his words began to wriggle through what little conscience he had while he stared at his hands. "Chuck," Malachi said slowly, evenly, feeling his way through his thoughts. "You told me to not act based on how I think *you* want me to act, but to do what I feel. I *feel* like we will sit here for hours waiting on… Nick… to extract a confession and a request for forgiveness. I don't *feel* like I can wait that long when there's an active threat to your life. Someone wants you dead because they think you're an abomination. I think you're the most perfect creation on this plane or any other, and I would sooner give my own existence away than see the wonder that is uniquely you disappear. So, I'm sorry for seeming impatient. I just care about you too much to see you

die because the winged freak wants to hold a h-holy mass." He dropped his gaze as guilt ate away at his insides, churning his stomach in a sickening whorl, knowing his words would push Chuck away.

A soft, warm hand grasped his jaw, and the most exquisite lips ever to exist touched his. Kelly was in his arms, kissing him. Clouds of awe, confusion, delight, and a healthy dose of what the fuck jumbled together as they swirled through him. Kelly turned to the others and jerked her thumb in a get out gesture before turning back and kissing him again. He heard Glenda clear her throat, Bennett cough in embarrassment, and Nick frown. Yes, the angel's disapproval was so strong, it was audible. A negative humming in the air. But none of that mattered. Kelly, his Kelly, was pressed against him, crushing her mouth to his and winding her arms around his neck.

Without fully understanding why this was happening, Malachi rose to his feet, Kelly still clinging to him, and lurched towards her room. He vaguely heard Glenda mention grabbing a late lunch and coming back later as she closed the front door, but he was too caught up in the woman wrapped around him to hear anyone's response. Stumbling to the bedroom, he shoved the door closed and set Kelly on her feet before finally lifting his lips from hers.

He studied her as she stood there, hair mussed, cheeks flushed. Her lips swollen from their steamy kiss, her eyes heavy-lidded and focused intensely on him. Her chest rose and fell rapidly, but most telling and intriguing of all, her aura was undeniably solid red. "Kelly?" he whispered, uncertainty and nerves creeping into his voice. "What are we doing?"

"Picking up where we left off this morning, I hope," she replied in a low, sultry tone.

36

Assume The Position

Malachi stared at the woman before him, debating whether or not to pinch his arm or just go with it. When he explained his actions—why he was being rude to the angel—he did not expect this type of response. His demon nature was willing to blindly accept it, but something stopped him and demanded he understand it. "Kelly," he moaned, banging the back of his head against the door, irritated at this newer, softer side of himself. "Help me out here, I'm dying to have you, but what is this all about? I thought you were mad at me for how I was treating Uncle Wingman?"

Grinning her sultry smile, she tugged on the hem of his t-shirt, pulling it up so far he had no choice but to take it off or be trapped in it. "Because, Malachi. You care about me so much that you're willing to lay your life down for your sworn enemy. You're willing to work with the other side to protect me. You go against your very nature to be with me because you care that deeply. I don't know many men, human or otherwise, who would do that. So, call me crazy; you're a demon, and I'm half angel, we shouldn't work, but dammit, we do."

"I..." He shook his head, then huffed out a wry laugh. "I don't know what to say." Snapping his gaze to hers, he paused. "Wait... yes, I do. Thank you, Kelly. Thank you for giving me a chance. For seeing *me*."

"Mal," she said, leaning into him. "Are you going to kiss me again?"

Grinning now, he picked her up again and carried her to the bed. "I'm going to do more than that." Gently laying her on the mattress, he stood, staring down at her. "Kelly, you are the most beautiful thing I've ever seen. I've seen a lot of things in my life. Good, bad, ugly, and depraved, but you... you were worth waiting for." Lowering himself over her, he took her face between his palms and smiled. "And I would wait another hundred years if that's what I had to do."

"Another hundred..." she murmured, then shook her head. "Later... get your hands on me."

"Yes, ma'am," he replied, lips against her throat. "Where would you like those hands?" he asked with a devious smile as his lips continued their journey down her neck to her shoulder. His fingers skimmed up her sides, raising her shirt as he traced her curves. "Here?" He feathered his hand over her stomach. "Or here?" The other hand splayed across her ribs, brushing the underside of her breast. Using one knee, he nudged her thighs wider and settled himself lower as he slipped the shirt over her head. Dropping his lips to her collarbone, he took the strap of her bra in his teeth and dragged it off her shoulder. His hand crept up to the slope of her breast and ran a fingertip over the edge of the lace. "Definitely here," he murmured as he pulled the material away from her skin.

His gaze drank her in, and he shuddered as he finished removing her bra. "Kelly," he breathed. "Even being a demon and knowing angels exist, this, you, how perfect you are, makes me believe in God."

Gasping, she grabbed his face between her palms. "You said it. The G word. Are you okay?"

Smiling shyly, he nodded. "I'm fine, I told you. You're changing me. And I mean it. Only H-Heaven could create something as beautiful as you." He moaned as her fingers curled into his waistband. "And now you're trying to kill me."

"No, I'm trying to get you naked. You talk too much." She smirked. "Get the rest of these clothes off!"

Raising one hand, Malachi snapped his fingers, and the rest of their clothing vanished, appearing neatly folded across the room on a chair. "Impatient little thing, aren't you? I wanted to savor you, but you're so bossy."

"Holy shit," she blurted, her eyes wide, staring at the pile of material in a chair. "Malachi, how did you—" Her words choked off on a gasp as he dropped one hand between her legs and teased his fingers over her center.

"I seem to remember you said I talked too much, and you wanted me to touch you?" he whispered seductively in her ear, leaning down so his chest was barely brushing hers. Pushing against her thighs with his, he laughingly told her, "Wider, Officer Charles, assume the position."

Twining her fingers in the unkempt locks of his hair, she suddenly tugged hard on them. "Do not," she demanded breathlessly as he ran his fingertips up and down over her inner thighs, "make police jokes. I swear to Lucifer and God both, Malachi, if you don't have your cock in me in about sixty seconds, I *will* handcuff you. And not in a fun way."

Malachi froze, and a large grin curved his lips up so hard his cheeks began to hurt. "Oh no, don't threaten me with a good time. I like a little pain. And I promise, my pain tolerance is a lot higher than you expect. But for fuck's sake, Kelly, you can't say stuff like that to me and not expect me to go a little feral. I don't want to hurt you." Her fingers tightened in his hair again as he slid one finger inside of her, moaning about how incredibly wet she was. He dropped his forehead to hers and captured her quivering lips

with his when she cried out. "That's my girl. I had no idea you were this needy for me. And I'm not even charming you. Hellfire and damnation, you really are going to be the end of me, aren't you?"

She arched her back as he took a nipple into his mouth and rolled it with his tongue. He hummed against her skin, reveling in how delicious she was. Her taste was warm and spicy, nothing overly exotic, just... Kelly. She was like satin or silk under his tongue and hands. Pressing his thumb to her clit, he began to stroke small circles over her while slipping another finger inside of her. He curled them upward, narrowing in precisely on the special place that had her writhing under him.

"Malachi!" she cried out, her body shuddering as he moved his mouth to her other breast, running his other hand up her throat, lightly squeezing as she gasped.

He gazed up at her from under his lashes, almost freezing at the sight of her head thrown back, cheeks flushed a deep rose pink, lips parted and damp, coming undone beneath him. Seeming to feel his stare, her gaze met his, and the desire he felt darkened his eyes until they were almost solid black. "Kelly," he rumbled in his chest, "I need you, but you are going to come in my hand before I have you." With his words, he sat back on his knees, keeping his one hand stroking between her thighs, the other wrapped around his cock. He was aching and throbbing, barely restraining himself from slamming into her as deep as he could. Withdrawing his fingers from her, he smirked at her whimper and slipped them around the base of his shaft, painting himself in her arousal. He slid two fingers from his other hand back inside her while he stroked himself now with the slippery coating.

Her eyes were drawn to him like a magnet, and she blurted, "Holy shit," as she took in the size of him.

"I'll take that as a compliment?" he asked in a husky voice with a hint of a laugh. "Never mind, I thought I told you to come!" he demanded, flames flickering in his eyes.

Like a magic spell, she obeyed his command and broke apart at his touch. He moaned as she screamed, her walls clamping around his fingers. Her breathing was rapid, and he could see her pulse pounding in her throat. As she shuddered, coming down from her release, her eyes blinked several times slowly as she focused on him. Leaning over her now, he hovered until his lips were inches from hers. He slid his fingers into his mouth, sucking them clean. "Mmm, I am definitely going to have to taste you longer next time, but for now, I want to be sure I meet my deadline for having my cock in you. I know we went a little over, but you didn't seem to mind."

Surging up and capturing his mouth with hers, she smirked against his lips. "Shut up," she mumbled. Tangling her legs with his, she suddenly flipped them over, and now she was straddling him.

Letting out a loud laugh, Malachi grasped her hips and lifted her over his straining shaft, then held her just above him. "Mmm, I love a woman who can take charge. Fuck that is such a turn on to have you manhandle me. But now, can you take it all at once? Or do you need me to be gentle? I'm going to enjoy this no matter what... but I want this to be exquisite for you." He lifted his hips slightly, teasing her entrance with the head of his cock, slowly rubbing back and forth while she squirmed, trying to lower herself on it. "C'mon now, don't be shy, speak up. Tell me what you want."

"Kinda... hard... to concentrate... when you're... doing *that!*" she panted. Glancing down at what he was teasing her with, she moaned, "I don't want to answer."

Malachi lifted his upper body and nibbled on her earlobe. "And why is that?" he inquired, pushing just a little further into her, then chuckling low at her whimper when he pulled back out.

"You're gonna make me say it..." she groaned and dug her fingers into his chest. "Look at me, do not get a big ego about this. But... I've never been with someone your... um... size before. Is that a demon thing? Cause I have been with other guys, and they weren't so... yeah, maybe go slow. Or is it better to rip off the bandage and just go for it? I don't know!" Her breath gusted out in a hard whoosh as he crushed her against him.

"Never be afraid to tell me what you need, Kelly. I can make you feel wonderful things. Immense pleasure, exquisite pain, everything in between. That's what I'm made for. So, whatever you need, I'm here for it. But only for you. No one else. Just you. Yours."

"Mine," she repeated. "Slow then, let me make sure I can handle you, then you can fuck me harder." She grinned innocently at his choked sound. Patting him on the cheek, she rocked forward, slipping down over the head of his cock again.

A satisfied sigh left her lips as he slowly inched deeper, stretching and filling her. He watched as her head rolled back, weightless on her shoulders, and she quivered in his arms. "That's my girl, take control, however you want it." He lifted her hands from where they rested on his chest and placed them on his shoulders. "Go on, Kelly, slide down and get comfortable, because once you are, I'm going to ruin you." His own head dropped back as she lowered herself further, and her walls clenched and squeezed him. "Oh, Satan, that feels amazing. Kelly, you are incredible."

A breathy gasp and moan slipped from her throat as she finally succeeded in taking all of him inside her. "Malachi," she called his name like a prayer, and his heart skipped a beat at the most beautiful sound he'd ever heard.

"Again," he begged. "Say my name like that again."

With the softest smile, she rolled her hips and breathed his name again, her aura flashing gold.

His cock jerked inside of her, and he felt tingling at the base of his spine. He was about to come, and he was nowhere near ready. Quickly, he thought of Hyacinth's threats, and it calmed him enough to get a grip on himself. "Lucifer's tits... Kelly... I need... I have to... fuck!" he was babbling now, but he couldn't help it. She was only sitting in his lap, and it was the most pleasure he'd ever experienced.

"Yes," she gasped.

"Thank you," he moaned as he lifted her, almost removing himself completely, before slamming into her again. Her scream was pure pleasure and music to his ears. His toes wanted to curl, and his fingers clamped hard on her hips. Lifting her again, he repeated the process several more times before he pulled out and threw her on her back. Flinging himself down over her, he lifted one leg to his shoulder and plunged into her again. A wordless shout slipped from his throat at how exquisitely wet and welcoming she was, how perfectly she gripped him. Her back arched and her hips ground against his, the friction nearly overwhelming. He began to pound relentlessly into her, grinning when she wrapped her other leg around his waist and dug her heel into his lower back, urging him on.

He felt it then, that telltale tightening of her channel, her walls clamping harder as her breathing went choppy and jagged. "Are you going to come again for me, Kelly?" he demanded in a low rumbling voice, purposely sending it over her skin like a physical caress. At her nod, he slowed and stroked deeper into her, angling for that spot he knew would send her over. As her breath caught and she tensed, her nails bit into his shoulders, drawing blood, but he didn't care. He stared in awe as her lips parted, and his name sang out across the room like the most beautiful hymn he'd ever heard. Not that he'd heard many, because they would normally make him vomit, but it was still the purest, most exquisite sound in the universe, accompanied by a flash of gold from her halo glow. He reached between

them, circling her clit with a finger, drawing out her orgasm until she went boneless beneath him.

“Ma-Malachi,” she breathed. “That... oh my G—” her words cut off as he clapped his hand over her mouth.

“No. Don’t say that. Please... still a demon. Never invoke that name while I’m fucking you. My name is the only one slipping between your lips. You can sing it like a hymn or say it like a p-prayer, because I’ll show you H-Heaven and Hell together, but the only name you scream when you come is your own personal demon’s. Malachi. Understand?” As she nodded, he lowered his lips to hers and kissed her deeply. With a sigh, he began thrusting again, but these were slow, deep slides, nothing like the frenzied pace from earlier. “Kelly,” he groaned, “you own me... heart and body.”

A moan of pleasure eased from her throat, and she tangled her fingers in his hair again. “Not soul?” she whispered back, pressing her damp, slick skin to his as he dropped her leg, and she wrapped it around his waist.

“Don’t have one, you’re my soul. You’re all I need,” he replied as his voice began to shake. His thighs started trembling, and he tightened in anticipation. The tingling at the base of his spine and cock were back, and he knew he was moments from losing himself and releasing into her. He opened his mouth to ask if she was alright with that, cursing himself for not checking sooner, when she grabbed his chin.

“I’ll gladly share my soul with you, Malachi,” she declared sincerely, while her fingers trapped him in a grip of steel. Velvet wrapped, as the saying went, because her skin was so soft, but still a firm hold, nonetheless. Her glowing gold was swirling with red, and it was mesmerizing.

That did it, he thought as a bolt of emotion shot through his body, wreaking havoc on his control and opening the floodgate for the torrent

he jetted into her. Crying out with a guttural groan, his arms buckled, and he almost collapsed, catching himself at the last moment.

Kelly snaked her arms around his back and pulled him the rest of the way down, wrapping herself around him. She held him as he trembled, still quaking with the aftershocks of his climax.

“Sorry…” he panted. “Meant to ask… if should pull out… but you… fuck… you…” He groaned and buried his face in her neck, soaking up the sensation of her slippery, hot skin against his own overheated body. “I lose my mind with you.”

“I’ll always help you find it.”

37

The Hair Envy is Real

Eventually, Malachi lifted himself and hurried to her bathroom for a warm cloth to help her clean up. He gently wiped her thighs and fussed over her to the point she laughed. Tilting his head, he tried to figure out what was funny. Was after-care not something he was supposed to do? He'd never done it before, so maybe he wasn't doing it right. The cloth fell from his fingers as it hit him. He'd never done this before. With anyone. In two centuries. But he hadn't hesitated here. Her amused chuckle brought him back to the present. "What?" he demanded, turning his palms up.

"You're so cute... I didn't know you had this whole mother hen side. It's sweet. And unexpected. I like it."

"Oh." He laughed ruefully. "Yeah, I might be going overboard here, but I want to take care of you and make sure you're okay. I've never done this part before. Am I doing it wrong?"

Shaking her head, she sat up and kissed him gently. "No, you're doing it just right. Lay down, I'll finish and be right back." She rose from the bed like a goddess emerging from the sea and sauntered to the bathroom.

Throat tightening at the sight, Malachi groaned and flopped back on the bed. Stretching his arms up over his head, he relaxed and took stock of how he felt. At peace. Content. Fulfilled. He smiled softly and thought about the fact that he'd never felt these things after sex before. Physically relaxed, yes, but never in his heart or satisfied the way he was now. The mattress dipped as Kelly crawled over to him, lowering her body next to his before she wrapped her arm and leg around him the way she did when she slept. Snuggling her head on his chest, she sighed happily and traced her fingers over his stomach.

Slowly, Malachi lowered his arms and pulled her tightly to him. "Kelly, that was incredible." He gently kissed the top of her head.

"*You* were incredible," she corrected quietly. "And you didn't even use your powers on me. I... uh... I hope that wasn't boring for you. I'm probably not as exciting as another demon would be."

Malachi froze, grimacing. It appeared they were going to have that discussion now. "Kelly, don't say that. You were fantastic. When you first slid down on me, I had to picture death threats from my former commander to keep from exploding like a teenager." He chuckled at her snort of disbelief. "I know you might think my life before was just a demonic orgy of sorts..." He glanced down, and his chest tightened at her small, nervous nod. Sighing, he continued, "I get it, I'm part incubus, so yeah, sex demon. But that's not all I am. My mother was a general in the fifth ward. She was a fierce warrior and amazing strategist. I look like my father, but I actually took after her more. I concentrated my powers on fighting and training to command legions. But looking like I do made it much harder for me. Remember, the uglier the better for demons, so I was constantly being underestimated."

Angling his body so he could face her better, he stared into her soft eyes, smiling gently at the anxious expression that was forcing her lips into

the cutest bow. He couldn't help leaning down and kissing her until she relaxed. "Not a virgin by any means, but also not a complete party demon. Kelly, full disclosure, I'm two hundred sixty-seven years old. So yeah, my list is longer, but in all that time, I've never been with anyone I cared about. Because I didn't care before, it's just not something I even considered. I care about you, and that made it feel incredible. I didn't even need my incubus power because you turned me on that much." Pressing his still hard cock against her hip, he added, "You always do," before rolling her on her back.

Hovering over her, he smiled gently as her lashes fluttered in surprise. "Kelly, this is because of *you.* No one else turns me on like this. One snap of my fingers and I could have anyone I wanted. But I don't have to because the only one I want, by some miracle, wants me back." Parting her thighs, he slid back into her, wrenching a gasp from her throat as her shoulders came off the bed and her fingers dug into his hips.

"Malachi!" she cried out, panting as he kept up his slow, deep thrusting.

Whispering dirty, unhinged things in her ear, he continued to torment her with his lazy pace, grinning harder as she begged him to go faster, harder. Finally, she grabbed his hair and yanked him closer.

"I swear if you don't fuck me harder right now, I'm taking you to the vet and paying them to use the biggest thermometer they have!" she snapped.

"I love it when you talk dirty," he replied before complying with her demand, taking her with a feral abandon. This time, he let some of his dark shadows slip out and around her, coating her skin and stroking her everywhere. He had them tweak her nipples and circle her clit, slipping inside with each snap of his hips, adding to the fullness of their joining. Moments later, she was pulsing around him, screaming her release as he watched, mesmerized by the vision of her coming undone beneath him. It quickly brought his own climax, even harder than the first, and he emptied himself once more, a hoarse cry slipping out as his body trembled.

Flopping next to her, he groaned. “You’re on your own for the cleanup duty this time, dirty girl. You wore me out. Not sorry about the mess.”

A quick burst of laughter erupted from her, and she clapped a hand over her mouth before running to the bathroom, the mix of their release running down her legs. When she came back, she was still smiling as she dropped down next to him. “I swear I don’t know why I put up with you.”

Grabbing her waist and pulling her back to his chest, he wrapped himself around her. “It’s the hair,” he murmured, nuzzling the back of her neck. “You’re obsessed with my hair. It’s longer than yours, so you have hair envy. Admit it.”

Snorting in disgust, she shook her head. “It’s not envy; I like my hair short. I like yours because it’s so pretty. But that’s not the only thing I like about you.” She was quiet for a moment, then in a smaller voice added, “Thank you, Malachi, for what you said earlier. I was a little in my head about it. I want to be enough for you, even after you’ve seen and done so much. I just have my small world here and... I don’t want you to get bored.”

“Never,” he insisted. “My world changed for the better when you came into my life. The day I met you, my punishment became a gift. I know it sounds cliché, but you really are the best thing that’s ever happened to me.”

“Same,” she replied, turning her head to smile back at him over her shoulder.

Taking advantage of the angle, he kissed her again. As they gazed at each other, he suddenly grinned. “I’m glad you didn’t know you were an angel when you first met me. Scared the shit out of me. Remember how I jumped back in the corner, and you thought I was too timid?” At her amused nod, he continued, “I could see your halo, so I knew you were at least part angel and that you were going to clock to what I was and smite me right there in that cage.”

Laughing now, she shook her head. "I remember, and when I said you were scared, you got mad and started barking like you were yelling at me. It intrigued me, and I had already decided I liked you." She turned to face him and trailed her fingers down his chest. "Hey… when you used to howl along with me to the radio, were you singing or was that a commentary on my vocal abilities?" Glaring, she poked him in the stomach.

"Singing along, I promise!" He batted his lashes innocently. "Since we're being honest here, when did you truly suspect I wasn't a dog?"

She was silent for a long moment. "Almost from the beginning. There was something about you that was different. The way you would respond, and I could tell you understood everything I said. At first, I wondered if it was just some incredible training. Then I suspected it was so much more, but I guess I was being selfish and didn't want to look too hard. I enjoyed your company and your keeping me in check if I got too silly. I should have said something sooner. I'm sorry I didn't, but I knew there was… something. Of course, now we know what it is, but I'm going to miss having a K-9 partner."

The hand that was lightly stroking her side stilled, and Malachi frowned, confused. "Miss it? Why would you miss it? I'm not going anywhere."

Pursing her lips, she scrunched her nose, and shook her head. "Mal, you aren't a real dog. I can't keep treating you like one. I know you were having fun. But…" she trailed off as he placed a finger over her lips.

"Kelly, it's more than fun. I need to be able to protect you, and I can't do that if you're at work for hours without me. I can't exactly show up as Evan and be your human partner; I don't have the necessary certifications to be an officer. Even if I did, there's no guarantee I'd be assigned to you. I really don't mind being the dog if it means I get to keep you safe and spend time with you. Think of it as my job, and that's my uniform, the same way you wear yours. Please, Kelly. We're good together, and I help you. It helps

me keep on the path of good to support your fight for justice. That may sound corny, but it really does work. And..."

Now it was his turn to be silent as she put her hand over his mouth with a grin. "Okay, Malachi. I understand. It does make sense. But it's hard to think of you like this,"—she waved at his naked body—"and that." She wrinkled her nose.

Humming quietly, Malachi traced her lips with his thumb. "Would it help to think of me as two different people? Partner, K-9 in dog form, and lover, Evan, ugh, at night?"

"Lover?" She chuckled, "Who says that?"

"I do," he offered quietly. "Because that's what I am. The one who cherishes and desires you beyond reason. The one who will follow you to protect and guard you, be whatever you need. The one who will hold you in the night and kiss you whenever you want. You are mine, Kelly, and others may look at you, but the only one touching you will be me."

She shivered under the intensity of his gaze. "I like that. But I don't want to call you Evan. I can't separate you in my head either. Maybe just... don't talk dirty to me when you have four legs, okay?"

"No guarantees." He grinned.

38

No Really, Angels are Jerks

After a lengthy steamy shower, in which he gave in to his need to taste her repeatedly until her legs gave out, they were dressed and holding hands on the sofa when Glenda and Nathan returned. Taking in Malachi's wet hair and Chuck's change of clothes, the witch beamed ear to ear as she playfully shook a finger at them.

"Get that out of your systems, naughty children?" she demanded. At their unabashed nods, she sighed and flopped on the other sofa. Patting the cushion near her, she motioned for Nathan to have a seat.

Gingerly lowering himself to the couch, Nathan glanced around, clearly still uncomfortable with the situation. "Uh, where's the angel?" he mumbled.

"He didn't go with you?" Chuck asked, surprise coloring her tone as she sat up straighter.

"Nuh-uh," Glenda happily advised. "He grumbled something about that's not what he meant by 'guarding her body' and poofed out!" She threw her hands out to demonstrate, nearly poking Nathan in the eye.

Smiling sweetly, she wiggled her fingers apologetically as she stared at her warily.

Squinting in suspicion, Chuck stared at her friend before crossing her arms over her chest and smirking. "Glenda..." she drawled, "behave!"

Turning innocent wide eyes towards Chuck, Glenda dramatically placed her hand over her chest. "Me? Whatever do you mean?"

Malachi chuckled then. "Oh, come on, Chuck, leave her alone. I bet Glenda adores a man in uniform."

Cocking her finger like a pistol, Glenda pointed at Malachi and clicked her tongue as she winked. "Caught me red-handed!" she cheered.

Glancing between them all, Nathan finally jolted as he realized what they were talking about. "Wait, me?" his voice rose in incredulity. "What did... why are... huh?" he sputtered, his mustache twitching like a nervous animal.

"Not important," Nick grumbled as he stalked into the living room and threw himself heavily into a chair. "You guys really should consider some soundproofing for that room if you're going to scream that loud. It was pretty embarrassing." He shook his head with righteous fervor.

"How? Where?" Chuck was the one stuttering now. "Were you here the whole time?"

Shrugging, Nick held up his hands. "I don't eat, didn't really have anywhere else to be. You know, you should listen to Malachi. He's right about needing to be near you to protect you."

Blinking rapidly, Chuck's face flushed deep scarlet. "Listen up, Uncle Nick," she snapped. "You might be family, and you obviously feel you're better than us, but you have no business snooping around my house and listening to two people who are supposed to be *alone,* when they are having a heartfelt conversation." She clenched her fists, drew in a deep breath, and

was no doubt about to lay into him harder when Malachi tapped her thigh. "What?" she barked, then bit her lip in shame.

"Sorry to interrupt what was surely about to be an epic rant." Malachi pointed at the angel while a wide smile stretched his mouth. "But did you hear him? Nick said I'm right!" His smile was triumphant and full of glee as he glanced at the others. A slight widening of Glenda's eyes was his only warning as he swung his gaze back to Chuck.

Her finger rapped him sharply on the tip of his nose as she flicked him hard. "Bad dog," she scolded, her lips quivering as she tried to rein in her laughter.

"The fuck?" he shouted, rubbing his nose as his eyes watered. "Not cool, Chuck. I just wanted to get back to the topic at hand. Did you leave your sense of humor in the bedroom? Damn violent woman." He continued to massage his face as he leaned away from her, glaring.

At that moment, Reena trotted in to see what the noise was all about. She glanced between Malachi and Chuck, tilting her head in inquiry.

"She hurt me!" Malachi told the little dog, pointing accusingly at Chuck.

Lifting her lip in a snarl, Reena howled like a Hellhound—if Hellhounds could be five pounds of spite—and jumped in Malachi's lap, glaring at Chuck evilly.

"Seriously? You're turning her against me?" Chuck demanded and threw herself back against the cushions. "Unbelievable."

Rolling with laughter, Glenda waved her hands. "Oh goddess be, you guys are hilarious. But let's get back to the point, can we?" She wiped her eyes and shook her head. Gesturing at Nick, she invited, "Go on then, Saint Nick, tell us what we need to know."

Barking out a laugh, Malachi slapped a hand over his mouth, muttering, "Saint Nick," between his fingers while Reena wheezed her own laugh from his lap.

Glaring at them, Nick's eyebrows bunched together. "Don't you start," he warned Glenda. Turning back to the others, he sighed. "I need to get out of here. I think you all might give me a headache, and it's not even physically possible." Pinching the bridge of his nose and squeezing his eyes closed in exasperation, Nick rolled his shoulders before opening his eyes again, gazing at Chuck. "You need to be careful. There's an active bounty on you. Malachi can protect you, and I have no doubt he would do whatever it takes to stop anyone from causing you harm."

Malachi nodded fervently. *Always,* he sent her, his tone low and brooding.

Chuck narrowed her eyes as if she suspected he was making a movie reference, so he simply smiled at her adoringly. It was the human version of his puppy eyes. When her glare softened in return, he mentally pumped a fist. *Works every time.*

"Adorable," muttered Glenda.

"Ahem," Nick interjected, crossing his arms while his expression was downright thunderous. "It's a wonder you humans live as long as you do. Not one iota of interest in saving your own lives."

Leaning forward, a mischievous gleam in his eye and a not-so-innocent smile curving his lips, Malachi pointed at Nathan. "Technically, he's the only pure human here and coincidentally the only one being quiet and listening to you. So, I feel like the kind and decent thing to do would be to acknowledge your error and apologize for your prejudicial commentary against humans. You've unfairly cast him in an ill light when his only crime was to avenge the death of your brother." He shook his head, slanting his

eyes down as if ashamed of the angel's behavior, clicking his tongue in disapproval.

Nick stared at Malachi without any sign of emotion. His features went preternaturally still, and his expression blandly neutral. He resembled a bust in a museum carved of granite.

Tense silence fell as the others watched the silent volley between the two sides of creation. Malachi grinned and wiggled his eyebrows; Nick continued his statue impression.

Suddenly, Malachi crowed in victory, laughing so hard he almost fell off the couch. The others saw it then, the slightest twitch under Nick's left eye. With a creeping slowness that was eerie and mechanical, Nick's head rotated until he was facing Nathan, and his inhuman stare was focused solely on the man. Malachi's gasps as he tried to control his laughter were the only sounds in the room.

For his part, Nathan did not flinch under the unnerving gaze, but his forehead went slightly dewy with a fine sheen of sweat as he remained still.

Finally, Nick cleared his throat and spoke. "My apologies to you for my slight, Nathan. I did not mean to broadly paint your species in such a derogatory and insulting way. I humbly ask your forgiveness for my thoughtless and hurtful commentary." He lowered his head in a small bow.

"Humph," Nathan muttered, then nodded in return. "I'll forgive you if you'll forgive me for not stopping Roger from killing your brother."

The room—which was fairly quiet before—was now more silent than a tomb. Even Malachi's muffled laughter had died out. He studied the older officer in admiration at his balls for his retort and how neatly he'd maneuvered the situation.

Nodding again, relaxing his shoulders now, Nick sighed. "Of course I forgive you." Cutting his eyes to Malachi, he glared in warning, as if daring him to say anything.

Malachi leered at him while flashing Hellfire through his eyes, daring right back.

Apparently deciding to be the bigger person, Nick stood and began pacing. Pausing mid-stride, he shook his arms out, and his wings unfurled behind him. Sighing in relief, he exclaimed, “Oh, that’s better.” Glancing around at their surprised expressions, he smiled sheepishly. “I didn’t have them out because it’s hard to sit in chairs with them.”

Humming in agreement, Malachi exclaimed, “Look, we can be on the same side of the issue. I agree, man, wings and chairs just do not mix. Especially—ironically—wingback chairs. Those are the worst. They pinch your feathers!”

A small, choked sound escaped Nathan then. He was staring at Malachi. “Y-you have wings too?” His wide eyes were roaming all over Malachi in disbelief.

“Yeah, I have a demon form. Remember I mentioned Blake saw it?” Malachi gently reminded him. “Do… you want to see it?” He tilted his head, wondering if this was curiosity or fear.

Nathan slowly nodded and placed his palms flat on his knees as if bracing himself for whatever was about to happen.

Rising to his feet, Malachi moved quickly to Nick’s side and smirked at the angel. “Hey, there, short stuff.” Waggling his eyebrows, he cackled and grew in size, slowly morphing into his full demon form. Unfurling his wings, he pretended he didn’t notice that he whacked Nick in the face as he towered over the angel.

“Insufferable spawn of Satan,” Nick grumbled, swatting at the feathers in front of him. “If you’re done with show and tell, I need to know about who gave Roger the forsaken blade.”

Turning, Malachi glanced down at Nick and sighed. “You call me the sweetest names, Nickerdoodle. But for an angel, you sure are rude. I’m not

showing off. Nathan wanted to see what a demon looks like. Considering some of the choices out there, you have to admit, I'm one of the better options. Give him a minute to adjust to seeing a 'spawn of Satan' in front of him. Also, I'm not actually a spawn of Satan. I have parents who are married. So not even a bastard, contrary to popular opinion. Neither of them is the Dark Lord, though. So quick to label people. Sheesh." He turned back to Nathan as the angel's face ran through a myriad of ever-darkening shades of red. "Doing okay, Nathan? Sorry about Mr. Insensitive over there." He jerked his thumb while smirking at the apoplectic sounds issuing from Nick, then continued on. "But yeah, this is my full demon form. This is what Blake saw when he attacked Chuck."

Studying Malachi and Nick with a calm, calculating gaze, Nathan strode closer and looked them both over in great detail. Finally, he shook his head. "The person I saw looked more like him,"—he pointed at Nick—"than him." His finger swung to Malachi briefly before raising it to tamp his mustache a few times. "But I see what you mean, Malachi. The halo thing and the shape of the wings were different. And like you said, the hair." Shaking his head in disgust, he huffed air through his lips. "Now I don't know what to do with this."

Malachi shrank back into his human form and clapped Nathan on the shoulder. "Hey, don't beat yourself up. You saw some type of supernatural being and stood up to it. Takes balls. Since you're a cop, I'm sure you're hell on details. Can you describe to us what she looked like?"

"Wait!" Glenda held up a finger. "Kelly, paper, pencil, come on." She snapped her fingers and waved for her to hurry. Once she had the supplies, she whispered some words over them. "Enchanted drawing skills spell," she explained. "Okay, now, go."

Tentatively, Nathan described the person who presented herself to him, claiming to be an angel and setting them down this road. As he spoke,

Glenda began to draw, quietly asking clarifying questions about the shape of various features. The scratching of her pencil on the paper and the soft murmurs of Nathan's words were the only sounds. Finally, when he was done, Glenda turned the page towards him. His face went pale, and he sat with a solid thump.

Chuck hurried to his side. "Nathan, are you okay? Is that her?" At his silent nod, she took the page from Glenda and handed it to Nick.

The paper shook violently in Nick's grip before his fingers fell lifelessly from the page. "Oh shit."

Malachi caught the paper and glanced at Nick in concern before he turned his gaze to it. Like Nick, he went pale, and his fingers trembled before they clenched the page, crumpling the edges of the picture. "Oh fuck! We're fucked! Royally fucked! Exquisitely fucked!"

"What?" Chuck and Glenda demanded in unison.

"Who is it?" Chuck added.

Staring at each other with wide eyes full of fear, Nick and Malachi supplied the answer.

"Amaryllis."

"The Defiler."

39

Well, That Escalated Quickly

"Amaryllis the Defiler isn't just any demon. She's even higher than an Archdemon. She's a Knight of Hell. The first, oldest, and most powerful of demons. They were the original warriors when Lucifer fell, personally trained by the first Knight, Cain. Yes, that Cain. Oh, fuck this is bad. This is very bad." Malachi paced across the living room, fingers tangled deep in his hair. Nick was pacing opposite him, his halo flickering erratically with his worry. The two shared agonized glances as they passed, both acknowledging their mutual misery and exquisite fucked-ness in this situation.

Nodding frantically, Nick added, "She's brutal. Unforgiving. I absolutely do *not* want to come face-to-face with her. It would not end well. For any of us. Quite frankly, Nathan, I'm surprised you survived your encounter with her the first time, much less telling her you wouldn't comply with her demands."

Nathan spread his hands in a confused gesture. "I... don't know what to tell you. She was very calm and seemed understanding. There was no

anger or yelling. She just smiled and poofed away." He wiggled his fingers to demonstrate.

"So strange," Nick muttered. He resumed pacing. "This is so very not good, regardless." He glanced at Malachi. "Open to feedback from you. She's a demon, so are you. Any ideas? Ways to ward Kelly? Hide her from sight?"

"So... should I go ahead and pick out my burial plot now?" Chuck drawled, causing both men to halt in their tracks. "Because you two are acting like some giant demonic monstrosity is going to puddle up in the middle of my kitchen any moment now. Or am I reading the room wrong?" She swung her finger back and forth between them before crossing her arms over her chest and popping a hip out.

Grinning, Malachi stalked over and placed his hands on her hips before he pulled her close. "Damn, I love it when you get all sarcastic and snippy like that. I think I might like getting tased by you."

"Mal," Chuck groaned as she tried to dial down her grin. "You're terrible. But thank you for calming down. Now explain. What's got you and Santa Claus over there in a twist?"

Blinking at her owlishly, Malachi was silent for about thirty seconds before he picked her up and kissed her hard. "Santa Claus. Saint Nick. Angel Nick. I'm so proud of you." Setting her back down, he pulled her to the sofa and onto his lap. "Okay, so I explained who she is. The reason Saint Nick and I are a little concerned..."

"Concerned," Glenda fake-coughed, calling him out.

Flipping her a middle finger, Malachi continued, "Worried. Okay, worried. Zip it, witch!" He pointed at Glenda, who mimed sealing her lips shut. Grin fading, his voice dropped lower, turning serious. "She's unstoppable. Only a very few demons or angels could take her on and hope to barely survive the encounter. So, if she's after you, neither Nick nor I could

defeat her head-on." He pinched his lower lip in thought, vaguely aware Nick was nodding along in agreement.

Flopping back in his chair, Nick nearly mirrored Malachi's expression and actions. "What I don't understand," he started in a shaking voice, "is *why*. I mean, yeah, Kelly is Nephilim, but we don't take as hard a stance on that as we used to. Especially when they do things like police work and fight for good and justice. Technically, she is an abomination—sorry, sweetheart—but no one puts out hits on them anymore. And Hell, you guys have never cared about that part inasmuch as you just like corrupting them for the extra boost their grace gives you. So, I don't understand why the push to end Gavin and Kelly."

"Agreed." Malachi nodded. "Next question: Does Amaryllis feel threatened by her? Is there some prophecy? Is there some deep political motivation we don't know about?"

Nick stood abruptly. "I can check on the prophecy part. I'll be back." With that, he blinked out of sight; the only sign he'd even been there was a warm summery scent.

"And you all call me dramatic," Malachi muttered under his breath, glancing at the others. "Look, I can't just pop back to Hell and ask about political machinations. It doesn't work like that. Everyone would lie, want something in return for the information, and I have nothing to give. Besides, thanks to Nick's guardian binding, I basically have my own halo, and no demon worth their brimstone is going to talk to me anymore."

Gasping, Chuck's fingers flew to her lips. "I didn't realize!" she cried. "You being my guardian assigned from Heaven, you've been ostracized as a demon, haven't you? Cut off from your family and home?"

With a slow nod, he smiled gently, just the slightest curve of his lips. "Yeah, I may have forgotten to mention that part. I... ugh... well, when I p-prayed for you, and H-Heaven answered, it left an indelible mark on

me. When they branded me as a Guardian on official holy business, you could say it canceled out my last two centuries of demon status to nothing. Which is what Hyacinth was threatening me with anyway, so I guess that's why he gave in so easily. The only difference is that there I would be begging for final death. But here, I have you."

"You have me ..." Chuck repeated. "Malachi, you gave up your whole life for me? That's it? I'm all you have left?" Her voice rose in pitch as incredulity set in.

Scratching his head in confusion, he squinted one eye and stared at her. "Kelly," he sighed, "I didn't have much in Hell. Families don't stay together; my parents barely acknowledge me. Yeah, I had a place to live and some possessions, but the constant battles, the debauchery, the sinning. It just... doesn't compare to what I have here with you. Is that wrong? I'm sorry, I'm new to this."

"Why, Malachi?" she inquired softly. "Why would you do that?"

He simply gazed at her with everything he felt in his entire being. Unsure how to explain it. Unsure if even after everything, she would accept it. Unable to say it out loud, he sent, *Don't you know?*

"Oh, for crying out loud, Kelly, can't you see he's in love with you? He's so head over heels, and he doesn't even know what that means, but he's there, and it's fucking adorable." Nathan laughed, shaking his head.

Malachi stared at Nathan in surprise, wondering how he could tell when Kelly couldn't. She didn't believe even he could have real, meaningful feelings at all until recently. A glance at Glenda showed she obviously knew as well, based on her warm, encouraging smile. His heart started pounding, and he clenched his fingers as his skin tingled like electric currents were running under it. He didn't know what to do. They were right, he was a fool in love with an angel who didn't even believe he was capable.

"I know," Chuck answered quietly, turning to face Malachi. "I think I'm ready to admit that, finally. Which is fortunate, because I love him, too."

Everything inside him stilled, and a feeling of peace wrapped around his body like a warm blanket. The throw pillow he'd been scrunching in his fists out of nervousness dropped to the floor, unnoticed. He swallowed heavily and lifted one hand, tracing his fingers through the strong pulsing red glow around Kelly's body. It swirled over his hand and tingled against his skin. His heart thumped, once, twice, bringing his attention back to himself. "I told Nick. I told him that's why I was able to pray for you. Because I love you. I didn't... I never thought you could..." He stared at her now, eyes wide, stinging with emotion. "Kelly, you love me?"

"I do, Malachi," she responded with a soft smile. "And I'm sorry I ever doubted you could feel the same. I know you do. I see how much it confuses you and spins you around. But you aren't fighting against it, you're fighting for it. For me. Which lets me know that, however wrong others might see me, or you, or us together, I don't care. You and I are right. We're meant to be together."

Folding her in his arms, he held her tightly against his body, sighing in relief as something unlocked in his chest. Warmth and pleasure spread through his veins, and he realized that right now, this moment, was the happiest he'd ever been in his life. "Kelly..." he whispered, emotion choking him, his eyes filled with burning tears, rendering him unable to see her clearly.

Well, that, and the power went out.

40

Fetch Me His Soul

Groans and other sounds of dismay filled the room as everyone scrambled for their phones to turn on their flashlights. Shining them around like a drunken disco, the occupants finally calmed when they saw everyone was still in the same place. "What happened?" Glenda demanded loudly. "You forget to pay your bill, girl?"

Shaking her head slowly, Chuck spoke in a low voice, "No, I paid it. Maybe there's something going on with the transformer or line. I'll check the neighbors." Moving warily towards the front window, she peeked outside the curtains and surveyed the homes around hers. "Huh," she murmured. "No one else's house is dark. Just mine." She eased back from the window and asked, "Malachi, are you able to sense if it's anything supernatural?"

Eyes closed, Malachi was already in tune with his surroundings, searching the area. He sensed darkness intent on harm, creeping into the backyard from the side. Growling low, he gave terse commands. "Glenda, Kelly, into the bedroom. Lock the door. Wait for me. I can get in under the door frame once it's safe. Do not open it, no matter what you hear, no matter

who they say they are. Nathan, with me. There are intruders in the back, and they fully plan to come after her. Not fucking happening."

"Malachi, I'm capable of facing an intruder," Chuck snapped angrily, her fists clenched at her sides, gritting her teeth. "Hello, police officer, not a helpless damsel in distress."

"I know," Malachi answered softly as he moved to her and ran his hands down her arms, noting how tense she was. Squeezing her hands, prying her fingers apart so he could weave his through them, he leaned down to her. "But you're also vulnerable to the type of blade he has, and you are mine. You just told me you love me. I need to be able to enjoy that without watching you possibly die in my arms. Because then I would go insane and burn the whole world down, probably start the apocalypse. So please, for the sake of the whole world, go to the bedroom where I know you're safe from this guy. I would never bench you if it weren't for that forsaken blade. Next time a homicidal maniac shows up, and he just has a regular gun, I'll hide behind you and whimper like a little bitch so you can redeem yourself. Deal?"

Her mouth opened and closed several times before she finally smirked and shook her head. "Fine. I'll do what you ask this time. Next time, lead with that whole magical weapon thing, okay?"

Smiling back, he tugged a lock of her hair in acknowledgement, then shifted into his canine form. He trotted over to Nathan and stared at him. *I'm going out through the dog door. I don't know if he knows what or who I am, so I'll feel that out and let you know.*

Nathan nodded his understanding and pulled his service weapon, then crouched by the door. He offered, "Good luck," as Malachi slipped through the flap.

In the yard, Malachi stood on the patio and let his tongue hang out, giving the impression he was just an average dog. He stared around with

a vapid expression and sniffed the air. The smell of nervous sweat and desperation was thick in the gathering dusk as his senses narrowed in on the invaders. The sour stench wafting from them was nearly palpable, and Malachi shook his head. These men were full of madness and religious fervor, but he was willing to bet these guys didn't know Chuck was a cop.

Concentrating, he realized the first man was absolutely terrified and the main source of the stench of fear. The second wasn't as afraid, but unfortunately for him, just as intent on harming Chuck. A low growl built in Malachi's throat at that thought. He finally knew true happiness and love, something that most demons thought was a myth, and he was not about to lose it to some misguided fanatics. Sending to Nathan, he advised, *two suspects, both male. On the west side of the house, moving towards the backyard. I'll keep them distracted; you want to slip out the front and circle around? If so, tap on the door twice. Quietly, I'll hear it.*

Waiting, he heard the faint taps to indicate Nathan had heard and agreed. With a feral grin, Malachi muted his sounds and crouched low, slinking towards the corner. He felt the men separate, one heading back towards the front. *Incoming,* he sent Nathan, *perp two heading back your way.* Silently, he crept closer, dragging the grass, and paused, ready to launch as soon as the asshole rounded the corner. Dismayed, Malachi realized the person with the forsaken blade and the darker soul was the one heading back to the front. The intruder coming towards him was just the terrified extra muscle.

A shaking hand holding a gun breached the edge of the house and was soon followed by the lean, rangy frame of an unkempt man whose eyes rolled wildly as he scanned the backyard. Unfortunately for him, he did what most amateurs did and only looked for threats level with his line of sight. He didn't look down at his feet, which was fine by Malachi, who was blending in with the lengthening shadows anyway. As soon as the man's

arm was over his head, Malachi leapt, biting his wrist, which forced him to drop the gun.

Ignoring the screaming, although it was rather delightful, he wrestled with the intruder and dragged him to the ground. Once the man was down, Malachi shifted to his natural form and grinned demonically at him. Given that he actually was a demon, it was even more unhinged than usual. Staring at the crying, babbling mess of a person beneath his claws, he shook his head in amused disgust mixed with a heavy dose of pity. This man was a type he knew well, and a favorite pick for corruption from demons. Meaning Amaryllis was definitely more interested in Chuck than he was comfortable with, and they were getting closer to her. He disliked everything about this and growled, the sound rattling around the small yard with an ominous echo from the brick walls surrounding it. The rumbling scared the scrawny pimple on Satan's ass even more, and he began screaming louder, shaking like a leaf.

Rolling his eyes, Malachi groaned, "For Lucifer's sake, will you shut the fuck up before I snap your putrid neck? Grow a damn pair." He lifted the man off the ground and shook him slightly for emphasis. "What was your goal here?" Huffing an impatient sigh as the man only whimpered while he dangled over the grass, Malachi tried to make his tone more reasonable. "Look, stop crying, and answer my questions, then I'll put you down, okay? I don't want to hurt you; I need to know about your orders."

"P-p-pro-promise?" stuttered the would-be attacker pathetically as he wiped snot on his sleeve.

Mentally cursing his luck, Malachi quickly agreed. "I so swear." He had to bite the inside of his cheek to keep from laughing as the man relaxed with the sarcastically intended formality. "Why are you here?"

"To kill the abomination," the man answered promptly, albeit breathlessly. "The bounty was to kill the woman with the short brown hair because she's an abomination against Heaven."

A snarl built in Malachi's throat, but he refrained from letting it out as his eyes lit with Hellfire. "She is not an abomination. Who set this bounty?"

"The angel!" blurted the man. "He told us she was a threat to Heaven and if we killed her, we would be accepted into Heaven when we died."

Chuckling low, Malachi leaned closer as he lowered the man to his feet but still kept a grip on his shirt. "Did this angel tell you what *kind* of abomination she is?"

Shaking his head frantically, he sputtered, "N-no, only that she was evil and needed to be taken down before she threatened the foundations of Heaven."

Nodding thoughtfully, Malachi tapped his claws absently on the man's shoulder, enjoying the way he flinched with each strike on his flesh. "What if I were to tell you that her only crime was being born? She's half angel, half human. And one-hundred percent cop. Did they tell you that? She's a police officer and armed to the teeth." At the choked gasp from the intruder, Malachi snorted in glee. "Not only that, but Heaven itself appointed me her guardian. Now, why do you think they would do that if they truly wanted her dead? I think you've been lied to, my friend. What do you think?"

A slow spread of horror dawned across the man's face as he stared into the fiery depths of Malachi's gaze. "A c-cop? She's a cop?"

"She's a cop, and I'm her demon. She's *mine,* so unfortunately for you, now I have to kill you. Because you don't threaten what's mine," Malachi delivered casually with a grin.

Mouth opening and closing rapidly while his hands fluttered like startled pigeons, the man finally squeaked out, “You promised!”

“I promised if you answered my questions, I would put you down and not hurt you. I did those things. Now, we can strike a new deal if you want. I can refrain from killing you, but I’ll need your soul in exchange.”

“My *SOUL*?”

“Hi, demon, remember?” Malachi snorted. “Of course that’s what I want. You think you have anything else I need?”

Slowly shaking his head, the shell of a man crumpled in on himself as he realized how well and truly fucked he was. “I have nothing,” he murmured. Raising his gaze, he threw his shoulders back in a last-ditch scramble to salvage his manhood. “Will it hurt?” he asked quietly. His voice steady and unwavering.

“A little,” Malachi admitted. “But not as much as me killing you. Tell you what, you tell me what this angel looked like, and I’ll reconsider letting you go as long as you leave my angel alone. I’m feeling nicer because she just told me she loves me.”

Blinking rapidly, the man began spouting a description of the angel. With a sinking feeling, Malachi decided the man must have truly seen an angel this time. That or the demon realized they were busted as a fake angel and upped their game. Regardless, Malachi realized two things at once. This guy was small potatoes, and he hadn’t heard from Nathan or the other intruder. Growling, he waved a claw negligently, then mumbled for the guy to get and stay lost. He barely noticed as the gangly man sprinted hard for the gate and was gone in a flash.

Shifting back to dog form, he slipped quietly through the door and let his senses roam. Right away, he could tell something was dreadfully wrong. He could smell blood and knew it wasn’t from the would-be assassin. The darkness was thick like heavy fog, much darker than it should be for the

time of day. Creeping forward, he heard another voice, Nick's, trying to coax Kelly and Glenda out of the room.

"Come on out, dearest niece, it's okay, everything's alright now," the voice reassured.

The growl building in his chest was getting hard to stifle, but Malachi choked it back, not wanting to alert anyone to his presence yet.

"You need to hurry," the man urged, his voice silky and comforting. "Malachi and Nathan are hurt; they need your help!"

I'm fine, stay put, Malachi sent to both ladies. *That's not Nick. I don't know who he is, but he has the blade and some spell that he's using to mimic angel Nick. I'm pretty sure Nathan is hurt badly. What do you want me to do? I can kill him, or check on Nathan, or my personal favorite, I can take his soul. It won't kill him, but he'll wish it had.*

The stillness was thick and tense, making his fur stand on end. Just when he began to worry Kelly hadn't heard him, his ears perked forward at her soft command.

"Malachi, fetch me his soul."

41

Souls and Soles- Brands matter

With an unearthly howl that echoed and rattled like an entire legion of demons was arriving, Malachi launched himself at the intruder. Snarling and frothing at the mouth like a rabid beast, he filled his eyes with flames and let shadows curl from his body. The dark tendrils expanded around his frame, making him appear larger, concealing his true form. All the man could see was glowing eyes of fire, wicked fangs, and deep writhing darkness.

A terrified bellow rent the air as the man raised his arms defensively, covering his face. The spell that made him look and sound like Nick fell away, revealing the attacker's true appearance. Just another gangly, sloppy man, almost identical to the one outside, he was utterly forgettable and average in every way. Height, weight, hair color, and even the size of his nose were boring.

As the enraged demon moved closer, the man blindly slashed with the blade, which had blood staining its length, still wet and dripping. Malachi's growl grew even more unhinged as he realized why Nathan was silent. The

blade wouldn't affect his demon hide any more than a regular one, but he still didn't want to get cut. Going in low, he bit the man's ankle, dropping him to the floor.

The intruder's grip on the blade did not slacken the way Malachi hoped as the jackass continued to flail his arms and clench his teeth. "Die demon!' he shrieked, while trying to slash wildly. "She's an abomination! She must be stopped!"

Rolling his eyes, Malachi shifted to full demon form, which was better suited for subduing enemies and removing souls. He flared his wings for dramatic effect, which was only ruined slightly when the feathers smacked the wall in the confines of the narrow hallway. Still, his horns glinted evilly as the Hellfire in his eyes lit the dim space. "You really think you can kill me, stupid mortal?" he laughed and shook his head. "You really have no idea who you're fucking with, do you?" Leaning down he easily plucked the blade from the man's fingers and studied it casually while gripping his captive's throat in his other hand. He absently lifted him and held him out at a distance while he continued to study the sword. Hefting it and taking a few experimental swings, Malachi shook his head in disgust.

"Seriously, this thing isn't even a full forsaken blade... It's like... a half-saken blade. It wouldn't even sting a full angel. Who gave you this? You could stab her, and she'd be like, 'Tis but a scratch!' and laugh it off." Malachi snorted and shook his head again. "So, back to my original question. Do you have any idea who you're fucking with? Because I'll be happy to enlighten you." He bared his teeth, his fangs showing their full razor-like lengths as he drew the sputtering, terrified man close enough to see the individual flames in his eyes. "I'm the demon in love with the woman you're trying to kill. So, it *really* pisses me off that you're here. Also, happy to bring up a sore subject, but she did order me to fetch your soul,

and I'm a *very* good boy." He leaned in closer. "This is where you scream, because I guarantee you it's going to hurt."

Lunging, Malachi slid his fangs into the man's throat, sucking hard and relishing that first pull of a sinner's blood. The agonized screams of exquisite pain filled the space, music to his Damned ears. He inhaled deeply, breathing in the glimmering part of the man that made up the complexity of his soul. It was certainly tarnished, and while not as sweet as the soul of a human who was otherwise 'good,' it was still delicious with its tang of darkness. He moaned indecently as the soul filled his throat, sliding down into his core like a silky caress. "Mmm… that's amazing. I do miss having souls to devour."

The man's form slumped to the floor in a boneless heap as the last of his soul oozed out of his body and into Malachi's. An uneasy groan rattled from his throat as he tried to regain his balance. Scrambling to sit up, his breath gasping and wheezing like an accordion, the man glared at Malachi. "Fuck you, I'm not telling you shit."

Rolling his eyes, Malachi chuckled. "Keep telling yourself that. I have your soul, remember? You're useless to me, Terry. I know everything I need to know about you and your pathetic experiences. I have no use for you; in fact, I would kill you, but that would create a mess for Chuck, so you get to live. Although now that you have no soul, it's not much of a life, is it?"

"That's what you did? You t-took my soul?" Terry's voice trembled. The shaking extended to his whole body as he quaked all over. "What… how… I don't…" he stumbled as he moved to his knees and shuffled towards Malachi pleadingly. "How do I live? How can I survive without my soul?"

"Fun fact, I don't fucking care. That's a you problem now, isn't it?" Malachi huffed. He glanced at the door. "Now, I need you to stay put while I tell her it's safe to come out." Glancing back at Terry, Malachi sneered.

"Stay, or I will hunt you down and kill you. Slowly. Painfully. Then I will paint a portrait of her with your blood."

Nodding frantically, visibly trying to rein in his terror, Terry scooted against the wall with a thud, one arm wrapped around his knees. The other holding the spot on his ankle where he'd been bitten, his eyes reflected nothing. He was now lost in the world.

Satisfied his prey wouldn't run, Malachi focused on the space beneath the door and willed himself into a cloud of ash and shadows. The nebulous mist slithered under the door and pooled on the other side before he reformed, quickly wrapping his wings around his body as a shoe came flying at his chest. "The fuck, Chuck?" he demanded as she readied another piece of footwear to launch his way. "It's me! Remember I told you I could get in without opening the door?"

She paused and stared at him warily. "Yeah, well, that other guy was using Nick's voice, so sorry if I'm not too trusting right now."

Glancing at Glenda, he shrugged. "Your friend has a teal dress with skeletons riding giant purple dildos, but somehow I'm the one who's concerning around here?" Winking roguishly, he leaned against the door and held out his arms to Chuck. His smile grew larger as the shoe hit the floor with a thump, and she launched herself into him. Wrapping her tightly against his body, he placed his cheek on the silky cap of her hair and sighed. "I've got you. I'm so proud of you, too. Look at you, not taking any shit. Ready to end my existence with a pair of Nikes. Brave woman."

"Only the best shoes for my demon," she muttered against his gray skin.

A chuckle built in his throat, until it boomed from him and filled the room with the rich sound. A mixture of relief and pure delight at her sassy comeback. Finally, he calmed his amusement and glanced into her eyes. "Alright, so now what do we do with the soulless cock sucker sitting in your hall? And we should probably check on Nathan." He grimaced, feeling

somewhat guilty for forgetting the other human, but being nice was still a little foreign to him.

Gasping and flinging the door open behind him, Chuck ducked under his wings and scrambled out of the bedroom. She kicked the intruder, Terry, as she passed while he still sat cowering in fear where Malachi had left him, and she started shouting for the other officer.

"Stop fussing over me like a damn child," Nathan huffed into his mustache as he shifted on the sofa, holding an ice pack to the back of his head. Glenda was indeed fussing—scolding him ferociously—while she placed the last suture in his arm. When she was done, she bandaged it and began cleaning up her supplies. They both ignored Malachi's quiet interjections, encouraging Glenda's tirade.

"Hear me well, Nathan Bennett. I *will* treat you like a child as long as you keep acting that way. Don't,"—she snapped and shoved a finger in his face—"roll your eyes at me. If you want, I can yank those sutures out and send you to the hospital, where you can explain that you got stabbed in the front yard of Officer Kelly Charles. The same Kelly Charles, your son tried to stab last night. So, what's it going to be, sir? Cause you want a scene? I can make a scene." Now her hands were firmly planted on her hips, and her eyes were narrowed on him in a defiant, dare-filled gaze.

Suddenly, Nathan laughed and held up his hands in defeat. "Okay, fine, I'm sorry, Miss Glenda. Thank you for helping me. I guess I'm just feeling my age and a little embarrassed some thug got the best of me. He did look like Nick, though; I didn't want to hurt an angel."

At Malachi's chuckle, they both turned to watch the man, Terry, as he sat shivering in a chair while Chuck interrogated him. Malachi was standing over her shoulder, still in demon form, making terrifying faces at him. Chuck couldn't see him, so he wasn't aware why the man kept flinching and twitching randomly.

He'd already jumped and screamed earlier when Reena trotted into the kitchen to inspect the visitor, having slept through most of the earlier ruckus. Terry was certain Reena was another demon, but she merely sniffed him in disdain, lapped up some water, and went out to the backyard.

Shaking her head, Glenda sighed, "Malachi, cut that out."

Slouching, he moved back from Chuck and frowned at Glenda. "What? Just having a little fun."

"You ate the man's soul, sugar, what else do you need to do to him?" she demanded, hands still on her hips.

Baring his fangs, Malachi swiveled back to Terry. "I don't know, Glenda, maybe flay him alive and dangle him over an open flame until his insides roast and burst?" At Chuck's involuntary noise of disgust, he shrugged. "The man *stabbed* Nathan and knocked him out. He was trying to get into where you two were. Did you think he just wanted to play Twister? He probably would have killed you, then Chuck." At her glare, he snorted. "He would have tried."

"And failed," Glenda added with a slight sniff of approval before turning back to Nathan, pretending she didn't see Malachi start leering at Terry again. "So, now what?" she asked him.

"Now what, what?" Nathan responded, then grimaced at Malachi's snort of amusement. Glancing up as the large demon moved over to them.

"I think what Glenda means," Malachi supplied before shimmering back into his human form, rolling his shoulders. "What do we do now? We've captured the intruder. You all won't let me kill him, but you can't

just let him go either. So, what's the story? What's the plan? Also, are you going to take Glenda to dinner?" He jerked his thumb towards where the witch was staring at him, open-mouthed and silent for once. "Because she wants you to. And she has this amazing dress she can wear. It's teal and has skeletons, and they're—"

"Malachi!" snapped Chuck, trying to choke back her laughter as Glenda's face turned a ruddy color in embarrassment.

Shrugging innocently, he spun on his heel and threw his hands in the air. "What? She's the one who made me look at it as a test. It's one of those... if I have to see it, so do you—things. It was traumatizing, really." He placed his hand dramatically over his heart and nodded wisely, his eyes overly wide and free of guile. Mostly.

Laughing out loud this time, Chuck shook her head as she stared at her friend, who was sputtering in indignation. "To be fair, Glenda, he does have you there. I was thinking, can you do that drawing spell again? Our friend Terry here has kindly agreed to give a description of the person who put the bounty on me."

Quickly regaining her composure, although she pointedly avoided looking at Nathan as she did it, Glenda gathered her supplies, muttered her spell, and began sketching. Although it took longer to gather the sketch because Terry wasn't trained to describe people the way Nathan was, they eventually had a working image of the supposed angel who had tricked him.

Passing it off to the others, Chuck's shoulders slumped, Nathan shook his head in disbelief, and muttered, "I'll be damned."

"I can arrange that if you want," Malachi offered helpfully before he glanced at the picture and cackled with unhinged glee.

42

Never Sucker Punch a Demon

"No, I *know* there's no way this is anything other than another demon trick, no offense, Malachi," Chuck insisted as she drove with Malachi, Nathan, and Glenda to meet up with the man in the drawing. After a heated debate, they agreed to drop Terry off on the other side of town with a promise to stay far away from them and never tell what happened, as if anyone would believe him that, despite stabbing a cop, and trying to kill another cop in her home, he had his soul sucked out by a demon and they let him go. Malachi hadn't approved, but he was outvoted. Besides, this new twist was too delicious to ignore.

"I refuse. Downright refuse to believe it!" Chuck repeated for the third time since they'd piled into her car. Shaking her head in disbelief, she glanced over at Malachi as he sat silently next to her. Glancing in the mirror, she met Nathan's stunned gaze and Glenda's amused grin.

The witch leaned forward and patted Chuck's shoulder companionably. "I don't know, honey, that boy has always seemed a little off to me."

Malachi pointed at Glenda and nodded. "Agreed. Also, he wears too much Axe body spray. And he sings Nickelback songs at karaoke."

Snorting in amusement, Chuck gave him some serious side-eye. "Mal, that's not enough of a reason to suspect someone of putting a hit on you. It's no secret you've never liked Jaxon. How many times did you pee on his shoes?" She grimaced. "That just sounds weird when you're in human form."

Chuckling, Nathan joined in. "For what it's worth, I've always thought Raifson was a bit of an idiot myself, but I also agree with Chuck. His questionable cologne choices and karaoke songs are not grounds for murder-for-hire. I still think it's a lead we have to follow."

Nodding stoically, Chuck's shoulders slumped. "I know, and I agree. It's just... Jaxon. We went to the academy together. He's like a brother to me. This doesn't seem like the kind of thing he would be behind. But I guess how well do you really know a person?" Her eyes zeroed in on Nathan in the mirror, then darted away in shame.

"It's okay, Chuck. I understand, and again, I'm so sorry I kept all of this from you. I never thought it would come to this." Nathan sat back in the seat and dropped his chin to his chest, staring at his tightly clasped hands. His sorrow was heavy in the air as the vehicle continued down the road, the only sound the hum of tires on the asphalt.

After a few minutes of uncomfortable silence, Malachi cleared his throat softly and glanced back toward Nathan. "Hey, I meant to ask, what did you do with the evidence and case files from last night and Chuck senior's box?"

"Huh?" Nathan started, his head flying up and eyes going wide with surprise. "What do you mean? I don't have them, never went near evidence."

"Wait..." Malachi spun to fully face him now, ignoring Chuck's protests. "I went to check on the evidence this morning. I needed to look at that

sword Blake used. It wasn't there. None of it was. And then I looked for Chuck's dad's case files, and those are missing too. When I sniffed the shelf, I detected the same darkness that's on you from association with your son." He stared at Nathan hard, confused and suspicious about the curveball they'd received. He was relieved they at least had the files he had previously liberated tucked away in Chuck's dresser at home. This turn of events had just thrown another wrench into an already sticky situation.

Nathan held up both palms to fend off any accusations as he quickly shook his head. "I'm telling you, I didn't go near evidence. I'm on temporary leave right now—just like Chuck—while this gets figured out. I wouldn't even be allowed in there. I came in and went straight to holding to see Blake. They only let me back there because they know me. I guess they felt sorry for me."

"But... if you didn't take that evidence..." Malachi quietly mused as he turned back to stare at Chuck. "Then who did?" He huffed and sighed in irritation, crossing his arms over his chest. "Seriously, after two centuries, I get feelings, a lover, and a fucking whodunit worthy of Agatha Christie herself all at the same time."

Chuck laughed low in her throat as she slowed for a red light.

"Two centuries?" Glenda inquired with a bawdy chuckle that shook her bangle bracelets. "Well, well, Mr. Malachi. Robbing the cradle a bit, aren't we?"

Blowing air through his lips in a rude noise, Malachi glared at her. "Maybe if Nathan ever asks *you* out. But in demon years, Kelly and I are essentially the same age. Focus, witch. If Nathan didn't take the files, we need to find out who."

"Agreed," Chuck offered quickly, before Glenda could offer another rebuttal. It was just as well because Malachi and the witch could trade snarky barbs and insults all night and still be friends in the morning. But

the clock was ticking. "We can question Jaxon about it when we get to his place."

Malachi grimaced at the thought of voluntarily entering the douche palace of delights, aka Jaxon's apartment, but knew it was necessary. He only hoped the man didn't wear Affliction shirts when he was off duty. When Chuck called to ask if she could come over, Jaxon was wary but quickly became happily surprised and accepted.

Turning into the parking lot of the complex where he lived, Chuck's grip on the steering wheel tightened. She took a deep, calming breath before easing the car into a guest spot. As she turned off the car, she blew out a heavy gust of air and rubbed her palms over her legs in a nervous gesture until Malachi squeezed her hand in reassurance. Nodding, she said, "Let's do this."

Jaxon's expression had gone from pleased to see Kelly, confused to see Glenda, resigned to see Malachi—or Evan as he knew him—and downright flabbergasted to find Nathan Bennett at the back of the group. The play of emotions running so clearly over his face had Malachi bouncing on his toes in glee until Chuck stomped his instep.

"Sorry," she offered sweetly with a bright, fake smile. "Thought I saw a spider."

Recovering himself, Jaxon shook his head and gestured silently for the group to come inside. Once they'd all made it into the living room of the small bachelor pad, he shut the door and spun to face them. He pointed at Chuck and then the others, seeming to be deciding what to say before

crossing his arms over his chest. "Anyone need a drink?" he offered in a flat, dutiful tone.

Malachi glanced around the surprisingly neat, tidy place and suspected Momma Raifson would have smacked him on the back of his head if he didn't offer refreshments to guests. Invited or otherwise. He was about to ask for something, but a glare from Chuck had him sighing in disappointment as he shook his head along with the others.

"Jax," Chuck started, "I'm sorry for the subterfuge, but some big things are going on, and we need your help."

Immediately, Jaxon perked up and rushed to sit beside her on the sofa. His expression went from confused to adoring in less than one second. Malachi leaned forward from her other side and stared unblinkingly at the other man to remind him of his presence.

"What's going on? I have to admit, I was a little surprised to see Bennett here with you," Jaxon admitted, then glanced at Glenda and did a double-take. "Wait," he gasped. "Weren't you the lady from the lobby? With the glass?" At her brief nod and small wave, he leaned back. "Hang on, I have a feeling *I'm* going to need a drink for this. Beer good for everyone?" At their nods, he stood and took a second to collect himself before sauntering into the kitchen.

In his absence, Chuck whirled to Malachi. "Anything?" she demanded.

Slowly, Malachi sighed with reluctance. For Chuck's sake, he didn't want Jaxon to be involved. But there was no denying the dark haze surrounding her friend. "It's a haze, like on Nathan. It's new too, because it certainly wasn't there this morning. I would have seen it."

"Seen what?" Jaxon asked as he hurried back in, an armful of beer bottles in his grip. He passed them out and settled back in before tipping his bottle towards Malachi. "Did you see something that helps explain this?" Now he waved the bottle at the others before taking a long pull.

Taking her own fortifying drink, Chuck turned to face her friend. "Jax, we're here because tonight two men tried to break into my home, intending to kill me." She held up a staying hand when he jolted and began to pepper her with questions. "Obviously, they didn't succeed. But my problem is that when I asked them who put them up to it, they described someone who sounded familiar. And the sketch, well, was unsettling really. Glenda?" She glanced at her friend, who handed over the sketch she'd produced from Terry's description.

"What the fuck?" Jaxon exclaimed as he slammed his beer on the table and studied the paper in his trembling grasp, blood draining from his face. "Chuck, Bennett, you gotta believe me, I didn't hire someone to kill you! Why would I do that? We're friends! You even helped Marla get the courage to ask me out. I would never... please Chuck!" He grasped her hands in his own now, the sketch falling to the floor. "I promise you!" He glanced at the others, desperation in his eyes as his pulse pounded in his throat, visible against the pale skin.

"Dammit," Malachi muttered. "He's telling the truth."

Leaning forward, Jaxon grabbed Malachi's arm and nodded frantically. "Yes! I am! Thank you, Evan, for believing me."

Disdainfully prying Jaxon's fingers from his arm, Malachi rolled his eyes. "I don't have a choice; it really wasn't you. Someone stole your image to deflect the blame and send us on a wild goose chase. Just like Terry was using Nick's image and voice. Jaxon, after you left us at the station this morning, where did you go? Who did you meet with? Tell us everything you did today."

Sitting back with a puzzled frown, Jaxon studied him. "Us? I didn't see you at the station. And who's Terry? Nick? Someone please explain this to me?" He glanced at Bennett and pointed at him.

"Look, Raifson," the other officer sighed as he pinched the bridge of his nose before continuing. "This is going to be hard to believe, but there's a lot at stake here. You're better off not knowing the details but just understanding that larger forces than our local precinct are at work, and you're being drawn in as a pawn or distraction of some sort. Let's just start from this morning when you saw Chuck and Malachi in the parking lot. Tell us your movements, who you spoke with until about five this evening. Anything stand out? Anyone new? Different?"

Slowly, Jaxon shook his head and pulled on his lower lip with his thumb and forefinger, thinking hard. "I just worked my regular shift today. I saw everyone who's in the shop as usual. And spoke with a few family members about ongoing case statuses. No one new there. Umm, wait." He snapped his fingers. "There's the new neighbor upstairs. She was unloading her car when I got here and trying to lug a giant box up the steps. I offered to carry it for her. She was grateful and offered me a glass of wine, which I declined, and then she asked if she could take my picture. Said she was an artist and liked to collect interesting faces." He shrugged. "I didn't see any harm in it, so I agreed. She snapped two photos on her phone and thanked me. That was it. Couldn't have been more than a few minutes."

Glenda rummaged in her oversized handbag and pulled out another sketch. "This wasn't her by chance, was it?" She held out the drawing of Amaryllis from earlier.

Gingerly pinching the paper in his fingers, as if afraid it would bite him, Jaxon stared at the image and groaned. "Shit, that is her."

Launching himself off the couch, Malachi grabbed Jaxon's shirt and yanked him nose to nose with him. "Which unit?" he growled.

"The heck, Evan?" Jaxon sputtered.

"Which one?" Malachi snarled, his eyes filling with Hellfire before he shook the other man. Jaxon's head snapped back and forth as he was

tossed on the couch. "Tell me!" roared the demon, growing more impatient with each second delaying him from confronting the Knight of Hell who wanted his Chuck dead.

A pair of strong arms wrapped around him from behind to keep him from grabbing Jaxon again. He could easily break Nathan's hold, but his awareness of Chuck's panicked shouts broke through his red haze of anger. Wilting in Bennet's arms, head dropping, chest heaving, he waved him off. "Sorry, I got a little crazy. I know better than to confront her head-on. But... we're so close. I won't let her hurt you, Kelly." He lifted his head and stared forlornly at her, the pain and fear bright in his gaze.

Closing the distance, she put a hand on his cheek. "I know, Malachi, I understand. But we have to be level-headed about this. And if you kill Jax, he can't tell you, can he? And you're not about to take on a Knight of Hell alone, are you?"

Shaking his head and dropping his gaze to the carpet, he pouted and grunted one salty word. "No."

"What the hell, Chuck? Why is your boyfriend attacking me? And what is this about a Knight of Hell? And," Jaxon's voice wound up both in volume and pitch until he nearly shrieked, "why did you call him Malachi? You got some sort of weird obsession with that dog!" He crawled upright on the sofa, looking ready to spring away from them any second as his eyes rolled wildly between them all.

"Ah fuck," Malachi muttered. "Guess we might as well read him in before he loses his shit." Glancing at Chuck, she nodded wearily. "Okay, listen close and shut up, Jaxon. This is going to be hard to follow, but you need to stick with me here, alright?" Rubbing his chin, he closed his eyes and thought about where to start. "My name isn't Evan, and I'm not Malachi's former owner. I *am* Malachi. I'm the dog, and the person. I'm actually a demon, and I was trapped in that dog's body and was Chuck's

K-9 partner until Glenda, who is a witch..." He paused and pointed at the bubbly woman who waved cheerfully from the chair where she perched, watching the drama unfold. "Yeah, the good witch freed me from the spell, and I got my human form back. Actually, you saw this version of me the next day. That's why she was getting me clothes. And she gave me that awful name, Evan."

Malachi paused and glared at Chuck for that, and she rolled her eyes before throwing her hands up in disgust. Chuckling, he turned back to Jaxon and studied the man. He looked a little green, but was following along quietly so far. "Right, so anyway, we figured out I could change between the dog and human, so I kept up my appearance as the dog."

Suddenly jumping to his feet, Jaxon moved closer to Malachi. "You were the dog the whole fucking time?" His voice was low and quiet.

"Yeah, dude, I was." Malachi grinned unrepentantly. Which was short-lived, as Jaxon reared back and punched him in the mouth. "What the fuck?" he sputtered through the blood that was dripping now.

"That's for pissing on my shoes!" Jaxon yelled, pointing at Malachi before laughing. "I knew there was something off about that damn dog. Always rolling his eyes and shrugging his shoulders like a smart ass."

Waving a hand and healing his injuries, Malachi glared at Jaxon. "Never, lay another finger on me unless you want me to bite your head off," he warned on a low growl.

Scoffing, Jaxon curled his fingers in a 'come on' gesture and held up his fists, snapping, "Bring it, bark boy!"

"Jax, don't—" Chuck tried to warn him, but she was too late.

43

Ruckus, Chaos, and Handcuffs

"I just wanted to scare him, I didn't think he'd pass out like a little punk-ass bitch," Malachi complained with heavy judgment in his tone. At Chuck's glare, he tossed his long hair over his shoulder and held up his hands, tipped with wicked talons. "Alright, so I hoped he would, but he hit me!" He gestured down at the prone form of Jaxon as he lay on the floor where he'd fallen like a sack of potatoes after his eyes rolled back in his head. Staring down at the man, Malachi shrugged. "Okay, so maybe I could have eased him into my demon form, but again, I reiterate, he sucker-punched me."

Sighing in annoyance, Chuck waved him off and grumbled under her breath about showing off.

Grinning, Malachi leaned down and tapped her shoulder. As she glanced up, his smile grew larger, and he let his hair slide silkily over his arms so it would brush hers, knowing she wouldn't be able to resist it. "But you love me," he reminded her quietly.

Wrapping a lock of his hair around her wrist, she pulled him lower so she could place a soft kiss on his mouth. "I do," she whispered, before raising her voice. "Which is why I'm going to forgive you, but earlier you were in a hurry to confront this other demon, and now we have to wait for Jax to wake up to tell us which apartment it was. You can't just go bang on other doors looking like that and not cause a ruckus." She waved her hands to indicate his demon form.

Pointing at his chest with indignation, Malachi arched an eyebrow. "Demon. Ruckus is practically my middle name. I live to create chaos."

Shaking her head, Chuck groaned. "No, not anymore. You're team 'good guys' now, remember?"

He opened his mouth to protest, then thought better of it. *If you promise to handcuff me later tonight, I promise I'll avoid causing any ruckus until then.*

Watching the slow rose color creep up her neck while her halo flashed red, he cheered in his head at the success his deal was gaining. He realized the advantages of being 'good' could bring him even better rewards than he originally thought.

"Deal," she whispered with a sultry smile. Her attention then turned back to Jaxon as he moaned and stirred.

"What happened?" Jaxon muttered and blinked slowly at Chuck. "Oh damn, Chuck, are you alright? I had the weirdest..." his voice trailed off as he caught sight of Malachi in his demon form looming over her shoulder. Scrambling back against the foot of the sofa, Jaxon's breathing sped up, and his eyelids fluttered again. "D-de-demon!" he pointed with a trembling finger.

Crouching down from his considerable height, Malachi leaned towards Jaxon and snapped his massive fingers in the other man's face. "Stop it!" he ordered, pushing some of his influence into him. "Man the fuck up right

now, Raifson. You're a cop, and you can handle seeing a demon in the flesh. Now sit up, take a deep breath, and tell us which unit that bitch Amaryllis is in."

Sitting quietly, Jaxon's trembling stopped, and his shoulders rolled back with the confidence Malachi had given him. Nodding once, he answered, "Right. Sorry. She was in the unit just to the right of the stairs. Apartment 2112."

Smirking, Malachi patted him on the shoulder. "Good job, Jaxon. And look, are we square on the pissing on the shoes thing? You did have it coming, and well, I was a dog then. Haven't pissed on you since I got my other forms back." He shrugged.

"Yeah," Jaxon mumbled. "We're good. Just uh... don't do it again, huh?"

Holding out his massive hand, claws and all, Malachi flashed his fangs as he offered to shake on it.

Gingerly, Jaxon reached out and took it, shaking on the deal. His eyes grew large then, and he paled. "Oh shit, did I just make a deal with a demon?" Snatching his hand back as if he'd been burned, he studied it, turning it this way and that, looking for any indication he'd been marked.

A booming laugh filled the room before Malachi clapped him on the back. "You did, but don't worry, I won't claim your soul this time." Rising back to his full height, he rolled his shoulders and stretched his neck. He extended his wings as far as they would go and flapped once. "Alright, let's do this!" Turning to the door, he started towards it, then paused. He glanced back at Chuck. "You know I believe in you, but you must also know you can't come with me. In fact,"—he spun to Glenda—"get her out of here. If this goes south, and I die, I need to know Amaryllis won't immediately kill Kelly."

His words were met with a cacophony of protests from everyone in the room. They all quieted down when Chuck stomped over and grabbed one of his wings, yanking him down to her level.

"Ow... Ow... Ow..." Malachi complained. "Dammit! I'd rather have your sharp elbows instead. Feathers are tender, you know?"

"No. I don't know. Because I haven't had time to learn more about this side of you yet. And I fully intend to. So, you better not fucking die, Malachi. Also, I'm not going anywhere, because if you *do* die, I'm going to go down fighting to avenge your death. I love you. I won't do this alone anymore. Not when I've finally found you. We go together or not at all. Got it?" Chuck crossed her arms under her breasts and snapped her teeth on the last word. Fury radiated off her small frame, and she practically vibrated with anger.

Under it all, Malachi could see the fear. Streaks of yellow and black were zipping through her glow. She was terrified. His heart swelled, and he went warm all over. Dropping to his knees, he pulled her against him and rested his forehead on hers. "Kelly, you stubborn, beautiful, perfect creature." Lowering his lips to hers, he kissed her gently. "I love you, too. So, I agree. Together." He entwined their fingers and stayed there for a moment, breathing her in. The mechanical racking of a rifle drew their attention across the room.

"As cute and really weird as this is, and you better believe I'm sending you my therapy bill," Jaxon deadpanned. "I'm not leaving my friend undefended. You may be a demon, but I'm a damn good shot. So is Nathan. Although I'm still a little confused why you're here when your son tried to kill Chuck, but I'll let that go for now." He handed the gun to Nathan, who bobbed his head once in thanks. "Chuck, you good?"

At her silent and surprised nod, he continued, "Glenda, do you need a weapon?"

The witch merely grinned and held up her hands, fire springing forth from her palms. "Locked and loaded, baby." She winked at Nathan, who was staring at her in open interest now.

"Witches are real, too. Check," Jaxon murmured and shook his head. Clearing his throat, he jerked a thumb to the open gun safe. "Last call for anyone wanting additional weaponry."

"Jax," Chuck called softly. "Please don't. This could ruin your career. I don't want you to be involved in this. I'm in too deep. So is Nathan. Glenda's a civilian, and no one outside of this room knows about Malachi. So, sit this one out. It's not worth your life."

Moving next to her, Jaxon smiled softly. "Kelly, do you remember graduation day? How your dad pinned my badge because I didn't have any family to do it? You and your dad were all I had; you became my family during the academy. And when he passed, that left me to live up to the promise I made him that I would always look after my little sister. I loved you too, you know? For the longest time, I wanted to be more than big brother Jax." He glanced up at Malachi's growl. "But I know we weren't meant to be. How were you meant to be with a demon? I don't get that, but that's another story for another time. The point is, I do love you. You *are* my sister, and I made a promise to big Chuck that I fully intend to keep. So no, little Chuck." He laughed softly as she punched his shoulder. "I will not sit this out. I'm all in." He turned his gaze to Malachi. "All in," he repeated firmly.

Wrapping an arm around the man's shoulder, Malachi smiled genuinely. "You know, I take back most of the references to you being a douche and dumbass. I like you, Jaxon. Although... do you have a middle name? Because that one..." he waggled his hand in a so-so gesture.

"Byron," Chuck declared with undisguised glee. "Jaxon Byron Raifson."

Eyes wide, Malachi choked down the nausea that engulfed him. "Ew, fuck no. Okay, Jaxon, it is." He turned towards the others. "Let's do this."

Malachi's body shook with the need to barge up the stairs and storm through the door—Hellfire blazing, of course. His hands practically itched with the desire to be coated in blood. But the need for stealth when surrounded by humans was not lost on him, so they quietly crept up the stairs under the cover of his and Glenda's quieting spells.

At the top of the landing, he rolled his shoulders and faced the unassuming door for unit 2112. There was a pleasant welcome mat and a wreath announcing how joyful fall was. The area was clean of leaves and other detritus that tended to collect around people's entryways. A simple brass knocker invited the visitor to announce their arrival in a basic way. No fancy cameras or video doorbells here.

Glenda pushed past the others and, with a deep fortifying breath, knocked firmly on the door. She clasped her hands demurely in front of her body while she glanced around casually, studying the empty landing with idle curiosity. After a few moments without response, she frowned and knocked again. Still, no answer. Glancing over her shoulder, she widened her eyes at Malachi in a silent, 'now what?'

Stepping forward, Malachi dissolved his body into ash and shadow, slipping slowly under the door, wary of any traps. He faintly heard Jaxon and Nathan's quiet exclamations of surprise at this ability. Ignoring them, he tuned in to the interior of the darkened living space. Casting his senses, he realized no one was home. Huffing out a disappointed sigh, he quickly ran through the rooms and double checked there was nothing amiss before returning to the front door to open it for his friends.

"She's not here," he announced flatly, trying not to let his anger show. Turning away, he stalked back through the home to search it more thoroughly. This time, for any indication of where or what Amaryllis was up

to. "Look for clues, I guess," he threw over his shoulder. Standing in the small single bedroom, he glanced around at the minimal furniture in the space—no homey touches like pictures or plants. No artwork graced the walls. Peeking in the closet, he found no clothing. The place was sterile, bland, staged. Huffing out an irritated breath, he clenched his fists and had to bite his tongue until he tasted blood to keep from punching the wall.

A pair of arms slipped around his waist as Chuck moved beside him and stood quietly. She seemed to understand his frustration and was offering her silent support when he was ready for it. Shoulders drooping in defeat, he shimmered back into his human form and pulled her closer.

"Dammit," he cursed softly. "This was just a setup to get Jaxon up here so she could use him to distract us." Shaking his head and holding her tightly, he bent his lips to Chuck's ear. "Why, Kelly? What are we missing?"

"I don't know, Malachi, but come to the living room with the others and let's see if we can come up with anything together."

Nodding, he turned to follow her when something caught his gaze under the edge of the bed. "Be right there," he murmured. "I just want to check the bathroom." He watched her head back to the front, where the rest of the group was gathering. As soon as she was out of sight, he reached down and snatched the object. A quick glance confirmed his suspicion, and his gut filled with a sickening sense of betrayal. Shoving it in his pocket, he hurried back to the living room with the others to hear their theories.

In the car, Malachi sat in brooding silence. He wasn't sure whether his concerns were correct or another wild lead. Staring out the window, watching

the streetlights pass in a hazy blur, he concentrated instead on how his breath fogged the glass. Wiping the condensation, he breathed on it again and used his finger to sketch a row of question marks in the haze before growling low in frustration.

"What's eating you, Malachi?" Glenda interrupted his musing.

"Just... frustrated." He sighed and glanced at the witch in the backseat. "Wondering how many more false trails we have to go down while people keep making threats on her life." He turned his gaze towards Kelly. The woman who loved him, in spite of being a demon. "I don't know what my next step is here. I need..." He swallowed heavily. "Help."

Nodding wisely, Glenda quietly added, "And you aren't used to asking for it. But you did once. You prayed, and it was answered. There's no shame in asking, Malachi. In fact, I think it makes you smarter and braver to recognize your limitations and speak up."

After pondering her words, Malachi sighed. "Thanks, Glenda. Speaking of helping, do you think Jaxon's okay with everything now?"

After the disappointing end to their search of the upstairs neighboring apartment, they'd returned to Jaxon's and filled him in on the rest of the details about Chuck's dad being an angel and her half-angel status. They left out the revelation that Nathan killed Roger for now. Only sharing that Nathan's son was corrupted by the demon, thus his involvement.

"He'll be fine," Nathan quietly huffed in his mustache. "Kid's made of stronger stuff than he seems."

The headlights of Chuck's car lit up the front of her house as she pulled into the driveway. "Alright, it's late. Why don't we all get some sleep and hit this again tomorrow? You want to come over after breakfast?" she offered quietly, fatigue clear in her voice.

Glenda and Nathan agreed and made their way to their own vehicles, waving as they left. Chuck stood on the front porch watching their tail-

lights disappear down the road before turning to Malachi and leaning against his chest.

Automatically, his arms went around her and held her tightly. "I know," he said. "I've got you. Let's get ready for bed. Go on, you first, and I'll check the perimeter and make sure everything is cleaned up and safe. I'll feed Reena, then join you."

"I thought you wanted me to handcuff you?" she smirked.

"I'll be quick!" he responded with a leer.

44

Whoa! Did Not See That Coming

After making the rounds outside of the house, Malachi did the same inside. Once he was certain there were no additional threats, he relaxed his shoulders a bit and blew out a harsh breath. He was standing in the kitchen, lights off, listening to Chuck going through her nighttime regimen. Assured that she was in the bathroom and wouldn't hear him, he softly called Reena to the room. Once he heard the telltale clicking of her toenails on the floor, he braced himself again and called out to the only person he knew that could possibly help.

"Nick, buddy, I really need you. I promise, no tricks. No messing with you. I need your help, please." His words were as heartfelt as he could make them.

A soft whisper of air across his cheek announced the arrival of the angel. He simply popped into the room and tilted his head. "Malachi."

Glaring, Malachi gritted his teeth. "So, you *can* show up without blasting me with your full power.

A bashful smile tilted the corners of Nick's lips. "Yeah, well, you kind of deserved it that second time. The first time was a mistake. Sorry about that."

Waving off his apology, Malachi glanced at Reena. "Hey, girl, you remember Nick, right? Chuck's uncle? We're going to go outside and talk in the backyard. Can you come with us and keep an eye out for Muriel? I don't want her snooping on us." He winked at his tiny friend and made his way to the door. Reena followed along, her curly tail springing with each excited step. It was obvious she was happy to participate in any subterfuge.

Nick was eyeing them warily as he followed Malachi out back. Once they stopped in the middle of the yard, he simply waited with folded hands.

"I wanted to give you an update," Malachi started. "After you left earlier to check on any rumors or prophecies upstairs, two men tried to break in and attack Chuck. We stopped them and they gave us a lead that an angel put them up to it. This time, the description truly sounded like an angel and not a demon pretending to be one."

"No!" Nick exclaimed in a thready voice. "It's not possible! There's no reason for anyone in Heaven to come after her. They would just do it themselves. We don't contract people to do our work for us." He shook his head vehemently to deny the implication.

Holding up his hands, Malachi patted the air between them. "Calm down there, I'm not saying it was. I believe it was a demon."

Stopping his muttered denials mid-sentence, Nick eyed Malachi suspiciously. "Huh, way to bury the lead there." He crossed his arms over his chest and stared expectantly. "Do tell."

"We had Glenda do another sketch. We recognized this guy, too. It was Jaxon. Chuck's friend at the station," Malachi explained.

Nick's chest puffed up, and his halo flashed bright gold. "Then what are we waiting for?" he demanded. "Let's go!" The angel spun and spread his

wings, preparing to fly or teleport or whatever angels did to get from one point to another.

Reaching out quickly, Malachi snatched Nick's arm and snapped, "Wait a minute, Nickelodeon. We already confronted him."

Groaning, Nick smacked Malachi's hand from his arm and whirled back to face him. A frown had bunched his blond eyebrows together and turned his lips down so hard, Malachi idly wondered if it would leave lines. He hoped so. Angels were too perfect already, it was entertaining to think of marring one.

"Maybe you could get to the point then?" Nick drawled, the sarcasm heavy in his tone.

"Or maybe—and hear me out—just maybe, you could shut the fuck up and let me tell the whole story before you go running off half-assed. Next time you interrupt, I'm going to let you fly off and wear your feathered ass out for nothing. No skin off my back." Malachi shrugged, laughing in his head that the angel actually believed he could be the snarkier of the two.

Blowing air harshly through his nose, Nick negligently waved for him to proceed.

Grinning, Malachi made a show of straightening his shirt and adjusting his stance. After running his hand through his hair and clearing his throat, he explained the rest of the story up until they returned to the house. He smiled expectantly at Nick then.

"And?" Nick growled through clenched teeth. His hands were now curled into fists at his sides, and his wings were trembling behind him.

"And I found a clue at Amaryllis' apartment," Malachi offered nonchalantly.

Nick went still in that weird, supernatural, statue-like way he had, staring at Malachi with wide eyes. The grinding of his teeth was audible, even over the slight ambient noise in the backyard.

"Hey, Re-Re, come here a second, would you?" Malachi called cheerfully. He winked at Nick. As she ran over, Malachi ignored the grumbling under the angel's breath. If he was right, the angel would soon be begging for forgiveness. "Hey, sweet girl," he cooed to the chuglet prancing happily at his feet. He scooped her up in his arms and tickled her belly like he usually did. "Okay, Reena, I have a very important question for you. Can you tell Uncle Nick what happened to your collar?"

Reena tilted her head and stared at him, confusion in her warm brown eyes. Her ears rotated towards him, and her underbite became more pronounced.

"What are you on about?" Nick demanded, throwing his hands out to the side in exasperation.

"Just... bear with me." Malachi tickled Reena's chin. "See, when I got home earlier, I noticed your collar was missing. I looked all over the house for it, but it was nowhere to be found. But that's okay. You know why?" He smiled softly at the little dog before setting her down and crouching in front of her. "Because I found it somewhere else. Under the edge of the bed at Amaryllis' apartment. The one where she set up the opportunity to get Jaxon involved and make us think he was out to get Chuck." Pausing, he pulled the lilac nylon loop from his pocket and shook it in front of her.

Nick was now silent, staring with bugged-out eyes at the demon and the small, unassuming brindle dog the size of a large cat.

Reena ducked her head and grumbled, pawing the ground as she muttered to herself. After another moment or two of silence, she stared up at Malachi with liquid eyes. A small whine came from her throat.

"Reena," he sighed. "Or should I go ahead and call you Amaryllis?"

Huffing out a small sigh, Reena sat back on her haunches and studied him while Nick sputtered in the background. A swirl of black shadows swirled around her tiny body, cloaking her in wisps of darkness and night.

The cloud of inky haze rose to the height of an average human female before receding, leaving a coppery-tressed, voluptuous woman who managed to appear breath-takingly exquisite and delicate despite being clad in full battle leathers that screamed lethality. A smirk curled her carmine lips and curved her high cheeks up towards her exotically slanted eyes. Eyes that were now trained on Malachi with a considering gaze.

"Ouch," she purred in a sultry tone that seemed to resonate in the still air. The world around them had grown quiet in anticipation. "Millennia of existence and I'm tripped up by a stupid dog collar."

"Amaryllis," Malachi murmured as he bowed his head respectfully. "Mistress of Darkness and Pain. It was barely visible. I nearly missed it. Had I not been lamenting my failure, I surely would not have seen it. Truly, you are a master of disguise and subterfuge."

A deep bubbling laugh poured from her lips as she threw her head back, letting her amusement ring through the night. "Stop, my dear. You damn me with your praise. Too bad I'm already damned. Oh, my darling Malachi, you have been a sheer delight to toy with these last few months, truly enjoyable."

Nodding, Malachi spoke low and calmly, resisting the urge to laugh at the sight of Nick trying not to piss himself behind the Knight of Hell standing casually in the backyard with them. "I see, and I am, of course, pleased to have been able to provide entertainment for you. If I may be so bold, might I inquire why you are trying to kill Kelly?"

A faraway look entered her eyes as she stared at something only she could see. "Take note, infant demon. There was a time I would absolutely crush you for even *thinking* of daring to question me. But, fortunately for you, I like you, so I'm willing to overlook it. For centuries, I've essentially been in stasis. When Hyacinth started his little plan to amass the power to become a Knight, it almost didn't register, but a nagging feeling prompted me to

pay attention, and I'm glad I did. At first, I wanted him to succeed because I needed a challenge. But *you* were far more interesting. Consorting with angels, witches, having feelings, living like a human." She glanced at the angel still trembling behind her.

As her gaze connected with Nick's, he squeaked slightly and bowed. "Mistress."

"*You* especially have been entertaining," she offered with a graceful nod. "Your banter with this one." She gestured at Malachi. "Well, I was half expecting you to kiss him any day. You, my dear, delicate angel, desperately need to get laid." At the choked gurgle from his throat, she laughed again, the sound underscored with the rattle of dead leaves skittering over cold ground.

Malachi shuddered. He could almost hear the Hellhounds howling within her laughter. "Oh damned one..." he started, loathe to be under her scrutiny, but knowing he needed to resolve this before Chuck got curious. As the fathomless depths of her eerie gaze settled on him again, he checked his chills and straightened his shoulders. "I wonder if we could return to why you have decided on this path, or rather, what is your desired outcome here? Because if you plan to kill us all, I would very much like to say goodbye to Kelly one last time."

Eying him with intense consideration, the elder demon nodded slowly. "I suppose there's no harm in telling you now that the charade is over." Sighing, she pointed at the ground and motioned with her finger as if summoning someone.

A burbling, squelching noise followed by the scent of decayed flowers filled the air as Hyacinth began to rise through the yard. As his head cleared the grass, he frowned and glared malevolently at Malachi. "You," he hissed, pointing a grubby finger at the lower demon. "You dare summon me? Who do you think you are? Where did you even get the power to do that?

Pissant excuse for a demon, I'd give you final death if it wasn't for that angel cloak you have. As soon as I make my way to the top, I'll strip you of that protection and have you writhing on the ground, begging me to kill you."

Grinning in undisguised glee, Malachi held up his hands in innocence. "I didn't summon you," he insisted and pointed over Hyacinth's shoulder.

Spinning on his gnarled feet, the bulbous demon stared at the waistline of the Knight of Hell who was watching him quietly with a bemused smile, hands propped on her hips. Her fingers twitched over the hilt of the sword belted at her side, and her fangs glinted as her lips parted with amusement when Hyacinth let out a strangled cough.

"Your Darkness!" he grunted, bowing down and groveling before her. "My deepest apologies for not immediately acknowledging your great presence. I was not aware you were here, but now I have only the most immense desire to serve you in any way I can."

"Is that so?" Amaryllis purred, her tone one of warning that had both Malachi and Nick taking a large step back. Then another. "And what if my desire was for you to demote yourself to a first-level demon and promote Malachi to your position instead. Would you do that for me, my precious little petal?" She dragged a sharp, talon-like nail over his shoulder, flicking the dirt on her finger in his face, making him flinch.

Swallowing heavily, Hyacinth clenched his teeth in disgust but finally nodded with reluctance. "If my Mistress commanded it," he choked out.

Slowly striding around the bent form of the demon, Amaryllis crouched by his side and leaned forward. "Then rise and tell me why it is that you felt a puny, shriveled root such as yourself was ready to challenge me to become a Knight?"

45

A Standing Invitation to Hell

Hyacinth jerked straight back toward Malachi as Amaryllis' question slammed into him like a wrecking ball. He shook his head vehemently side to side in denial of her accusation. "Never would I think to challenge you, oh Dark Mistress. Queen of my family line. I haven't nearly the strength to even *dream* such a thing." Hyacinth's beady yellow eyes flitted to the side and glared at Malachi, who had moved away when the filthy plant-shaped demon jumped. "Him." He pointed accusingly at Malachi now. "It was his plot, and I punished him by sending him here to foil his ill-imagined attempts."

Blowing air through his lips in a rude noise, Malachi shook his head in amusement. There was no point in defending himself. He knew Hyacinth wasn't aware that Amaryllis had been masquerading as Reena, and thus had witnessed their conversations. Crossing his arms over his chest, he simply stared at Hyacinth with interest, eager to see how this would play out.

His former commander was staring back at him now in concern, not understanding why Malachi wasn't protesting his lie.

"Hi!" Nick called cheerfully, leaning out from behind Amaryllis, his halo now beaming bright gold and wings spreading with a subtle glow. "Remember me? I'm Nick. I put the guardian spell on Malachi because I uncovered your plot to kill my niece, Kelly. You remember, the one you undertook so you could get the power to do the thing you're saying you didn't want to do? I guess I shouldn't be surprised you're lying. I mean, you are a demon. But seriously? Do you even—"

"Be at ease, Heavenly one," Amaryllis murmured with a feline smile, stopping Nick's rant with a small wave. He immediately stepped back and bowed his head. "Your defense of one of my kind is appreciated and noted. I'm impressed, Nick, that you would speak on Malachi's behalf. Especially with as many times as he got your name wrong."

Malachi chuckled low in his throat, then mimed zipping his lips as everyone turned to stare at him—Nick with irritation, Amaryllis with amusement, and Hyacinth with bewilderment.

Hyacinth was shaking now. Not much, but enough to have a fine trickle of dust floating from his body to pool at his feet. "I wanted him to take her soul for the glory of Hell! I didn't know she was an angel until I came to check on the progress of his punishment."

Leaning down, she caressed her hand over his wrinkled, leathery cheek, mocking the way a lover would do the same. "Oh, sweet Hyacinth, don't lie to me," she pleaded, her tone laced with insincerity, before it firmed. "You of all demons should know better. I know all the sordid details. I've been here the whole time, and you never knew. You told me all about your plot the day you decided to give Malachi his powers back."

Shaking his head—still in frantic denial—Hyacinth whined, "Mistress, I have not seen you in decades. How could I have told you?"

Grinning, Amaryllis yipped in a small dog's voice, then shimmered as she shrank into the tiny body of the brindle psycho menace that had been following Malachi for months. She panted and barked at Hyacinth, wagging her curly tail so hard it shook her whole ass.

It should have been hard for a creature as leathery and dark as Hyacinth to go pale, but he made a valiant effort. A dull, ashy gray coursed over his hide, making him look like a long-buried corpse. His mouth hung open slightly, and he stumbled back several ungainly steps. "Y-y-you were the other dog?" he squeaked, horror etching his features as the realization cascaded through him.

Appearing back in her regular form, Amaryllis smiled knowingly. "Oh yes, and that little mission you sent me on to wake Malachi up so you could set your trap? I was laughing the whole way. Really, very unimaginative of you." She shook her head and clicked her tongue. "Tsk, tsk." Heaving a weary sigh, she firmed her gaze at him with a stern glare. "Now, I repeat my earlier question. How is it you thought you had enough of a sack to take me on?"

As Hyacinth started to deny it, Amaryllis drew her sword and pointed the tip into the hollow of his throat before he could blink. "Do. Not. Lie. Again!" she roared, the rumble of her booming voice sounding like thunder echoing through the neighborhood. Car alarms began wailing around them, along with the sound of glass breaking as patio furniture in nearby backyards shattered.

A circle of Hellfire appeared around Hyacinth, writhing and licking at his heels with wicked glee. The flames reached for him with a hint of screaming souls as they danced wildly around his cowering form.

"I see I'm interrupting something here," Chuck's clear and firm voice announced. "Is this a private party or can anyone join?" She sauntered out in her tiny lace camisole and sleep-shorts, pressing herself to Malachi's side.

"Amaryllis, I presume?" Her gaze was steady; no hint of fear in her body or her aura.

Malachi stared at the small woman with amazement, simply mesmerized by the sheer audacity of her actions. "Kelly, may I introduce to you Amaryllis the Defiler, First Knight of Hell, our Lady of Evil, Mistress of Darkness."

Waving him off with impatience, Amaryllis moved closer to Chuck and studied her intently. "You are a brave little thing, aren't you?" She shook her hair back. "I've been impressed by you. I'd apologize for trying to have you killed, but I'm not sorry. I am, however, done with that. It was just a test for your Malachi and this one." She jerked her thumb negligently at Hyacinth, who was cowering in the center of the circle of Hellfire that was shrinking around him with agonizing slowness.

"I see," Chuck answered, pinching her lower lip between her thumb and forefinger, deep thought creasing her brow and narrowing her gaze on the unfortunate demon in the midst of the flaming torment. "Well, I'm sure it would be lovely to meet you under other circumstances, but did I hear you say you're done trying to kill me?"

"You did." Amaryllis chuckled. "I was sharing with your Malachi that I've been bored, and his escapades have provided me with much entertainment. I never truly wanted you dead. It was just something to do."

"Something to—" Chuck thundered before Malachi clapped his palm over her mouth, stopping what surely would have been another epic rant.

He quickly thought to her, *millennium-old demon Chuck. She doesn't think the way we do. Your whole life span is but a blink of an eye to her. Don't antagonize her.*

"Wise words, young one," Amaryllis chuckled. Glancing back at Chuck, she expanded on his words. "It was not personal. I was watching to see what Hyacinth was up to. When I learned of his plot, I decided to personally

monitor the situation to alleviate my boredom. To my everlasting delight, your charming demon lover here showed up and immediately drew me in. I watched you two develop emotions for each other. It's strange. I've never felt anything but rage and the ache to destroy. But you gave me fascination, curiosity, desire, and a whole list of things it will take me decades to understand. So no, Chuck, I'm not going to kill you. Or Malachi. Not even Nick. Hyacinth, however, he will be turned into an example of what happens when you cross me."

Demonstrating the lightning speed and decision-making that made her so feared, Amaryllis spun and skewered the demon with her sword before anyone even realized she'd moved. With an anticlimactic gurgle, Hyacinth dangled on the blade as she lifted it and rested it on her shoulder. The grotesque demon was stuck there, making pitiful mewling sounds.

"I'm going to hang him on my front gate to greet visitors. Not that I have many." Spinning to face Nick, Amaryllis aimed a sultry smile at him. Her red eyes drank him in, head to toe. "Maybe you'd like to be the first visitor from Heaven," she purred. "I would like to discuss more demon-angel... interactions with you."

Staring at her with eyes nearly falling from his skull, Nick slowly nodded as his wings trembled only slightly. "Yeah, I'll uh... I'll see if that's doable."

Malachi burst into laughter then. "See, I wasn't that bad, Nicodemus. We demons really are an enjoyable sort once you get to know us."

Amaryllis chuckled as he grimaced when Chuck elbowed him, exclaiming, "I like her. And him." She gestured at the angel who was now blushing and pulling on the collar of his robe, as if he couldn't breathe. Not that he needed to. "This is where I leave you. But don't worry. I'll leave the real Reena here in my place, so you don't miss me too much. She's been enjoying Real Housewives reruns in my parlor for the past few months.

She does seem a little homesick, though." She snapped her fingers, and a brindle Chuglet appeared, curly tail wagging, making excited piggy snorts.

Squinting, Amaryllis stared at Chuck and sighed. "I took your files, too. Didn't want Malachi to figure out it was two different demons yet." Waving her hand negligently, all the missing evidence showed up in a heap on the patio table, one folder sliding to the ground with a loud plop. A chuckle had the demon's shoulders bouncing with her amusement.

A choking whimper sounded from Hyacinth as he slid farther along her blade, the black ichor of his blood sluggishly dripping to the ground. "M-Mistress?" he pleaded weakly.

Huffing an irritated sigh, Amaryllis straightened and gave a jaunty wave. "Well, I'll be off. But I think I'll check in here and there to see how this works. I'm so intrigued by the thought of feelings. I thought they would be a burden, but you,"—she pointed at Malachi—"seem to like them."

Wrapping his arms tightly around Kelly, he nodded. "I do like them. I'd give up my immortality to spend the rest of my life with her."

Tapping a talon on her chin, Amaryllis studied him thoughtfully. "And I believe you would. I won't ask you for that. For now."

Feeling Kelly trying to lurch forward, he held her tightly around the waist and clapped his hand over her mouth once more, hoping she didn't bite him for doing it again. He was worried she was about to say something he would regret if Amaryllis took offense. "Wait!" Malachi called as the higher demon made to depart. At her impatient glare, he swallowed hard. "If I may beg another question, my darkest lady?" He bowed deferentially, forcing Kelly to bow as well. At the other demon's small nod, he hurried on before she changed her mind. "What of Kelly's father, Gavin? Why did you make his friends kill him?" He felt Kelly slump in his grasp, and he was grateful he'd known what she was going to ask and prevented her from making a grave mistake.

"Oh, I didn't," chuckled Amaryllis as she shook the sword, grinning at Hyacinth's moan. "That was this foul creature masquerading as me. It's what caught my attention in the first place. It also gave me the idea to be the dog so I could watch him continue his plot. He was trying to use the full angel's grace, but your associate foiled his plan when he killed the other man, releasing that grace back to Heaven." With that, Amaryllis dissolved into a cloud of shadows and another tortured scream from Hyacinth. The heavy smell of brimstone lingered long after she'd gone.

46

No Collars in Bed

Malachi, Chuck, and Nick simply stared at each other in silence for several minutes after Amaryllis' departure. No one knew quite where to begin. Her revelations had been shocking to say the least. Finally, Malachi turned Kelly to face him and searched her eyes. He figured the truth about her father must have had some ill effect on her, but he saw only relief. "You okay?" he murmured, trying to determine where her head was at.

"Strangely,"—she nodded slowly—"I am. Thank you. For asking. I admit I was mad at first that you stopped me, but I guess you were trying to protect me. You knew the right way to approach it. But now... I know what happened and why. We were just pawns in some stupid power struggle with demons. And the one who started it is being punished in a way I could never accomplish, so in a sense, you could say I got some justice." She sighed and gazed at him with concern, tightening the corners of her mouth. "Are *you* okay? You were a pawn, too."

He started to deny it but realized the truth in her words; he was just a small part of the larger game. "I'm not happy about being used like

that, but the outcome is beyond anything I could have imagined. I have you." His hands dropped from her arms suddenly as a new dark thought slithered into his head, planting a seed of doubt. "That is, if you still... if you would... after what those demons did to you. I guess I can understand if you don't want me around anymore. I mean... I'm a demon too, and although I would never betray you like that, I get it if it's too much." He stared at the ground where Reena—the real Reena—sat with one paw on his foot in solidarity. Her gaze told him she was with him, even if Kelly wasn't.

Shaking her head, Kelly slipped her fingers into his hair and tugged him down so she could kiss him, hard. When she finally leaned back, slightly breathless, she smiled sadly. "Malachi, humans do bad things all the time, but that doesn't make me want to stay away from them. I just need to find the good ones. I found the good in you, and I'm keeping you. No takebacks. I love you, and you are my demon. Got it?"

"Got it," he replied, grinning against her lips before capturing them again with his own. Glancing up as he heard a slight rustle, he noticed Nick was gone. Smirking, he waggled his eyebrows. "Think Nickle went to see a certain demon at her palace? Could be the scandal of the century!"

Shuddering, Chuck shook her head. "I hope not. She's a little too blood-thirsty."

"That reminds me," he snapped as his eyebrows drew together in a thunderous expression. Leaning back, he grabbed her shoulders tightly, giving her a slight shake. "What the actual fuck were you thinking, just strolling out here all casual like when the very fucking demon I told you wanted you dead was here?"

"You were out here," she offered simply and shrugged. "I figured if she were going to kill me, you would attack her. And if she killed you, well... I

didn't want to be here if you weren't with me. Seemed better we went out together—fighting."

Humbled, Malachi lowered his forehead to hers. "I *still* don't know what I did to deserve your love, but I will absolutely never let it go. You are the bravest and most terrifying creature I know." He gazed into her eyes and let his lips curve with a feral edge. "Kelly?"

"Yeah?"

"Still have those handcuffs ready?"

Four months later

"I don't get it, man." Jaxon pointed at Malachi with a chicken wing. "You don't *have* to be the dog anymore, so why do you still do it? I mean... don't you worry about, like, I don't know, fleas?" The officer glanced around to make sure no one else could hear them in the noisy bar. It was karaoke night at their usual bar, and Marla had gone to the ladies' room with Chuck. Nathan chuckled into his beer at the question.

"Yeah, I don't get fleas," Malachi replied dryly. "I can give you some if you'd like."

Jaxon quickly shook his head and dropped the wing on his plate, his interest in the food suddenly gone. "No, thank you! I didn't mean anything by it; I'm just curious."

Sighing, Malachi ran a hand through the unruly waves of his hair. "I know, but it lets me spend time with Chuck, and I get to keep protecting her. I can't do that as Evan." He made sarcastic finger quotes around the

name he used in mixed company. Marla and Jaxon were a serious couple now, but she still wasn't aware of the secret shared between the others.

"Is she still in danger?" Nathan murmured as he watched the ladies wander back towards the table.

"Not actively, but she is a Nephilim, so some supernatural may take offense to that at some point. Besides, doing police work keeps me on the straight and narrow. At least, she thinks it does." Malachi grinned and gave a conspiratorial wink to the other men before Chuck perched back on the high barstool next to him.

Glenda giggled as her name was called to take her turn at the microphone. No one was surprised when her song of choice was, "I Put a Spell on You". It was fitting for the witch, and she belted it out with the gusto that had finally won over Nathan. The two were a couple now. The stoic, straightlaced cop and the boisterous, colorful witch.

Blake had spent some time in a psychiatric facility after Chuck pleaded for leniency on his behalf. He was doing much better now and working through his rocky relationship with his father.

Reena was still addicted to daytime television, but she moved her dog bed to Malachi's old room since he'd moved into the master bedroom with Chuck. Apparently, that was too much reality, and she didn't like to watch their activities.

"Mal," Chuck murmured in his ear as she leaned on his shoulder, distracting him from his thoughts. "I got you something."

"It better not be another rawhide bone," he declared with a grimace, frowning at her amused snort. She'd given him a dog treat that resembled a brontosaurus femur as a joke a month ago. He promptly regifted the chew toy to Reena, who dragged the massive bone around the house triumphantly, despite it being twice her size.

"Better," she promised solemnly, then ruined it by grinning at him with a sultry smile. "This... is for you." She handed him a small, black box tied with purple ribbon and topped with an enormous black bow that was much larger than the box.

Glancing at her suspiciously, he saw her aura was streaked with red, and she watched him anxiously. He realized it was not a trick this time, but a genuine present that she had put real thought into. Nervous, but excited, he removed the bow, absently sticking it on Jaxon's head while ignoring the man's protests. Slowly lifting the lid, he peered inside to find a velvet drawstring pouch nestled snugly within. He arched one eyebrow at her as she watched him closely, biting her bottom lip in anticipation. Gingerly, he pulled the pouch from the box and tugged the strings to open it. Something heavy and metallic clinked inside as the cloth shifted. Taking a deep breath, Malachi poured the contents into one palm and stared at the gift.

A pair of handcuffs lay in his hand. Matte black with a strange finish that seemed to absorb all light shining on it. He could feel something ancient and borderline dangerous emanating from the otherwise innocuous-seeming object. Turning them over, he peered closer, noting runes etched into the surface. He studied them intently before breaking into a huge grin.

"You always turn to shadows and escape when I use my regular ones. I wanted to even the playing field," Kelly explained in a low voice laced with breathless uncertainty.

Staring into her wide eyes that were trained on him, Malachi grabbed her shoulders and yanked her against him hard enough that he pulled her right off her barstool. Crushing his mouth to hers, he kissed her so passionately that the entire bar filled with cheers and catcalls. After he finally released her and set her gently back in her seat with a dazed expression, he leaned

his forehead against hers. “So, you got me handcuffs I can’t escape from,” he breathed. “I’m assuming Glenda etched those runes?”

She nodded mutely as she came back to herself. “I’m... uh... I guess you like them?” A wobbly, relieved smile curved her lips.

“I *love* them,” he corrected and dangled the dark promise of the metal between them. “And we are so using these tonight.”

“A demon with a bondage fetish and a half-angel police officer,” she chuckled. “What a pair we are. Just don’t ever wear your K-9 collar to bed again.” She wagged a finger at him admonishingly.

“No guarantees!”

Thank You

Thank you for reading

How To Tell If Your K-9 Is A Demon

(I hope you enjoyed reading it as much as I loved writing it.)
Love this book? Don't forget to leave a review!

Every review matters, and it matters a *lot!*
Head over to Amazon, Goodreads, or wherever you purchased this book
to leave a review for me.
Malachi sends wet sloppy kisses if you do!

Want a sneak peek?

Turn the page for a taste of the next series, Compulsions of the Damned.

One touch. That's all it takes to change your life for better or worse. For those under the Compulsion of the Caretaker, life is lonely and fraught with misery.

Meet Wendy Lace, the sassy bartender who has lived her whole life thinking there was something wrong with her. She doesn't feel things the way others do, in fact she doesn't feel much at all. She can't stand to be touched and thinks she's alone in a world of normal people. Always armed and finding her way, she's just making it through another shift when a dark, brooding stranger turns out to have more in common with her than she expected.

Damien – Not the Antichrist – Richards is resigned to the fact that he is destined to die young and alone. But he's going to get as much out of his life and music as he can before he goes. A last-minute booking for his band at a new venue brings him face to face with destiny and a glimpse at what things could truly be.

That is, if the demon and the serial killer stalking them all would give them a break.

Chapter 1- Arcane Fate

"I hate it when guys order Blowjobs." Carrie sighed dramatically as she slid up to the bar to pick up the order for her rowdy table of frat boys. They'd already been admonished once to keep their hands off the staff. "Like... they think asking for a Blowjob means I'm going to take them to the storeroom and suck them off because they're funny." She rolled her eyes and groaned, clearly exasperated.

Wendy's sleek eyebrows bunched, a dark slash against her pale skin. "Want me to stab them for ya?" she inquired eagerly, grinning at the petite brunette leaning over the bar.

Carrie paused a moment—seriously contemplating it—then sighed wistfully, shaking her head. "Nah, too many witnesses. Plus, like diamonds, felonies are forever."

Wendy let out a deep belly laugh. Carrie was always good for a quick comeback. She eyed the table of frat boys watching Carrie bend over and smirked as she caught their attention. Pulling her dagger from the little sheath in her corset, she slowly ran it over her tongue while she stared them down. They now watched her with undisguised lust as she stabbed two cherries out of her water glass. Lifting them to her lips, she licked them sensually before sucking them off the blade. She winked as she crushed the fruit between her teeth. The guys swallowed hard and turned back to the table.

Carrie pointed at her friend while her cotton candy pink painted lips quirked as she tried not to laugh. "That... that is why I love you."

Chuckling, Wendy playfully shook a finger. "You better! You'll get a bigger tip. Hopefully they're too busy debating which one of them is going to swagger over here and get shut down by me, to pinch your ass again. But if they do."-she stabbed the dagger forcefully into the dark wood of the bar- "Let me know."

The grinning waitress took the shots to her table and dropped them off without incident before making her way to her other customers.

Wendy glanced at the clock behind the bar, noting it was 8:50 p.m. The band for the evening should be starting soon. It was a new one for them, a last-minute change as the band originally slotted for the evening cancelled on short notice. This replacement group was local and seemed to be drawing a larger than usual crowd.

She reached for a fresh glass then paused, the feeling like someone was watching her skittered over her skin. A cool sensation, a slight prickle on her neck. Stretching she thought, *probably that new tattoo itch*. She'd sat for it the afternoon before, and the heat in the crowded bar wasn't helping. Normally, she wouldn't have done it right before a night shift, but her co-worker Brad had called in sick and the owner, Mike, begged her to cover. There was no way the other bartender, Chase, could work this crowd by himself. Between the new band playing, and the harvest festival in town, they were packed.

"Wendy! Thank you, please marry me!" Chase called over his shoulder as he bustled behind the bar to drop off the cases of beer he was lugging in to restock.

"Sorry Chase, not my type!" She grinned at him. He was everyone's type. Stunning, with wavy tousled blond hair, green eyes that lit up when he was happy — which was pretty much always — and a full mouth made for

kissing. He was thoughtful, kind, had rock-hard abs and a fantastic tush. He was the All-American guy that most girls dreamed of dating.

Not Wendy, other girls.

The good guy vibe wasn't attractive to her. Not that she liked bad boys either. She was pretty sure she was dead inside, not attracted to anyone.

"You're killing me babe," Chase moaned dramatically as he set the beer down and turned to grab more. He smacked her butt in passing, and she waved her knife at him, growling in mock ferociousness. Spinning back, he grabbed her waist and pulled her close. "God it turns me on when you do that, crazy chick." He kissed her noisily on the cheek and scurried off laughing like a cartoon villain.

Wendy laughed too, shaking her head at his antics. Chase had asked her out a couple of times, but she kept turning him down. He finally understood it wasn't him personally, she just didn't date. Anyone. Now he enjoyed teasing her, and she enjoyed it, too. It made her feel normal. If she wasn't feeling it, he was great about listening. He really was a wonderful friend. She sighed; she didn't understand why she didn't like him that way, he truly was the perfect guy.

Hearing a lusty sigh echoing her own, Wendy turned. Carrie was back to pick up another order and had witnessed the exchange. Carrie was nuts about Chase, but he didn't seem to notice her that way.

"I wish he would look at me the way he looks at you. It's not fair, you don't even like him like that and he still likes you more. What gives?" the small woman moaned.

Mike, the owner, strolled over then. "Carrie, I pay you to serve tables, not moon over my bartenders. Get your butt out there." He patted her on the cheek and smiled to show he was joking as she ran off giggling.

The staff all thought Mike was the best boss in the world. He was friendly, easy-going, understanding, and clear in his expectations. The

burly affable man was the main reason Wendy loved working at the bar; he looked after them all.

"Wendy, you're a life saver and I adore you. But... no stabbing anyone tonight, okay?" Mike told her, warily eyeing the dagger in her hand.

Smothering a groan, Wendy sheathed it and muttered, "It was one time, and he totally had it coming." As Mike shook his head, she added, "Even the police agreed with me!"

Three months prior, a particularly rowdy man didn't like that Wendy cut him off when it was obvious he'd had too much to drink. The man's friends tried to get him to leave but he became belligerent and broke a beer bottle on the bar then tried to cut her with it. Wendy had stabbed the man through the hand with one of the knives she always carried, pinning him to the bartop. The police weren't too happy with her at first, but after watching the security video, and taking statements, they agreed she had cause.

Nodding, Mike huffed, "Yeah, but man the lawyers had a field day with that one. And the news stories." He shook his head ruefully.

Wendy grinned and pinched his cheek. "Oh, come on you grumpy bear, that got this place so much free advertising, our tips tripled! Hey, if business slows down let me know, and I'll stab someone else!"

He just snorted and shook his head, holding the bar pass-through open for Chase as he came back with another few cases.

"Mike," Chase called, "there's a guy out back with a delivery. Some special vodka you ordered?"

Mike nodded his thanks and hurried off. The house lights went down then, and a drummer began tapping out a few rhythms to check his set up. The band for the evening was about to begin.

"Hey, Chase," Wendy shouted over the surge of cheering. "Who's the band tonight? Some new group for us I heard?"

He nodded as he unloaded the bottles into the back of the fridge. "Yeah, some metal band." He paused and stared at her with his brows scrunched. "Good Kitty, I think? Or was that last night's band? Umm. Crap. I can't remember."

"Arcane Fate."

The two words trickled into her ear from a voice made of velvet and smoke. Wendy felt that prickling sensation crawling over her neck again, like a gentle caress. She turned to see a man leaning against the counter, in the darkest part of the shadows. One hand rested on the bar, lightly tapping a guitar pick on the lacquered, scarred surface, a small tattoo of some kind on his wrist.

She moved slowly toward him, drawn by unseen forces. Staring, she tried to make out his features in the low light and smoky air. He had silky jet-black hair, long, down to his shoulder on one side, shorter and spiky on the other. He was tall and lean, but very muscular. She couldn't tell what color his eyes were, but his lips were full and pulled into a sensual smile. Several silver rings glinted in his ears, his nose, and lower lip. The thin, slender hoops were barely visible in the haze surrounding him. She could just make out the edges of more tattoos peeking out from his shirt sleeves.

"Arcane Fate?" she repeated breathlessly as the drummer began to run a few longer riffs to warm up and heavy bass notes joined the beat. The crowd was cheering even louder now as the show became imminent.

The man holding her hostage with his gaze nodded once. "That's the name of the band, Arcane Fate." He shrugged then leaned in and she could now see his eyes were green like Chase's, but softer, with dark secrets in their jade depths instead of shining emerald innocence. Those eyes spoke of desires to be explored and sins to be committed. "If I asked you for a whiskey neat, would you stick me with that little steel of yours?"

Her mouth went as dry as the desert, and she shook her head slowly side to side.

He arched one eyebrow and her heart fluttered at how his lips curved into a wicked pout before he murmured, "That's too bad."

Swallowing hard, she smiled back before whirling to pour the drink. Shivering slightly, she pulled in a deep breath through her nose as the force of the man's gaze released her. She noticed Chase was watching her with a perplexed expression. She gave him a questioning shrug in return and mouthed *what?*

Chase waggled his eyebrows suggestively then made a kissy face at her. She glared at him, a silent promise to kill him later and turned back to the dark man with his drink.

His fingers brushed hers as he picked it up and their eyes locked. He seemed surprised and cocked his head to the side. "I have to go up there. I'll be back. Start a tab for me?"

She nodded and he turned to make his way to the stage, but she realized she didn't know anything about him. "Wait!" Wendy called, her voice shaking with something she didn't understand. "I... I need your name. For the tab."

Those lips curved again before they parted on a single word. "Damien."

Printed in Dunstable, United Kingdom

80937263R00211

Made in the USA
Middletown, DE
27 September 2024

61094962R00119